DAVID WLECHINSKY, AMY WALLACE,
IRA BASEN & JANE FARROW

THE BOOK

OF LISTS

The Original Compendium
of Curious Information,

Canadian Edition

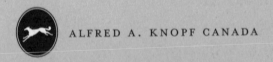

ALFRED A. KNOPF CANADA

PUBLISHED BY ALFRED A. KNOPF CANADA

Original edition copyright © 1977, 1980, 1983, 2004 David Wallechinsky and Amy Wallace
Canadian edition copyright © 2005 Ira Basen and Jane Farrow
Published by agreement with Canongate Books Ltd., Edinburgh, Scotland

www.randomhouse.ca

Photo Credits
Chapter 1—Copyright © *The People's Almanac* Photographic Archives; Chapter 2—Film still from *McKenna of the Mounted* ; Chapter 3—Library and Archives Canada/ Credit: Duncan Cameron (PA–180804); Chapter 4—Paul V. Galvin Library collection; Chapter 5—Library and Archives Canada/ Credit: Claude-Charles Bacqueville de La Potherie (CFC305 B326); Chapter 6—City of Vancouver Archives, CVA 1184–2559; Chapter 7—Copyright © Frank Micoletta/Getty Image; Chapter 8—Steve Patterson/Glaucomys.org; Chapter 9—Jeff Goode/*Toronto Star*; Chapter 10—Copyright © M. Ponomareff/PonoPresse; Chapter 11—Copyright © Brian Willer - Toronto; Chapter 12—J.H. Webster/Hudson's Bay Co. Archives/Archives of Manitoba (HBCA 1987/363-E-152/4); Chapter 13—Library and Archives Canada/Montreal Star collection (PA-209767); Chapter 14—Niagara Falls (Ont.) Public Library - Digital Collections - George Bailey; Chapter 15—Saskatchewan Archives Board (S-B4121)

Pages 506 to 507 constitute a continuation of the copyright page. Also included is a key to
    contributors.

LIBRARY AND ARCHIVES CANADA CATALOGUING IN PUBLICATION

The book of lists / David Wallechinsky ... [et al.]. — Canadian ed.

Includes index.
ISBN 0-676-97720-0

1. Handbooks, vade-mecums, etc. 2. Curiosities and wonders.
3. Curiosities and wonders—Canada. I. Wallechinsky, David, 1948–   .

AG106.B66 2005   031.02   C2005-901023-1

Text design: CS Richardson

First Canadian Edition

Printed and bound in the United States of America

10 9 8 7 6 5 4 3 2 1

CONTENTS

INTRODUCTION AND ACKNOWLEDGMENTS
FROM DAVID WALLECHINSKY AND AMY WALLACE

Acknowledgments

The authors warmly thank Flora Wallechinsky for long hours of typing, organizing and troubleshooting, Elijah and Aaron Wallechinsky and Macho Boubekour for help with typing, and Jaime Loucky for his creative research. Our love and thanks to our mother for her support and encouragement. To Chris Fishel, for his wonderful work and ingenuity as staff writer; to Danny Biederman for organising the celebrity lists; to Scott Bradley, for his work as researcher and writer of celebrity biographies and as editor with Amy; to Allison Berry, for abstracting texts and research. Warm thanks to Jamie Byng, our publisher at Canongate Books, whose vision and enthusiasm inspired us throughout. And with gratitude to Canongate's wonderful and enthusiastic staff, including our two editors, Helen Bleck and Nick Rennison. Thanks also to our agents, Ed Victor, for his long, long support of *The Book of Lists* series, and Wendy Shmalz, the model of equanimity and humour. And special thanks to Jeremy Beadle for being available for consultations, for providing good advice and for always being a friend in need.

Amy would like to extend special thanks to Allison Berry for helping to keep her life running and to Scott Bradley for having saved his school lunch money at 13 to buy *The Book of Lists*, only to grow up to become part of its creation; and to Richard Jennings for support and keeping the wolves from the door.

This edition would not have been possible without the many people who worked on previous editions of *The Book of Lists*, in particular Vicki Baker, Carol Orsag-Madigan, Anita Taylor, Helen Ginsburg, Elizabethe Kempthorne, Judy Knipe, Fern Bryant, Roger Fadness, Lee Clayton and Torene Svitil.

Most of all, we wish to thank the millions of readers who wondered, and the many who asked "When is the next *Book of Lists* coming out?" We welcome ideas and contributions from our readers for future editions; and thank you all for helping us create a genre that has lasted for three decades, and is more popular than ever.

The authors can be reached at viciousgnu@aol.com

Introduction

As Oscar Wilde observed, the only sin is to be bored. We believe it is an equal sin to be boring, and if the great wit was correct, then the authors and millions of *Book of Lists* readers are quite unblemished by sin: for we place a high value on curiosity.

The original 1977 volume of *The Book of Lists*, and its all-new sequels, inspired nearly 200 imitation volumes. These have included books of lists about movies, rock 'n' roll, Judaism, the Bible, general sports, and countless other subjects. The books spawned games, toilet paper with lists on it, CD-ROMs, calendars and television shows. We had no idea that *The Book of Lists* would become a bestseller, let alone a phenomenon. We thought we were just having fun.

The Book of Lists rose to number 1 on the bestseller lists, and was published all over the world. Young readers wrote to tell us they'd bought our book for fun, and were using it to spice up their schoolwork. Older readers locked themselves in bathrooms, curled up in bed, took the book to parties and demanded more editions. We invited their contributions, which came pouring in, and we featured many of them in the editions that followed.

Although we are pleased to have popularised a genre that so many people enjoy, we do not pretend to have been its founders. That honour goes to the Reverend Nathaniel Wanley, author of *Wonders of the Little World,* a book of lists first published in 1678. We didn't know about the Reverend Wanley when we wrote our own Book of Lists, but a glance through his table of contents shows striking similarities: "Of such People and Nations as have been scourged and afflicted by small and contemptible things," "Of such as having been extremely Wild, and Prodigal, or Debauched in their Youth, have afterwards proved excellent Persons," "Of such as have been seized with an extraordinary joy, at what hath followed there-upon."

The trend never died down, and in recent years has had a dazzling renaissance. We appear to live in an age in which the volume of information available to us is far too overwhelming for our minds to process. The everyday lists we all make are a balm to a cluttered mind; list-making puts things in order, it clarifies, it helps coax truth from the cracks of the universe, and it invites our favourite question: "What if . . . ?"

In the present volume, we have updated our readers' favourite lists, prepared an array of new material, and included lists from a wide variety of notables and celebrities. We owe much of the inspiration for this volume to our father, Irving Wallace, who always hoped we'd continue to compile new editions. Whenever possible, we have concentrated on lists that cause readers to laugh out loud, gasp, shake their heads in wonder, or call out "Wait until you hear this!" To quote Mark Twain's introduction to *The Adventures of Huckleberry Finn:* "Persons attempting to find a motive in this narrative will be prosecuted; persons attempting to find a moral in it will be banished; persons attempting to find a plot in it will be shot."

INTRODUCTION AND ACKNOWLEDGMENTS FROM IRA BASEN AND JANE FARROW

IT WAS HARD NOT TO FEEL intimidated about joining forces with the Wallace and Wallechinsky list machine. The first *Book of Lists*, by David, Amy and their father, Irving, was brilliant. David and Amy have subsequently spent several decades filing away obscure pieces of information to be included in future books of lists. And here we were, two CBC radio producers, whose brains gear more towards finding interesting people to talk to on the radio than to trying to find a Canadian who had died laughing.

Sometimes we got lucky. We hadn't really expected to be able to add Canadian content to a list of "famous events that happened in the bathtub," until we stumbled across the fact that former prime minister R.B. Bennett had died in his. It also turns out that you can actually learn a few things about the differences between Canada and the United States by working on a book of lists such as this. We realized that our showbiz celebrity culture is not nearly as developed as theirs; our stars aren't larger than life. We could find no examples of a public kiss that equalled the buzz created by Britney and Madonna, or scenes left out of Canadian films that could rise to the level of the lost production number from *The Wizard of Oz.* So we started looking in different places. Our mobsters don't have nicknames as colourful as their American counterparts, but our athletes do. And while the American version of the book had a list of "15 Actors Who Became Politicians," we flipped it around to suit our needs: "12 Canadian Sports Heroes Who Became Politicians." Finally, we couldn't find an instance of Canadians rioting after a trial verdict, but we had no trouble finding fans going wild after Stanley Cup games and rock concerts.

We want to thank our "experts" who took us deep into their areas of specialization to come up with some truly wonderful lists. Two whose names are not attached to their lists are Robert Williams, the Director of the Centre for Election Studies at the University of Waterloo, who contributed a list on the highs and lows of Canadian elections, and our CBC buddy Nick Purdon who, luckily for us, happens to have a fascination with wilderness expeditions that ended in disaster. We are grateful for the assistance of the brilliant and patient library staff at the CBC and the University of Toronto libraries. We also want to thank some close friends and colleagues who generously indulged our needling inquiries about Canadian law (Debra Parkes and Pam Shime), rowdy rock fans (Greig Dymond) and all things environmental (Lorraine Johnson).

Our trusted editor, Michael Schellenberg, did a wonderful job of keeping us focused and motivated. He could be depended on for encouraging words at the right moment, and more importantly, came through with a few steak dinners at critical junctures. Most of all, we thank Michael for being organized, driven and infallible—in other words, the editorial equivalent of a border collie. Thanks to Kate Cassaday for compiling the first round of the manuscript; our copy editor, Sue Sumeraj, for sticking to the facts and crossing the t's; Deirdre Molina, Knopf Canada's capable managing editor, for grace under pressure; Martha Magor, for her able assistance; Bao-Nghi Nhan, our intrepid photo researcher; and finally, the always elegant executive publisher Louise Dennys, for giving us a shot at the big time.

Jane would like to single out her own guiding light, Sophie Hackett, for all the love and support on the home front, and Ira would like to acknowledge the names on his most important list: Lynn, Joanna, Andrea, Rochelle and Nathaniel.

We spent many hours in libraries and on the Internet researching these lists, knowing all the while that our greatest resource will ultimately be you, the reader. That's why we really are looking forward to hearing from you, even if your letters begin "I can't believe you missed . . ." So if you know about a cat who covered hundreds of miles to come home, or a noteworthy Canadian who hated his or her portrait, or a famously naked Canadian woman, please get in touch. That's why they invented second editions.

Ira and Jane
The Canadian editors can be reached at bookoflists@randomhouse.com

CHAPTER 1   **PEOPLE**

ABOVE: *Francesco Lentini, the Three-Legged Man, with one of his five children*

1

AGES OF 30 PEOPLE HAD THEY LIVED TO 2006

1. Dylan Thomas (1914–53), poet: 92
2. John F. Kennedy (1917–63), president: 89
3. Pierre Laporte (1921–70), politician: 85
4. René Lévesque (1922–87), politician: 84
5. Malcolm X (1925–65), civil rights activist: 81
6. Marilyn Monroe (1926–62), actress: 80
7. Margaret Laurence (1926–87), novelist: 80
8. Ernesto "Che" Guevara (1928–67), revolutionary leader: 78
9. Anne Frank (1929–45), diarist: 77
10. Martin Luther King Jr. (1929–68), clergyman and civil rights leader: 77
11. James Dean (1931–55), actor: 75
12. Glenn Gould (1932–82), pianist: 74
13. Sylvia Plath (1932–63), poet: 74
14. Elvis Presley (1935–77), singer: 71
15. Barbara Frum (1937–92), broadcaster: 69
16. John Lennon (1940–80), musician: 66
17. Ritchie Valens (1941–59), singer: 65
18. Gwendolyn McEwen (1941–87), poet: 65
19. Jimi Hendrix (1942–70), musician: 64
20. Janis Joplin (1943–70), singer: 63
21. Jim Morrison (1943–71), musician: 61
22. Bob Marley (1945–81), singer: 59
23. John Belushi (1949–82), comedian: 57
24. John Candy (1950–94), actor: 56
25. Gilles Villeneuve (1950–82), race car driver: 56
26. Terry Fox (1958–81), runner: 48
27. Princess Diana (1961–97), royalty: 45
28. Kurt Cobain (1967–94), musician: 39
29. River Phoenix (1970–93), actor: 36
30. Michel Trudeau (1975–98), hiker: 31

11 MEN WHO CRIED IN PUBLIC

1. Todd Bertuzzi, hockey player

On March 8, 2004, Todd Bertuzzi of the Vancouver Canucks delivered a vicious sucker punch to Steve Moore of the Colorado Avalanche in an NHL game in Vancouver. Moore suffered a concussion and broke several bones in his neck. Two days later, Bertuzzi appeared in front of the media and sobbed uncontrollably as he offered his "apology" to Steve Moore. "I just want to apologize for what happened out there," said Bertuzzi, wiping his eyes with a napkin. "I had no intention of hurting you." Many observers viewed Bertuzzi's tearful performance with a dash of cynicism, noting that feeling sorry for "what happened out there" is not quite the same thing as taking personal responsibility for seriously injuring a fellow hockey player.

2. Jesus Christ, religious leader

After Lazarus died, Jesus led his disciples to visit Lazarus's sisters, Mary and Martha. When the friends of Lazarus agreed to show Jesus the cave where Lazarus's body was laid, Jesus wept.

3. Bill Clinton, American president

On the morning of his inauguration, President Clinton and his family attended services at Washington's Metropolitan African Methodist Episcopal church. As the choir sang hymns, tears rolled down Clinton's cheeks. Clinton teared up frequently as his years in office continued. Once, when caught on camera laughing and joking at a funeral, Clinton suddenly realized he was being filmed. Having learned "the Nixon lesson," he instantly grew serious, and tears came to his eyes. Right-wing TV host Rush Limbaugh played the tape in slow motion repeatedly, sending his studio audience into fits of mirth. Tom Lutz, the author of *Crying: The Natural & Cultural History of Tears*, observed that crying for male politicians was "a 1990s version of kissing babies."

4. David, warrior king

When David and his troops returned to the city of Ziklag, after being sent home by the princes of the Philistines, they discovered that the Amalekites had invaded the city and taken captive all of the women and children, including David's two wives. David and his followers immediately "lifted up their voices and wept until they had no more power to weep."

5. John Diefenbaker, Canadian prime minister

Diefenbaker shed a few tears when the Canadian flag was first hoisted on February 15, 1965. A fierce defender of the Red Ensign, he vigorously opposed the new maple leaf design chosen by Prime Minister Lester B. Pearson. Commenting on the flag ceremony a few days later, he said, "As leader of Her Majesty's Loyal Opposition, and as an officer of Parliament, I was present at the raising of that flag. It was my duty to be there because I believe in Parliament. I confess, too, that I had a heavy heart. I was not aware that tears fell from my eyes until I saw the picture. But I cannot change my convictions."

6. Wayne Gretzky, hockey player

Hockey's Great One routinely choked up—while winning games, getting awards, addressing the media, retiring and once when talking about his wife's acting career. But his most memorable tears streamed down his face at the press conference announcing his trade from Edmonton to Los Angeles in 1988. Edmonton owner Peter Pocklington accused him of crying "alligator tears," and fans responded by burning Pocklington in effigy outside the arena.

7. Michael Jordan, basketball player

Michael Jordan cried openly when, while playing with the Chicago Bulls, he won his first NBA title in 1991, and this drew no comment from the press. Then, when he won his fourth title in 1996, he wept once more, falling onto the floor in a fetal position and sobbing when the game ended. This time, TV announcers explained that Jordan's father had been murdered a year and a half before; the game was played on Father's Day, and Jordan had made an incredible comeback after retiring for two years.

8. Laurier LaPierre, broadcaster

The most talked-about tear ever shed on Canadian television fell from the eye of Laurier LaPierre, the mercurial co-host of CBC's controversial current affairs program *This Hour Has Seven Days*, in the spring of 1966. It happened while LaPierre was watching a taped interview with the mother of Stephen Truscott. At the age of 14, Truscott had been convicted and sentenced to hang for the murder of a 12-year-old girl, a conviction that was later overturned. When the interview ended, LaPierre slowly rubbed a tear from his eye and proceeded to link the Truscott case to the debate over capital punishment that was about to begin in Parliament. CBC management was outraged and publicly condemned LaPierre's "unprofessional" conduct. In a statement he later came to regret, CBC president Alphonse Ouimet questioned whether the tear was real. The following year, LaPierre was fired from the program. The CBC cited the incident as proof that LaPierre was unable to control his emotions or his bias on air.

9. Richard Nixon, American president

During a 1977 television interview, Nixon told David Frost, "I never cry—except in public." Nixon's most famous public weep occurred in 1952 after he made his notorious "Checkers speech" and Dwight Eisenhower decided to allow him to remain on the Republican ticket as the vice-presidential candidate. Watching this performance, Nixon's college drama coach, Albert Upton, who had taught the future politician how to cry, remarked, "Here goes my actor."

10. Nikolai Ryzhkov, Russian prime minister

Ryzhkov was prime minister during Mikhail Gorbachev's reign. He received his nickname, "The Weeping Bolshevik," for crying in front of the press when visiting Armenia after the brutal earthquake of 1988. Opposition critics treated him as an object of ridicule, a pathetic clown. Running for Parliament in 1995, he countered accusations that tears proved him too weak to hold a position of power, implying that others would have wept had they seen the same horrors. By changing public opinion to that of viewing tears not as a weakness but as a sign of humanity, Ryzhkov won the election.

11. Norman Schwarzkopf, American military leader

Towards the end of the 1991 Persian Gulf War, General Schwarzkopf was interviewed on television by Barbara Walters. His eyes welled up with tears as he answered personal questions. Walters said, "Generals don't cry." Schwarzkopf replied, "Grant, after Shiloh, went back and cried.

Sherman went back and cried . . . and these are tough old guys . . . Lincoln cried." He added that he held back his tears in front of his troops during the war for the purpose of morale; although he could cry in front of them during a Christmas Eve service, where he was embodying the role of father figure, rather than commanding officer.

IF 36 FAMOUS MEN WERE KNOWN BY THEIR MOTHERS' MAIDEN NAMES

In our society, a married woman loses part of her identity through taking her husband's family name. Should her children happen to become famous, her husband's family is immortalized, while her own family is consigned to oblivion. (Picasso is one of the few famous men who chose to use his mother's name, partly because it was less common than Ruiz, his father's name.) It seems fitting to turn the spotlight, for once, on the maternal branch responsible for contributing half the genetic endowment of the world's immortals and mortals.

1. William Arden (Shakespeare)
2. Isaac Ayscough (Newton)
3. George Ball (Washington)
4. John Bannerman (Diefenbaker)
5. Charles Barrow (Dickens)
6. Jean Boisvert (Chrétien)
7. Frank Buchar (Mahovlich)
8. Milton Carbonell (Acorn)
9. Joey DeVannah (Smallwood)
10. Frank Garaventi (Sinatra)
11. Osama Ghanem (bin Laden)
12. George Bernard Gurly (Shaw)
13. Ernest Hall (Hemingway)
14. Abraham Hanks (Lincoln)
15. Charlie Hill (Chaplin)
16. Arnold Jedrny (Schwarzenegger)
17. Winston Jerome (Churchill)
18. Ludwig Keverich (van Beethoven)
19. Leonard Klinitsky-Klein (Cohen)
20. Albert Koch (Einstein)

21. Johann Sebastian Lämmerhirt (Bach)
22. Robertson McKay (Davies)
23. Sigmund Nathanson (Freud)
24. Brian O'Shea (Mulroney)
25. Wolfgang Amadeus Pertl (Mozart)
26. Stephen Pillsbury (King)
27. Karl Pressburg (Marx)
28. Tiger Punsawad (Woods)
29. Napoleon Ramolino (Bonaparte)
30. Thomas Randolph (Jefferson)
31. Earl Robertson (Birney)
32. Michael Scruse (Jackson)
33. Mick Scutts (Jagger)
34. John A. Shaw (Macdonald)
35. Alexander Graham Symonds (Bell)
36. Charles Wedgwood (Darwin)

—M.B.T. & Cdn. Eds.

9 PEOPLE WITH EXTRA LIMBS AND DIGITS
1. Myrtle Corbin (1868–19??)
"The woman from Texas with four legs" was the only freak who could challenge the "King of Freaks" Frank Lentini as a box-office attraction. ("Freak" expresses dramatic physical deviation from the norm and was not offensive to those in the sideshows.) The body of a twin grew from between Myrtle's legs, well developed from the waist down and completely functional. Myrtle was married and, according to her billing, had five children—three from her own body and two from her twin's.

2. Jean Baptista Dos Santos (1843–?)
Born in Cuba, Jean (or Juan) was a good-looking, well-proportioned boy who happened to have two fully-functioning penises and an extra pair of legs behind and between his own, united along their length. His mental and physical capacities were considered above normal and so, according to one report, was his "animal passion" and sexual functioning. He was exhibited in Havana in 1865 and later in Paris, where he is

alleged to have had an affair with the three-legged courtesan Blanche Dumas, who had two vaginas.

3. Foldi Family

Written up in the book *Anomalies and Curiosities of Medicine* in 1896, the Foldi family was described as living in the tribe of the Hyabites in "Arabia" for many generations. Each member of the large family had 24 digits. They confined their marriages to other members of the tribe, so the trait was usually inherited. In fact, if a baby was born with only 10 fingers and 10 toes, it was sacrificed as the product of adultery.

4. Laloo (1874–1905)

Laloo was a Muslim born in Oovonin, Oudh, India. He had an extra set of arms, legs and sex organs from a headless twin attached to his body at the neck. He, too, travelled with carnivals and circuses in the U.S. and Europe and was written up in many medical textbooks. He married in Philadelphia in 1894, and his wife travelled with him. His "parasitic twin" was male, but the circuses liked to advertise it as female to add to Laloo's strangeness.

5. Francesco Lentini (1889–1966)

For years acknowledged as the "King of Freaks," Frank Lentini had three legs, two sets of genital organs, four feet and sixteen toes. In order to counter his depression at being deformed, Lentini's parents took him to an institution for handicapped children, where he saw boys and girls who were far worse off than he was. "From that time to this," he would later recall, "I've never complained. I think life is beautiful and I enjoy living it." He could use the third leg, which grew out of the base of his spine, as a stool. In his circus act, he used it to kick a football the length of the sideshow tent. Born in Rosolini, Sicily, he moved to the U.S. at the age of nine. He married and raised four children.

6. Jean Libbera (1884–1934)

"The Man with Two Bodies" was born in Rome. He travelled with several circuses displaying his miniature "twin," named Jacques. Jacques had hips, thighs, arms and legs. A German doctor, using X-rays, found a rudimentary structure resembling a head inside Jean's body. Jean covered

8

Jacques with a cape when he went out. Walking with his wife and four children, he looked just like any other family man.

7. Louise L. (1869–?)

Known as "La Dame à Quatre Jambes" ("the lady with four legs"), Louise was born in France. Attached to her pelvis was a second, rudimentary pelvis from which grew two atrophied legs. There were two rudimentary breasts where the legs joined her body. In spite of this handicap, Louise not only married but gave birth to two healthy daughters.

8. Shivshankari Yamanappa Mootageri (1978–)

A young woman from Karnataka, India, Shivshankari has a third leg with nine toes growing out of the middle of her body. She views her anomaly as a divine blessing and supports her family by exhibiting herself locally.

9. Betty Lou Williams (1932–55)

Betty Lou Williams was the daughter of poor black sharecroppers. She looked pretty and shapely in her two-piece bathing suit on the sideshow stage—but growing out of her left side was the bottom half of a body, with two legs and one misplaced arm. Betty, who died at the age of 23, made a good living during the Depression. Her friends say she died of a broken heart, jilted by a man she loved. However, the more probable cause of her death was complications from an asthma attack, aggravated by the second head inside her body.

10 FAMOUS NOSES

1. Rudolf I of Hapsburg (1218–91), German king and Holy Roman Emperor

According to one historian of anatomy, Rudolf "had so large a nose that no artist would ever paint its full dimension."

2. Michelangelo (1475–1564), Italian artist

Michelangelo's nose was so squashed against his face that, in the words of one historian, "his forehead almost overhangs the nose." As a boy, Michelangelo had mercilessly teased the painter Pietro Torrigiano while Torrigiano was trying to study some art inside a church. Angered, Torrigiano turned on young Michelangelo and, in his own words, "dealt him such a blow on the nose that I felt the bone and the cartilage yield under my fist as if they had been made of crisp wafer. And so he'll go with my mark on him to his dying day."

3. Matthew Parker (1504–75), English clergyman
Matthew Parker's name entered the English language as "Nosey Parker"— meaning someone who pokes his nose into other people's business. Parker was Archbishop of Canterbury under Queen Elizabeth I. Though shy and modest, he was over-inquisitive about Church matters, and his enemies began to call him "Nosey" Parker.

4. Tycho Brahe (1546–1601), Danish astronomer
Brahe lost the bridge of his nose in a swordfight when he was 20 and replaced it with a silver one.

5. Cyrano de Bergerac (1619–55), French dramatist
He really was a living person. He is said to have fought 1,000 duels over insults concerning his enormous nose.

6. "Flat Nose" George Curry (1865–1900), bank robber
A Prince Edward Islander who made his mark robbing banks and trains in the American west in the 1890s, Curry got his name after being kicked in the nose by a horse. A bona fide member of the Wild Bunch, his partners in crime included Butch Cassidy and the Sundance Kid. His luck ran out in April 1900, when he was gunned down by a posse near Thompson, Utah. According to some accounts, his distinctive flat nose helped victims and lawmen identify him.

7. Kate Elder, "alias" Fisher, American brothel owner, 1870s
Elder was famous in the Wild West as "Big Nose" Kate. Her nose was of the bulbous variety. She ran a house of ill repute in Dodge City, Kansas, and was the mistress of bad man Doc Holliday. Once, when Holliday, in an argument over a poker hand, slit his opponent's throat and was about to be arrested, "Big Nose" Kate set the livery stable afire, creating a distraction that allowed her lover to escape.

8. George Chuvalo (1937–), heavyweight boxer

The most famous nose in Canadian boxing was first broken when it was just 15 years old. George Chuvalo of Toronto was sparring with the Ontario Amateur Heavyweight Champion when he got caught flush on the nose with a solid punch. Over a professional career that lasted more than 20 years and through more than 90 fights, that nose was bloodied and broken countless times and absorbed thousands of punches. And today, it looks as if it carries the scars of every one. Chuvalo's nose jigs and jags in all the wrong places: it's flat where it should be pointed, and broad where it should be narrow. But like the true heavyweight that he is, George Chuvalo wears it as a badge of honour.

9. Eddie Shack (1937–), hockey player

There is no entry in the hockey record book for "biggest nose on an NHL player," but if there was, the honour would surely belong to Eddie Shack. And "Eddie the Entertainer" was never shy about sticking that nose in the face of his opponents during a fiery professional career that lasted 17 seasons. Which is why the lingering image many hockey fans have of Shack is of blood flowing from his famous nose following a fight. And it is why reporters dubbed him "the Pugnacious Pinocchio." When his career ended in the 1970s, Shack turned his prominent proboscis into a marketing tool. As the corporate spokesperson for the Pop Shoppe, a soft drink company, he boasted, "I've got a nose for value." And he famously insured the nose for $1 million with Lloyds of London, in front of hoards of reporters and photographers.

10. Mehmet Ozyurek, Longest Nose contest winner

Ozyurek is the only two-time winner of the Longest Nose competition in Rise, Turkey. Proudly displaying his 3½-inch (8 cm) nose, he won the inaugural contest in 1997 and then regained the title in 2000.

—I.W., J.Be. & Cdn. Eds.

10 MEETINGS BETWEEN FAMOUS PEOPLE AND PEOPLE NOT YET FAMOUS

1. New York City, 1789. George Washington is introduced to Washington Irving

As the president browsed in a Broadway shop, a servant of the Irving family spotted him from the street and hustled inside with six-year-old Washington Irving in tow. Informed that the lad had been named after him, the chief executive stroked the head that later would conjure up Rip Van Winkle and wished the boy well. *Note:* This pat on the head has been passed on through generations of Americans to the present-day recipient. An older Washington Irving bestowed it upon his publisher, George Putnam, who in turn gave it to young Allan Nevins, the future Pulitzer Prize—winning historian. Years later, at an informal gathering at the Irving Wallace home, Nevins conferred the historic pat on 10-year-old Amy Wallace, saying, "Amy, I pat you on behalf of General George Washington." Amy refused to wash her hair for a week afterwards. As *The Book of Lists* was going to print, she bestowed the historic pat upon baby Daniel, son of the owners of Clementines, one of Los Angeles' most popular restaurants.

2. London, England, 1836. Elizabeth Barrett Browning attends a dinner for William Wordsworth

Elizabeth Barrett, not yet either married to Robert Browning or very well known, was a great admirer of Wordsworth. John Kenyon, a friend of the Barrett family, arranged for Elizabeth to attend a dinner in the poet's honour. Although she was nervous (she said that she trembled "in my soul and my body") about being seated next to Wordsworth, he was kind and even recited one of Dante's sonnets for her entertainment. Eight years later, Barrett paid tribute to Wordsworth by mentioning him in "Lady Geraldine's Courtship."

3. Leghorn, Italy, 1897. Enrico Caruso sings for Giacomo Puccini

Near the beginning of his career, Caruso was hired by Arturo Lisciarelli to star as Rudolfo in a production of Puccini's *La Bohème*. Lisciarelli took advantage of Caruso's eagerness to sing the part by booking him for a mere 15 lire per performance, but added, rather vaguely, that the fee would be increased to 1,000 lire if Puccini liked him. When Caruso found out that Puccini lived nearby, he made a 25-mile (40 km) trip to see the composer at his villa. After Caruso sang several measures, Puccini exclaimed, "Who sent you? God?" Despite the composer's praises, Lisciarelli held Caruso to the original terms of his contract.

4. Saskatoon, 1910. John Diefenbaker sells a newspaper to Wilfrid Laurier

Laurier was in Saskatoon to lay the cornerstone of a building at the University of Saskatchewan. As he left the train station, he was approached by a 15-year-old newsboy named John Diefenbaker. The prime minister paid Diefenbaker for a paper, inquired as to the state of the newspaper business and offered his hope that the young boy would one day grow up to be a great man. In his speech later that day, Laurier spoke about his meeting with the newsboy, who apparently ended the conversation by saying, "I can't waste any more time on you, Prime Minister. I must get about my work."

5. New York City, 1910. Sarah Bernhardt meets Lillian Gish in the wings

Before going west to become a star in D.W. Griffith's epic films, Miss Gish landed a dancing role in Sarah Bernhardt's show. As they waited together in the wings for the opening curtain, the Divine Sarah stroked the young girl's delicate curls admiringly and uttered something to her in French, a language Miss Gish had never before heard.

6. New York City, c. 1945. Nancy Reagan dates Clark Gable

Gable dated the future first lady—then known as Nancy Davis and an aspiring actress—on three occasions during a visit to New York. Although gossip columnists speculated about a possible marriage, the relationship never was particularly romantic. Gable simply enjoyed seeing the town with Nancy and making her laugh, while she hero-worshipped Gable and wondered how long it would last. Once, when they attended a party, she was convinced that Gable would leave her the moment a more glamorous woman appeared. When he stayed, it gave her self-confidence a great boost.

7. Gainesville, Florida, 1962. Tom Petty meets Elvis Presley

When future rock star Petty was 11 years old, Elvis arrived in his hometown to shoot scenes for the movie *Follow That Dream*. Since his uncle was involved with making the film, Petty was able to visit the set and meet the king of rock 'n' roll. Petty remembered, "He didn't have much to say to us, but for a kid at an impressionable age, he was an incredible sight." Straight away, Petty traded his slingshot for a friend's collection of Elvis records.

13

8. Washington, D.C., 1963. Bill Clinton shakes hands with John F. Kennedy

In the summer of 1963, Clinton was named one of the delegates to Boys Nation, an American Legion program in which a select group of high school juniors travelled to Washington to watch national politics in action. The highlight of the trip was the delegates' visit to the White House, where a gangly, crew-cut Clinton briefly shook hands with President Kennedy. The moment was recorded for posterity (and future Clinton campaigns) in a photo and on film. When Clinton returned home to Arkansas, he was set on a political career. His mother, Virginia Kelley, remembered, "I'd never seen him so excited about something. When he came back from Washington, holding this picture of himself with Jack Kennedy, and the expression on his face—I just knew that politics was the answer for him."

9. Cheltenham, England, Literary Festival, 1963. John Fowles meets Iris Murdoch

When bestselling author John Fowles was on the verge of success, but not yet famous, he was a panellist at the Cheltenham Festival. He was prepared to attack the famous authoress Iris Murdoch, but instead found her "a gentle creature with a good mind." Mrs. Fowles felt Murdoch ignored them. Years later, when Fowles's fame was enormous, Murdoch invited the Fowleses to lunch. He recorded the following exchange in his diary:

> I.M.: Are you religious?
> J.F.: Not at all . . .
> I.M.: Nor am I.
> J.F.: in the normal sense of the word.
> I.M.: Ah. (long Pinter-like silence, contemplation of the lawn outside.) I expect you have a nice intellectual circle at Lyme Regis? [The extremely remote country area where Fowles lived.]
> J.F.: Are you mad?

10. Ottawa, 1969. Allan Rock takes John Lennon on a Mystery Tour of Ottawa

Lennon arrived in the nation's capital by train from Montreal, where he was bedded down with Yoko Ono as part of their Year of Peace tour. They had come because future Liberal cabinet minister Allan Rock, then the 21-year-old president of the University of Ottawa's Student Union, had promised them a meeting with Prime Minister Trudeau. After speaking to some students at the university about peace, Lennon, Ono and Rock piled into Rock's Volkswagen fastback for a tour of the city. They drove up to the front door of 24 Sussex Drive and knocked on the door. Alas, the prime minister wasn't home. Lennon scribbled a note for Trudeau and left it with the housekeeper. Six months later, Lennon was back in Ottawa, and this time he was able to get his visit with the prime minister (see Chapter 3).

—W.A.D., C.F. & Cdn. Eds.

CHARLOTTE GRAY'S 10 WOMEN WHO LIVEN UP CANADIAN HISTORY

A graduate of Oxford University, Charlotte Gray came to Canada in 1979 and quickly established herself as a keen observer of Canadian history, politics and culture. To date, Charlotte has written five bestselling books of biography and popular history, including Sisters in the Wilderness, The Lives of Susanna Moodie and Catharine Parr Traill; Canada, A Portrait in Letters 1800–2000; *and (most recently)* The Museum Called Canada. *She is an adjunct research professor in history at Carleton University and is currently at work on a biography of Alexander Graham Bell.*

1. Charlotte Whitton (1896–1975)

A brilliant academic who crusaded tirelessly on behalf of children, Charlotte was a feisty and controversial woman who became Canada's first woman mayor when she was elected mayor of Ottawa in 1951. During 10 stormy years in office, she sought to prove one of her characteristically blunt dictums: "Whatever women do, they must do twice as well as men to be thought half so good . . . luckily, it's not difficult." (She also said, "Call me anything you like, but don't call me a lady." No wonder *Reader's Digest* called her "hell on wheels.")

2. Mary Ann Shadd Cary (1823–93)

Born into an African-American family in Delaware that was active in the Underground Railway, Mary Ann immigrated to Canada in 1850, married a Toronto man and founded a racially integrated school in Chatham, Ontario. She campaigned energetically against slavery and those who took advantage of freed slaves. Afterwards, she returned to the U.S. and became the first black female lawyer there, but not before she had taught a whole generation of new Canadians that "Self-reliance is the Fine Road to Independence."

3. E. Pauline Johnson, Tekahionwake (1861–1913)

The fiery daughter of a Mohawk chief and an English gentlewoman, Pauline was our first coast-to-coast celebrity. In wealthy cities and in every one-horse town across the West, she would sweep onto the stage in fringed buckskin, or an elegant silk evening gown, and mesmerize audiences with her Indian ballads, love poems and lyrical verses about nature. She embodied our dual identity—part British, part other—and in her best-known poem, "The Song My Paddle Sings," she celebrated the national love affair with canoes.

4. Laure Gaudreault (1889–1975)

An elementary school teacher in Charlevoix while still in her teens, Laure realized that the working conditions of teachers—especially women teachers—in rural Quebec lagged far behind those of their counterparts in Quebec City. So she got busy, first organizing a vigorous union for female teachers, then editing a union newspaper, then working for a consolidated union for all teachers in Quebec. Even when she retired, in 1961, she didn't slow down. She founded another union, this time for retired schoolteachers like herself.

5. Belinda Mulroney (1869–1964)

A coal-miner's daughter from Pennsylvania, Belinda opened first a saloon, and then a hotel, in 1897, during the Klondike gold rush, and became the richest woman in the Yukon. She brought all the materials over Chilkoot Pass herself and hired a cook from San Francisco and a manager from L.A. Prim and plain, she went on to become the only woman mining-manager in the Yukon, and made another fortune.

6. Thérèse Forget Casgrain (1896–1981)

Born into the affluent Montreal establishment, Thérèse married a lawyer and cabinet minister and seemed headed for a comfortable and conventional life. But she emerged as the *grande dame* of radical causes within Quebec. All her life, she campaigned for women's rights, and she was also active on behalf of children, consumers, charitable organizations, musicians and the poor. She always wore her pearls, and she believed that "The true liberation of women cannot take place without the liberation of men." Thérèse ran for Parliament as a Liberal, then decided the Liberals were too middle-of-the-road and joined the left-wing CCF (precursor of the New Democratic Party).

7. Asayo Murakami (1898–2003)

Murakami's life represents a triumph of spirit over circumstance. She arrived in Canada from Japan in 1923 as a 25-year-old "Picture Bride," to marry a man who had paid $250 for her passage. The groom she had never met was all wrong ("he was not my type . . . so very short"), so she laboured for three years in a fish cannery to pay off the $250 to him. She then married a Japanese fisherman in British Columbia and happily raised eight children with him while facing the hardship of internment during the Second World War on a Manitoba sugar beet farm. On her 100th birthday, she revealed to her family that she had two more daughters in Japan by a first husband who had abandoned her.

8. Lili St. Cyr (1918–99)

Born Marie Van Schaak in Minneapolis, Lili was neither a francophone nor a Canadian. But in 1944 she changed her name, crossed the border and scandalized and seduced Montreal with a burlesque act in which she emerged from an onstage bubble bath with the bubbles selectively clinging to her salient parts. She was eventually charged with obscenity, but her acquittal in 1951 confirmed that, while Toronto was all about money, Montreal was all about fun.

9. Léa Roback (1903–2000)

One of nine children of Polish Jewish immigrants to Montreal, Léa travelled in Europe in the 1920s and 1930s, and saw the rise of Nazism. She returned to Montreal in 1932 and began a lifelong career of social action and grassroots militancy. Soon she was organizing Marxist study groups, working in a Marxist bookstore and unionizing the garment industry, where working conditions were appalling. Cheerful and outspoken, she remarked that her favourite activity was "standing on a street corner, passing out leaflets, because it is how you come to understand what people are about."

10. Judy LaMarsh (1924–80)

One of the first women cabinet ministers in Canada, between 1963 and 1968 Judy established the fundamentals of medicare and the Royal Commission on the Status of Women, introduced groundbreaking legislation, including the Canada Pension Plan, and presided over the Centennial Year celebrations. She is best remembered, however, for outrageous hats and locker room language within political circles unaccustomed to mouthy women who elbowed their way onto the front bench.

10 DISPARAGING SOBRIQUETS

1. Charles The Simple (879–929), King of the Franks

Son of Louis the Stammerer, Charles III owes his nickname to his policy of making concessions to the Norse invaders to prevent the complete disintegration of his kingdom. In one concession, Charles gave Rollo, the Norse chieftain, his daughter in marriage and the fiefdom of Normandy. This act, among others, was unpopular with his barons, who later deposed and imprisoned him.

2. Louis The Sluggard (966?–987), King of the Franks

His short reign (986–87) marked the end of the Carolingian line. Noted for his self-indulgence, Louis V died at an early age due to a hunting accident. He was also known as "Louis the Do-Nothing"—but historians have noted that since the power of the kingdom was in the hands of the noblemen, there was little that he could do.

3. Ethelred The Unready (968–1016), King of England

Ethelred II's sobriquet is a result of his inability to repel the Danish invasion of England. At first he paid tribute to the Danes, but their raids continued and he was forced to abandon England for Normandy in 1013. In a more generous vein, he has also been called "Ethelred the Ill-Advised."

4. Louis The Fat (1081–1137), King of France

Like his father Philip I, Louis VI was fat. At the age of 46, because of his extreme corpulence, he was unable to mount his horse. Yet he was a popular Capetian monarch and was also referred to as "Louis the Wide-Awake" because of the peace and prosperity of his reign.

5. Louis The Quarreller (1289–1316), King of France

"*Louis le Hutin*" can be translated as "Louis the Stubborn" or "Louis the Quarreller." Louis X's brief reign (1314–16) ended when he died of pleurisy caused by overindulging in cold wine after becoming overheated playing ball.

6. Charles The Bad (1332–87), King of Navarre

Charles II was "bad" because of his treacherous nature. His notoriety grew during the Hundred Years War, when he forced John II of France to grant him lands in Normandy, one of several attempts to further his personal ambition to occupy the French throne.

7. Pedro The Cruel (1334–69), King of Castile

In an age when kings and nobles were unlikely to be mild-mannered and forgiving pacifists, Pedro's nickname indicates that his brutality and violence were seen as something exceptional. Guilty of a series of murders, including his wife's, he was eventually overthrown and killed by his own brother. Attempts by later apologists to get him renamed "*El Justiciero*" ("Executioner of Justice") failed, and history still remembers him as "cruel."

8. Ferdinand The Inconstant (1345–83), King of Portugal

Ferdinand I earned his sobriquet by jilting the daughter of the king of Castile for the more beautiful Leonora Telles, a Portuguese noble-woman. He was also inconsistent in his political policies towards England and Castile.

9. Charles The Mad (1368–1422), King of France

Charles VI assumed the throne at the age of 12, when he was referred to as "Charles the Well-Beloved." In 1392 he became ill, suffering fever and convulsions—the first of 44 attacks he would subsequently endure. The bouts of madness—during which he sometimes tore his clothing and broke furniture—continued to plague him sporadically for the last 30 years of his reign.

10. Ivan The Terrible (1530–84), Czar of Russia

As a young ruler, Ivan IV tortured animals and tossed dogs from rooftops. Torture and executions were common throughout his reign. In 1570 he marched on Novgorod and killed thousands in a five-week binge—some of them children, who were thrown into the icy river. In 1580 he killed his own son in a mad rage.

—D.P.M.

12 FAMOUS PEOPLE WHO WERE EXPELLED FROM SCHOOL

1. Tori Amos (1963–), singer and songwriter

At the age of five, Amos was the youngest person accepted to the Peabody Conservatory in Baltimore, Maryland. Six years later, she was expelled for refusing to read sheet music. The experience inspired the title of her first album, *Y Kant Tori Read?*

2. Conrad Black (1944–), media mogul and author

Conrad Black hated going to Upper Canada College, the elite private boys' school in Toronto. In 1959 he and two other students stole answers to an exam and sold them to their classmates. The trio made almost $5,000, but the scheme unravelled when one of their "customers" got caught walking into the exam with his prepared answers. The boy fessed up to authorities and, in Black's words, "sang like a canary flying backwards at three in the morning." Black was promptly expelled from UCC and next attended Trinity College School in Port Hope. He despised this school too, and, as Peter C. Newman reports in his biography *The Establishment Man*, after a short time TCS "strongly suggested that Conrad would be happier elsewhere."

3. Humphrey Bogart (1899–1957), actor

The son of a successful physician with inherited wealth, young Bogart was sent to Phillips Academy of Andover, Massachusetts, and after a year was thrown out for "irreverence" and "uncontrollable high spirits." Since attending Yale was suddenly out of the question, Bogie joined the U.S. Navy.

4. Tina Brown (1953–), magazine editor

Former editor-in-chief of *Vanity Fair* and *The New Yorker*, Brown was expelled from three boarding schools by the time she was 16. "I got other girls to run away," she recalled, "and I organized protests because we weren't allowed to change our underpants." At one school, the head-mistress found her diary, "and opened it where I had described her bosom as an unidentified flying object."

5. Jean Chrétien (1934–), Canadian prime minister

While attending boarding school in Trois-Rivières in the spring of 1952, former prime minister Jean Chrétien got caught trying to sneak back into the school after a night of carousing with his classmates and was expelled. Rather than face his strict father with the news of his expulsion, he arranged to lay low at a friend's place in Montreal and wait out the rest of the spring term. He returned to Shawinigan when "school" let out, his father still unaware of his expulsion. As the summer progressed, Chrétien made inquiries about going to another college in Prince Edward Island, but that summer he fell in love with his future wife, Aline, and lost interest in moving hundreds of miles away from Shawinigan. As Chrétien faced the dilemma of coming clean with his father or leaving Quebec, his brother Maurice saved the day by pleading with the Trois-Rivières school to take Jean back, which they did.

6. Jackie Collins (1941–), novelist

At 16, Collins was expelled from Francis Holland School in England for (among other crimes) truancy, smoking behind a tree during lacrosse, selling readings from her diary of naughty limericks and waving at the neighbourhood flasher. Says Collins, "I was a *bad* girl." She later sent her own daughters to the same school.

7. Salvador Dali (1904–89), artist

In 1926 Spanish ultra-modernist painter Salvador Dali was expelled from the Escuela Nacional de Bellas Artes de San Fernando in Madrid when he refused to allow his professors to critique his paintings.

8. Gustave Flaubert (1821–80), author

The 18-year-old Flaubert was first in his philosophy class at the Collège Royal. Nevertheless, he led a revolt against a substitute teacher, and when the noisy students were ordered to copy 1,000 lines of poetry as punishment, Flaubert organized a petition in protest. The headmaster was unmoved, and Flaubert and two other boys were expelled.

9. William Randolph Hearst (1863–1951), plutocrat

In 1885 American newspaper publisher William Randolph Hearst was expelled from Harvard, halfway through his junior year. He had given each of his professors a chamber pot adorned with the professor's name and picture.

10. Benito Mussolini (1883–1945), dictator

At the age of nine, Mussolini was sent 20 miles (32 km) from home to a boarding school in Faenza, Italy, run by Salesian priests. The recalcitrant youth was nearly expelled for throwing an inkpot at a teacher who had struck him with a ruler. Finally he went too far—he stabbed a fellow student in the buttocks with a knife. The future dictator was permanently dismissed.

11. Richard Pryor (1940–), comedian

Pryor was expelled from a Catholic grammar school in Peoria, Illinois, when the nuns discovered that his grandmother ran a string of brothels. At 16, he was expelled from Central High School for punching a science teacher named Mr. Think.

12. Leon Trotsky (1879–1940), political leader

At approximately the age of 10, Russian Communist leader Leon Trotsky was expelled from secondary school in Odessa after he incited his classmates to howl at their teacher. Trotsky, however, was the school's best pupil and was readmitted the following year.

—R.J.F., the Eds. & Cdn. Eds.

10 PEOPLE WITH THE MOST SQUARE MILES OF THE EARTH'S SURFACE NAMED AFTER THEM

		Square miles
I.	Amerigo Vespucci, Italian explorer	
	Total area:	16,243,000
	North America	9,360,000
	South America	6,883,000
2.	Victoria, British queen	
	Total area:	1,188,100
	Queensland (Australia)	666,790
	Victoria (Australia)	227,620
	Great Victoria Desert (Australia)	127,000
	Victoria Island (Canada)	83,000
	Victoria Island (Antarctica)	60,000
	Lake Victoria (Africa)	26,000
	Victoria Strait (Canada)	6,000
3.	Maud, Norwegian queen	
	Total area:	1,102,000
	Queen Maud Land (Antarctica)	1,081,000
	Queen Maud Mountains (Antarctica)	15,000
	Queen Maud Gulf (Canada)	6,000
4.	James Weddell, British seal hunter and explorer	
	Weddell Sea (Antarctica)	1,080,000
5.	Abel Janzoon Tasman, Dutch explorer	
	Total area:	925,100
	Tasman Sea (Pacific Ocean)	900,000
	Tasmania (Australia)	24,900
	Tasman Peninsula (Australia)	200
6.	Christopher Columbus, Italian explorer	
	Total area:	923,350
	Colombia	440,830

British Columbia (Canada)	365,950
Columbia Plateau (U.S.)	100,000
District of Columbia and 10 U.S. counties named for Columbus (combined area)	6,790
Colón Department (Honduras)	3,430
Colón Department (Panama)	3,150

7. Vitus Bering, Russian explorer
      Bering Sea (Arctic Ocean)   879,000

8. Ibn-Saud, Saudi king
      Saudi Arabia   865,000

9. Charles Wilkes, U.S. naval officer
      Wilkes Land (Antarctica)   660,000

10. Willem Barents, Dutch explorer
      Barents Sea (Arctic Ocean)   592,000

—C.F.

8 UNNAMED WOMEN OF THE BIBLE

1. Noah's Wife

She is mentioned five times in the book of Genesis, but only in the context of being one of a group who is present. This is surprising considering how talented and efficient she must have been to have been suddenly uprooted from her home and asked to set up housekeeping in a gopherwood ark filled with birds, snakes, insects and full-grown animals of every species. This woman, who kept everything in order in the ark for 12 months, is known to us today, not by her own name, but only as "Noah's wife" (Gen. 6:18; 7:7 and 13; 8:16 and 18).

2. The Pharaoh's Daughter

Her father, probably Ramses II, decreed that it was necessary to kill all male children born to the Hebrews because the Hebrew population in Egypt was growing too quickly. One day the pharaoh's daughter was bathing in the Nile with her attendants when she noticed a basket containing a three-month-old baby boy. She realized that he was a Hebrew child and decided to raise him rather than allow him to be killed by her father. The baby's sister, Miriam, was standing nearby and offered to find a Hebrew woman to suckle the child. The baby's mother, Jochebed, conveniently close at hand, was summoned and hired as a nurse to care for the child. The pharaoh's daughter later named the baby Moshe, or Moses, and he grew up to become the greatest leader and teacher in the history of the Jews. The woman who saved his life and raised and educated him was known in various history books as Thermuthis, Myrrina or Mercis. However, the authors of the Bible referred to her only as "the pharaoh's daughter" (Exod. 2:5–10).

3. The Woman Patriot of Thebez

Abimelech was a tyrant who ruled over Shechem for three years during the 12th century BC. Having taken power by slaughtering 69 of his 79 brothers, he continued his bloody ways by killing the entire population of the town of Shechem when they revolted against him. Moving on to the neighbouring town of Thebez, he was about to set it ablaze when "a certain woman" appeared on the roof of the town tower and dropped a piece of a millstone on Abimelech's head, crushing his skull. Humiliated by the prospect of being killed by a woman, Abimelech ordered one of his followers to run him through with a sword. With Abimelech dead, his supporters dispersed and Thebez was saved (Judg. 9:50–55).

4. The Wise Woman of Abel

When Sheba, the son of Bichri, led a revolt against King David, David sent his commander-in-chief, Joab, to track down the rebel and kill him. Joab finally found the culprit hiding in the walled city of Abel. Joab and his soldiers began the destruction of the city, but stopped when a wise woman called out to them to discuss the situation. Joab explained that if the people of Abel turned the rebel Sheba over to him, he and his soldiers would leave them alone. The wise woman easily convinced her people that this was a good deal. Sheba was quickly decapitated, his head thrown over the wall to Joab, and the city of Abel was saved (II Sam. 20:15–22).

5. Barzillai's Daughter

When this Gileadite woman married, she retained her own name rather than take her husband's. In fact, her husband, a priest, took *her* family's name. Despite this early display of feminism, or perhaps because of it, the Bible authors do not tell us her name, but refer to her merely as "one of the daughters of Barzillai" (Neh.7:63).

6. The Shulamite Sweetheart

According to some scholars, the Song of Songs tells the story of a young Shulamite maiden who attracted the attention of King Solomon. He forced her to come to Jerusalem and tried to convince her to marry him, but she resisted him and insisted on remaining faithful to her shepherd lover. Eventually Solomon gave up and allowed her to return home, while he was forced to continue living with the 700 women he had already married (Song of Solomon).

7. Herodias's Daughter

Known to the historian Josephus as Salome, this most famous of all dancers is not given a name in the New Testament. King Herod was so impressed by the dancing of Herodias's daughter that he offered her any gift, including half his kingdom. After consulting her mother, who was angry with John the Baptist for publicly denouncing her as an incestuous adulterer, she asked for the head of John the Baptist on a platter. She got it and promptly turned over the grisly prize to her mom (Matt. 14:6; Mark 6:22).

8. The Adulterous Woman

Caught in the act of adultery, this woman was brought before Jesus by the scribes and Pharisees, who pointed out that the law required that such an offence be punished by stoning. Jesus ignored them at first and then said, "He that is without sin among you, let him first cast a stone at her." One by one her accusers slithered away, and she was not punished (John 8:3–11).

8 FAKE "DE"S

1. Honoré de Balzac

The great French novelist was the son of a civil servant named Balzac. He added the aristocratic "de" to his name and passed it on to his son.

2. Pierre-Augustin Caron de Beaumarchais

The author of *The Barber of Seville*, the most popular comedy of the 18th century, Caron was the son of a watchmaker. He married a widow and took over her husband's position at court, as well as his property. One of those properties was in Beaumarchais, which name he then appended to his own.

3. Amor De Cosmos

Born William Alexander Smith, Amor De Cosmos was one of the founding fathers of British Columbia. A reformer and liberal at heart, he was elected several times in and around Vancouver and Victoria and served simultaneously as the premier of British Columbia and a federal member of Parliament from 1872 to 1874. In 1854 he changed his name to something that he felt was more memorable than Bill Smith. *Amor de cosmos* means "lover of the universe." His name was a factor in one electoral defeat when he was forced to run as "William Alexander Smith commonly known as Amor De Cosmos." When one voter could not say the full name at the polling station, his vote was disqualified, and De Cosmos's opponent George Gordon won by a single vote.

4. Fabre d'Eglantine

Born Philippe Fabre, he was a popular playwright and politician who is credited with creating the names of the months and days that were used in the French Revolutionary calendar. Accused of "moderacy," he was guillotined on April 5, 1794.

5. Daniel Defoe

Born Daniel Foe, he had already adopted his "de" before he wrote his famous novels *Robinson Crusoe* and *Moll Flanders*.

6. Mazo de la Roche

The popular author of 16 books in the Whiteoaks of Jalna series was born Mazo Roche in Newmarket, Ontario, in 1879, the daughter of William

Roche and Alberta Lundy. Why she decided to add "de la" to her name is not exactly clear, but in both her fiction and real life, Mazo de la Roche liked to live in a world of illusion. Part of that illusion appears to be that her family was descended from French aristocracy.

7. André de Toth

Born Andreas Toth in Hungary, he transformed into a "de," moved to Hollywood and became a successful director of violent Westerns and action dramas. He also directed the 3-D classic *House of Wax* (1953).

8. Dame Ninette de Valois

Born Edris Stannus and married to Arthur Connell, she was known as a dancer, a choreographer and the founder of what became the Royal Ballet, as well as the Royal Ballet School. She died on March 8, 2001, at the age of 92.

JAN WONG'S 10 FAVOURITE DINNER GUESTS OF ALL TIME

A journalist and author, Jan Wong's books include Red China Blues: My Long March from Mao to Now *(1996) and* Jan Wong's China: Reports from a Not-So-Foreign Correspondent *(1999). In her celebrity lunch column for* The Globe and Mail, *she dissected the likes of Yo-Yo Ma, Suzanne Somers, Margaret Atwood and Mordecai Richler. The columns were published in* Lunch with Jan Wong *(2000).*

The success of a great dinner party lies in the seating arrangements. Of course, I'd put Hitler between the only black and the only Jew. Martin Luther King Jr. and his dream would be Hitler's worst nightmare. Mao would sit between Cleopatra and my grandfather, Chong Hooie. A peasant who arrived in Canada in 1881 (and who died before I was born), Grandfather Chong would enjoy meeting a fellow peasant who transformed China. Mao and Cleopatra would likely hit it off. He liked a pretty face; to her, power was an aphrodisiac.

Joan of Arc and Mozart could discuss peaking at an early age. Galileo would find a common bond with Joan, who was burned at the stake for heresy that included cross-dressing. During the Inquisition, Galileo was forced to recant his shocking theory that the earth revolved around the sun.

As hostess, I'd seat myself between Shakespeare and the Virgin Mary. I always wanted to ask Will how he came up with those great plot lines. But I wouldn't discuss children with Mary. Like every mother, she'd say her son was perfect. Instead, I'd ask how tough it was convincing Joseph of the Immaculate Conception.

Seating plan:

<table>
<tr><td colspan="2" align="center">Me</td></tr>
<tr><td>1. The Virgin Mary</td><td>6. Shakespeare</td></tr>
<tr><td>2. Hitler</td><td>7. My grandfather</td></tr>
<tr><td>3. Martin Luther King Jr.</td><td>8. Mao</td></tr>
<tr><td>4. Joan of Arc</td><td>9. Cleopatra</td></tr>
<tr><td>5. Mozart</td><td>10. Galileo</td></tr>
</table>

6 PEOPLE WHOSE NAMES WERE CHANGED BY ACCIDENT

1. Irving Berlin (1888–1989), songwriter

He was born Israel Baline, but the sheet music for his first composition, "Marie from Sunny Italy," credited the song to "I. Berlin." Baline preferred the mistake over his actual name.

2. William Faulkner (1897–1962), novelist

After William Falkner's first book, *The Marble Faun* (1924), was published, he discovered that a *u* had been inserted into his last name. He decided to live with the new spelling rather than go through the hassle of correcting the error.

3. Ulysses S. Grant (1822–85), general and U.S. president

The future Civil War general was born Hiram Ulysses Grant. The prospect of entering the U.S. Military Academy with the initials "H.U.G." embarrassed him, so the new cadet reversed the order of his names and started signing himself U.H. Grant. He soon learned that Rep. Thomas L. Hamer, who had sponsored his appointment to West Point, had mistakenly enrolled him as Ulysses Simpson Grant, "Simpson" being the maiden name of Grant's mother. Grant, finding nothing objectionable in the initials "U.S.G.," adopted the new name.

4. Buddy Holly (1936–59), singer and songwriter
When Charles "Buddy" Holley signed his first contract with Decca Records, his last name was misspelled as "Holly." Reasoning that others in the recording industry would make the same error, Buddy kept the new spelling.

5. Dionne Warwick (1940–), singer
When her first record, "Don't Make Me Over," was released in 1962, a printing error made Dionne Warrick over into Dionne Warwick.

6. Oprah Winfrey (1954–), television personality
Her parents intended to name her "Orpah" after Ruth's sister-in-law in the Old Testament. However, the name was misspelled "Oprah" on her birth certificate. Winfrey has used it ever since.

—C.F.

6 ALMOST INDESTRUCTIBLE PEOPLE
1. Grigori Rasputin
The Russian mystic and orgiast held enormous political power at the court of the Romanovs from 1905 until his murder in 1916. That this decadent, vulgar peasant should hold such sway over the Empress Alexandra infuriated a group of five power-hungry aristocrats, who set out to destroy him. They arranged for Rasputin to take midnight tea at the home of Prince Felix Yussupov. Some accounts say that Rasputin drank voluminous amounts of poisoned or opiated wine and remained unaffected, to Yussupov's great consternation.

The frightened prince contrived an excuse to go upstairs, where the waiting gang furnished him with a gun, then followed him downstairs. According to Rasputin's daughter, Maria, the men assaulted her father and "used him sexually." Then Yussupov shot him. Again, according to Maria, they viciously beat Rasputin and castrated him, flinging the famed penis across the room. One of the conspirators—a doctor—pronounced the victim dead, but Yussupov, feeling uneasy, began to shake the body violently. The corpse's eyelids twitched—and opened. Suddenly, Rasputin jumped to his feet and gripped Yussupov by the shoulders. Terrorized, Prince Felix pulled himself free. Rasputin fell to the floor, and the other men dashed upstairs. In the midst of the brouhaha, they heard noises in the hallway: Rasputin had crawled up the stairs after them. Two more shots were fired into him, and again he was beaten with harrowing violence. The men (still doubting his death) bound Rasputin's wrists. Carrying him to a frozen river, they thrust his body through a hole in the ice. Rasputin was still alive. The icy water revived him, and he struggled against his bonds. When his body was found two days later, his scarred wrists and water-filled lungs gave this proof, as did his freed right hand, which was frozen in the sign of the cross.

2. Samuel Dombey

Dombey was a black gravedigger in post–Civil War Orleans. Because he worked for such low rates, his fellow gravediggers decided to put an end to their competition. They called upon a certain Dr. Beauregard, reputed to have magical powers, to use his $50 (U.S.) "supreme curse" involving an owl's head. The next morning, as Dombey began to dig a new grave, he heard a loud explosion. Someone, apparently injured, staggered from a nearby clump of bushes. There Dombey found a gun that, overloaded with buckshot, had blown up. Later, a much-bandaged Dr. Beauregard threatened to curse anyone who questioned him.

The gravediggers took matters into their own hands. They placed a keg of explosive powder under the cot in the tool shed where Dombey took his daily nap and lit it while he slept. The explosion blasted Dombey out the doorway and plopped him 20 feet (6 m) away. The tool shed was completely destroyed, but Dombey was unhurt. The local police nick-named him "Indestructible Sam."

But the best (or worst) was yet to come: Indestructible Sam was soon captured by masked men and taken in a boat to Lake Pontchartrain. Sam's hands and feet were tied, and he was dumped into the depths of the lake. These particular depths, however, turned out to be only 2 feet (60 cm); Sam wriggled free of his bonds and walked ashore.

Next, Dombey's foes tried arson—and as Dombey ran from his burning home, he received a full load of buckshot in his chest. Firemen saved the house and rushed Sam to the hospital, where he lived up to his nickname.

Sam had the last laugh. He continued to dig graves and died at 98, having outlived every one of his jealous competitors.

3. Michael Malloy

In 1933, a down-and-out drunken Irishman became the victim of an extraordinary series of murder attempts. Malloy was a bum who frequented the speakeasy of one Anthony Marino in the Bronx. Marino and four of his friends, themselves hard up, had recently pulled off an insurance scam, murdering Marino's girlfriend and collecting on her policy; pitiful Michael Malloy seemed a good next bet. The gang took out three policies on him. Figuring Malloy would simply drink himself to death, Marino gave him unlimited credit at the bar. This scheme failed— Malloy's liver knew no bounds. The bartender, Joseph Murphy, was in on the plot and substituted antifreeze for Malloy's whisky. Malloy asked for a refill and happily put away six shots before passing out on the floor; after a few hours, he perked up and requested another drink. For a week Malloy guzzled antifreeze non-stop. Straight turpentine worked no better, and neither did horse liniment laced with rat poison. A meal of rotten oysters marinated in wood alcohol brought Malloy back for seconds. In an ultimate moment of culinary inspiration, Murphy devised a sandwich for his victim: spoiled sardines mixed with carpet tacks. Malloy came back for more.

The gang's next tactic was to dump the drunk into a bank of wet snow and pour water over him on a night when the temperature had sunk to −14°F (−26°C). No luck. So Marino hired a professional killer, who drove a taxi straight at Malloy at 45 mph (72 kph), throwing him into the air—and then ran over him again for good measure. After a disappearance of three weeks, Malloy walked into the bar, told the boys he'd been hospitalized because of a nasty car accident, and was "sure ready for drink."

Finally, the desperate murderers succeeded—they stuffed a rubber hose into Malloy's mouth and attached it to a gas jet until his face turned purple. The scheme was discovered, and four members of the five-man

"Murder Trust" (as the tabloids dubbed Marino and Co.) died in the electric chair. One New York reporter speculated that if Mike Malloy had sat in the electric chair, he would have shorted out every circuit in Sing Sing.

4. Herbert "The Cat" Noble

This Dallas racketeer earned his nickname after the first nine attempts on his life. He was shot at so often that he was also called "The Clay Pigeon." His third moniker was "The Sieve" because he had been riddled by so many bullets. The murder attempts were made by another Dallas gangster, the crude, illiterate "Benny the Cowboy" Binion. A retired police captain revealed the details of their rivalry to Ed Reid and Ovid Demaris, authors of *The Green Felt Jungle*, an exposé of Las Vegas crime. Binion was taking a 25% cut of Noble's crap games and wanted to up it to 40%. Noble refused, and the fireworks began.

In a dramatic car chase, Binion's thugs splattered Noble's car with bullets, and one slug lodged in Noble's spine. Binion moved to Las Vegas, but the feud continued long-distance—Benny wanted to save face by employing hired killers to nail Noble. Hollis "Lois" Green, a depraved murderer, succeeded in wounding Noble on his third attempt. The following year, in 1949, explosives were found attached to Noble's car, and he was soon shot again. Real tragedy struck when Noble's beloved wife, Mildred, was literally blown to bits by an explosion of nitrogelatin planted in his car. This loss unhinged Noble's mind—his prematurely grey hair (he was 41) turned snow white, he lost 50 pounds (23 kg) and he began to drink heavily. Another shooting put him in the hospital, where he was fired upon from across the street.

Noble's attempts at retaliation included equipping a plane with bombs to drop on Binion's home, but Noble was shot again before he could carry out his plan. Next, Noble miraculously survived the bombing of his business and a nitroglycerine explosion in one of his planes. Binion finally killed Herbert the same gruesome way he killed Mildred—with nitrogelatin hidden near Noble's mailbox. On August 7, 1951, the top part of Noble's body was blown right over a tree—there was nothing left of the bottom. The retired police captain who revealed all this commented, "I think Noble had more downright cold-blooded nerve than anyone I've ever known. He was ice in water in a tight place."

5. Bernadette Scott

Between 1979 and 1981, Peter Scott, a British computer programmer, made seven attempts to kill his 23-year-old wife after taking out a $530,000 (U.S.) insurance policy on her. First, he put mercury into a strawberry flan, but he put in so much mercury that it slithered out. Next, Peter served Bernadette a poisoned mackerel, but she survived her meal. Once in Yugoslavia and again in England, Peter tried to get her to sit on the edge of a cliff, but she refused. When Bernadette was in bed with chicken pox, her husband set the house on fire, but the blaze was discovered in time. His next arson attempt met with the same result. Bernadette had her first suspicion of foul play when Peter convinced her to stand in the middle of the street while he drove their car towards her, saying he wanted to "test the suspension." He accelerated, but he swerved away moments before impact. "I was going to run her over but I didn't have the courage," he later confessed to the police. Pleading guilty to several charges, he was jailed for life. The Scotts had been married for two years.

6. Alan Urwin

According to the *Daily Mirror*, after his wife left him, Urwin, a 46-year-old former miner from Sunderland, England, made seven suicide attempts in a three-month period in 1995. Having survived three drug overdoses, he wound an electrical wire about his body, got into a tub of water and plugged the wires into an outlet. The fuse blew out and he suffered a minor electric shock. He then tried to hang himself with the same piece of wire, but it snapped and he fell to the floor, very much alive. For his sixth attempt, he broke a gas pipe in his bedroom and lay next to it. When this didn't kill him, he lit a match. The explosion blew away the gable end of his semi-detached house, along with the windows and part of the roof. He was pulled out of the wreckage suffering nothing worse than some flash burns. He was convicted of arson and placed on two years' probation. A few months later, he was on speaking terms with his ex-wife and was considerably more cheerful.

6 PEOPLE WHO CAME SECOND IN HISTORY

1. The second pope

After St. Peter, a shadowy figure known as St. Linus the Martyr reigned as the second pope from AD 67 to 79. He was probably a Jew, and was most certainly born in Tuscany, Italy.

2. The second Cromwell to be Lord Protector of England

On September 3, 1658, Oliver Cromwell, the Lord Protector of England, died, nominating as his successor his eldest surviving son, Richard. Not the man his father was, Richard survived as ruler of the country for less than a year and was dismissed by Parliament in May 1659. Twelve months later, the monarchy was restored in the shape of Charles II, and Richard Cromwell fled to the Continent. Allowed to return to England in 1680, he became a farmer in Hertfordshire and died in 1712 at the age of 85.

3. The second woman to take her seat in the Canadian House of Commons

In 1935 Martha Louise Black became the second woman to be elected to the House of Commons when she won the Yukon riding for the Conservatives despite a Liberal sweep in the rest of the country. Born in Chicago in 1866, she arrived in the Yukon with her father during the height of the gold rush in 1899. In 1904 she married George Black, a local Dawson City lawyer. In 1912 George was appointed Commissioner of the Yukon, and in 1921 he was elected to Parliament. He held the seat until 1935, when he was forced to step aside due to ill health. Martha ran in his place and won the seat, becoming one of only two women in the House (Agnes Macphail was the other). But Martha Black always believed her husband was better suited to political life than she was, and she gladly stepped aside in the 1940 election to allow George to regain the seat.

4. The second führer of the Third Reich

If the Third Reich had survived the thousand years its founder predicted it would, there would have been very many Reichsführers. In fact, there were two. After Hitler's suicide in his Berlin bunker on April 30, 1945, the dubious honour of being the second führer of Nazi Germany was bestowed on Admiral Karl Dönitz. Eight days later the new führer agreed to terms of unconditional surrender to the Allied forces. Tried at the Nuremberg War Trials, he was sentenced to 10 years' imprisonment, which he served in Spandau Prison on the western fringes of Berlin. Dönitz died in 1980.

5. The second man to run a mile in less than four minutes

Just 46 days after Roger Bannister ran the first sub-four-minute mile, the Australian athlete John Landy became the second man in history to break the four-minute barrier. Running in a race in Finland, Landy beat Bannister's record-breaking time by nearly two seconds. The stage was set for an epic confrontation between the two men, which took place in the so-called "Miracle Mile" at the Empire and Commonwealth Games in Vancouver on August 7, 1954. Landy led from the start but, in the home straight, looking over his left shoulder to see where his rival was, he was overtaken by Bannister on his right. Landy tried to respond but was beaten to the tape. In later life, Landy was elected governor of the Australian state of Victoria.

6. The second person to swim across Lake Ontario

When Marilyn Bell became the first person to swim across Lake Ontario on September 9, 1954, she attracted headlines all around the world. Many people were stunned that a 16-year-old schoolgirl was the first to meet one of swimming's greatest challenges. When 36-year-old John Jaremey became the second person to cross the lake two summers later, he didn't get nearly as much recognition, even though 21 men had already failed in their attempts to make the swim. A Toronto steamfitter, Jaremey left Niagara-on-the-Lake at 5:47 a.m. on July 22, 1956, and when he arrived at the Eastern Gap lighthouse at 3:02 the following morning, he was greeted by 12,000 cheering spectators.

VICKI GABEREAU'S 10 FAVOURITE PEOPLE TO INTERVIEW

Vicki Gabereau has been in the radio and/or television business for 30 years, as a researcher, producer and on-air type at CBC and CTV. "I guess I will keep at it until dementia takes over or I get it right. I should say, this list could have included another 1,000. Next time."

1. Pierre Berton

Pierre never let me down, except maybe the first time I interviewed him, when he thought it would be funny if he didn't answer the questions. So "yes" and "no" was pretty much all I got. His biggest complaint was that too many interviewers neglected to read whichever one of his 50 books he was flogging. One time, knowing that I had just received the 1,000-page book the day before, he agreed to fake it, just this once. But, of course, he didn't fake it. In answer to my lame question about Tecumseh, he replied, "You ought to know that, Vicki, you've read the book."

2. Carol Channing

She has never gone unnoticed. She is a spectacle in all ways, and will, luckily, say whatever is on her not-insubstantial mind. She is tiny of body but tall, with an enormous head, giant eyes, big, big hair and a mouth like a bear cave. She is still working in her 80s. When she came to my studio, the whole building was in an uproar, people were desperate to see her, and she spoke to everyone who approached. We had lunch together. I was enchanted.

3. Andrew Jones

He was a paleo-archaeologist, also known as a paleo-scatologist, and this was, and continues to be, the goofiest interview I have ever conducted. An Englishman who specializes in 500-year-old latrines is not that easy to dig up. Apparently what we ate half a millennium ago holds a fascination for some. Who knew? He had found a particularly interesting bit of human excrement (now mercifully petrified) in an excavation where they were building the new Lloyds Bank. They have, it is reported, kept the aforementioned item in a glass case on display in the lobby.

4. Jack Webster

Jack was one of the greatest broadcasters who ever lived. He was certainly the loudest. A Scot from Glasgow with an impressive newspaper background, he came to Vancouver, and he ate the town for lunch. For many years he held court on open-line radio, and then he conquered television. As a kid, I begged him to let me watch him do his radio program. He was our watchdog, ranting and raving and taking apart politicians, the police force, the courts—all transgressors were fair game. He and I won a radio award for a loony interview that involved a bottle of Scotch. His wife said she could hear the ice clinking.

5. Tom Robbins

A prolific American writer and cultural icon of my generation (read old, now), Tom Robbins is a quiet man with a ragingly funny take on the world. We have had three encounters, each one delightful. He has a trick, and it's a good one, a kind of parlour entertainment, a party piece suitable for dinner parties and talk shows. He can yell like Tarzan. It could wake the dead. When questioned by Canada Customs some years ago about his reason for visiting Vancouver, he said he was coming to do my show . . . "Oh yeah, well if you're Tom Robbins, do the yell." He did. They let him in.

6. Jann Arden

Jann has the voice of an angel and the mouth of a 19th-century stevedore. For that we are all grateful. Our ratings are never higher than when she appears, which makes me think it is high time she had her own TV platform. She is the most fearless of entertainers, and watching her work an audience is like witnessing lightning strike. She has a take-no-prisoners style of comedy, and I know almost no one who can keep up with her . . . Not I; I just let the reins go loose.

7. Peter Ustinov

He is the only man for whom I would have waited a week, not just the seven hours I cooled my heels in the English countryside while he shot scenes for a Poirot turn. When he was finally able to free himself, he should have been exhausted, but he was a firecracker and he could hardly wait to try out his Canadian accent. It was pretty good, too, better than mine, maybe.

8. George Chuvalo

George was a superb pugilist. He really was a contender. In my extreme youth, I watched a lot of boxing with my father, who was an enthusiast.

Unfortunately, I never saw Chuvalo fight, except on film. He was impressive, fearless and sure-footed. I am sure he was never knocked down, not even the great Muhammad Ali could shake him. His personal life brought him the real blows: the deaths of three sons and his first wife brought him to his knees. He now dedicates his life to helping people overcome substance abuse.

9. Elton John

In the first part of his life he was also known as Reg Dwight, and sometimes even now his old cronies will call him that. I interviewed him in Las Vegas, and I think I was a nervous wreck until he came into the room. He talked about his parents and his childhood; his new show at Caesars Palace, The Red Piano; his new record—all the bits one would expect. But then he went off on another road . . . he wants to build a retirement home for aging rock 'n' rollers and buddies of his, somewhere in Italy, a nice villa, perhaps. The rockers with the walkers. Sign me up.

10. Julia Child

She died two days short of her 92nd birthday, a life packed with adventure and beauty. She came to my radio studio when she was a mere kid in her 80s. She was the proselytizer of good cooking . . . butter, salt, sugar and plenty of it was her mantra. It worked for her and millions of fans, professional and amateur, around the world. I use her cookbooks weekly and hear her darling cracked voice on every page.

10 THINGS DOUGLAS COUPLAND FIGURED OUT ABOUT TERRY FOX WHILE DOING A BOOK ABOUT HIM

Doug Coupland is the author of many novels, most recently including Generation X: Tales for an Accelerated Culture *(1991),* Girlfriend in a Coma *(1998),* Hey Nostradamus! *(2003) and* Eleanor Rigby *(2004). All of the proceeds of* Terry *will go to the Terry Fox Foundation (www.terryfoxrun.org).*

1. Everyone thinks his cheeks were sunburnt, but it was actually mostly his left cheek, the one that faces the sun while running westward.

2. He received more mail than anybody in Canadian history.

3. He never once brought up the subject of running anywhere else but Canada.

4. The run was to have ended in Vancouver's Stanley Park on December 8, 1980.

5. No one knows if the run either speeded up his cancer or slowed it down.

6. He liked Hank Williams music.

7. He wore nine shoes during the Marathon of Hope—eight on his left, real foot and just the one on his prosthetic right foot.

8. He'd actually completed two-thirds of his planned run, not just half.

9. There's no known record of anybody else running more than 10 marathons in a row. Terry ran 143.

10. If he had the same cancer today, chances are he'd be alive and still have both his legs. Cancer research works.

CHAPTER 2   # MOVIES AND TELEVISION

ABOVE: *Wayward Mountie is stripped of his tunic and his honour in* McKenna of the Mounted

15 ACTORS AND ACTRESSES WHO TURNED DOWN GREAT ROLES

1. Marlon Brando

Turned down the role of Frankie, the musician-junkie, in *The Man with the Golden Arm* (1955). Frank Sinatra got the part and re-established his career with an electrifying performance.

2. Montgomery Clift

Expressed enthusiasm for the role of the young writer in *Sunset Boulevard* (1950), but later turned it down, claiming that his audience would not accept his playing love scenes with a woman who was 35 years older. William Holden starred with Gloria Swanson in the widely acclaimed film.

3. Sean Connery

Long a fan-favourite to play Gandalf, the venerable wizard from J.R.R. Tolkien's Lord of the Rings trilogy, the star turned the role down because he did not want to spend 18 months filming in New Zealand. Sir Ian McKellan eventually played the role in the film trilogy to wide acclaim. After the massive success of the first film, *The Fellowship of the Ring*, Connery said, "I had never read Tolkien and the script when they sent it to me, I didn't understand . . . bobbits, hobbits . . . I will see it."

4. Bette Davis

Turned down the role of Scarlett O'Hara in *Gone with the Wind* (1939). The role went to Vivien Leigh. Davis thought that her co-star was going to be Errol Flynn, with whom she refused to work.

5. W.C. Fields

Could have played the title role in *The Wizard of Oz* (1939). The part was written for Fields, who would have played the Wizard as a cynical con man. But he turned down the part, purportedly because he wanted $100,000 (U.S.) and MGM only offered him $75,000. However, a letter signed by Fields's agent asserts that Fields rejected the offer in order to devote all his time to writing *You Can't Cheat an Honest Man*. Frank Morgan ended up playing the Wizard.

6. Jane Fonda

Turned down *Bonnie and Clyde* (1967). The role of Bonnie Parker went to Faye Dunaway. Fonda, living in France at the time, did not want to move to the U.S. for the role.

7. Cary Grant

Producers Albert Broccoli and Harry Saltzman, who had bought the film rights to Ian Fleming's James Bond novels, originally approached Cary Grant about playing 007. Grant declined because he did not want to become involved in a film series. Instead, Sean Connery was cast as Bond, starting with *Dr. No* (1962). Fleming's comment on this casting choice: "He's not exactly what I had in mind."

8–9. Gene Hackman and Michelle Pfeiffer

Orion Pictures acquired the film rights to *The Silence of the Lambs* in 1988 because Gene Hackman had expressed an interest in directing and writing the screenplay for it. He would also star as serial killer Hannibal Lecter. By mid-1989, Hackman had dropped out of the project. Jonathan Demme took over as director and offered the female lead of FBI agent-in-training Clarice Starling to Michelle Pfeiffer, with whom he had worked in *Married to the Mob* (1988). Pfeiffer felt the film was too dark and decided not to be in it. When *The Silence of the Lambs* was made in 1990, the lead roles were played by Anthony Hopkins and Jodie Foster. Both won Academy Awards for their performances.

10. Hedy Lamarr

Turned down the role of Ilsa in *Casablanca* (1942). Ingrid Bergman took over and, with Bogart, made film history. Lamarr had not wanted to work with an unfinished script.

11. Burt Lancaster

Turned down the lead in *Ben-Hur* (1959). The role of Judah Ben-Hur went to Charlton Heston, who won an Academy Award and added another hit to his career of spectacular blockbusters.

12–13. Ewan McGregor and Will Smith

Both of these stars turned down the role of Neo, which eventually went to Keanu Reeves, in the blockbuster science fiction epic *The Matrix*. McGregor starred as the young Obi-Wan Kenobi in *Star Wars: The Phantom Menace* instead, while Smith—who went on to star in the film version of Isaac Asimov's *I, Robot*—admitted, "I watched Keanu's performance—and very rarely do I say this—but I would have messed it up. I would have absolutely messed up *The Matrix*. At that point I wasn't smart enough as an actor to let the movie be."

14. Sarah Polley

The outspoken Canadian actress got her start playing Sara Stanley in the much-loved Canadian TV series *Road to Avonlea* and quickly found big-screen success in films such as *The Sweet Hereafter* (1997), directed by Atom Egoyan. She was offered and almost accepted the female lead in Cameron Crowe's film *Almost Famous* (2000). Polley's part as "Penny Lane," a lovelorn groupie, eventually went to Kate Hudson, which quickly established her as a bankable Hollywood star.

15. Robert Redford

Turned down the role of Ben Braddock in *The Graduate* (1967). The role made an instant star of Dustin Hoffman. Redford thought he could not project the right amount of naïveté.

—R.S., C.F. & Cdn. Eds.

NORMAN JEWISON'S 10 MOST IMPORTANT FILMS

Maverick film director Norman Jewison is one of Canada's greatest cinematic talents. He has been nominated for seven Academy Awards, as both director and producer. He rose to prominence directing such classics as In the Heat of the Night *(1967),* The Thomas Crown Affair *(1968),* Fiddler on the Roof *(1971),* Jesus Christ Superstar *(1973),* Rollerball *(1975) and* Moonstruck *(1987). Jewison has said that "feature films are the literature of our generation. They express the social conscience of a country: films are forever."*

1. *The Bicycle Thief* (1949), directed by Vittorio De Sica
A film that haunts me still.

2. *The Grapes of Wrath* (1940), directed by John Ford
A great translation from a great book.

3. *Citizen Kane* (1941), directed by Orson Welles
Probably the best American movie.

4. *8½* (1963), directed by Federico Fellini
I love almost every film of Fellini's, but *8½* is my favourite.

5. *The 400 Blows* (1959), directed by François Truffaut
Truffaut's film moved me deeply and had an effect on my style of filmmaking.

6. *The Battle of Algiers* (1965), directed by Gillo Pontecorvo
The most daring analysis of modern revolution and terrorism.

7. *The Third Man* (1949), directed by Carol Reed
The Third Man is almost a perfectly constructed film.

8. *Mon Oncle Antoine* (1971), directed by Claude Jutra
I had to include the one Canadian film that I believe is a classic.

9. *City Lights* (1931), directed by Charles Chaplin
Everything that Chaplin did I enjoyed. *City Lights* is comedy artfully done.

10. *Gunga Din* (1939), directed by George Stevens
I have to include this film based on a Kipling poem because it's the first movie I can remember that made me want to be a filmmaker.

15 FILM SCENES LEFT ON THE CUTTING-ROOM FLOOR

1. *Frankenstein* (1931)

In one scene, the monster (Boris Karloff) walks through a forest and comes upon a little girl, Maria, who is throwing flowers into a pond. The monster joins her in the activity but soon runs out of flowers. At a loss for something to throw into the water, he looks at Maria and moves towards her. In all American prints of the movie, the scene ends here. But as originally filmed, the action continues to show the monster grabbing Maria, hurling her into the lake and then departing in confusion when Maria fails to float as the flowers did. This bit was deleted because Karloff, objecting to the director's interpretation of the scene, felt that the monster should have gently put Maria into the lake. Though Karloff's intentions were good, the scene's omission suggests a crueller death for Maria, since a subsequent scene shows her bloodied corpse being carried through the village by her father.

2. *King Kong* (1933)

The original *King Kong* was released four times between 1933 and 1952, and each release saw the cutting of additional scenes. Though many of the outtakes—including the censored sequence in which Kong peels off Fay Wray's clothes—were restored in 1971, one cut scene has never been found. It is the clip in which Kong shakes four sailors off a log bridge, causing them to fall into a ravine, where they are eaten alive by giant spiders. When the movie—with spider sequence intact—was previewed in San Bernardino, California, in late January 1933, members of the audience screamed and either left the theatre or talked about the grisly sequence throughout the remainder of the film. Said the film's producer, Merian C. Cooper, "It stopped the picture cold, so the next day back at the studio, I took it out myself."

3. *Tarzan and His Mate* (1934)

Considered by many to be the best of the Tarzan films, *Tarzan and His Mate* included a scene in which Tarzan (Johnny Weissmuller), standing on a tree limb with Jane (Maureen O'Sullivan), pulls at Jane's scanty outfit and persuades her to dive into a lake with him. The two swim for a while and eventually surface. When Jane rises out of the water, one of her breasts is fully exposed. Because various groups, including official censors of the Hays Office, criticized the scene for being too erotic, it was cut by MGM.

4. The Wizard of Oz (1939)

The Wizard of Oz originally contained an elaborate production number called "The Jitter Bug," which cost $80,000 (U.S.) and took five weeks to shoot. In the scene, Dorothy, the Scarecrow, the Cowardly Lion and the Tin Woodsman are on their way to the witch's castle when they are attacked by "jitter bugs"—furry pink and blue mosquito-like "rascals" that give one "the jitters" as they buzz about in the air. When, after its first preview, the movie was judged too long, MGM officials decided to sacrifice the jitter bug scene. They reasoned that it added little to the plot and, because a dance by the same name had just become popular, they feared it might date the picture. (Another number was also cut for previews because some felt it slowed the pacing, but it was eventually restored. Its title was . . . "Over the Rainbow.")

5. The Big Sleep (1946)

This movie is famed as a classic despite its notoriously difficult-to-follow plot. As originally filmed, it included an aid for the viewer: Philip Marlowe (Humphrey Bogart) and a DA meet and have a conversation that summarizes the plot. The film was finished in 1945, but was held back from release until the studio finished rolling out its backlog of World War II films. During the delay, the decision was made to reshoot several scenes to play up the chemistry between Bogart and Lauren Bacall. A scene was also added, in which Bogart and Bacall meet in a nightclub and flirt while ostensibly talking about horse racing. In order to keep the running time of the film the same, the scene of Marlowe and the DA was cut.

6. Sunset Boulevard (1950)

Billy Wilder's film classic about an aging Hollywood film queen and a down-on-his-luck screenwriter originally incorporated a framing sequence that opened and closed the story at the Los Angeles County Morgue. In a scene described by Wilder as one of the best he'd ever shot, the body of Joe Gillis (William Holden) is rolled into the morgue to join three dozen other corpses, some of whom—in voice-over—tell Gillis how they died. Eventually Gillis tells his story, which takes us to a flashback of his affair with Norma Desmond (Gloria Swanson). The movie was previewed with this opening in Illinois and Long Island. Because both audiences inappropriately found the morgue scene hilarious, the film's release was delayed six months so that a new beginning could be shot in which police find Gillis's corpse floating in Norma's pool while Gillis's voice narrates the events leading to his death.

7. *Limelight* (1952)

Charlie Chaplin's film about a vaudeville comic on the decline features a scene in which Chaplin, as the elderly Calvero, makes his comeback in a music hall sketch. The routine, which originally ran to 10 minutes, has Calvero performing onstage with an old colleague, played by Buster Keaton. It has been said that while Chaplin was good, Keaton was sensational. Consequently, Chaplin allowed only a small portion of the scene to remain in release prints.

8. *The Seven Year Itch* (1955)

Originally, the movie included a scene of Marilyn Monroe in the bathtub, getting her toe stuck in the faucet. Although Monroe remained covered by bubbles, the scene ran afoul of the Hollywood censors, so director Billy Wilder cut it.

9. *Spartacus* (1960)

Of the 167 days it took Stanley Kubrick to shoot *Spartacus*, six weeks were spent directing an elaborate battle sequence in which 8,500 extras dramatized the clash between Roman troops and Spartacus's slave army. Several scenes in the battle drew the ire of the Legion of Decency and were therefore cut. These included shots of men being dismembered. (Dwarfs with false torsos and an armless man with a phony "break-away" limb were used to give authenticity.) Seven years later, when the Oscar-winning film was reissued, an additional 22 minutes were chopped out, including a scene in which Varinia (Jean Simmons) watches Spartacus (Kirk Douglas) writhe in agony on a cross. Her line "Oh, please die, my darling" was excised, and the scene was cut to make it appear that Spartacus was already dead. These cuts were restored to the film in the early '90s.

10. *Splendor in the Grass* (1961)

As filmed, *Splendor in the Grass* included a sequence in which Wilma Dean Loomis (Natalie Wood) takes a bath while arguing with her mother (Audrey Christie). The bickering finally becomes so intense that Wilma jumps out of the tub and runs nude down a hallway to her bedroom, where the camera cuts to a close-up of her bare legs kicking hysterically on the mattress. Both the Hollywood censors and the Catholic Legion of Decency objected to the hallway display. Consequently, director Elia Kazan dropped the piece, leaving an abrupt jump from tub to bed.

11. *Dr. No* (1962)

The first of the James Bond films ended with Honey Ryder (Ursula Andress) being attacked by crabs when Bond (Sean Connery) rescues her. The crabs moved too slowly to look truly menacing, so the ending was reshot without them.

12. *Everything You Always Wanted to Know about Sex But Were Afraid to Ask* (1972)

"What Makes a Man a Homosexual?" was one of the many vignettes filmed for the Woody Allen movie using the title of Dr. David Reuben's bestselling book. The sequence stars Allen as a common spider anxious to court a black widow (Louise Lasser). After doing a mating dance on Lasser's web, Allen makes love to the widow, only to be devoured by her afterwards. The scene was finally cut out of the film because Allen couldn't come up with a suitable way to end the piece.

13. *Big* (1988)

In this film, Tom Hanks plays Josh, a 12-year-old who becomes an adult literally overnight when he makes a wish on a machine at a carnival. While an adult, Josh falls in love with a woman named Susan (Elizabeth Perkins), but he has to leave her behind when he makes another wish to become 12 again. In the original version, there was an additional scene at the end, in which Josh is back at school and a new girl named Susan arrives. The implication is that Susan went back to the carnival machine to make herself Josh's age. Due to negative audience feedback, the scene was cut from the movie.

14. *Jerry Maguire* (1996)

Jerry Maguire originally included a fictional Reebok advertisement starring Rod Tidwell (Cuba Gooding Jr.), which was cut from the film by director Cameron Crowe. However, when the movie was broadcast on the Showtime cable network, the commercial was restored, playing under the closing credits. Reportedly, the scene was put back in because of a lawsuit filed by Reebok against Columbia Pictures over the terms of product placement in the film.

15. *Titanic* (1997)

The film ends with Rose (Gloria Stuart) going to the deck of the research ship investigating the *Titanic* wreck, leaning over the railing and dropping a necklace with the valuable Heart of the Ocean diamond into the ocean. As originally filmed, the crew members of the research ship see Rose, mistakenly believe that she is planning to jump overboard and try to talk her out of committing suicide. When they realize what she is actually doing, they try to persuade her to preserve the necklace. Director James Cameron decided that he wanted the scene to focus on Rose, so he reshot it with her alone.

—D.B. & C.F.

17 CANADIAN MUSICIANS AND THE MOVIES THEY'VE BEEN IN

1. Bryan Adams

Adams played a gas station attendant in *Pink Cadillac* (1989), which starred Clint Eastwood and Bernadette Peters.

2. Paul Anka

Anka's most memorable film role probably came when he played himself in the groundbreaking 1962 National Film Board documentary *Lonely Boy*. He has appeared in at least eight other films. He starred in his first movie in 1959 at the age of 18, when he played Jimmy Parlow in the film *Girls Town*. He followed that up with *The Private Lives of Adam and Eve* (1960) and *Look in Any Window* (1961). He played an army ranger in the 1962 D-Day epic *The Longest Day*. He did three forgettable films in the 1990s: *Captain Ron* (1992), *Ordinary Magic* (1993) and *Mad Dog Time* (1996). In 2001 he played a pit boss in the film *3000 Miles to Graceland*, which was set in Las Vegas during an Elvis convention and starred Kurt Russell and Kevin Costner.

3. Michael Bublé
By the time this popular young Vancouver crooner released his best-selling debut album in 2003, he had already made three movie appearances: he had a bit part as a singer in the film *Duets* (2000), which starred Gwyneth Paltrow and Huey Lewis; he played Van Martin in the 2001 airhead comedy *Totally Blonde*; and he was Hap in the 2003 Canadian film *The Snow Walker*, based on the book by Farley Mowat.

4. Leonard Cohen
Cohen played himself in the wonderful 1965 NFB documentary *Ladies and Gentlemen . . . Mr. Leonard Cohen*, directed by Donald Brittain and Don Owen. Two years later, he played a singer in *The Ernie Game*, which was written and directed by Owen and starred Jackie Burroughs.

5–6. Jim Cuddy and Greg Keelor
Cuddy, Keelor and the other members of Blue Rodeo played themselves in the 1990 hit *Postcards from the Edge*, which was directed by Mike Nichols, written by Carrie Fisher, and starred Meryl Streep and Shirley MacLaine.

7. Burton Cummings
Cummings played Rick in the 1982 flick *Melanie*. The movie, which starred Glynnis O'Connor and Paul Sorvino, was the story of a young woman's battle to regain custody of her son.

8. Gord Downie
Downie and the rest of the Tragically Hip crew were the Team Kingston curling team in Paul Gross's 2002 comedy *Men with Brooms*.

9. Ronnie Hawkins
Canada's favourite hillbilly has appeared in several notable movies. In 1980 he played Wolcott in the colossally unsuccessful *Heaven's Gate*. He also played a bar singer in the 1987 production of *Meatballs III*, and he was Desi in *Boozecan* (1994). Perhaps his most unusual role was as Bob Dylan in *Renaldo and Clara* (1978), a movie that Dylan wrote and directed. His

most recent appearance was in 2002, when he played a gas station attendant in the Red Green movie *Duct Tape Forever*.

10. k.d. lang
Lang's first screen role was as Kotzebue in the 1991 film *Salmonberries*. She followed that in 1994 with *Teresa's Tattoo*, and then in 1999 she played Hilary in the thriller *Eye of the Beholder*, alongside fellow Canadians Jason Priestley and Geneviève Bujold.

11. Gordon Lightfoot
Lightfoot played U.S. Marshal Morrie Nathan in the seldom-seen 1982 drama *Harry Tracy, Desperado*. The movie starred Bruce Dern and fellow Canuck Helen Shaver.

12. Alanis Morissette
The Ottawa rocker has appeared in two movies, *Dogma* (1999) and *Jay and Silent Bob Strike Back* (2001). Both were written and directed by Kevin Smith, and in both movies Alanis played the role of God.

13. Robbie Robertson
Robertson played himself and also produced *The Last Waltz* (1978), perhaps the best concert movie ever made. He followed that up with roles in two less impressive films: he was Patch in *Carny* (1980), a movie he also produced, and Roger in *The Crossing Guard* (1995), which was written and directed by Sean Penn.

14. Shania Twain
Shania played herself in the 2004 David O. Russell film *I ♥ Huckabees*.

15–16. Martha and Rufus Wainwright
The musical progenies of Kate McGarrigle and Loudon Wainwright III appeared as lounge singers at the Cocoanut Grove in Martin Scorsese's 2004 Howard Hughes biopic *The Aviator*. In 2005 Rufus can also be seen in the role of Jeremy in *Heights*, a drama set in New York City.

17. Neil Young

Young's first acting role came in a 1982 film called *Neil Young: Human Highway*, in which, despite the movie's title, he played a character called Lionel Switch. He followed that up in 1987 with a role as a truck driver in the romance *Made in Heaven*. He was Westy in *'68* (1988) and Rick in *Love at Large* (1990). He returned to the big screen in 2003 with *Greendale*, a musical look at the lives and struggles of people in a small fictional town named Greendale. Young wrote and directed the movie. A lot of critics and fans were left shaking their heads, trying to figure out what exactly the beloved rock star was trying to say. Young himself made a cameo appearance as his alter ego Bernard Shakey, playing the role of Wayne Newton.

STEPHEN KING'S 6 SCARIEST SCENES EVER CAPTURED ON FILM

One of the most popular, prolific and influential writers in the history of American literature, Stephen King was born on September 21, 1947, in Portland, Maine. Beginning with the 1974 publication of Carrie, *King's bestselling output has included such novels as* The Stand, Pet Sematary, It, Misery, The Green Mile *and* Bag of Bones. *Hit movies adapted from King's works include* The Shining (*directed by Stanley Kubrick*), The Dead Zone (*directed by David Cronenberg*) *and* The Shawshank Redemption.

1. *Wait Until Dark* (1967), directed by Terence Young
The moment near the conclusion, when [Alan] Arkin jumps out at Audrey Hepburn, is a real scare.

2. *Carrie* (1976), directed by Brian De Palma
The dream sequence at the end, when Sissy Spacek thrusts her hand out of the ground and grabs Amy Irving. I knew it was coming and still felt as if I'd swallowed a snow cone whole.

3. *I Bury the Living* (1958), directed by Albert Band
In this almost-forgotten movie, there is a chilling sequence when [Richard] Boone begins to maniacally remove the black pins in the filled graveyard plots and to replace them with white pins.

4. *The Texas Chainsaw Massacre* (1974), directed by Tobe Hopper

The moment when the corpse seems to leap out of the freezer like a hideous jack-in-the-box.

5. *Night of the Living Dead* (1968), directed by George Romero

The scene where the little girl stabs her mother to death with a garden trowel in the cellar . . . "Mother, please, I can do it myself."

6. *Psycho* (1960), directed by Alfred Hitchcock

The shower scene, of course.

Source: Gabe Essoe, *The Book of Movie Lists* (Westport: Arlington House, 1981).

8 MEMORABLE LINES ERRONEOUSLY ATTRIBUTED TO FILM STARS

1. "Smile when you say that, pardner."

What Gary Cooper actually said to Walter Huston in *The Virginian* (1929) was, "If you want to call me that, smile."

2. "Me Tarzan, you Jane."

Johnny Weissmuller's first Tarzan role was in *Tarzan, the Ape Man* (1932). He introduced himself to co-star Maureen O'Sullivan by thumping his chest and announcing, "Tarzan." He then gingerly tapped *her* chest and said, "Jane."

3. "You dirty rat."

In fact, James Cagney never uttered this line in any of his roles as a hard-boiled gangster. It has often been used by impersonators, however, to typify Cagney's tough-guy image.

4. "Come with me to the Casbah."

Charles Boyer cast seductive glances at Hedy Lamarr throughout *Algiers* (1938), but he never did make this suggestion. Delivered with a French accent, the line appeals to many Boyer imitators who enjoy saying, "Come weez mee . . ."

5. "Why don't you come up and see me sometime?"

Cary Grant found himself the recipient of Mae West's lusty invitation, "Why don't you come up sometime and see me?" in *She Done Him Wrong* (1933).

6. "Play it again, Sam."

In *Casablanca* (1942), Ingrid Bergman dropped in unexpectedly at old lover Humphrey Bogart's nightclub, where she asked the piano player to "Play it, Sam," referring to the song "As Time Goes By." Although Bogart's character was shocked at hearing the song that reminded him so painfully of his lost love; he also made Sam play it again—but the words he used were, "You played it for her, you can play it for me . . . play it."

7. "Judy, Judy, Judy."

Cary Grant has never exclaimed this line in any film, but imitators often use it to display their Cary Grant–like accents.

8. "I want to be alone."

In the 1932 film *Grand Hotel*, Greta Garbo's character said, "I want to be let alone." In 1955, retired film star Greta Garbo—despairing of ever being free of publicity—repeated it. The melodramatic misinterpretation, however, is the way most people have heard and quoted it.

—K.P.

12 MOVIE STARS (AND 1 NEWS ANCHOR) AND HOW THEY WERE DISCOVERED

1. Pamela Anderson

Comox, British Columbia, native Pamela Anderson was spotted at a B.C. Lions football game in Vancouver in 1989. A cameraman roaming the stands for crowd shots locked onto the 22-year-old blonde beauty in a tight Labatt's Blue T-shirt, causing the crowd to cheer. Labatt's quickly signed her up as their "Blue Girl," and Pamela was soon adorning the walls of bars across Canada. Within the year she was on the cover of *Playboy* and two years later she got the starring role in the TV series *Baywatch*.

2. Ellen Burstyn

She was cast in her first major role in *Tropic of Cancer* (1969) on the basis of a political speech that director Joseph Strick heard her delivering.

3. Gary Cooper

Working as a stunt man, he was noticed by director Henry King on the set of *The Winning of Barbara Worth* at Samuel Goldwyn Studios in 1926.

4. Errol Flynn

He was discovered by Cinesound Studios casting director John Warwick in Sydney, Australia, in 1932. Warwick found some amateur footage of Flynn taken in 1930 by Dr. Herman F. Erben, a filmmaker and tropical-disease specialist who had chartered navigator Flynn's schooner for a tour of New Guinea headhunter territory.

5. Rock Hudson

Hudson, whose original name was Roy Fitzgerald, was working as a truck driver for the Budget Pack Company in 1954 when another driver offered to arrange a meeting between Fitzgerald and agent Henry Willson. In spite of Fitzgerald's professed lack of faith in his acting abilities, Willson took the aspiring actor under his wing, changed his name to Rock Hudson and launched his career.

6. Janet Leigh

She was a psychology student when MGM star Norma Shearer happened to see a photo of her at a ski lodge in northern California where her parents were employed. Shearer took it to the studio, with the result that Leigh was given a role in *The Romance of Rosy Ridge* (1947).

7. Gina Lollobrigida

An art student in Rome, she was stopped on the street by director Mario Costa. She let loose a torrent of abuse about men who accost defenceless girls and only when she paused for breath was he able to explain that he wanted to screen-test her for *Elisir d'Amore* (1946). She won the part.

8. Carole Lombard

She met director Allan Dwan in Los Angeles in the spring of 1921. Dwan watched 12-year-old Carole—then tomboy Jane Alice Peters—playing baseball outside the home of his friends Al and Rita Kaufman.

9. Ryan O'Neal

He was befriended by actor Richard Egan in 1962 at the gymnasium where both Egan and O'Neal worked out. "It was just a matter of Ryan himself being so impressive," said Egan.

10. Telly Savalas

He was teaching adult-education classes in Garden City, New Jersey, when an agent asked him if he knew an actor who could speak with a European accent. He tried out himself and landed a part in *Armstrong Circle Theater* on television.

11. Charlize Theron

The South African–born actress studied dance and modelled in Milan and New York before heading to Los Angeles to pursue her dream of acting. After several difficult months in L.A., Theron's discovery came in a Hollywood Boulevard bank. When a teller refused to cash an out-of-town cheque for her, she threw an enormous tantrum that caught the attention of veteran talent manager John Crosby, who happened to be standing nearby. Crosby handed her his business card as she was being thrown out of the bank, and she signed with him.

12. John Wayne

He was spotted by director Raoul Walsh at Hollywood's Fox lot in 1928. Walsh was on his way to the administration building when he noticed Wayne—then Marion Morrison, a studio prop man—loading furniture from a warehouse onto a truck.

+1. Peter Mansbridge

"Trans Air flight 106 for Thompson, The Pas and Winnipeg, now ready for boarding at gate one." It's hard to believe that one simple flight announcement, delivered at an airport in Churchill, Manitoba, would be the launching pad for one of the most successful careers in Canadian broadcasting. But that is exactly what happened in the case of CBC anchor Peter Mansbridge. He was a 20-year-old baggage handler in September 1968, when a busy ticket agent asked him to make the now-famous flight announcement. The manager of the CBC station in Churchill was at the airport that day. He knew a radio voice when he heard one. He approached Mansbridge and asked if he would be interested in working the night shift at the station. Mansbridge said yes, and so began a career that has lasted more than 35 years.

—D.B., C.F. & Cdn. Eds.

CHRIS TURNER'S 10 BEST CANADIAN REFERENCES ON *THE SIMPSONS*

Simpsons creator Matt Groening's father was born in Saskatchewan, Homer Simpson is an honorary citizen of Winnipeg, and the main freeway running through Springfield is Route 401—yes, there are few American pop culture institutions as rich in Canadiana as *The Simpsons*. There have been dozens of references to Canadian people and places over the 16 years (and counting) of the series' run. Here are the 10 best ones to date, selected by former military base brat Chris Turner, whose critically acclaimed book *Planet Simpson* was published in 2004.

1. Winnipeg: One Great City!
Episode FABF16 ("Midnight Rx")
Original Airdate: January 16, 2005
Prescription drugs are in short supply in Springfield after Mr. Burns cancels his employees' drug plan at the nuclear power plant and the Retirement Castle follows suit. This sets the stage for the most Canuckophilic episode in *Simpsons* history, as Homer takes it upon himself to lead repeated drug-buying missions to Canada—Manitoba, to be exact—where Mounties abound, Flanders-like passersby offer visitors a "puff on a reeferino," and the TV blares the "Canadian News and Lost Mitten Update." One mercy errand takes Homer and his co-conspirators to Winnipeg, roaring past a sign at the city limits that reads: "NOW ENTERING WINNIPEG. WE WERE BORN HERE, WHAT'S YOUR EXCUSE?" One of the upstanding citizens of much-maligned Winterpeg—a good-natured senior citizen named Johnny—gets in a sly

counterpunch before the Springfieldianites head home, however. "We really appreciate your help, Johnny," Homer tells him. "Is there any way we can repay you?" Johnny gives his chin a scratch. "Well, I always wanted to see a man with the IQ of a child executed by the state," he says, referring to an execution carried out in Texas just before George W. Bush vacated the governor's office. "We don't get that up here."

2. The Simpson Family Visits Toronto

Episode DABF06 ("The Bart Wants What It Wants")
Original Airdate: February 17, 2002

In the first instance ever of four-toed Simpson feet falling upon Canadian soil, Bart and the rest of the Simpson family travel en masse to Toronto in this episode's final act in pursuit of Greta, Bart's erstwhile girlfriend and the daughter of action hero Rainier Wolfcastle. "It's so clean and bland," Marge announces as the Simpsons step off the bus in the T-Dot. "I'm home!" The Simpsons find Greta at Paramountie Studios, on the set of her father's new movie, but she wants nothing to do with Bart, so he and his pal Milhouse content themselves with becoming starters on the Canadian Olympic basketball team. This episode features references to the CN Tower, the weak Canadian dollar, curling and the Toronto headquarters of the little-known organization Dodgers of Foreign Wars.

3. Broadest. Canadian. Accent. Ever.

Episode 3F23 ("You Only Move Twice")
Original Airdate: November 3, 1996

When the Simpsons move to a posh high-tech enclave called Cypress Creek, Bart soon finds himself in the remedial class, where he joins a motley crew of "arsonists and kids with mittens pinned to their jackets all year round." Among these misfits is a seemingly normal boy named Gordy. Bart asks him how he wound up in the remedial class. "I moved here from Canada, and they think I'm slow, eh?" Gordy replies, in a syncopated series of flattened soft vowels and drawn-out long vowels that might stand as the broadest parody of a Canadian accent in the history of American pop culture. A genuine Canuck from rural northern Ontario who spent his teenage years in Ireland and then had a mild stroke *might* sound a *little* like Gordy, but the accent is otherwise purely Simpsonian.

4. True Patriot Love, Simpson-Style

Episode EABF16 ("The Bart of War")
Original Airdate: May 18, 2002

It's an ugly day for baseball when the rivalry between Springfield's competing scout troupes (the "Pre-Teen Braves" and the "Calvary Kids") leads to a botched rendition of "The Star-Spangled Banner" before a Springfield Isotopes game. In response, the agitated crowd takes to rioting—until Sideshow Mel (Krusty the Klown's hula-skirted sidekick) makes a peace overture. "Let us end this mindless violence," he bellows, "and join our hands in song." Captain McAllister (Springfield's beloved salty sea captain) immediately seconds the motion. "Aye," he says. "Not a hymn to war, like our national anthem, but a sweet, soothing hymn, like the national anthem of Canada." The assembled throng promptly joins hands to form the outline of a maple leaf and sings a rousing rendition of "O Canada."

5. Homer Shows His Rider Pride

Episode 7F23 ("When Flanders Failed")
Original Airdate: October 3, 1991

How desperate for entertainment does Homer Simpson become on the afternoon he refuses to attend the Flanders family's barbecue? So desperate that he finds himself staring blankly at "exciting 15th-round action" of the Canadian Football League Draft on TV—setting up a brief but brilliantly obscure reference to the oddest of oddball CFL rules. "So," an announcer enthuses in a Canadian accent as broad as the open prairie, "the Saskatchewan Roughriders have scored only four *rouges* all last season." And now we know, as Homer does, how many single points the Riders scored that year on unreturned punts and missed field goals.

6. Bartie Mnemonic

Episode DABF20 ("Bart vs. Lisa vs. 3rd Grade")
Original Airdate: November 17, 2002

Lisa does so well on the Elementary School Achievement Test that she's promoted to the third grade, Bart does so poorly that he's demoted to the third grade, and soon the Simpson kids are working side by side on the same homework. And that's how we learn that Bart has committed to memory an impressive range of mnemonic devices about Canadian geography and history. "Quiet Nerds Burp Only Near School," he announces to his bewildered sister, then explains: "That's how you remember the four original provinces of Canada—Quebec, New Brunswick, Ontario, Nova Scotia." Bart's also got mnemonics for Canada's principal exports ("Dogs Eat Barf Solely On Wednesday, Mabel") and for its Governors General ("Clowns Love Haircuts, So Should Lee Marvin's Valet"), but he never provides Lisa—or us—with the answer keys to these phrases.

7. News Homer Can Use
Episode 9F05 ("Marge Gets a Job")
Original Airdate: November 5, 1992
When Marge gets a job at the Springfield Nuclear Power Plant, she arrives home eager to discuss this exciting new phase of her career with her husband. Homer, seated at the kitchen table and desperate for *anything* to provide an excuse not to talk about his disapproval of her decision to join him at the power plant, seizes the newspaper lying in front of him. "'Canada to Hold Referendum,'" he reads with heavily forced interest. "Sorry, Marge—can't talk now." No word ever did emerge on whether Homer was a "Oui" or a "Non" supporter.

8. Every Immigrant's First (Or Possibly Second) Choice
Episode 8F01 ("Mr. Lisa Goes to Washington")
Original Airdate: September 26, 2001
Budding young polemicist Lisa Simpson handily wins the preliminary round of the *Reading Digest* patriotic essay contest, so the Simpsons are off to Washington, D.C., for the finals. Lisa loses out in the end to an adorable immigrant boy named Trong Van Dinh, whose essay, "U.S.A. A-O.K.," features a rare reference to Canada's equal footing with our southern neighbour in matters of freedom and opportunity. "When my family arrived in this country four months ago," Trong recites, "we spoke no English and had no money in our pockets. Today, we own a nation-wide chain of wheel-balancing centres. Where else but in America, or possibly Canada, could our family find such opportunity?"

9. Beauty, Eh?

Episode AABF20 ("Thirty Minutes over Tokyo")
Original Airdate: May 16, 1999

On the Simpsons' ill-fated trip to Japan, they wind up so desperate for money that they become contestants on a sadistic game show, narrowly escaping with their lives. As Homer and his brood exit stage right, the show's host, Wink, introduces the next segment: "Coming up next—a Canadian couple who say they are deathly afraid of scorpions." Cut to a shot of said couple being bombarded with live scorpions. "Sting those Canucks!" Wink enthuses. Homer, evidently a fan of the legendary *SCTV* duo Bob and Doug McKenzie, joins in the cheerleading: "Take that, you stupid hosers!"

10. Vive Le Québec Libre!

Episode AABF09 ("Homer to the Max")
Original Airdate: February 7, 1999

After legally changing his name to "Max Power," Homer finds himself brought into the inner circle of Springfield's cultural elite. He and his wife are soon invited to a hip garden party, where Marge winds up slow dancing with none other than President Bill Clinton. "Are you sure it's a federal law that I have to dance with you?" Marge asks warily. "You know, I'd change that law if I could, Marge," Clinton replies. "But I can't." Just then, an aide comes up and whispers in Clinton's ear. "Aw, shoot," the president tells Marge. "Quebec's got the bomb. Well, I gotta go. But, look, if you're ever near the White House, there's a tool shed out back. I'm in there most of the day."

ANTHONY BOURDAIN'S 10 GRITTIEST, MOST UNCOMPROMISING CRIME FILMS

"Extreme chef" Anthony Bourdain, born in New York in 1956, rose from dishwasher to executive chef at Brasserie Les Halles in New York City via a stint with the CIA (Culinary Institute of America). He is the author of two novels, Gone Bamboo *(1995) and* Bone in the Throat *(1997), as well as* Kitchen Confidential *(2000), "part autobiography, part restaurant-goer's survival manual."*

Is it good? Is it realistic? (That leaves out *The Godfather*.) Is it a timeless "how-to"? Those are the criteria here. No good guys or bad guys—just a moral quagmire of betrayal, lust, greed and crushing, grim inevitability. That's my recipe for a good time at the movies!

1. *The Friends of Eddie Coyle* (1973), directed by Peter Yates

You can smell the beer on Robert Mitchum as aging hood/part-time informer Eddie, running out one last scam in a swamp of atmospheric betrayal.

2. *Get Carter* (1971), directed by Mike Hodges

Maybe the most vicious, hardcore—and magnificent—revenge melodrama ever filmed. Accept no substitutes. (The Stallone remake was a sin against God.)

3. *Bob Le Flambeur* (1955), directed by Jean-Pierre Melville

Elegant, beautiful, sad and wise caper movie. And the hero gets away!

4. *Rififi* (1956), directed by Jules Dassin

The *Citizen Kane* of caper flicks.

5. *The Killing* (1956), directed by Stanley Kubrick

Seedy, delicious—and with Sterling Hayden! Pure crack for film nerds.

6. *The Asphalt Jungle* (1950), directed by John Huston

The jumbo, king-Hell noir to beat all noirs. A crime masterpiece told from the criminals' point of view.

7. *Goodfellas* (1990), directed by Martin Scorsese

Simply the best American movie ever made. Every word, every move, every inflection thoroughly believable. And funny—as only real mobsters can be.

8. *Mean Streets* (1973), directed by Martin Scorsese

Scorsese's breathtaking low-budget portrait of small-time hoods in Little Italy. It changed everything.

9. *Thief* (1981), directed by Michael Mann

An underrated classic. James Caan as a professional safecracker—just out of prison—trying to steal his way to a "normal" life. Beautiful, grimly realistic, technically groundbreaking.

10. *The Long Good Friday* (1980), directed by John Mackenzie

Bob Hoskins owned this part. And yet a shatteringly good Helen Mirren still steals the movie. Brit-crime at its very, very best.

15 HOLLYWOOD MOVIES ABOUT THE MOUNTIES

1. *Steele of the Royal Mounted* (1925)
2. *Glenister of the Mounted* (1926)
3. *Moran of the Mounted* (1926)
4. *Law of the Mounted* (1928)
5. *Honor of the Mounted* (1932)
6. *McKenna of the Mounted* (1932)
7. *Mason of the Mounted* (1932)
8. *Code of the Mounted* (1936)
9. *O'Malley of the Mounted* (1936)
10. *King of the Royal Mounted* (1936)
11. *Renfrew of the Royal Mounted* (1937)
12. *Susannah of the Mounties* (1939)
13. *Outpost of the Mounties* (1939)
14. *Morton of the Mounted* (1940)
15. *Gene Autry and the Mounties* (1951)

Source: Pierre Berton, *Hollywood's Canada: The Americanization of Our National Image* (Toronto: McClelland and Stewart, 1975).

RON MANN'S 10 FAVOURITE DOCUMENTARIES

Auteur filmmaker and hopped-up cultural historian Ron Mann has made some of Canada's most original and compelling documentaries. His subjects have ranged from beat poetry (Poetry in Motion, *1982) and comic books* (Comic Book Confidential, *1988) to dance crazes* (Twist, *1992) and marijuana* (Grass, *1999). In 2003 he finished* Go Further *about Woody Harrelson's bus ride down the West Coast of the U.S. to publicize his Simple Organic Living Tour.*

1. *Electrocuting an Elephant* (1903), directed by Thomas Edison
This "real life" shock doc by Thomas Edison predates the acerbic "Mondo Cane" social commentary films by some 60 years. After watching this film, you will join PETA.

2. *This is Cinerama* (1952), directed by Merian C. Cooper, Gunther Von Fritsch, Michael Todd Jr., Ernest B. Shoedsack
The opening scene was a roller coaster ride that caused the person sitting in front of me to puke. A thrilling spectacle, *Cinerama* paved the way for 3-D and IMAX.

3. *Pull My Daisy* (1959), directed by Alfred Leslie and Robert Frank
Allen Ginsberg, Gregory Corso and other "beats" play themselves as Jack Kerouac improvises narration to David Amram's score. With cinematography by photographer Robert Frank and co-direction by painter Alfred Leslie, *Pull My Daisy* is all things beat and beatific.

4. *Jazz on a Summer's Day* (1959), directed by Bert Stern
One of the greatest performance films of all time. Filmed at the Newport Jazz Festival, Bert Stern's cameras capture inspired performances from the giants of jazz, gospel and rock 'n' roll.

5. *Harvest of Shame* (1960), directed by Edward R. Murrow
Murrow's hard-hitting television documentary about the exploitation of U.S. migrant workers aired on U.S. Thanksgiving and ruffled feathers. The U.S. State Department called it anti-American and tried to stop CBS from broadcasting it in the U.K.

6. *Kennedy Assassination* (1963), directed by Abraham Zapruder
Zapruder didn't blink as his lone camera caught Kennedy's assassination. The only film I know where actual frame numbers are discussed.

7. *Mills of the Gods* (1965), directed by Beryl Fox
The '60s series *This Hour Has Seven Days*, produced by the CBC, created a number of politically charged documentaries. *Mills of the Gods*, however, stands out for being the first film that challenged the U.S. role in Vietnam.

8. *Woodstock* (1970), directed by Michael Wadleigh

Peace, love and music without the rain, mud and standing in line for toilets. Made by and for the counterculture, Woodstock is the revolution televised and more.

9. *Eyes on the Prize* (1987), directed by Henry Hampton

Hampton's epic PBS series brought to life the history of the American Civil Rights Movement. Unbelievably, *The New York Times* recently reported that *Eyes on the Prize* may never be broadcast again due to licensing restrictions of archival footage.

10. *Mr. Hoover & I* (1989), directed by Emile de Antonio

America's radical documentary filmmaker Emile de Antonio turns the camera on himself to discuss art and politics in Cold War America.

11 MOVIES THAT WERE PART OF HISTORY

1. *Manhattan Melodrama*

This film starred William Powell and Clark Gable as two streetwise city kids who grew up in opposite directions—one good, the other headed for the electric chair. The plot was old hat, even in 1934, but the film was enough to draw John Dillinger into the cinema with the "lady in red." He had just left the cinema when the tipped-off G-men sprang their trap and killed him in the ensuing fight.

2. *Grand Illusion*

Directed by pacifist Jean Renoir and starring Erich von Stroheim, this movie was being shown when the German army marched into Vienna in 1938. Not surprisingly, Nazi storm troopers invaded the cinema and confiscated the WWI anti-war classic in mid-reel.

3. *The Great Dictator*

Produced by, directed by and starring Charlie Chaplin in 1940, *The Great Dictator* was a brilliant political satire of Nazi Germany. Hitler ordered all prints of the film banned, but when curiosity got the better of him he had one brought in through Portugal and viewed it himself in complete privacy—not once, but twice. History does not record his views on the film.

4. Rock Around the Clock

This was a raucous celebration of rock 'n' roll starring Bill Haley and his Comets. In London, its young audience took the message to heart in September 1954. After seeing the film, more than 3,000 Teddy boys left the cinema to stage one of the biggest riots in Britain up to that time.

5. Foxfire

Starring Jane Russell and Jeff Chandler, this film—a Universal production dealing with a dedicated mining engineer and his socialite wife—was playing in the tourist-section cinema of the *Andrea Doria* on the foggy night in July 1956 when the liner collided with the *Stockholm*. The film was in its last reel when the collision occurred. Fifty people lost their lives in the tragedy.

6. Can-Can

A 20th Century Fox production starring Frank Sinatra, Shirley MacLaine and Maurice Chevalier, *Can-Can* was just a little too lavish for the taste of Soviet premier Nikita Khrushchev during his 1959 visit to the studio where it was being filmed. The Cold War heated up briefly when Khrushchev reacted with shocked indignation at the "perversity" and "decadence" of dancer MacLaine's flamboyantly raised skirts.

7. War is Hell

A double bill featuring two B-style war movies was playing at the Texas Theater in Dallas, where Lee Harvey Oswald was captured after the assassination of John F. Kennedy in 1963. *War is Hell*, starring Tony Russell, had just begun when Oswald called attention to himself by ducking into the cinema without paying the 90¢ admission. He was apprehended by the police amid the sound of onscreen gunfire.

8. I Am Curious Yellow

This Swedish film, which starred Lena Nyman as a sexually active political sociologist, was a shocking sensation in 1969. But on October 6, 1969, Jackie Onassis was the one making headlines after she allegedly gave a professional judo chop to a New York news photographer who took pictures of her leaving the cinema that was showing the film.

9. *Mohammed, Messenger of God*

Directed by Moustapha Akkad, this picture, which purported to be an unbiased, authentic study, evoked the wrath of the Hanafi Muslim sect, which assumed that the film would depict the image of the Prophet, an act they consider blasphemous. Demanding that the film be withdrawn from the Washington, D.C., cinema where it was opening, small bands of Hanafi gunmen invaded the local city hall and two other buildings on March 10, 1977, killing one man and holding more than 100 hostages for two days before surrendering. Their protest turned out to be much ado about nothing. The Prophet was neither seen nor heard in the film; instead, actors addressed the camera as if it were the Prophet standing before them.

10. *The Deer (Gavaznha)*

This Iranian film was being shown at the Cinema Rex in Abadan, Iran, on August 19, 1977, when arsonists set fire to the building, killing at least 377 people (an additional 45 bodies were discovered later in the charred ruins, but these were not included in the official government totals). Police arrested 10 members of a Muslim extremist group that opposed the shah's reforms and had been implicated in other cinema and restaurant fires. However, another version of this incident was sent to the authors by an eyewitness who claims that police chained shut the cinema doors and fended off the crowd outside with clubs and M-16s. The fire department, only 10 minutes from the theatre, reportedly did not arrive until the fire had burned itself out. Surprisingly, this witness found that most of the people had been burned to death in their seats.

11. *Taxi Driver*

John Hinckley, Jr., an underachiever from a well-to-do family, watched *Taxi Driver* (1976) more than a dozen times and became obsessed with Jodie Foster, who played a teenaged prostitute in the film. By this time, the actress was a student at Yale, where Hinckley left letters for her and tried to contact her by phone. Frustrated in his attempts to court Foster, Hinckley, apparently inspired by scenes in *Taxi Driver* in which Travis Bickle (Robert DeNiro) plots to kill a presidential candidate, began stalking President Jimmy Carter and then his successor Ronald

Reagan. On March 30, 1981, after writing a final letter of dedication to Foster, Hinckley pulled a revolver and shot Reagan outside the Washington Hilton. Reagan was wounded in the shooting, along with Press Secretary James Brady, Secret Service agent Timothy McCarty, and Washington, DC, police officer Thomas Delaharty. At a jury trial the next year, Hinckley was found not guilty by reason of insanity. He was sent to St. Elizabeth's Hospital in Washington, DC, where he still resides.

—R.S.

CHAPTER 3   # THE ARTS

ABOVE: *John Lennon and Yoko Ono discuss world peace with
Prime Minister Pierre Trudeau (Ottawa: December 23, 1969)*

71

15 ART RIOTS

1. The "Old Price" Riots (Covent Garden Theatre, London, 1809)

After the Covent Garden Theatre burned to the ground in 1808, a new building was put up the following year and the management of the theatre took the opportunity to raise prices from six shillings to seven shillings for boxes and from three shillings and sixpence to four shillings for most other seats. Outraged by the rise, the audience at the first performance in the new theatre constantly interrupted the playing of *Macbeth* with loud shouts of "Old Prices! Old Prices!" Soldiers were sent into the gallery to quell the disturbances, but the gallery-goers, further angered by the fact that in the badly designed new theatre they could see little more than the legs of the actors, continued to cause mayhem. In fact, they continued to do so at every performance for the next three months, bringing rattles, whistles, trumpets and farmyard animals into the theatre to cause maximum disruption. Eventually, the management, under the famous actor and impresario John Philip Kemble, bowed to the pressure and returned seats to the old prices. Kemble appeared onstage to make a public apology to the rioting audience.

2. The Appearance of William Macready at the Astor Place Opera House (New York, May 10, 1849)

William Macready, a close friend of Charles Dickens, was the most famous English actor of his day and, when he travelled to the U.S. to perform there, he fully expected to receive the kind of acclaim he was used to in London. Instead, he found himself at the centre of a fierce controversy involving a rival actor, the American Edwin Forrest. Patriotic Americans championed Forrest over Macready, whom they saw as an arrogant, patronizing foreigner. On May 10, 1849, thousands of Forrest supporters gathered outside the Astor Place Opera House, where Macready was due to perform. Stones were hurled at the building and the police attempting to protect it. As the violence grew worse, the militia was summoned and eventually opened fire on the crowd. Twenty-three people were killed and hundreds injured.

3. Premiere Performance of the Marquise de Morny's Pantomime Play *Rêve d'Égypte* (Moulin Rouge, Paris, January 3, 1907)

Set in the pharaohs' Egypt, this pantomime featured the controversial French writer and music-hall actress Colette and her friend and *inamorata*, the Marquise de Morny. The women portrayed reunited lovers, with the marquise playing the male role. Colette had said, "I become my parts," and it was so on that night, for when the lovers embraced in a long kiss, Colette, almost nude, displayed uninhibited passion. The marquise's husband, his friends and the audience were outraged. When the curtain came down, the audience was in an ugly mood, and its outrage boiled over into a riotous affair, with people throwing objects at the performers and beating each other with their umbrellas.

4. Premiere Performance of Arnold Schönberg's *Pierrot Lunaire* (Berlin, 1912)

In 1912 Schönberg had yet to develop his 12-tone system, but his composing had already evolved towards music severe in style, terse in form, atonal, with melodies that were sombre and unadorned. *Pierrot Lunaire* was such a work, and it provoked hostility, riots and scandal. Blows were traded amid hysteria and laughter. One critic wrote: "If this is music, then I pray my Creator not let me hear it again." Even years later, repercussions were still felt, as a man from the premiere audience brought assault charges against another man. In court, a physician testified that the music had been so jarring as to awaken peculiar neuroses.

5. The Armory Show (International Exhibition of Modern Art) (The Armory of the 69th Cavalry Regiment, New York, February–March, 1913)

In 1913 Americans viewed a major exhibit of European and American art, and most were not impressed. The 1,600 predominantly modern works assembled at the armory included the art of Picasso, Matisse and Duchamp. Modern American art was represented by the works of such artists as John Sloan, John Marin and Maurice Prendergast. But most Americans were not ready for the brave new visual worlds. Demonstrations unprecedented in the U.S. marred the show. Howls of laughter and derision were common, and a frenzied mob threatened to destroy canvases, particularly the Cubist paintings and Duchamp's *Nude Descending a Staircase*. Nevertheless, the exhibition was a great success, stirring up curiosity and gaining a few supporters.

6. Premiere Performance of Igor Stravinsky's *Rite of Spring* and the Accompanying Ballet by Nijinsky (Théâtre des Champs Élysées, Paris, May 29, 1913)

The music performed that night was so revolutionary in concept that many in the audience perceived it as musical anarchy. Also, Nijinsky's dancing was too sensual for the moral and aesthetic palates of many of the ballet lovers. Together, the music and dance shocked the audience. Whistling and catcalls rocked the theatre, and sympathetic patrons tried, without success, to silence the upheaval. Fistfights cropped up in the aisles, and gendarmes arrived to expel the worst of the offenders, but pandemonium soon broke out anew and continued until the end of the performance. Years later, the composer-conductor Pierre Boulez referred to the *Rite* as "the cornerstone of modern music."

7. Dada Performance (Salle Gaveau, Paris, May 26, 1920)

Well known for provoking their audiences to riotous protest, the Dadaists (who opposed bourgeois values) went all out at this performance—one that many claim was the climax of the Paris Dada anti-art movement. The performers appeared onstage to present their poems, manifestos and sketches in outrageous attire. André Breton had a revolver tied to each temple, Paul Eluard was dressed as a ballerina, and the others wore tubes or funnels on their heads. These outfits, together with the content of the program, which attacked art, philosophy, ethics and just about everything the bourgeoisie held sacred, pushed the audience beyond its endurance. Tomatoes, eggs and beefsteaks were thrown at the performers amid a tremendous uproar. Naturally, the Dadaists considered the evening a great success.

8. Performance of Music for Piano by George Antheil (The Philharmonie, Budapest, 1923)

A composer of avant-garde music that was considered anti-romantic and anti-expressive, Antheil was often subjected to hostile audiences. As a result, he began carrying a gun hidden in a shoulder holster whenever he performed. His opening concert in Budapest provoked the audience because of its harsh and unfamiliar sounds, and a riot broke out. The following night, determined that his music be heard, Antheil ordered the ushers to lock all the doors. Then, with the audience's full attention on him, he pulled out his gun and placed it on the piano, where it remained for the rest of an uninterrupted performance.

9. Fourth Performance of Sean O'Casey's *The Plough and the Stars* (Abbey Theatre, Dublin, February 11, 1926)

In the second act of O'Casey's play, set during the 1916 Easter Rebellion against the British, actors portraying Irish heroes brought the national flag onto the stage, set up as a tavern. Many patriots in the audience took this as an insult to the men who had died in the Free Ireland struggle. This emotional issue touched off a riot that included fights between members of the audience and the actors. William Butler Yeats, the esteemed poet and senior director of the theatre, called the police and then took to the stage to castigate the audience. Later, there was a threat to blow up the theatre. During subsequent performances, the police were present, as were the stench of stink bombs and occasional outbursts, but no more riots erupted.

10. Initial Screenings of Luis Buñuel and Salvador Dali's *L'Âge d'or* (Paris, December 1930)

A film that bombards the viewer with violent and erotic surrealistic imagery, *L'Âge d'or* is concerned with the malice and hypocrisy of man. It vigorously scorns the conventions and institutions of bourgeois society. As expected, bourgeois society was not delighted with the film. One newspaper called it "obscene, repellent and paltry," and another commented that "country, family and religion are dragged through the mud." An article in an extreme rightist paper incited reactionary young Frenchmen, and they launched an attack on the theatre that did not stop for six days. By that time, 120,000 francs' worth of damage had been done. Due to the violent controversy, the film was not shown again publicly for more than 35 years.

11. Unveiling of Mural by Diego Rivera (Hotel del Prado, Mexico City, June 1948)

Diego Rivera's mural *Dream of a Sunday Afternoon in the Alameda*, commissioned for the dining room of the new Hotel del Prado in 1948, showed Mexican historian Ignacio Ramirez holding an open book. The words *Dios no existe* ("God does not exist") were clearly printed on one page. Consequently, Archbishop L.M. Martinez refused to bless the government-owned structure, and a mob of youths stormed into the dining room and scraped away the words with a knife. When Rivera restored the words with a fountain pen, local students threatened to obliterate them as often as Rivera replaced them. The hotel had the mural covered, and while its fate remained in limbo, Rivera was denied entrance to a movie house and his home was vandalized. Eventually, a priest who preferred to remain anonymous quietly blessed the hotel.

12. Concert by Paul Robeson (Peekskill, New York, September 4, 1949)

When the Cold War intensified, Robeson came under increasing fire for his leftist political views. A benefit concert for the Civil Rights Congress by Robeson and other liberal singers in Peekskill, New York, scheduled for August 27, 1949, had to be cancelled when a mob of anti-Communists reinforced by the Ku Klux Klan smashed chairs and beat concertgoers. Robeson returned on September 4 to sing for a crowd of 10,000 in a field outside Peekskill. Supporters formed a human shield around Robeson as he performed songs including "Go Down Moses" and "Ol' Man River." At the end of the show, concertgoers found themselves having to run a gauntlet of stone-throwers lining the exit. Singer Pete Seeger used the stones thrown at his car to build a chimney for his house. Hundreds were injured trying to leave the show. A year later, Robeson was blacklisted after he refused to sign an affidavit disclaiming his membership of the Communist Party.

13. Appearance of Lenny Bruce (The Establishment Club, London, 1962)

During Bruce's engagement at the "liberal" cabaret, the freewheeling social satirist offered his unorthodox views on pornography, sex and drugs, among other topics. Each night, patrons responded uproariously with shouting, walkouts and fistfights. Russian poet Yevgeny Yevtushenko left in disgust, as did playwright John Osborne. The manager of the club was punched in the nose by the escort of actress Siobhan McKenna. Soon, Bruce was declared an undesirable alien and deported from Britain. His obscenity trials still lay ahead of him.

14. Unauthorized Exhibit of Modern Art (Moscow, September 15, 1974)

A group of Russian artists whose paintings were in many styles—except Social Realism, the official art of the U.S.S.R.—was unable to obtain either permission or a building for its exhibit, so it was set up on a muddy field in southeast Moscow. Soviet police met this challenge by driving bulldozers and high-pressure water trucks through the exhibit grounds, sending men, women and children fleeing in panic. Plainclothes officials trampled many paintings underfoot, and the police burned others. Thirty foreign diplomats watched while artists were beaten up, newsmen were manhandled and U.S. consul Leonard Willems was shoved around. The police defended these actions, saying that the bulldozers and trucks were building "a park of rest and culture." Two weeks later, to appease the U.S.—its détente partner—and to court world opinion, the Soviet government gave permission for a similar exhibit.

15. "Blood and Honey" Exhibits (Serbia, June–August 2002)

A series of confrontations occurred when "Blood and Honey," a collection of pictures taken on the battlefields of the former Yugoslavia by American photographer Ron Haviv, was displayed in Serbian cities. On June 5, a group of 40 people disrupted the exhibition in Užice, protesting that the pictures were anti-Serb. A month later, in Čačak, a gang of skinheads burst into the gallery during the opening of the exhibition and attacked organizer Ivan Zlatic, leaving him badly injured. When the exhibit opened in Kragujevac in August, protestors, many wearing T-shirts declaring war criminal Radovan Karadzic a "Serbian hero," greeted visitors with shouts of "Traitors!" Police arrived on the scene but did not react as the demonstrators continued to hurl insults at people entering the gallery. Exhibit organizers decided to postpone the opening to avoid a major confrontation.

—E.H.C.

4 DAYS IN THE LIFE OF JOHN LENNON

1. May 30, 1969—John and Yoko record "Give Peace a Chance" in a Montreal hotel room

The famous recording session took place at about 11:00 p.m. in Lennon's room at the Queen Elizabeth Hotel. It was produced by a young Montreal producer and jazz musician named André Perry, who had been hired by Lennon's record company, EMI. Conditions were hardly ideal for recording. The room was small and filled with people, the ceilings were low, and the acoustics were terrible. Perry had one 4-track Ampex tape machine with four microphones—one for Lennon and his guitar, one for Tommy Smothers and two for everyone else in the room. The group, which included Timothy Leary, Toronto rabbi Abraham Feinberg, musician Petula Clark and members of the Canadian Radha Krishna Temple, did one quick sound check and then recorded the song in one take. After everyone left, at about 2:00 a.m., Perry also recorded John and Yoko singing the flip side of the record, "Remember Love."

2. September 13, 1969—Lennon performs solo for the first time at a Toronto concert

The Toronto Rock & Roll Revival Concert was possibly the greatest concert ever held in Canada, featuring such stars as Chuck Berry, Little Richard, Alice Cooper, the Doors, Jerry Lee Lewis and a new musical ensemble called John Lennon and the Plastic Ono Band. The organizers had wanted the full complement of Beatles, but the concert was put together so hastily that it was not possible to get them all together. So John brought Yoko Ono and some friends, including Eric Clapton, over with him from London to perform without the Beatles for the first time. John looked almost messianic onstage, wearing a white robe and a heavy beard. Yoko hid behind a giant pillow and shrieked for most of the concert. But the gig appears to have helped Lennon make an important decision. When he got back to London, he informed Paul, George and Ringo that he was no longer interested in being a Beatle.

3. December 22, 1969—Lennon gives secret testimony to the Le Dain Commission

Three days before Christmas 1969, John Lennon and Yoko Ono met secretly with two members of the Le Dain Commission, which had been established by the Trudeau government to investigate Canada's marijuana laws. The session was held in secret because the Commission suspected that the RCMP was harassing and sometimes even arresting people who appeared in front of them in public sessions. They were concerned that the same fate might befall the famous Beatle. In his testimony, Lennon urged that marijuana be legalized, and that its sale be controlled by the government to keep money out of the hands of the pushers. He also condemned the use of hard drugs, including LSD, which, he said, had "burned my head off." He strongly supported the Commission's efforts to reform the country's marijuana laws. "We honestly think a place like Canada looks like the only hope," Lennon told the commissioners. "Canada is America without being American, without that . . . 'We-are-the-mighty-whatever scene.' Canada's image is just about getting groovy, you know."

4. December 23, 1969—Lennon talks peace with Prime Minister Pierre Trudeau

This was a meeting between a politician who often behaved like a rock star and a rock star who, by 1969, was behaving much like a politician. The location was the Prime Minister's Office. The discussion was scheduled to last just 15 minutes, and was to be followed by a 15-minute photo op, but it ended up lasting much longer. Most of the conversation dealt with the world situation and Lennon's campaign for peace. Both men agreed that a climate of mutual trust had to be created in which disarmament and peaceful diplomatic relations could begin. When it was over, Lennon said, "If all politicians were like Mr. Trudeau, there would be peace." Trudeau replied, "I must say that 'Give Peace a Chance' has always seemed to me to be sensible advice."

THE ARTS

8 RARE ABILITIES OF GLENN GOULD

1. As an infant, Glenn rarely cried, but by the age of three months he had begun to hum, loudly and persistently. His mother would hold him on her knee in front of the piano keys, and unlike most children, who would thump or pound the notes, Glenn would strike one key at a time, letting the note decay into silence before playing another.

2. Glenn loved to sing, and by the time he was three it was clear that he had perfect pitch. He could detect subtle differences between flats and sharps, and when asked to sing any specific note—a C-sharp, for example—was able to hit the note perfectly every time.

3. Glenn could read music before he could read words, and could play piano pieces from memory that he had heard just once.

4. When learning new piano pieces, Glenn would take the sheet music into his room and study it quietly, then play a concerto, for instance, completely from memory. This exceptionally rare musical ability is akin to being able to read a manual on how to drive, then get in a car and drive on busy streets or highways.

5. At 14, Glenn had an epiphany about his ability to hear music on different levels. While he was practising a fugue by Mozart, someone

switched on a vacuum cleaner near the piano, thus drowning out the noise of the piano notes being struck. Instead of being distracted, Glenn found the mechanical wall of sound quite pleasing because it allowed him to hear the music "in his head" louder than the music being made on the piano. By heightening his physical and inner experience of the music, he was able to distinguish between the "perfect" music he heard in his mind and the sometimes less than perfect music he was producing on the instrument. Armed with this crucial distinction, he became an unstinting perfectionist in all of his performances and recordings. At times, he created this shroud of mechanical noise while he practised by loudly playing TV Westerns or Beatles records simultaneously.

6. At 22, Glenn first performed his unique interpretation of Bach's Goldberg Variations in public on October 16, 1954, in Toronto. He was drawn to their complex contrapuntal phrasing and mathematical precision and worked on the compositions painstakingly for months in the quiet of his family's Lake Simcoe cottage. Glenn's distinctive mannerisms and fidgeting were already very much in evidence. He swayed, hummed, sang along and conducted with one hand while playing with the other. Unfortunately, only a dozen or so people attended the concert because it was the same night that Hurricane Hazel was flooding streets, toppling buildings and wreaking havoc on the city. Within a year, he recorded his career-defining performance of the Goldberg Variations in New York for Columbia Masterworks. It was an instant success and, since then, has never been out of print.

7. At the age of 35, Glenn created a new art form: contrapuntal radio. Asked by CBC radio to come up with an original production that celebrated Canada's centennial year, 1967, he set out to explore his fascination with solitude and the effect of the northern geography, climate and isolation on Canadian identity. The resulting documentary, *The Idea of North*, layered human voices on top of each other in a manner reminiscent of contrapuntal music composition to create a dense, impressionistic, non-linear narrative. Provocative and original, this work and other contrapuntal essays and documentaries cemented his reputation as a radio genius.

8. Glenn's hearing was so refined that he was able to hear things on audio tape that most people around him couldn't. He could tell exactly what tape deck was used to record a specific performance by almost imperceptible changes in the quality of the sound and tape hiss.

10 COMPOSERS WHO DIED IN UNUSUAL CIRCUMSTANCES

1. Jean-Baptiste Lully (1632–87)

The creator of French grand opera, Lully was a great favourite of King Louis XIV. It was Lully's custom to conduct ensembles by pounding the floor with a large pointed cane. While conducting a Te Deum for the king's benefit, he accidentally struck his foot so violently that he developed an infection. Gangrene set in, followed by blood poisoning, which led to his death.

2. Johann Schobert (1720–67)

A popular composer of chamber music, Schobert died in his Paris home after eating mushrooms that were, in fact, toadstools. One of his friends, a servant and all of the members of his immediate family, with the exception of one young child, also died from ingesting the poisonous mushrooms.

3. Pyotr Ilyich Tchaikovsky (1840–93)

On October 28, 1893, the illustrious Russian composer conducted the first performance of his Symphony No. 6 in B Minor in St. Petersburg. Called the "Pathetic Symphony" because of its melancholic air, it was not well received. Four days later, Tchaikovsky—already feeling ill—knowingly drank a glass of unboiled water, even though a cholera epidemic was raging throughout the city. His death on November 6 set off a flurry of rumours that, despondent over the reaction to his symphony, he had committed suicide by purposely contracting cholera.

4. Ernest Chausson (1855–99)

Chausson was a wealthy man who switched from the study of law to the composition of chamber music. His career was cut short when he lost control of his bicycle while riding down a steep slope near his home in Limay, France. He crashed into a wall and died instantly.

5. Enrique Granados Campina (1867–1916)

One of the foremost composers of Spanish nationalist music, Granados overcame his terror of deep water and sailed to New York City to hear an operatic adaptation of his piano compositions. He braved the return journey as a passenger on the SS *Sussex* and was drowned in the English Channel when the ship was torpedoed by a German submarine. The tragedy was compounded because, by agreeing to play at a reception given by President Wilson, Granados had missed the boat on which he was originally scheduled to return to Spain.

6. Alexander Scriabin (1872–1915)

This innovative Russian composer developed a pustule on his lip in the spring of 1915 but elected to ignore it. Soon the pustule developed into a carbuncle, which disfigured much of his face. Bedridden with a fever of 106°F (41°C), Scriabin allowed surgeons to lance his lip several times, but blood poisoning set in and he was dead within hours. No death mask could be cast because of the hideous scarring caused by the emergency surgery.

7. Mieczyslaw Karlowicz (1876–1909)

Considered the greatest Polish composer of the late Romantic era, Karlowicz blended aspects of nationalist music with the ultra-Romantic tradition of Richard Strauss. He was also one of the first of his countrymen to popularize skiing. On one of his frequent solo skiing expeditions in the Tatra Mountains, he was buried by an avalanche.

8. Anton von Webern (1883–1945)

A brilliant composer whose unconventional music was banned by the Nazis in 1938, Webern was killed because of a tragic mistake. While staying with his daughter in the small Austrian town of Mittersill, he inadvertently failed to respond to a wartime curfew warning and was shot by an overzealous American soldier. The guilt-ridden soldier spent his last years in an asylum.

9. Alban Berg (1885–1935)

An outstanding student of Arnold Schönberg, Berg—like Scriabin—died from blood poisoning caused by a carbuncle. In Berg's case, the abscess was located in the small of his back and was the result of an insect bite.

10. Wallingford Riegger (1885–1961)

One of the first American composers to employ Schönberg's system of composition, Riegger met his end when he became entangled in the leashes of two fighting dogs. He fell to the ground and sustained a serious head injury. Emergency brain surgery proved futile, and he died shortly thereafter.

—D.W.B. & C.Ro.

STIRRING OPENING LINES OF 11 NATIONAL ANTHEMS

1. Algeria

We swear by the lightning that destroys,
By the streams of generous blood being shed
By the bright flags that wave
That we are in revolt . . .

2. Bolivia

Bolivians, propitious fate has crowned our hopes . . .

3. Burkina Faso

Against the humiliating bondage of a thousand years
Rapacity came from afar to subjugate them
For a hundred years.
Against the cynical malice in the shape
Of neocolonialism and its petty local servants,
Many gave in and certain others resisted.

4. Guinea-Bissau

Sun, sweat, verdure and sea,
Centuries of pain and hope;
This is the land of our ancestors.

5. Luxembourg

Where slow you see the Alzette flow,
The Sura play wild pranks . . .

6. Oman

O Lord, protect for us Our Majesty the Sultan
And the people in our land,
With honour and peace.
May he live long, strong and supported,
Glorified by his leadership.
For him we shall lay down our lives.

7. Paraguay

To the peoples of unhappy America,
Three centuries under a sceptre oppressed.
But one day, with their passion arising,
"Enough," they said and broke the sceptre.

8. Senegal

Everyone strum your koras,
Strike the balafons,
The red lion has roared,
The tamer of the bush with one leap,
Has scattered the gloom.

9. Taiwan

The three principles of democracy our party does revere.

10. Uruguay

Eastern landsmen, our country or the tomb!

11. USSR

Unbreakable union of freeborn republics,
Great Russia has welded forever to stand;
Thy might was created by the will of our peoples,
Now flourish in unity, great Soviet land!

JAY FERGUSON'S 10 PERFECT POP SONGS

Sloan guitarist, singer and songwriter Jay Ferguson began building his record collection at age nine with the soundtrack to Grease. *At 19 Jay hosted a radio show on Dalhousie's CKDU-FM. When fellow Haligonian and friend Chris Murphy heard Jay playing My Bloody Valentine tunes on the show, it cemented his desire to form a band with him. They first played together in Kearney Lake Road, and then formed Sloan in 1991. Fourteen years later, the fabulous pop four-piece has eight albums and a greatest hits package to their credit.*

1. "Instant Karma," John Lennon
I love the story that this song was written in the morning, recorded in the afternoon, mixed that night and available in the stores a couple weeks later. The perfect instant pop song and the perfect instant production.

2. "Never Understand," The Jesus and Mary Chain
Changed my life when I heard it. Buried way below the layers of feedback is a simple pop melody that I used to play 20 times in a row just to try to decipher it.

3. "We Can Work It Out," The Beatles
It's been said before, but it's true—the meeting of the minds. The perfect showcase of McCartney the optimist and Lennon the realist in just over two minutes.

4. "Where or When," Rodgers and Hart (Dave Edmunds version)
A romantic lyric set to a dreamlike melody about meeting someone you feel like you've known all your life. Edmunds tops Sinatra's version here by taking the Phil Spector approach and turning this 1937 hit into a floating soft wall of guitars and vocals. Another perfectly catchy track that doesn't even have a real chorus.

5. "Someday We'll Be Together," Diana Ross and the Supremes
This song is the bittersweet flip side of the situation in "Where or When." With only three well-arranged chords, and an almost lazy delivery from Ms. Ross, this tune is a perfect example of what distinguishes a good pop song from a great one—it's melancholy at heart with a glimmer of hope on the horizon.

6. "Too Young," Phoenix

Okay . . . it's recent, but it's up there. I remember hearing this for the first time in Amsterdam in the summer of 2000 while on tour. I played it over and over on headphones. It blew me away. A super melody over clever chord structure—like Todd Rundgren and Michael Jackson together at last.

7. "Dreams," Fleetwood Mac

Yet another lyric about the dissolution of the relationship between Lindsey Buckingham and Stevie Nicks, but the words still ring universal. A very economical structure—the whole song is basically two chords, yet all the melodic variations in the verse and chorus mask its simplicity, rendering it a pop classic.

8. "Billie Jean," Michael Jackson

An undeniably perfect song. A guilty pleasure for me when it was released—I thought it was uncool to like Michael Jackson when everybody else was into new wave or punk—but now it's clearly one of the greats. One of the most instantly recognizable opening beats of all time and also his best lyric.

9. "Up the Junction," Squeeze

I love a pop song that crams a novel into three minutes without sacrificing all the minute details. Another melancholy lyric of a relationship that started one way and ended up another. And the lack of a chorus doesn't hurt it one bit.

10. "You're My Favorite Waste of Time," Marshall Crenshaw

Another record that I instantly loved. Heavy Beatles influence, raw 4-track sound, great vocal and a fantastic chorus that Bette Midler must have liked as well. Crenshaw went on to write many perfect pop songs, but this one, recorded on the cheap at home, will always be hard to beat. I dig the way he says "hit it" right before the guitar solo.

WHERE 14 CANADIAN BANDS GOT THEIR NAMES

1. Barenaked Ladies

A provocative but puerile name the band came up with while bored and hanging out at a Dylan concert. The name has grabbed people's attention, as it was intended to do, including that of Toronto mayor June Rowlands, who banned the group from playing at City Hall on January 6, 1992, because, she claimed, the name objectified women.

2. Coney Hatch

This Toronto bar band of the 1980s was named after a town in England that was home to a notorious lunatic asylum.

3. 54–40

Vancouver's indie mavericks of the '80s named themselves after an unkept campaign promise made by 11th U.S. president James Polk to annex most of Canada, from the 54th to the 40th parallel.

4. The Guess Who

Randy Bachman and Burton Cummings first made music together under this name in 1966. The intent of the name was to make people wonder who was this hot new British supergroup.

5. Klaatu

A Toronto trio formed in 1971 that named itself after a character in the 1951 sci-fi movie *The Day the Earth Stood Still*. The band assiduously avoided all publicity, and for a while the rock press speculated that Klaatu was in fact a sub-group of the Beatles. Their song "Calling Occupants (of Interplanetary Craft)" became an international hit when the Carpenters covered it in 1977.

6. Men Without Hats

Ivan and Stefan Doroschuk of Montreal, the brothers behind the monster '80s hit "Safety Dance," say the name of the band was meant to suggest that they were nonconformists.

7. Nickelback

The story goes that bass player Mike Kroeger used to work at Starbucks, where he uttered the phrase "Here's your nickel back" all day long.

8. Rough Trade

The creative duo of Kevan Staples and Carole Pope first began singing folk songs in Yorkville under the moniker the Bullwhip Brothers. In 1975 they changed their sound and name, becoming Rough Trade, a gay slang term for a sadistic or violent sexual partner.

9. Rush

Apparently the band was having trouble coming up with a name, and in the final rush to get one John Rustley's older brother yelled, "Hey, why don't you call your band RUSH?"

10. The Sadies

The reigning kings of cowpunk twang derived their moniker from two sources: the Sadie Hawkins dances, where women asked men to dance, and the name of one of the gangs featured in the 1979 cult film *The Warriors*.

11. Skinny Puppy

A Vancouver-based techno outfit that chose this name to convey the sense of an abused, neglected animal.

12. Sloan

Sloan was the nickname of a bass-playing friend of the band, Jason Larsen. His one-time boss had a French accent and referred to Jason as the "slow one," which sounded more like "sloan" when he said it, hence the nickname.

13. Teenage Head

An obvious sexual reference, the name for these Hamilton punk pioneers was lifted directly from a Flaming Groovies song title. MCA tried to clean them up for American audiences in 1983 by adding an *s* to their name, a move that backfired utterly with their small but dedicated "party till you puke" fan base.

14. The Tragically Hip

The hard-rocking Kingston-based band formed in 1983 was apparently inspired by a video titled "Elephant Parts," made by former Monkee Michael Nesmith.

11 PEOPLE WHO HATED PORTRAITS OF THEMSELVES

1–5. Jacob Von Loon, Volckert Janz, Willem Von Doeyenburg, Jachem De Neve, Aernout Van Der Meije

Rembrandt's group portrait of the board of directors of the cloth-makers' guild, although judged by modern critics to be a great painting, was thought by its conservative subjects to be too radical in approach. Today it serves as a trademark for a cigar company.

6. Mary Riddle (d. 1892)

Mrs. Riddle, a cousin of American impressionist Mary Cassatt, once gave the artist a blue-and-white china tea set. In gratitude, Cassatt painted a portrait of Riddle seated at a table on which the set was prominently displayed. The Riddle family refused to accept the portrait, complaining that Mrs. Riddle's nose was too large. Cassatt, who noted, "You may be sure it was like her," put the picture away in storage until 1915. *Lady at the Tea Table* now hangs in the Metropolitan Museum of Art in New York City.

7. Mme Michel Lévy (1857–1919), French publisher's wife

Impressionist Édouard Manet painted Mme Lévy in the last year of his life. She later sold the portrait because she felt it didn't do justice to her beauty.

8. Winston Churchill (1874–1965), British statesman

"Disgusting," said Lord Hailsham, Churchill's good friend, of Graham Sutherland's portrait. "A beautiful work," said Nye Bevan, Churchill's bitter foe. Churchill called it "a remarkable example of modern art." Churchill hated modern art. So did Lady Churchill. In 1955 she retrieved the portrait, valued at $300,000 (U.S.), from its hiding place behind a cellar boiler, smashed it to the floor and then tossed it in the incinerator. Another portrait of Sir Winston, done by his painting instructor, Sir Walter Sickert, also met with her disfavour. She put her foot through it.

9. Lyndon Johnson (1908–73), U.S. president

L.B.J. called Peter Hurd's portrait "the ugliest thing I ever saw in my whole life." Lady Bird Johnson hoped she would never see another like it if she "lived to be 1,000." Nevertheless, the Johnsons were unable to prevent its hanging in the Smithsonian Portrait Gallery in Washington, D.C.

10. Philip Mountbatten (1921–), British prince consort, the Duke of Edinburgh

In 2003, the Royal Society for the Encouragement of Arts, Manufactures and Commerce, commissioned an official portrait of its long-time president, Prince Philip, to hang in its headquarters. The Prince himself chose artist Stuart Pearson Wright, who had once gained notoriety for a portrait of six presidents of the British Academy gathered around a table decorated with a dead chicken. The most distinguishing feature of Wright's portrait of the Prince was his abnormally long, scrawny and severely wrinkled neck. The RSA was delighted with the portrait, but the same cannot be said for either the artist or the subject. The most positive comment the Prince could come up with was that the portrait was okay "as long as I don't have to have it on my wall."

11. Henry Kissinger (1923–), U.S. secretary of state

Gardner Cox's portrait was to have hung in the State Department, but Kissinger felt he had been "reduced." A spokesman said it "made him look something like a dwarf." Cox rejected the request to rework the portrait, forfeiting his $12,000 (U.S.) commission, saying he liked the painting the way it was.

—R.W.S. & Cdn. Eds.

8 VALUABLE ART WORKS FOUND UNEXPECTEDLY (AND 1 CANADIAN CONTROVERSY)

1. In a farmer's field

In 1820 a Greek peasant named Yorgos was digging in his field on the island of Milos when he unearthed several carved blocks of stone. He burrowed deeper and found four statues—three figures of Hermes and one of Aphrodite, the goddess of love. Three weeks later, the Choiseul archaeological expedition arrived by ship, purchased the Aphrodite, and took it to France. Louis XVIII gave it the name Venus de Milo and presented it to the Louvre in Paris, where it became one of the most famous works of art in the world.

2. Beneath a street

On February 21, 1978, electrical workers were putting down lines on a busy street corner in Mexico City when they discovered a 20-ton stone bas-relief of the Aztec night goddess, Coyolxauhqui. It is believed to have been sculpted in the early 15th century and buried prior to the destruction of the Aztec civilization by the Spanish conquistadors in 1521. The stone was moved 200 yards (183 m) from the site to the Museum of the Great Temple.

3. In a hole in the ground

In 1978 more than 500 movies dating from 1903 to 1929 were dug out of a hole in the ground in Dawson City, Yukon. Under normal circumstances, the 35-mm nitrate films would have been destroyed, but the permafrost had preserved them perfectly.

4. Under a bed

Joanne Perez, the widow of vaudeville performer Pepito the Spanish Clown, cleaned out the area underneath her bed and discovered the only existing copy of the pilot for the TV series *I Love Lucy*. Pepito had coached Lucille Ball and had guest-starred in the pilot. Ball and her husband, Desi Arnaz, had given the copy to Pepito as a gift in 1951, and it had remained under the bed for 30 years.

5. On a wall

A middle-aged couple in a suburb of Milwaukee, Wisconsin, asked an art prospector to appraise a painting in their home. While he was there, he examined another painting that the couple had thought was a reproduction of a work by Vincent Van Gogh. It turned out to be an 1886 original. On March 10, 1991, the painting *Still Life with Flowers* sold at auction for $1,400,000 (U.S.).

6. In a trunk in an attic

In 1961 Barbara Testa, a Hollywood librarian, inherited six steamer trunks that had belonged to her grandfather James Fraser Gluck, a Buffalo, New York, lawyer who died in 1895. Over the next three decades she gradually sifted through the contents of the trunks, until one day in the autumn of 1990 she came upon 665 pages that turned out to be the original handwritten manuscript of the first half of Mark Twain's *Huckleberry Finn*. The two halves of the great American novel were finally reunited at the Buffalo and Erie County Public Library.

7. At a flea market

A Philadelphia financial analyst was browsing at a flea market in Adamstown, Pennsylvania, when he was attracted by a wooden picture frame. He paid $4 for it. Back at his home, he removed the old torn painting in the frame and found a folded document between the canvas and the wood backing. It turned out to be a 1776 copy of the Declaration of Independence—one of 24 known to remain. On June 13, 1991, Sotheby's auction house in New York sold the copy for $2,420,000 (U.S.).

8. Masquerading as a bicycle rack

For years, employees of the God's House Tower Archaeology Museum in Southampton, England, propped their bikes against a 27-inch (69 cm) black rock in the basement. In 2000 two Egyptologists investigating the museum's holdings identified the bike rack as a seventh-century BC Egyptian statue portraying King Taharqa, a Kushite monarch from the region that is modern Sudan. Karen Wordley, the Southampton city council's curator of archaeological collections, said it was a "mystery" how the sculpture ended up in the museum basement.

+1. In an Ottawa home

On May 11, 2001, *The Globe and Mail* reported that a 1603 portrait of Shakespeare as a young man had turned up in the suburban Ottawa home of Lloyd Sullivan, a retired engineer. A portrait of a young man with a subversive smile and twinkly eyes, it was signed by John Sanders and done in oils on an oak panel. This caused a sensation in art circles. If the Sanders portrait was real, it would be the only known painting of

Shakespeare made during his lifetime. Scientists duly set about investigating the painting and have concluded that the painting was done with wood, paint and paper that came from the early 17th century. What they can't say for sure is if it is a picture of the Bard himself. That remains a source of debate, but regardless, the painting is worth a small fortune and is no longer kept under a bed.

DIZZY GILLESPIE'S 10 GREATEST JAZZ MUSICIANS

Jazz legend John Birks "Dizzy" Gillespie was born in Cheraw, South Carolina, on October 21, 1917. After learning to play piano at the age of four, he taught himself to play the trombone, but had switched to the trumpet by the time he was twelve. The leading exponent of "bebop" jazz, Gillespie was famous for conducting big bands, for playing trumpet (many consider him the greatest trumpeter in history), and for his work with Earl "Fatha" Hines and Charlie Parker, among others. He died on January 6, 1993, at the age of 75, and the world mourned the loss of a true jazz giant. He prepared this list for The Book of Lists *in 1980.*

1. Charlie Parker
2. Art Tatum
3. Coleman Hawkins
4. Benny Carter
5. Lester Young
6. Roy Eldridge
7. J.J. Johnson
8. Kenny Clarke
9. Oscar Pettiford
10. Miles Davis

TOP 10 PRICES PAID FOR CANADIAN PAINTINGS AT AUCTION IN 2004

1.	Paul Kane, *Scene in the Northwest* (c. 1845)	$4,600,000
2.	Lawren Harris, *Baffin Island* (1930)	$2,200,000
3.	Paul Kane, *Portrait of Maungwudaus* (c. 1851)	$2,200,000
4.	Jean-Paul Riopelle, *Untitled* (1955)	$1,610,000
5.	James Wilson Morrice, *Effet de Neige* (?)	$1,500,000
6.	Lawren Harris, *Winter in the Northern Woods* (c. 1915–18)	$1,400,000

7.	Jean-Paul Riopelle, *Composition* (1951)	$1,311,000
8.	Emily Carr, *Quiet* (c. 1942)	$975,000
9.	Lawren Harris, *Lake Superior III* (c. 1923–24)	$960,000
10.	Emily Carr, *War Canoes, Alert Bay* (1912)	$925,000

Source: Canadian Art Sales Index 2004.

JOHNNY CASH'S 10 GREATEST COUNTRY SONGS OF ALL TIME

Johnny Cash, widely considered to be the greatest country music singer and composer in history, died in September 2003 at the age of 71. Known as "The Man in Black" (he always wore black), Cash recorded more than 1,500 songs. Cash contributed this list to The Book of Lists *in 1977.*

1. "I Walk the Line," Johnny Cash
2. "I Can't Stop Loving You," Don Gibson
3. "Wildwood Flower," Carter Family
4. "Folsom Prison Blues," Johnny Cash
5. "Candy Kisses," George Morgan
6. "I'm Movin' On," Hank Snow
7. "Walking the Floor over You," Ernest Tubb
8. "He'll Have to Go," Joe Allison and Audrey Allison
9. "Great Speckle Bird," Carter Family
10. "Cold, Cold Heart," Hank Williams

6 CANADIAN CONCERTS WHERE THE FANS WENT WILD

1. The Festival Express, Toronto, 1970

The Festival Express was Canada's answer to the epic concerts that brought together the twin tribes of rockers and hippies for a peace-loving music extravaganza. Montreal, Toronto, Winnipeg and Calgary had signed on for the tour, which travelled by private train between gigs and featured such rock royalty as the Band, Janis Joplin, Buddy Guy, Traffic, the Grateful Dead, and Canadian acts Ian and Sylvia and Robert Charlebois. The tour hit a snag early on, when the first gig in Montreal was cancelled by Mayor Jean Drapeau, who feared mayhem in light of the much-publicized hedonism and occasional violence associated with other festivals, including Woodstock and Altamont. So the Festival Express rolled down the highway to Toronto to kick things off on June 27. Waiting for them there was a large contingent of the May 4th Movement (M4M), anti-Vietnam protestors who drew inspiration from the Kent State killings of four students by Ohio Guardsmen. They dubbed the event the RRRRip-Off Express, claiming that live music should be free, even though the two-day music fest was only charging $14 for a pass. Two thousand protestors stormed the gates, 350 of whom gained entry. Outside, the rest of the M4M mob sparred with 160 policemen, throwing garbage cans, bottles and rocks. Ten officers and 20 youths were injured, and 29 arrests were made. The situation was defused when the Grateful Dead agreed to play a free concert in nearby Coronation Park for the gatecrashers. When Janis Joplin took the stage later that night, she said, "Man, I never expected this of Toronto. You're really looking beautiful, man." The Festival Express continued, although M4M demonstrations were also held in Winnipeg and Calgary. The hippie paradise of a week-long trans-Canadian party and jam session on the train has achieved legendary status in the annals of rock and roll history.

2. The Clash, Vancouver, 1978

The Clash played Vancouver for the first time in 1978 at the Commodore Ballroom. The place was packed with punks revved up at the prospect of slam-dancing on the spring-loaded dance floor. A local act, the Dishrags, got things going with a punishing, sneer-filled set, then Bo Diddley took the stage with his odd rectangular-shaped guitar and let rip with his epic riff "Hey, Bo Diddley." The punks were polite for a few songs, but clearly failed to grasp why Clash lead singer Joe Strummer would invite this old guy along for the tour. The beer and joints were starting to kick in, along with the catcalls, so Bo cut his set short. When the Clash took the stage, pandemonium hit. The punks paid tribute to their heroes by slamming into each other, jumping onstage, throwing drinks and beer bottles at the band, and spitting at them. The Clash withstood the controlled riot for four songs, ducking and dodging the fusillade, then Strummer interrupted the music to mock them: "If anybody had any balls they'd be throwing wine bottles!" At the end of the shortened set, Strummer, clearly peeved at the lack of respect shown one of the greats of rock and roll, pulled Bo Diddley out onstage for the encore to jam with them on "I Fought the Law."

3. Teenage Head, Toronto, August 20, 1981

It was a hot August night at Toronto's lakeshore amusement park. Youth had come from far and wide to attend the free concert by one of Canada's hottest punk acts. But before the gig had even started, police had closed the front gate, saying the venue was full to capacity. A crowd gathered at the gate, quickly noting that there were only a handful of police officers facing several hundred excited fans. A few rowdy ringleaders climbed the fence and beckoned the crowd to follow and storm the turnstiles. They were beaten back by the cops once, but they persisted by forcing open the gate. The crowd surged forward as the cops tried in vain to stop them. By the time reinforcements arrived, a full-scale riot was in progress. Lakeshore Boulevard was closed down as police in cruisers and boats, on horseback and in riot gear swung their batons while being pelted by garbage, bottles and rocks. Largely oblivious to the goings-on, Teenage Head continued to rock out as the melee continued for three hours. Dozens of fans and cops were injured, and 24 people were eventually arrested. The riot was front-page news in 90-odd North American news-papers, and Ontario Place pulled the plug on free rock concerts forever.

4. The Jackson Victory Tour, Montreal, 1984

The Jackson Victory Tour of 1984 was hyped as the biggest music event of the century. It was the first time all six brothers had played together since the '60s, and in the intervening years Michael had hit the big time with mega-million-selling albums *Off the Wall* and *Thriller*. The entire tour sold out before the Jacksons hit the road, including several dates in Vancouver, Montreal and Toronto. The first show in Montreal, on September 17, went off without a hitch, but the next night the mood changed. Word had spread that the show was bloated and overpriced, the tour merchandise was tacky and ridiculously expensive, and, as usual, the sound quality at the Big O was horrible. The capacity crowd grew restless as the show was delayed two hours while security patted down concertgoers for weapons or alcohol. When a local radio jock announced that scalpers were selling off their unsold tickets for $5 each, Montrealers rushed down to the stadium for a last-minute bargain. Venue staff made a foolish decision to close the doors, thus preventing all ticket holders from coming into the stadium, even those who had paid full price. An unruly mob formed outside the gates, bent on getting even with the greedy promoters and rock stars. First they swarmed the T-shirt vendor booths and threw all their inventory into the crowd. Next they took up the metal stanchions and used them as battering rams to break into the stadium. When the glass doors shattered, they ran in and got lost in the crowd. Security finally did the right thing and radioed for the show to start, in order to quell the looming melee that could spill out into the audience of 58,000. With a huge explosion of pyrotechnics, the Jacksons took the stage and broke into the tune "Wanna Be Startin' Something."

5. Guns N' Roses, Montreal, 1992

Guns N' Roses concerts in Canada have been the occasion for two separate riots. The first unfolded in Montreal's Olympic Stadium on August 8, 1992. Front man Axl Rose, famous for his tantrums on and off the stage, incited a riot when he complained about the sound system, and seemed to imply he had a sore throat before walking offstage 50 minutes into the show. This came after Axl had made the audience of 57,000 wait for two hours before taking the stage. Fans were enraged, and began removing the bolts from their stadium seats and throwing them on the stage. Elsewhere they looted concession stands, set fires, smashed windows and damaged 30 police cruisers. Of the 300-odd police officers who tangled with the mob, 8 were slightly injured, along with 3 concertgoers. Damages ran into the hundreds of thousands of dollars, and 12 people were arrested.

6. Guns N' Roses, Vancouver, 2002

The second Guns N' Roses riot was in Vancouver on November 7, 2002. The band was ready to kick off the North American leg of its Chinese Democracy Tour, but front man Axl was AWOL. He called 10 minutes before showtime to say that his plane couldn't get off the ground in Los Angeles due to inclement weather. When the cancellation was announced to the 8,000 fans, they rampaged through the streets of Vancouver. Their fury may have been fuelled in part by the memory of another Guns N' Roses last-minute cancellation in Vancouver, in 1992. Dozens of glass doors and windows were smashed, fireworks were set off, and rocks, beer bottles and cement bricks were thrown at the 120 police officers called out to quell the riot, who used pepper spray, attack dogs and batons to disperse the mob. Damages were estimated at over $350,000 and 12 people were arrested. Some fans were angry and proclaimed they would never listen to

Guns N' Roses again, while others felt it fit in with the band's badass attitude. One fan who was arrested declared that "the riot kicked ass. It's like I told the cops—now that's how you start a motherfuckin' world tour!"

23 EARLY NAMES OF FAMOUS BANDS

In the music business, you have to hit not only the right chords, but also the right name. Here's a quiz to test your knowledge.

1.	Angel and the Snakes	a.	Bachman Turner Overdrive
2.	Composition of Sound	b.	The Bangles
3.	Big Thing	c.	The Beach Boys
4.	Artistics	d.	The Beatles
5.	Carl and the Passions	e.	Bill Haley and His Comets
6.	Primettes	f.	Black Sabbath
7.	Tom and Jerry	g.	Blondie
8.	Johnny and the Moondog	h.	The Byrds
9.	Caesar and Cleo	i.	Champagne Music Makers
10.	Honolulu Fruit Gum Band		(Lawrence Welk)
11.	Bravebelt	j.	Chicago
12.	Polka Tulk	k.	Creedence Clearwater Revival
13.	Bangs	l.	Depeche Mode
14.	Beefeaters	m.	The Guess Who
15.	Falling Spikes	n.	Led Zeppelin
16.	Sparrow	o.	Lynyrd Skynyrd
17.	My Backyard	p.	The Mamas and the Papas
18.	The New Journeymen	q.	Simon and Garfunkel
19.	The Elgins	r.	Sonny and Cher
20.	The Four Aces of Western Swing	s.	Steppenwolf
21.	The Golliwogs	t.	The Supremes
22.	The New Yardbirds	u.	Talking Heads
23.	Chad Allan and the Expressions	v.	The Temptations
		w.	Velvet Underground

Answers: 1 (g), 2 (l), 3 (j), 4 (u), 5 (c), 6 (t), 7 (q), 8 (d), 9 (r), 10 (i), 11 (a), 12 (f), 13 (b), 14 (h), 15 (w), 16 (s), 17 (o), 18 (p), 19 (v), 20 (e), 21 (k), 22 (n), 23 (m)

DR. DEMENTO'S 8 WORST SONG TITLES OF ALL TIME

Radio personality Dr. Demento's private collection of more than 200,000 records is said to be one of the world's largest.

What's a really bad song title? One that's offensive or inarticulate, I'd say, or one that doesn't readily identify the song it's attached to (Bob Dylan did that for kicks in the '60s). I think we can leave those alone for now.

Then there are the sort of song titles (often from country music) that are often rather clever, to be truthful, but induce the same sort of groans that often greet a really good pun when heard for the first time.

Some of those are included on this list, along with others that induce groans for altogether different reasons. Qualifiers: 1) This list does not duplicate my two earlier *Book of Lists* contributions. 2) All of these songs have been heard at least once on *The Dr. Demento Show* (I actually like most of them).

After each song title, the composer credits are shown first (in parentheses) followed by the artist on the recording played on the show.

1. "Booger on My Beer Mug" (Dr. Peter Rizzo), Sneaky Pete

2. "Grope Me Gently, Airport Security Guard" (Larry Weaver), Larry Weaver

3. "Who Put the Benzedrine in Mrs. Murphy's Ovaltine" (Harry Gibson), Harry the Hipster (inspired by the Bing Crosby hit "Who Put the Overalls in Mrs. Murphy's Chowder")

4. "The Five Constipated Men of the Bible" (Scott Hendricks), Axel the Sot

5. "The Day Ted Nugent Killed All the Animals" (Wally Pleasant), Wally Pleasant

6. "I'm Selling Mom's Urine on eBay" (Tommy Womack), Tommy Womack

7. "He Went to Sleep—the Hogs Ate Him" (Ray Starr, N. Nath, G.C. Redd), the Stanley Brothers

8. "Flushed You from the Toilets of My Heart" (J.D. Blackfoot, Johnny Durzo), J.D. Blackfoot (pronounced "hort." Not to be confused with the marginally less groan-inducing "Flushed from the Bathroom of Your Heart," a different song, written by Jack Clement and popularized by Johnny Cash.)

6 CANADIAN MUSIC PRODUCERS OF NOTE

Canada's cultural contribution to the world of comedy and satire is well known. But Canadians have also done very well at home and abroad when it comes to calling the shots in a sound studio.

1. Bob Ezrin

One of the most commercially successful producers of the 1970s, Toronto-raised Bob Ezrin got his start working alongside Guess Who producer Jack Richardson. Within a year, he struck gold, taking Alice Cooper into the big time with *Love It to Death* and later *School's Out*. Other hits soon followed, including Aerosmith's *Get Your Wings*, Kiss's *Destroyer* and his career-defining production, Pink Floyd's *The Wall*. A string of pop and rock albums followed in the 1980s with bands such as Aerosmith, Poco, Lee Aaron, Kansas, Peter Gabriel, Rod Stewart, Lou Reed and Nils Lofgren. His most recent credits include producing tracks for Jane's Addiction, Kula Shaker, the Jayhawks and Nine Inch Nails.

2. Bruce Fairbairn

A major force in rock music during the 1980s, Bruce Fairbairn started producing his own band, Prism, and then got behind the board for Loverboy's hits "Turn Me Loose" and "The Kid Is Hot Tonight." Other hard-rock acts soon came knocking, first Blue Oyster Cult, then Bon Jovi, for whom he produced the 12-million-copy seller *Slippery When Wet*. Working out of his Vancouver studios, Little Mountain Sound and the Armoury, a steady stream of hit albums followed for Aerosmith, AC/DC, Poison, Van Halen, Kiss, Yes and the Cranberries. He died on May 17, 1999, at the age of 49 in his Vancouver home.

3. David Foster

David Foster is one of pop music's most influential producers and songwriters. Born in Victoria, B.C., Foster played keyboards in a couple of bands, but when he moved to L.A., he worked regularly as a session player. His greatest success has come as a songwriter and producer for other people, specializing in the "adult contemporary" niche. Some of the musicians he's made hits for include Celine Dion, Barbra Streisand, Whitney Houston, Toni Braxton, Madonna, Mariah Carey, Garth Brooks, Earth Wind & Fire, Paul McCartney, Lionel Richie and Michael Jackson. Foster has 14 Grammys to his name, including three for Producer of the Year, and also holds the record for Grammy nominations.

4. Daniel Lanois

Daniel and his brother Bob started recording bands in their mother's basement on a 4-track deck. By the '80s they had their own studio, Grant Avenue Sound, in Hamilton, Ontario. Early success came with the Parachute Club and Martha and the Muffins, but it was Dan's collaboration with experimental genius Brian Eno that got him noticed internationally. Lanois promptly knocked out a string of hit albums for the likes of Peter Gabriel, U2, Bob Dylan, Robbie Robertson, Emmylou Harris, Ron Sexsmith and Luscious Jackson. He has also had success as a composer and solo performer, with four albums to his credit.

5. Jack Richardson

Dubbed the dean of Canadian record producers, Jack Richardson's string of hit productions began in the '60s with the Guess Who and extended internationally to Alice Cooper, Bob Seger, Pink Floyd, Peter Gabriel, Rough Trade and the Bay City Rollers.

6. Robbie Robertson

Best known as the singer and creative force behind the Band, Robbie Robertson is a gifted musician, songwriter, guitarist and producer. One of his first ventures in producing was Neil Diamond's *Beautiful Noise*, but he soon got involved in writing and producing soundtracks for Martin Scorsese films, including *Raging Bull*, *The King of Comedy*, *The Color of Money* and *Gangs of New York*. He co-produced his own solo album in 1987 with Daniel Lanois and has won the Juno for Producer of the Year for his work with Native songwriters and musicians.

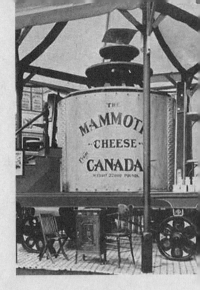

CHAPTER 4　　　　　　　**FOOD AND HEALTH**

ABOVE: *Eleven tons of prime Canadian cheddar on display at the 1893 Chicago World's fair*

103

5 BODY PARTS NAMED AFTER ITALIANS

1. Organ of Corti

The organ of hearing in the middle ear. Alfonso Corti (1822–78) was an Italian nobleman who studied medicine and anatomy in Vienna, writing his thesis on the cardiovascular system of reptiles. He published his findings on the inner ear in 1851, the year that he inherited estates and titles from his father and retired from scientific research.

2. Eustachian Tube

A tube leading from the middle ear to the throat. Its purpose is to equalize pressure in the ear. It is named after Bartolommeo Eustachio (c. 1513–74), considered one of the fathers of anatomy, who lived much of his life in Rome, working as a physician to leading churchmen, including two future saints, Charles Borromeo and Philip Neri.

It has been suggested that Eustachio's discovery of the connection between the middle ear and the pharynx was known to Shakespeare and gave the playwright the means of murder (poison poured in the ear) used by Claudius to kill Hamlet's father.

3. Fallopian Tubes

The pair of tubes that conduct the egg from the ovary to the uterus in the female. They are named after Gabriel Fallopius (1523–62), who spent much of his adult life as a professor of anatomy at Pisa and Padua (early attempts to practise as a surgeon resulted in the deaths of several patients, and Fallopius decided that an academic career was a safer option). He coined the word "vagina" and also invented a kind of contraceptive sheath, which he tested out on more than 1,000 men in what was, perhaps, the first medical trial of condom efficacy.

4. Ruffini's Corpuscles

Sensory nerve-endings that respond to warmth. Named after Angelo Ruffini (1864–1929), who used gold chloride to stain microscope slides of anatomical specimens, thus revealing the tiny and sensitive corpuscles. Ruffini began his career as a country doctor but ended it as a professor at the University of Bologna. His major researches were into the embryology of birds and amphibians.

5. Sertoli Cells

Cells of the testis that serve to nourish sperm cells. Named after histologist Enrico Sertoli (1842–1910), who discovered them in 1865, when he was still a postgraduate student of physiology in Vienna. The year after his discovery, Sertoli returned to his native country to fight for Italian forces against an invading army from Austria. His later life was spent as a professor of anatomy and physiology in Milan.

—K.A.M. & N.R.

10 MAMMOTH CHEESES

1. The 28½-ton Cheddar

The world's largest block of cheese was 6 feet (1.8 m) high, 32 feet (9.8 m) long and 4½ feet (1.4 m) wide. It was commissioned in 1995 by Loblaws supermarket and made by the Agropur dairy cooperative of Quebec. At 57,508 pounds (26,090 kg), the giant cheddar was equivalent to the amount of cheese eaten by 2,500 Canadians in one year.

2. The 17½-ton Cheddar

Known as the "Golden Giant," this enormous chunk of cheese was 14½ feet (4.4 m) long, 6½ feet (2 m) wide and 6 feet (1.8 m) high. Produced in 1964 by Steve's Cheese of Denmark, Wisconsin, for the Wisconsin Cheese Foundation, it required 183 tons of milk—the daily production of 16,000 cows. After its manufacture, the cheese was shipped via a special tractor-trailer, called the Cheese-Mobile, to the Wisconsin Pavilion at the New York World's Fair. A refrigerated glass enclosure remained its home until 1965. It was then cut up into 2-pound (1 kg) pieces that were put on display until 1968, when they were sold for $3 per package. At the 1978 Wisconsin Cheese Makers' Association convention, the two remaining pieces of the cheese were auctioned off for $200 each.

3. The 11-ton Cheddar

Twelve Canadian cheese makers collaborated to make a cheese for display at the 1893 Chicago World's Fair. The "Canadian Mite" was 6 feet (1.8 m) tall and 28 feet (8.5 m) in circumference. When the Mite was put on display at the fair's Canadian pavilion, it broke through the floor, and had to be placed on reinforced concrete at the agricultural building. In 1943 a concrete replica of the cheese was unveiled alongside the railroad tracks in Perth, Ontario, to commemorate the 50th anniversary of the cheese. For the 100th anniversary in 1983, Perth organized a week-long celebration.

4. The 6-ton Cheddar

This giant was produced by upstate New York cheese makers under the direction of W.L. Kilsey for the 1937 New York State Fair at Syracuse. Production began on July 12, 1937. It took seven weeks to cure and had to be turned frequently to ensure even ripening. It used the milk of 6,000 cows.

5. The 4-ton Cheddar

Made by Canadian cheese makers, this 7,000-pound-plus (3,175 kg) giant excited spectators at the 1883 Toronto Fair. Mortician-poet James McIntyre immortalized it in the following cheesy verses:

> We have thee, mammoth cheese,
> Lying quietly at your ease;
> Gently fanned by evening breeze,
> Thy fair form no flies dare seize.

6. The 1,400-pound (635 kg) Cheddar

Bestowed upon U.S. president Andrew Jackson by a New York State cheese maker in 1837, this three-quarter-ton monster ripened in the vestibule of the White House for nearly two years. It was served to the entire city of Washington, D.C., when Jackson threw open the doors of the White House to celebrate Washington's Birthday. According to eye-witnesses, the whole atmosphere for a half-mile around was infected with cheese. The birthday cheddar was devoured in less than two hours. Only a tiny morsel was saved for the president.

7. The 1,200-pound (544 kg) Cheshire

In 1801 President Thomas Jefferson received this cheddar-like tribute from the tiny town of Cheshire in the Berkshire Mountains of

Massachusetts. Named the "Ultra-Democratic, Anti-Federalist Cheese of Cheshire," it was shipped to Washington, D.C., by sled, boat and wagon to honour Jefferson's triumph over the Federalists. The originator of the cheese was a preacher named John Leland, who took advantage of all the fuss and publicity to proselytize for his church. Duly impressed, Jefferson donated $200 to Leland's congregation.

8. The 1,100-pound (500 kg) Cheddar

The Great Pennard Cheese, 9 feet (2.7 m) in diameter, was a wedding gift to Queen Victoria in 1840. Puzzled and somewhat embarrassed by not knowing what to do with it, the Queen was relieved when its makers asked if they could borrow it to exhibit around England. But when they tried to return the grubby, show-worn cheese, Victoria refused to accept it. After lengthy quarrels over its disposition, the cheddar was finally surrendered to the British Chancery, where it gradually disappeared. In 1989, John Green of West Pennard recreated the Great Pennard Cheese, but added 100 pounds (45 kg).

9. The 1,000-pound (454 kg) Luni Cheese

One of the lesser-known wonders of the ancient world, the 1,000-pound (454 kg) Luni cheese, named after an ancient town in northern Italy, was reported by Pliny in his *Natural History* around AD 77. Manufactured in what is now Tuscany, near the famous Carrara marble quarries in central Italy, the Luni cheese was probably made from a mixture of cow's and goat's milk. It is supposed to have tasted like a cross between cheddar and Parmesan.

10. The 1,000-pound (454 kg) Cheddar

The largest cheese to travel halfway around the world, this half-ton cheddar was taken to London all the way from New Zealand. It was the star attraction at the Wembley Exposition of 1924.

—S.R. & C.F.

12 HAIR TIPS FOR MEN FROM *NATIONAL HOME MONTHLY*, 1938

In the 1930s and '40s, *National Home Monthly* proudly billed itself as "Canada's Greatest Magazine." Its main competitor for the loyalty of Canadian women readers, *Chatelaine*, might have taken issue with that designation, but there is no doubt that the Winnipeg-based monthly presented a highly popular mix of fiction, essays, recipes, beauty secrets and other domestic tips. Most of its advice was aimed at women, but writers would occasionally offer some tips for male grooming, such as these pointers for proper male hair care, from February 1938.

Things that are BAD for your hair

1. Tight-fitting hats
2. Cold showers on the unprotected head
3. Salt water not rinsed out of the hair after a swim
4. Deep, warm bed pillows (try flat pillows or do without one)
5. An unbalanced diet, particularly one lacking in the vitamins provided by fruits, vegetables, leafy green things
6. Strain and over-exertion (take exertion in moderation; don't go in for weekend marathons. Leave business worries at the office)

Things that are GOOD for your hair

7. A weekly shampoo, thoroughly rinsed out
8. Daily brushing
9. Hair pulling (some doctors say that the fussing, combing, curling, and rearranging that women constantly give their hair exercises the muscles of the scalp. They suggest tugging gently at the hair, taking small tufts and pulling, as a substitute exercise for men's hair)
10. A sound regime, good diet, rest and recreation (falling hair and early greyness are often a symptom of failing health)
11. Exercise—in moderation
12. Sunlight—in moderation

9 FOODS INVENTED BY CANADIANS

1. Canola Oil

Invented in 1974 at the University of Manitoba, canola oil is pressed from the seeds of the yellow rapeseed plant. In order to appeal to consumers, that name was dropped in favour of Canola, a contraction of "Canadian oil." It has become one of the most popular cooking oils in the world.

2. Ginger Ale

John McLaughlin was a chemist and pharmacist who opened a soda water bottling business in 1890. While experimenting with adding flavours to the bubbly water, he hit upon the additive of ginger root. The resulting drink, Pale Dry Ginger Ale, was an instant hit with thirsty Canadians and Americans. It was patented in 1907 as Canada Dry Ginger Ale.

3. Instant Mashed Potatoes

Instant mashed potatoes were invented by Edward A. Asselbergs in 1962. He came up with this novel use for Canada's staple vegetable crop while working for the Department of Agriculture. The dehydrated flakes were never a big hit with diners, but they continue to be widely used in the creation of convenience food and military rations.

4. Marquis Wheat

The short growing season and harsh climate of the Canadian prairies led to the development of the hardy Marquis wheat between 1902 and 1910. Sir Charles Saunders crossed Red Fife and Hard Red Calcutta wheat to create a rust-resistant variety that yielded big crops before the killing frosts of fall. By 1920 Marquis wheat accounted for 90% of all wheat grown in western Canada.

5. McIntosh Apples

McIntosh apples were discovered and first grown by United Empire Loyalist John McIntosh in 1811. While clearing land on his farm near Ottawa, he found a small stand of 20 or so apple trees growing wild. He transplanted them into his own orchard, but they all died—except one, which was exceptionally sturdy and healthy. Most importantly, the apple tree produced abundant quantities of tasty bright red apples. Neighbours and fruit growers sought out this hardy new variety, the McIntosh Red, for their own orchards, and over the years, hundreds of cuttings and graftings produced similarly robust apple trees ideally suited to the Canadian climate. All McIntosh apple trees descend from this one tree, which stopped producing fruit in 1908 and died in 1910.

6. Pablum

A mixture of ground and precooked wheat, oat and cornmeal, Pablum was invented in 1930 by three pediatricians at Toronto's Hospital for Sick Children: Alan Brown, Theodore Drake and Fred Tisdall. At the time it was created, Pablum revolutionized infant nutrition because it was affordable, nutritious and easy to prepare. As a word, Pablum has gone on to become synonymous with anything that is bland and mushy.

7. Poutine

Although many claim responsibility for inventing the greasy, gooey combination of squeaky cheese curds, gravy and french fries, the first poutine was made by restaurant owner Fernand Lachance in 1957 in Warwick, Quebec. He sold the regional specialty for 35 cents, mixing the curds and fries together in a paper bag, and warned diners that it would be messy but delicious. Many variations on the original recipe exist, including one deluxe version with foie gras served in Montreal's Pied de Cochon bistro.

8. Processed Cheese

J.L. Kraft grew up on a dairy farm in Stevensville, Ontario. While working as a grocer, he was struck by the amount of cheese that went to waste when the dry outer rind was scraped off to reach the moist, fresh interior. He experimented with ways to use these bits of old cheese using double boilers and preservatives. Eventually, he found a way to stabilize the new dairy product, which he called processed cheese.

9. Yukon Gold Potato

This hybrid potato was invented by researchers at the University of Guelph in Ontario in 1980. Named after the Yukon gold rush, it has been hailed as the perfect multi-purpose potato because its smooth, yellow, waxy flesh does well when boiled, mashed or baked. The same team developed the Red Gold, a less popular hybrid, while a team of New Brunswick researchers came up with the Rochdale Gold, which hit their local grocery stores in 2002.

12 FAMOUS INSOMNIACS

1. Barbara Amiel, journalist
Amiel is a lifelong insomniac. "My earliest memory as a child of four was being sedated to sleep," she once recalled.

2. Tallulah Bankhead, actress
Bankhead suffered from severe insomnia. She hired young homosexual "caddies" to keep her company, and one of their most important duties was to hold her hand until she drifted off to sleep.

3. Marlene Dietrich, actress
Dietrich said the only thing that lulled her to sleep was a sardine-and-onion sandwich on rye.

4. Alexandre Dumas, author
Dumas suffered from terrible insomnia, and after trying many remedies, he was advised by a famous doctor to get out of bed when he couldn't sleep. He began to take late-night strolls, and eventually started to sleep through the night.

5. W.C. Fields, actor
The aging Fields resorted to unusual methods to go to sleep. He would stretch out in a barber's chair (he had always enjoyed getting haircuts) with towels wrapped around him, until he felt drowsy. Sometimes he could only get to sleep by stretching out on his pool table. On his worst nights, he could only fall asleep under a beach umbrella being sprinkled by a garden hose. He told a friend that "somehow a moratorium is declared on all my troubles when it is raining."

6. Judy Garland, actress and singer
As a teenager, Garland was prescribed amphetamines to control her weight. As the years went by, she took so many that she sometimes stayed

up three or four days running. She added sleeping pills to her regime, and her insomnia and addiction increased. She eventually died of a drug overdose.

7. Glenn Gould, musician and composer
Pianist Glenn Gould was a lifelong insomniac. He usually stayed up into the early morning hours, working or talking on the phone. He rarely slept without the help of tranquilizers. The Goldberg Variations, a sequence of short compositions Bach composed at the behest of Count von Kaiserling as musical therapy for his abiding insomnia, became Gould's career-defining performance.

8. Franz Kafka, author
Kafka, miserable with insomnia, kept a diary detailing his suffering. For October 2, 1911, he wrote, "Sleepless night. The third in a row. I fall asleep soundly, but after an hour I wake up, as though I had laid my head in the wrong hole."

9. Amy Lowell, poet
Whenever she stayed in a hotel, Lowell would hire five rooms—one to sleep in and empty rooms above, below and on either side to guarantee quiet.

10. Groucho Marx, comic actor
Marx first began to have insomnia when the stock market crashed in 1929 and he lost $240,000 in 48 hours. When he couldn't sleep, he would phone people up in the middle of the night and insult them.

11. Theodore Roosevelt, U.S. president
His insomnia cure was a shot of cognac in a glass of milk.

12. Mark Twain, author
An irritable insomniac, Twain once threw a pillow at the window of his bedroom while he was a guest in a friend's house. When the satisfying crash let in what he thought was fresh air, he fell asleep at last. In the morning he discovered that he had broken a glass-enclosed bookcase.

JULIA CHILD'S 10 FAVOURITE COOKBOOKS (BESIDES HER OWN)

Star of the Emmy-winning TV show The French Chef, *Julia Child delighted millions of viewers with her culinary feats and energetic style. She also had several bestselling cookbooks to her credit, including* Mastering the Art of French Cooking, *co-authored with Simon Beck and Louisette Bertholle, and* From Julia Child's Kitchen, *a compendium of her favourite recipes. She died in 2004.*

1. *The Classic Italian Cookbook* and its sequel, by Marcella Hazan
2. *The Art of Eating*, by M.F.K. Fisher
3. *Larousse Gastronomique*
4. *La Technique*, by Jacques Pépin
5. *The Cuisines of Mexico* and its sequel, by Diana Kennedy
6. *American Cooking and the Theory and Practice of Good Cooking*, by James A. Beard
7. *The Key to Chinese Cooking*, by Irene Kuo
8. *The Art of Making Sausages, Pâtés, and Other Charcuterie*, by Jane Grigson
9. *The Joy of Cooking*, by Irma Rombauer and Marion Becker
10. *French Provincial Cooking*, by Elizabeth David

10 NOTABLE EVENTS THAT HAPPENED UNDER THE INFLUENCE OF ALCOHOL

1. The Hanging of Captain Kidd (1701)

Captain William Kidd was sentenced to death for murder and piracy and led to the gallows at London's Execution Dock on May 23, 1701. The execution itself was a fiasco. As a large group of spectators sang a series of ballads in honour of the pirate, a very drunk public executioner attempted to hang Kidd, who was so smashed that he could hardly stand. Then the rope broke and Kidd fell over into the mud. Though a second attempt at hanging the prisoner succeeded, the sheriff in charge was later harshly criticized in a published editorial for the bungled performance.

2. The Boston Tea Party (1773)

In Boston, Massachusetts, 50 colonials and members of the Committee of Correspondence met at the home of a printer named Benjamin Edes at about 4:00 p.m. on December 16, 1773. Later that evening, they intended to destroy the tea aboard three ships in Boston Harbor as a protest against the British government's taxation of the American colonies. To bolster their resolve, Edes filled a massive punch bowl with a potent rum concoction. Edes's son Peter had the job of keeping the bowl filled, which proved to be an almost impossible task because of the ardour with which the patriots drank. Shortly after 6:00 p.m., the men, most of whom were now in a noisy, festive mood, with a few staggering noticeably, departed and marched to Griffin's Wharf, where the tea ships were anchored. For the next three hours they sobered up, a number becoming violently ill, as they dumped heavy tea chests into the harbour—and set off the American Revolution.

3. The Charlottetown Conference (1864)

Confederation might have happened without the champagne and the wine. But the Canadian cabinet ministers who set sail from Quebec aboard the steamer *Queen Victoria* on August 29, 1864, bound for Charlottetown, were not prepared to leave anything to chance. Their mission was to convince reluctant politicians from New Brunswick, Nova Scotia and Prince Edward Island to abandon their plan for Maritime union and join with them in a larger Canadian federation. In the ship's hold were many cases of champagne and wine. After two days of inconclusive meetings, the Canadians invited the Maritimers for a late Saturday lunch aboard the *Queen Victoria*. The trap was set. Historian P.B. Waite wrote that "champagne flowed like water, and union talk with it. The occasion took hold of everyone. Champagne and union!" So much progress was made that according to George Brown, by the time the lunch ended many hours later, "the union was thereupon formally completed and proclaimed!"

4. Lincoln's Assassination (1865)

On April 14, 1865, actor John Wilkes Booth began drinking at the Kirkwood House bar in Washington, D.C., at 3:00 in the afternoon. At 4:00 p.m. he arrived at Deery's Saloon and ordered a bottle of brandy. Two hours later he was drinking whisky at Taltavul's Saloon, next door to Ford's Theater. Having made the final arrangements for his impending crime, Booth returned at 9:30 to Taltavul's, where President Abraham Lincoln's valet, Charles Forbes, his coachman, Francis Burns, and his bodyguard, John Parker, an alcoholic policeman, were all drinking. At 10:15, while Parker continued to imbibe—thus leaving the president unprotected—Booth left, went next door to Ford's Theater, and shot Lincoln. Meanwhile, George Atzerodt, Booth's fellow conspirator, who was supposed to assassinate Vice President Andrew Johnson, had become so intoxicated and frightened that he abandoned the plan.

5. The Third Battle of the Aisne River (1918)

In May 1918, during the First World War, General Erich Ludendorff's German troops reached the Marne River at Château-Thierry, only 37 miles (60 km) from Paris, during the Third Battle of the Aisne River. On the verge of capturing Paris, but after living without any luxuries for years, the German soldiers invaded France's champagne provinces, where well-stocked wine cellars abounded. Drunkenness quickly spread through the ranks; even the German military police joined the revelries. In the village of Fismes on the morning of May 30, the bodies of soldiers who had passed out littered the streets, making it difficult for trucks to drive through the town on their way to the front lines. The intoxication and subsequent hangovers afflicting the Germans slowed their advance and halted it completely in certain sectors. This enabled the French and Americans to establish new defensive lines, counterattack and end Ludendorff's offensive, which proved to be the Germans' last chance for victory in the war.

6. The Filming of *My Little Chickadee* (1940)

As in almost all of his films, W.C. Fields was intoxicated throughout the production of *My Little Chickadee*. After drinking two to four martinis with his breakfast each morning, Fields arrived at Universal Studios with a cocktail shaker full of martinis. Apparently at his comic best when drunk, Fields consumed two bottles of gin each day during the filming. Fields's inebriated behaviour often infuriated his co-star, Mae West, especially once, when in an overly affectionate mood he prodded and pinched her generous figure and called her "my little brood mare." Although he often required an afternoon nap to diminish the effects of his drinking, Fields was never incapacitated by alcohol during his performance in the movie.

7. The Writing of *A Clockwork Orange* (1962)

Even though his work sometimes dealt with projected future worlds, English author Anthony Burgess developed his novels from his personal experiences. For example, the brutal rape scene in *A Clockwork Orange* was derived from an incident in which his wife was mugged during the Second World War, resulting in the death of their expected child. While writing *A Clockwork Orange*, Burgess became so emotionally involved that he frequently had to calm himself by means of alcohol. As he admitted, "I had to write *A Clockwork Orange* in a state of near drunkenness, in order to deal with material that upset me so much."

8. The *Exxon Valdez* Oil Spill (1989)

After striking a reef, the *Exxon Valdez* spilled 250,000 barrels of oil into Alaska's Prince William Sound, forming a slick that covered 2,600 square miles (4,180 sq. km) and washed onto 1,000 miles (1,600 km) of coastline. At the time of the accident, Captain Joseph Hazelwood was below deck, having left at the helm Third Mate Gregory Cousins, who was not certified to pilot the tanker in Prince William Sound. After the collision, Hazelwood attempted to pilot the tanker off the reef, despite warnings that the ship might break up if he succeeded. Hazelwood also failed to sound a general alarm. In addition, Hazelwood was observed chain-smoking on the bridge until Coast Guard officers arrived and warned him that he could set the whole ship on fire. One of the Coast Guard officers who boarded the ship two and a half hours after the collision reported that Hazelwood's breath smelled of alcohol. When a blood test was administered—a full nine hours after the accident—Hazelwood's blood alcohol level was above the legal level permissible when operating a ship. Although Hazelwood admitted that he had drunk alcohol while ashore earlier that day (and witnesses spotted him drinking in two different bars), he denied being impaired at the time of the accident and insisted that the blood alcohol test was inaccurate. Indeed, although a jury convicted Hazelwood on misdemeanour negligence charges (later overturned), he was acquitted of operating a ship while under the influence of alcohol. On the other hand, an investigation by the National Transportation Safety Board concluded that Hazelwood had left the bridge because of "impairment from alcohol."

9. The Failed Soviet Coup (1991)

In a last-ditch attempt to undo the reforms of glasnost, on August 19, 1991, Communist Party hardliners attempted to overthrow Soviet premier Mikhail Gorbachev. The coup collapsed two days later in the face of resistance led by Boris Yeltsin, president of the Russian republic. The plotters' failure to act decisively against Yeltsin ensured the failure of the coup. Heavy alcohol consumption contributed to the ineptitude of the plotters. Former Soviet vice-president Gennady Yanayev, the front man for the coup, drank heavily throughout the affair, and was found "in an alcoholic haze" in his office when the coup collapsed. Another plotter, former prime minister Valentin Pavlov, began drinking the first night of the coup, by his own admission. When Pavlov tried unsuccessfully to convince the government to declare a state of emergency, he appeared sick "or more likely drunk" according to Deputy Prime Minister Shcherbakov. The failed coup ultimately led to the complete disintegration of the Soviet Union.

10. The Death of Princess Diana (1997)

On August 31, 1997, Diana, her boyfriend, Dodi al-Fayed, and their driver, Henri Paul, were killed in a car crash in a tunnel in Paris. Paul had been driving at more than 100 mph (160 kph) when he apparently clipped another car and lost control. An investigation found that Paul's blood alcohol level was three times the legal limit. There were also traces of antidepressants in his blood. Conspiracy theorists—including Dodi's father, Mohammed al-Fayed—have disputed the blood test results. They note that two bodyguards who were with Paul shortly before the crash said that he did not appear drunk and that he acted normally.

—R.J.F. & C.F.

10 TASTY DISHES FEATURED IN THE PAGES OF *MACLEAN'S* MAGAZINE, 1940

1. Sour Cream Jam Cake
2. Tomato Peanut Butter Soup
3. Grape Nuts Mousse
4. Pea and Celery Loaf
5. Vegetable Pie with Peanut Butter Crust

6. Rice Pudding with Molasses
7. Lemon Prune Pie
8. Peanut Butter Cake
9. Coconut Bread Pudding with Jam and Meringue
10. Orange Tapioca Soup

8 GREAT SAUSAGE EVENTS

1. Comic Sausage

Epicharmus, a Greek dramatist who lived during the golden age of Sophocles and Aeschylus, wrote a comedy titled *Orya* ("The Sausage") around 500 BC. Because the play exists today only as a fragment, we will never know exactly what the Greeks thought was funny about sausage.

2. Heathen Sausage

The ancient Romans were so fond of pork sausage spiced with pine nuts and pepper that the dish became a staple of the annual Lupercalian and Floralian festivals. Since these pagan celebrations usually degenerated into orgiastic rites, the early Christians looked upon them with disapproval. When Constantine the Great, a Christian, became emperor in AD 324, he outlawed the production and consumption of the sinful sausage. But the Romans refused to cooperate and developed a flourishing black market in sausage. They continued to eat the bootlegged delicacies throughout the reigns of several Christian emperors until the ban was finally lifted.

3. Fatal Sausage

At a simple peasant meal in Wildbad, Germany, in 1793, 13 people shared a single sausage. Within hours they became seriously ill, and six of them died. Their disease became known as botulism—a word coined from the Latin for sausage, *botulus*. The powerfully toxic bacteria *Clostridium botulinum* inside the sausage could have been easily killed by boiling it for two minutes. Once in the body, botulism toxins attack the nervous system, causing paralysis of all muscles, which brings on death by suffocation.

4. Human Sausage

Adolph Luetgert, a Chicago sausage maker, was so fond of entertaining his mistresses that he had a bed installed in his factory. Louisa Luetgert was aware of her husband's infidelities and, in 1897, their marriage took a dramatic turn for the worse. Louisa subsequently disappeared, and when the police arrived to search Luetgert's factory, they found human teeth and bones—as well as two gold rings engraved "L.L."—at the bottom of a sausage vat. During his well-publicized trial, Luetgert maintained his innocence, but he was convicted of murder and spent the rest of his life in prison.

5. Muckraking Sausage

Upton Sinclair's novel *The Jungle*, an exposé of conditions in the Chicago stockyards and meat industry, contained shocking descriptions: "There was never the least attention paid to what was cut up for sausage . . . there would be meat stored in great piles . . . thousands of rats would race about on it . . . these rats were nuisances, and the packers would put poisoned bread out for them; they would die, and then rats, bread, and meat would go into the hoppers together." Americans were deeply alarmed by the filth described, and in the same year the book was published, Congress passed the Pure Food and Drug Act of 1906.

6. Insolent Sausage

In October 1981, Joseph Guillou, an engineer on the Moroccan tanker *Al Ghassani*, was arrested, fined £50 and sentenced to two years in jail for insulting Morocco's King Hassan. Guillou's offence was hanging a sausage on the hook normally reserved for a portrait of the monarch. A sausage, said Guillou, was "more useful than a picture of the king."

7. Victim Sausage

During home games at Miller Park, the Milwaukee Brewers baseball team holds "sausage races" in which people costumed as different types of sausages run around the park between innings. During a game on July 9, 2003, as the runners passed the visiting team's dugout, Randall Simon, the first baseman for the Pittsburgh Pirates, struck the Italian sausage, Mandy Block, with his bat, knocking her to the ground. After the game, Simon was handcuffed by Milwaukee County sheriff's deputies, taken to a police station and fined $432 (U.S.) for disorderly conduct. The sausage whacking was broadcast repeatedly, but Block ignored the controversy, accepting Simon's apology. When he returned to Miller Park later in the season, Simon bought Italian sausages for a section of fans. Block was recognized by the National Hot Dog and Sausage Council with a certificate of bravery. "I'm proud of it," Block said. "I didn't even know there was a hot dog council."

8. The Last Red Hot

In October 2004 the last hot dog ever sold at a Montreal Expos baseball game was auctioned off on eBay for $2,605—700 times its original stadium price. It was purchased by Expo fan Guy Laliberté, the founder of the Montreal-based Cirque du Soleil. The sausage, minus the bun, is now floating in a jar of formaldehyde, while a replica has been mounted as a trophy. The hot dog auction was the brainchild of a Montreal disc jockey who gave away four tickets to the final game on the condition that the winner bring back the last red hot. Rémy Coté hovered by the concession stand after every inning, afraid they would run out feeding the 30,000 fans who showed up for the last game. Early in the eighth inning, Coté's patience paid off. Just before the concession stand closed, they sold him what they said was the last of the Expos' red hots. The money raised was donated to charity and, after 36 years in Montreal, the Expos moved to Washington, D.C.

—K.P. & Cdn. Eds.

5 REALLY UNUSUAL MEDICAL CONDITIONS

"Nothing is too wonderful to be true" —Michael Faraday

1. Dr. Strangelove Syndrome

Officially known as Alien Hand Syndrome, this bizarre neurological disorder afflicts thousands of people. It is caused by damage to certain parts of the brain, and causes one of a person's hands to act independently of the other and of its owner's wishes. For example, the misbehaving hand may do the opposite of what the normal one is doing: If a person is trying to button a shirt with one hand, the other will follow along and undo

120

the buttons. If one hand pulls up trousers, the other will pull them down. Sometimes the hand may become aggressive—pinching, slapping or punching the patient; in at least one case, it tried to strangle its owner. Says neurologist Rachelle Doody, "Often a patient will sit on the hand, but eventually it gets loose and starts doing everything again."

2. Foreign Accent Syndrome

There are about 50 recorded cases of foreign accent syndrome, in which people who have suffered strokes or other injuries adopt a new accent. For example, Tiffany Roberts of Florida suffered a stroke and then began speaking with an English accent. She even adopted such anglicisms as "bloody" and "loo." Ms. Roberts had never been to Great Britain, and was not a fan of British television shows.

Perhaps the oddest case concerned a Norwegian woman who fell into a coma after being hit on the head by shrapnel during an air raid in 1941. When she woke up, she spoke with a thick German accent. She was then ostracized by her neighbours.

3. Mary Hart Epilepsy

The case of Dianne Neale, 49, appeared in the *New England Journal of Medicine*. In a much-publicized 1991 incident, Neale apparently suffered epileptic seizures at hearing the voice of *Entertainment Tonight* co-host Mary Hart. Neale experienced an upset stomach, a sense of pressure in her head and confusion. Laboratory tests confirmed the abnormal electrical discharges in her brain, and Neale held a press conference to insist that she was not crazy and resented being the object of jokes. She said she bore no hard feelings towards Hart, who apologized on the air for the situation.

(In another bizarre case, the theme from the show *Growing Pains* brought 27-year-old Janet Richardson out of a coma. She had been unresponsive for five days after falling out of bed and hitting her head, until, according to her sister, the TV theme "woke her up.")

4. Mud Wrestler's Rash

Twenty-four men and women wrestled in calf-deep mud at the University of Washington. Within 36 hours, seven of the wrestlers were covered with patches of "pus-filled red bumps similar to pimples," and the rest succumbed later. Bumps were on areas not covered by bathing suits—one unlucky victim had wrestled in the nude. The dermatitis palastraie limosae, or "muddy wrestling rash," may have been caused by manure-tainted mud.

5. Uncombable Hair Syndrome

Also known as "hair felting," this condition causes hair to form a tangled mass. In a case reported in 1993 in the *Archives of Dermatology*, a 39-year-old woman's hair fell out and was replaced by dry, coarse, curly hair that was so tangled it was impossible to comb. It lacked knots, kinks or twists that would explain the tangling. The hairs themselves were strangely shaped: the cross-sections were triangular, grooved or shaped like kidneys instead of circular. The usual solution to the condition is to cut off the solidified mass of hair. In one case, a woman from Indiana wanted to keep her hair, having spent 24 years growing it. After two and a half months of lubricating her hair with olive oil and separating the strands with knitting needles, her hair returned to normal.

—C.F.

5-YEAR SURVIVAL RATES FOR 25 TYPES OF CANCER

		Total Survival (%)
I.	Prostate	99.8
2.	Thyroid	96.6
3.	Testis	96.0
4.	Melanoma of the skin	91.6
5.	Breast	88.2
6.	Corpus uteri	85.3
7.	Lymphoma (Hodgkin's)	85.3
8.	Urinary bladder	81.8
9.	Cervix uteri	73.3
10.	Leukemia (lymphocytic)	71.4
II.	Larynx	65.6
12.	Rectum	64.7
13.	Kidney and renal pelvis	64.6
14.	Colon	63.9
15.	Lymphoma (non-Hodgkin's)	60.2

16.	Oral cavity and pharynx	60.0
17.	Ovary	44.6
18.	Brain and nervous system	33.3
19.	Myeloma	32.4
20.	Leukemia (myeloid and monocytic)	25.6
21.	Stomach	23.2
22.	Lung and bronchus	15.3
23.	Oesophagus	14.9
24.	Liver and intrahep	9.7
25.	Pancreas	4.6

Source: SEER Cancer Statistics Review 1975–2001 (National Cancer Institute).

10 AFFLICTIONS AND THEIR PATRON SAINTS

1. Cancer

A young 14th-century Italian, Peregrine Laziosi, once demonstrated against the papacy, but was converted and became famous for his preaching and his holiness. When he developed cancer on his foot and doctors were about to amputate, he prayed all night and was miraculously cured. He became the patron saint of cancer victims.

2. Epilepsy

St. Vitus expelled an evil spirit from a Roman emperor's child, and so became the patron of people suffering from diseases typified by convulsions—epilepsy, chorea (or St. Vitus's dance) and other neurological disorders. He is also considered the patron saint of dancers, comedians and actors.

3–4. Hemorrhoids and Venereal Disease

St. Fiacre, a seventh-century holy man who set up a hospice for travellers in France, was known for miraculously healing his visitors of a variety of ills, including venereal disease and hemorrhoids. In addition, cab drivers call on him as their protector because the Hôtel St-Fiacre in Paris was the first establishment to offer coaches for hire.

5. Mental Illness

The remains of St. Dympna, a seventh-century Irish princess murdered by her father when she tried to escape his incestuous desires, are kept in a church in Gheel, Belgium. Dympna became the patron saint of the mentally ill when many insane or mentally handicapped people were cured after visiting her shrine.

6. Paralysis

St. Giles, a hermit who lived near Arles, France, in the seventh century, became the patron of the lame and the crippled. He had protected a deer that was being hunted and took an arrow that had been meant for the animal.

7. Rabies

According to legend, St. Hubert (eighth century) converted to Christianity when during a hunt he saw a stag bearing a cross in its antlers. He became the patron saint of hunters and, because of his connection with wild animals, rabies victims.

8. Skin Diseases

The patron saint of pig herders, St. Anthony was also the fourth-century Egyptian monk who established the world's first Christian monastery. Because pork fat was used to dress wounds, he became the intercessor for people with skin problems. One type of skin inflammation is known as St. Anthony's fire.

9. Throat Infections

St. Blaise (fourth century) cured a young boy who was near death from a fishbone caught in his throat. To this day, Catholics celebrate the blessing of throats. Blaise is also the patron saint of wool combers (his enemies used iron combs on his flesh) and of wild animals (he once lived in a cave among the animals).

10. Toothaches

The intercessor for those with toothaches (and the patron saint of dentists) is St. Apollonia. She lived in Alexandria, Egypt, during the third century, at a time when gangs roamed the city and tortured Christians.

When artists drew Apollonia, they showed her holding either a gold tooth or a set of pincers—her teeth were pulled out by a mob when she refused to give up her Christianity.

9 BODY PARTS YOU DIDN'T KNOW HAD NAMES

1. Eponychium
Another term for the cuticle of the fingernail, a narrow band of epidermal tissue that extends down over the margin of the nail wall.

2. Frenum Glandis
Found in the male reproductive system, this delicate fold of skin attaches the foreskin to the undersurface of the glans.

3. Glabella
A flattened area of the frontal bone (forehead area) between the frontal eminences and the superciliary arches (eyebrows), just above the nose.

4. Lunnule
The white crescent-shaped mark at the base of a fingernail.

5. Otoliths
Particles of calcium carbonate in the utricles and saccules of the inner ears. The otoliths respond to gravity by sliding in the direction of the ground and causing sensitive hairs to bend, thus generating nervous impulses important in maintaining equilibrium.

6. Phalanx
One of the bones of the fingers or toes. There are two phalanges in each thumb and big toe, while there are three phalanges in all other fingers and toes, making a total of 14 in each hand or foot.

7. Philtrum
The vertical groove in the middle portion of the upper lip.

8. Pudendum

A collective name for the external genitalia of the female; also known as the vulva. It includes the mons pubis, the labia majora and the labia minora.

9. Canthus

The corners of the eye where the upper and lower eyelids meet.

—K.A.M. & N.R.

CHAPTER 5   ANIMALS

ABOVE: *Copper engraving of a Canadian beaver drawn from written descriptions provided by Fort Nelson voyageurs (circa 1722)*

THE CAT CAME BACK: 9 CATS WHO TRAVELLED LONG DISTANCES TO RETURN HOME

1. Sugar—1,500 miles (2,414 km)

Sugar, a two-year-old part-Persian, had a hip deformity that made her uncomfortable during car travel. Consequently, she was left behind with a neighbour when her family left Anderson, California, for Gage, Oklahoma. Two weeks later, Sugar disappeared. Fourteen months later, she turned up in Gage on her old owner's doorstep—having travelled 100 miles (160 km) a month to reach a place she had never been. The case was investigated in person by the famous parapsychologist J.B. Rhine, who observed Sugar and interviewed witnesses.

2. Minosch—1,500 miles (2,414 km)

In 1981 Mehmet Tunc, a Turkish "guest worker" in Germany, went home with his cat and family for a vacation. At the Turkish border, Minosch disappeared. Sixty-one days later, back on the island of Sylt, in northern Germany, the family heard a faint scratching at the door. It was a bedraggled Minosch.

3. Silky—1,472 miles (2,369 km)

Shaun Philips and his father, Ken, lost Silky at Gin Gin, about 200 miles (320 km) north of Brisbane, Australia. That was in the summer of 1977. On March 28, 1978, Silky turned up at Mr. Philips's house in a Melbourne suburb. According to his owner, "he was as thin as a wisp and stank to high heavens."

4. Howie—1,200 miles (1,931 km)

In 1978 this three-year-old Persian walked home from the Gold Coast in Queensland, Australia, to Adelaide—a trip that took a year. Said his owner, Kirsten Hicks, 15, "although its white coat was matted and filthy and its paws were sore and bleeding, Howie was actually purring."

5. Rusty—950 miles (1,529 km)

Rusty distinguished himself by setting an American all-time speed record for a cat return. In 1949 this ginger tom travelled from Boston, Massachusetts, to Chicago, Illinois, in 83 days. It is speculated that he hitched rides on cars, trucks and trains.

6. Ninja—850 miles (1,368 km)

Brent Todd and his family moved from Farmington, Utah, to Mill Creek, a suburb of Seattle, Washington, in April 1996, taking with them their eight-year-old tomcat, Ninja. After a week, Ninja jumped over the fence of the new yard and disappeared. More than a year later, on May 25, 1997, Ninja turned up on the porch of the Todds' former home in Farmington, waiting to be let inside and fed. He was thin and scraggly, but his distinctive caterwaul was recognized by the Todds' former neighbours, Marilyn and John Parker. Mrs. Parker offered to send Ninja back to the Todds, but they decided to let him stay.

7. Ernie—600 miles (966 km)

In September 1994, Ernie jumped from the truck of Chris and Jennifer Trevino while it was travelling 60 mph (97 kph) down the highway 600 miles (966 km) west of their home. A week later, Ernie showed up at the Trevino home in Victoria, Texas. When Mrs. Trevino called the cat by name, he came forward and rubbed his face against Mr. Trevino's leg.

8. Gringo—480 miles (773 km)

The Servoz family lost their pet tom, Gringo, from their home in Lamarche-sur-Seine, France, in December 1982. The following July they learned that the cat had moved to the French Riviera. Wishing to escape the cold winter, he had made the journey south in a week and appeared at their summer home, where neighbours took care of him.

9. Muddy Water White—450 miles (724 km)

On June 23 or 24, 1985, Muddy Water White jumped out of a van driven by his owner, Barbara Paule, in Dayton, Ohio. Almost exactly three years later, he returned to his home in Pennsylvania. "He came and just flopped down like he was home," said Mrs. Paule. She fed him for three days before realizing he was Muddy Water White, an identification that was confirmed by the local vet.

10 ANIMALS THAT HAVE EATEN HUMANS

1. Bears

The North American bear, although smaller and less aggressive than the grizzly, can be deadly and has been responsible for many harmful attacks on humans. In 1963, when the Alaskan blueberry crop was poor, hungry black bears attacked at least four people, one of whom they killed.

2. Crocodiles

Estuarine crocodiles are the most effective man-eaters on earth, killing approximately 2,000 people a year. On the night of February 19, 1945, they were responsible for the most devastating animal attack on human beings in recorded history. British troops had trapped 1,000 Japanese infantrymen, many of whom were wounded, in a swampy area in the Bay of Bengal. The noise of gunfire and the smell of blood attracted hundreds of crocodiles, and by evening the British could hear terrible screams. The following morning, only 20 Japanese were found alive.

3. Giant Squid

The giant squid is the most highly developed of the invertebrates. Its eyes are almost exact replicas of human eyes. It has 10 arms, and its body can reach up to 65 feet (20 m) in length. Often confused with the octopus, which attacks humans only when threatened, the giant squid is a carnivorous predator. One notable incident occurred on March 25, 1941, when the British ship *Britannia* sank in the Atlantic Ocean. As a dozen survivors clung to their lifeboat, a giant squid reached its arms around the body of a man and pulled him below. Male squid sometimes eat the female after mating.

4. Komodo Dragons

The world's largest lizard, the Komodo dragon can reach 10 feet (3 m) in length and weigh more than 300 pounds (136 kg). They are the top predators on the handful of Indonesian islands where they live. Their prey normally consists of deer, wild goats and pigs, but they will eat anything they can catch, including the occasional human. Komodo dragons devour their prey completely, including the bones. All that was left of a French tourist killed in 1986 was his bloodstained shoes. All that was left of a German tourist eaten in 1988 was his mangled glasses.

5. Leopards

Considered one of the most dangerous animals to hunt, the leopard is quick and stealthy and is seldom observed. In the central provinces of India, leopards have been known to invade native huts to find their prey. One, known as the Panawar man-eater, is reputed to have killed 400 people. It was shot in 1910 by Jim Corbett, who also killed the Champawat man-eating tigress the following year.

6. Lions

Like tigers, lions do not usually attack humans. Man-eating lions usually hunt in prides, or groups, although occasionally single lions and pairs have become man-eaters. In October 1943, a lone lion was shot in the Kasama District of what is now Zambia after it had killed 40 people.

7. Pumas (Mountain Lions)

Pumas have been known to catch prey seven to eight times their own size: a 100-pound (45 kg) female has been seen killing an 800-pound (360 kg) bull elk. In recent years, as people have built subdivisions in the mountains of the western U.S., attacks by pumas on humans have exploded. Since 1970 there have been more than 40 attacks, at least 7 of them fatal. In 1994 two female joggers in California were killed and partly consumed by female pumas.

8. Pythons

Pythons are quite capable of killing people, and several such incidents have been reported since they became a trendy pet in the 1990s. However, most reports of pythons actually eating humans have proven untrue. A picture circulating on the Internet of a boy allegedly recovered from a python's digestive tract is a hoax. However, there is at least one credible report. In 1992 a group of children playing in a mango plantation near Durban, South Africa, was attacked by a 20-foot (6 m) rock python, which swallowed one of them. Craig Smith, the owner of a snake park, declared, "I've dealt with a few cases like this and I always dispel them as absolute rubbish. But in my opinion this one did happen."

9. Sharks

Of the 200 to 250 species of shark, only 18 are known to be dangerous to humans. The most notable are the great white, the mako, the tiger, the white-tipped, the Ganges River and the hammerhead. The best known of all individual "rogue" shark attacks occurred on July 12, 1916. Twelve-year-old Lester Stilwell was swimming in Matawan Creek, New Jersey, 15 to 20 miles (24 to 32 km) inland, when he was attacked by a great white shark. Both he and his would-be rescuer were killed. In 10 days, four people were killed over a 60-mile (97 km) stretch of the New Jersey coast. Two days after the last attack, an 8½-foot (2.5 m) great white was netted just 4 miles (6 km) from the mouth of the creek. According to the Florida Museum of Natural History, between 1670 and 2003 there were 833 confirmed unprovoked shark attacks in the U.S., 52 of which were fatal.

10. Tigers

A tigress known as the Champawat man-eater killed 438 people in the Himalayas in Nepal between 1903 and 1911. Tigers do not usually hunt humans, unless the animals are old or injured, or have become accustomed to the taste of human flesh.

Note: and two who would not

While it is almost certain that wolves have preyed on human beings at some time in history, there are no confirmed reports of unprovoked attacks on humans by North American wolves. Likewise, there are no confirmed reports of piranha-caused deaths. Observers in the river regions of northeastern South America do report that many natives have lost fingers, toes or penny-sized chunks of flesh while bathing in piranha-infested waters. A school of piranhas can strip a wounded alligator of flesh in five minutes, but they are generally sluggish in their movements.

—D.L. & C.F.

13 FASCINATING FACTS ABOUT BEAVERS

The beaver, which has come to represent Canada as the eagle does the U.S. and the lion Britain, is a flat-tailed, slow-witted, toothy rodent known to bite off its own testicles or to stand under its own falling trees.
—June Callwood

Beavers have an image problem that stems largely from their instinctive drive to build dams and cause floods. They also defecate in drinking water, leading to giardia (a.k.a. beaver fever) among humans. They feed on crops such as corn and soybeans and have been known to cause considerable damage to forests.

But before we write off beavers as chubby, buck-toothed pests, let's not forget their core qualities of industriousness and ingenuity—they are mother nature's chief engineers. And everyone knows they have nice fur (as proven by the fur trade). We offer this list in the hope that we can learn to accept and even honour our national animal with the praise it so richly deserves.

1. Giant beavers roamed Eurasia and North America in the Pleistocene era, rubbing shoulders with mastodons and mammoths. They were 10 feet (3 m) in length, including tail—just smaller than a MINI Cooper—and weighed up to 800 pounds (360 kg).

2. The modern beaver is the second-largest rodent in the world (the capybara of South America is the first). An average adult beaver weighs 35 to 70 pounds (16 to 32 kg) and measures 4 feet (1.3 m) long, including a 12-inch (30 cm) tail.

3. A large adult beaver skin yielded enough fur for 18 beaver hats, popular in the 19th century. Despite this, the beaver was hunted and trapped almost to the point of extinction. They are firmly established once more, thanks to a conservation movement started by Grey Owl, the infamous English immigrant who posed as a Metis in the 1930s.

4. Grey Owl claimed to have compiled a "beaver dictionary" by listening to the utterings of his two pet beavers, Rawhide and Jellyroll. He stated that he could recognize 49 words and expressions that were intelligible to

all beavers, but the manuscript of this dictionary is now missing and presumed lost forever.

5. Beavers are well adapted to working underwater. A secondary, transparent eyelid allows them to see, and specialized ducts allow them to close off their ears, nostrils and lips so they can chew without drowning.

6. The two chisel-like upper front teeth of the beaver grow continuously and are sharpened by the act of gnawing on trees. They are not "buck" teeth, but point inwards to facilitate chewing wood.

7. Beavers groom themselves constantly to keep their pelt waterproofed with the oil (castoreum) they produce in two glands near the anus. Castoreum also keeps their soft, fine under-fur from matting. Moisture never penetrates their skin, even after a long time swimming underwater.

8. There is a misconception that male beavers will bite off their own testicles if provoked, which dates back to Aesop's fables. At that time, the beaver was hunted for its castoreum, which people believed was produced in the testicles. A story popular at the time held that beavers would see a hunter coming and would bite off their testicles and toss them to the hunter to avoid being killed. If they were chased again, they would flash the hunter to show that they had already made the "ultimate sacrifice."

9. Contrary to popular legend, beavers do not know how to fell a tree so that it falls in a certain direction. Beaver remains have been found that show that the trees they were chewing fell towards them, pinching and crushing their skulls.

10. The urge to build dams stems from an instinctive aversion to the sound of running water. Beavers will try desperately to stem the flow, thereby flooding their surroundings to create a pond deep enough that the water won't freeze in winter. They eat sticks in these lean months, so they spend the entire fall submerging twigs in the pond and poking them into the muddy bottom to store them.

11. Female beavers do most of the engineering work and lodge planning, while male beavers concentrate on inspecting the structure and patching leaks.

12. Beavers are monogamous and mate for life.

13. Beavers are critical participants in creating and maintaining wetland environments and minimizing damage caused by spring floods.

11 EXAMPLES OF UNUSUAL ANIMAL MATING HABITS

1. Geese

Two male geese may form a homosexual bond and prefer each other's company to any female's. Sometimes, however, a female may interpose herself between them during such a courtship and be quickly fertilized. They will accept her, and weeks later the happy family of three can be seen attending to its tiny newborn goslings.

2. Grasshoppers

Why are grasshoppers so noisy? It's because they're singing to woo their partners. They have as many as 400 distinct songs, which they sing during their courtship and mating cycles. Some males have a different song for each distinct mating period—for example, there may be a flirting song, then a mating song.

3. Hippopotami

Hippos have their own form of aromatherapy. Hippos attract mates by marking territory, urinating and defecating at the same time. Then, an enamoured hippo will twirl its tail like a propeller to spread this delicious slop in every direction. This attracts lovers, and a pair will begin foreplay, which consists of splashing around in the water before settling down to business.

4. Lynx Spiders

When a male lynx spider feels the urge, he will capture his beauty in his web and wrap her in silk. Offering her this elegant meal (the silken web) is his way of wooing. When the mood is right, the female, distracted by her feast, will allow her suitor to mount her and begin mating. Oblivious, she ignores him and enjoys her supper.

5. Penguins

Penguins prefer to be "married," but they suffer long separations due to their migratory habits. When reunited, a pair will stand breast to breast, heads thrown back, singing loudly, with outstretched flippers trembling. Two weeks after a pair is formed, their union is consummated. The male makes his intentions known by laying his head across his partner's stomach. They go on a long trek to find privacy, but the actual process of intercourse takes only three minutes. Neither penguin will mate again that year.

The male Adélie penguin must select his mate from a colony of more than a million, and he indicates his choice by rolling a stone at the female's feet. Stones are scarce at mating time because many are needed to build walls around nests. It becomes commonplace for penguins to steal them from one another. If she accepts this gift, they stand belly to belly and sing a mating song.

6. Porcupines

The answer to one of our oldest jokes: "How do porcupines do it?" "Veeery carefully!" is not quite true. The truth is more bizarre than dangerous. Females are only receptive for a few hours a year. As summer approaches, young females become nervous and very excited. Next, they go off their food and stick close by the males and mope. Meanwhile, the male becomes aggressive with other males and begins a period of carefully sniffing every place the female of his choice urinates and smelling her all over. This is a tremendous aphrodisiac. While she is sulking by his side, he begins to "sing."

When he is ready to make love, the female runs away if she's not ready. If she is in the mood, they both rear up and face each other, belly to belly. Then, males spray their ladies with a tremendous stream of urine, soaking their loved one from head to foot—the stream can shoot as far as 7 feet (2 m). If they're not ready, females respond by: 1) objecting verbally; 2) hitting with front paws like boxers; 3) trying to bite; or 4) shaking off the urine. When ready, they accept the bath. This routine can go on for weeks. Six months after the beginning of courtship, the female will accept any male she has been close to. The spines and quills of both go relaxed and flat, and the male enters from behind. Mating continues until the male is worn out. Every time he tries to stop, the female wants to continue. If he has given up, she chooses another partner, only now *she* acts out the male role. To "cool off," females engage in the same courtship series, step by step, in reverse order.

It is advised never to stand close to a cage that contains courting porcupines.

7. Red-Sided Garter Snakes

These snakes are small and poisonous, and live in Canada and the north-western U.S. Their highly unusual mating takes place during an enormous orgy. Twenty-five thousand snakes slither together in a large den, eager to copulate. In that pile, one female may have as many as 100 males vying for her. These "nesting balls" grow as large as 2 feet (60 cm) high. Now and then, a female is crushed under the heavy mound—and the males are so randy that they continue to copulate, becoming the only necrophiliac snakes!

8. Seagulls

Lesbian mating is practised by between 8% and 14% of the seagulls on the Santa Barbara Islands, off the California coast. Lesbian gulls go through all the motions of mating, and they lay sterile eggs. Homosexual behaviour is also known in geese, ostriches, cichlid fish, squid, rats and monkeys.

9. Squid

Squid begin mating with a circling nuptial dance. Pairs of squid revolve around across a "spawning bed" 650 feet (200 m) in diameter. At daybreak they begin having sex and continue all day long—they only take a break so the female can drive down and deposit eggs. When she returns to the circle, the two go at it again. As twilight falls, the pair goes offshore to eat and rest. At the first sign of sunlight, they return to their spot and do it all over again. This routine can last up to two weeks, ensuring a healthy population of squid.

10. Uganda Kobs

Exhaustion is the frequent fate of the male Uganda kob, an African antelope. Like many species of birds and mammals, the kob roams in a social group until the mating season, when the dominant male establishes a mating territory, or lek. But the females decide which territory they wish to enter and then pick the male they think most attractive. He then mates with all the females until he is too weak to continue (usually due to lack of food) and is replaced by another.

11. White-Fronted Parrots

These birds, native to Mexico and Central America, are believed to be the only species besides humans to kiss. Before actually mating, male and female will lock their beaks and gently flick their tongues together. If kissing is satisfying for both parties, the male boldly takes the next step, regurgitating his food for his girlfriend, to show his love. White-fronted parrots also share parenting, unlike many other species. When the female lays her one egg, both parents take turns incubating it. When the baby hatches, the couple feed and care for their offspring together.

15 CHILDREN WHO MAY HAVE LIVED WITH WILD ANIMALS

1–2. Romulus and Remus (8th century BC)

Twin brothers Romulus and Remus were allegedly raised by a wolf after being abandoned in the countryside by their uncle. A number of years later they were rescued by a shepherd, and they went on to found the city of Rome in 753 BC. Scholars long considered their childhood adventures to be mythical, but recent studies of children known to have lived with animals have demonstrated that there could well be an element of truth to the Romulus and Remus legend.

3. Hessian Wolf-Boy (1344)

In 1344 hunters in the German kingdom of Hesse captured a boy between 7 and 12 years of age who had been living in the wild. Wolves had brought him food and dug holes to shelter him at night. The boy ran on all fours and had an extraordinary ability to leap long distances. Treated as a freak by his human captors, he died shortly after his return to civilization because of an enforced diet of cooked food.

4. Lithuanian Bear-Boy (1661)

In 1661, in a Lithuanian forest, a party of hunters discovered a boy living with a group of bears. The hunters captured him even though he resisted by biting and clawing them. Taken to Warsaw, Poland, and christened Joseph, the boy continued to eat raw meat and graze on grass. Although he never dropped the habit of growling like a bear, Joseph acquired a limited vocabulary and became the servant of a Polish nobleman.

5. Irish Sheep-Boy (1672)

In 1672 a 16-year-old boy was found trapped in a hunter's net in the hills of southern Ireland. Since running away from his parents' home as a young child, the boy had lived with a herd of wild sheep. He was healthy and muscular even though he ate only grass and hay. After his capture he was taken to the Netherlands, where he was cared for in Amsterdam by Dr. Nicholas Tulp. The boy never learned human speech, but continued to bleat like a sheep throughout his life.

6. Fraumark Bear-Girl (1767)

In 1767 two hunters captured a girl who attacked them after they shot her bear companion in the mountains near the village of Fraumark, Hungary. The tall, muscular 18-year-old girl had lived with bears since infancy. Later she was locked up in an asylum in the town of Karpfen because she refused to wear clothes or eat anything but raw meat and tree bark.

7. Wild Boy of Aveyron (1800)

In 1800 hunters captured a 17-year-old boy who had lived alone in the forest of Aveyron, France, since he was an infant. Given the name Victor, the boy was not happy living in civilized society and repeatedly tried to escape. He also growled and gnashed his teeth at first, but later became adjusted to being with humans. When he died at the age of 40, he had learned only three words.

8. Dina Sanichar (1867)

In 1867 a hunting party found a seven-year-old boy living with wolves in a cave in the jungles of Bulandshahr, India. Taken to the Sekandra Orphanage near Agra and given the name Dina Sanichar, the boy refused to wear clothes and sharpened his teeth by gnawing on bones. For 28 years he lived at the orphanage, but he never learned to talk. In 1895 he died of tuberculosis aggravated by the one human habit he had adopted—smoking tobacco.

9. Tarzancito (1933)

In December 1933 a woodcutter captured a boy about five years of age in the jungles of Ahuachapán province in El Salvador. The boy, nicknamed "Tarzancito," had lived alone since infancy, subsisting on a diet of wild fruit and raw fish. Newspaper correspondent Ernie Pyle, who met Tarzancito, reported that when the boy first returned to human society, he communicated by howling and frequently attacked and bit people. Eventually Tarzancito learned to talk and adjusted to human life.

10. Cachari Leopard-Boy (1938)

In 1938 an English sportsman found an eight-year-old boy living with a leopard and her cubs in the north Cachar Hills of India. The boy, who had been carried off by the leopard five years earlier, was returned to his family of peasant farmers. Although nearly blind, he could identify different individuals and objects by his extremely well-developed sense of smell.

11. Misha Defonesca (1945)

When she was seven years old, Misha's mother and father were seized by Nazis. She was hidden in a safe house, but, worried that she might be turned over to the Germans, she ran off and lived in the wild. For the next four years, as the Second World War raged, Defonesca wandered through Europe, covering more than 3,000 miles (4800 km). During this time, she lived on raw berries, raw meat and food stolen from farmhouses. On occasion, she lived with packs of wolves. She later recalled, "In all my travels, the only time I ever slept deeply was when I was with wolves. . . . The days with my wolf family multiplied. I have no idea how many months I spent with them, but I wanted it to last forever—it was far better than returning to the world of my own kind. . . . Those were the most beautiful days I had ever experienced."

12. Saharan Gazelle-Boy (1960)

In September 1960 Basque poet Jean Claude Armen discovered and observed a boy who was approximately eight years old living with a herd of gazelles in the desert regions of the Western Sahara. For two months

Armen studied the boy, whom he speculated was the orphaned child of some nomadic Saharan Moorish family. The boy travelled on all fours, grazed on grass, dug roots, and seemed to be thoroughly accepted by the gazelles as a member of the herd. Since the boy appeared happy, Armen left him with his gazelle family. American soldiers attempted to capture the boy in 1966 and 1970, but without success.

13. Shamdeo the Wolf-Boy (1972)

This boy was taken to the Catholic mission at Sultanpur, a town in Punjab, India, by a man who allegedly had found him living in a forest with wolves. The boy, estimated to be three or four years old at the time, was covered with matted hair and had calluses on his elbows, palms and knees. According to Father Joseph de Souza, Shamdeo learned to stand upright in five months, and within two years he was doing chores around the mission. He communicated by sign language. Father Joseph also noted that the boy no longer caught and ate live chickens, but he was still drawn by the scent of blood. That Shamdeo actually lived with wolves has not been authenticated.

14. John Ssebunya (1991)

In 1991 Ugandan villagers treed and captured a little boy living with a pack of monkeys. One of the villagers identified the child as John Ssebunya, who had fled the village three years earlier when his father had murdered his mother and then disappeared. John was adopted by Paul and Molly Wasswa, who ran an orphanage. Several experts who studied John were convinced that John really had lived with monkeys. When left with a group of monkeys, he approached them from the side with open palms in classic simian fashion. He also had an unusual lopsided gait and pulled his lips back when he smiled. He tended to greet people with a powerful hug, the way monkeys greet each other. After some time in the orphanage, John learned to talk and to sing. In 1999 he visited Great Britain as part of the Pearl of Africa Children's Choir. That same year, he was the subject of a BBC documentary, *Living Proof*.

15. Bello of Nigeria (1996)

In 1996 a boy about two years of age was found by hunters living with chimps in the Folgore forest in Nigeria. He was taken to the Maliki Torrey

children's home, where the staff named him Bello. Mentally and physically disabled, with a misshapen forehead, sloping right shoulder and protruding chest, he was apparently abandoned by his parents, members of
the nomadic Fulari tribe. When he first arrived at the home, Bello walked
like a chimp. As of 2002 he still could not speak, but made chimp-like
noises.

—R.J.F. & C.F.

THE DAY OF EXTINCTION FOR 8 BIRDS
1. Great Auk, June 3, 1844
This large flightless bird similar to a penguin nested along both coasts of
the North Atlantic. In Canada, great auks were found in Newfoundland,
New Brunswick and Nova Scotia. The great auk was the first bird known
as a "penguin"; when explorers from the northern hemisphere came
across the similar but unrelated species in the Antarctic, they transferred
the name to the new bird. The last recorded breeding place of the great
auk was Eldey Island, off the coast of Iceland. At the beginning of June
1844, three men, part of an expedition funded by an Icelandic bird collector called Carl Siemsen, landed on the island. They found and killed
two auks, among other birds gathered on the island's cliffs, and took away
an egg, which was later sold to an apothecary in Reykjavik for £9. There
has since been no confirmed sighting of a great auk on Eldey Island or
anywhere else.

2. Labrador Duck, December 12, 1872
This small black and white duck bred in Canada's Maritime provinces
and migrated as far south as Chesapeake Bay in the winter. A strong and
hardy species, its decline remains a mystery but is likely due to a combination of a severe reduction in its invertebrate food supply and predation
and egg-collecting by humans. The last reported Labrador duck was shot
down over Long Island in 1872.

3. Guadalupe Island Caracara, December 1, 1900
A large brown hawk with a black head and grey striped wings, the caracara
was last seen alive and collected by R.H. Beck in 1900. One of the few

cases in which a bird was deliberately exterminated, the caracara was poisoned and shot by goatherds, who thought it was killing the kids in their herds.

4. Passenger Pigeon, September 1, 1914

These brownish-grey pigeons were once so numerous that a passing flock could darken the sky for days. As recently as 1810, an estimated 2 billion pigeons were sighted in one flock. But massive hunting by settlers and a century of forest destruction eliminated the passenger and its native forest habitat. In 1869, 7.5 million pigeons were captured in a single nesting raid. In 1909 a $1,500 (U.S.) reward was offered for a live nesting pair, but not one could be found. Martha, the last of the passenger pigeons, died of old age in 1914 in the Cincinnati Zoo.

5. Carolina Parakeet, February 21, 1918

The striking green and yellow Carolina parakeet was once common in the forests of the eastern and southern U.S., but because of the widespread crop destruction it caused, farmers hunted the bird to extinction. The last Carolina parakeet, an old male named Incas, died in the Cincinnati Zoo. The zoo's general manager believed it died of grief over the loss of Lady Jane, its mate of 30 years, the previous summer.

6. Heath Hen, March 11, 1932

A relative of the prairie chicken native to the East Coast of the U.S., the heath hen was once so common around Boston that servants sometimes stipulated before accepting employment that heath hen not be served to them more than a few times a week. But the bird was hunted to extinction, and the last heath hen, alone since December 1928, passed away in Martha's Vineyard at the age of eight, after the harsh winter of 1932.

7. Euler's Flycatcher, September 26, 1955

Known only from two specimens and one sighting, Euler's flycatcher was an 8½-inch (22 cm) olive and dusky yellow bird. The flycatcher was believed by James Bond (the authority on Caribbean birds, not Ian Fleming's 007) to have perished in Jamaica in 1955, during Hurricane Janet.

8. Dusky Seaside Sparrow, June 18, 1987

This sparrow was once common in the marshes of Merritt Island, Florida, and along the nearby St. John's River. In the 1960s, Merritt Island was flooded to deal with the mosquito problem at the Kennedy Space Center, while the marshes along the St. John's were drained for highway construction. Pesticides and pollution also contributed to the bird's demise. In 1977, the last five dusky seaside sparrows were captured. Unfortunately, they were all male, with no female to perpetuate the species. The five were relocated to Disney World's Discovery Island to live out their last days. The last one, an aged male blind in one eye, named Orange Band, died 10 years later.

—D.L.

7 ANIMAL SPECIES EXTINCT IN CANADA

Ten animal species have been eradicated in Canada since European settlers arrived on the shores of North America. The three extinct species of bird—great auks, Labrador ducks and passenger pigeons—are discussed in the previous list. These are the other seven extinctions.

1. Sea Mink—1894

This seacoast carnivore's rocky shoreline habitat stretched from the Maritimes to Maine. Twice as large as regular minks, it was prized by hunters for its valuable fur and oil. Hunted to extinction, the last sea mink was killed on Campobello Island in New Brunswick in 1894.

2. Eelgrass Limpet—1929

A small saltwater mollusc that was once found along the North Atlantic shoreline, the eelgrass limpet died out when eelgrass, its sole food supply, was afflicted by a deadly infestation of slime mould. The demise of 90% of the eelgrass also caused a collapse in the scallop fishery and a decline in the population of migratory waterfowl.

3. Dawson's Caribou—1930s

Little is known about this subspecies of the woodland caribou that roamed the northern extremes of the Queen Charlotte Islands of British

Columbia. Its decline is generally attributed to overhunting and deterioration of habitat.

4. Deepwater Cisco—1952

Deepwater cisco (or chub) were found in Lakes Erie, Huron and Michigan. A commercial fishery that caught and "smoked" the silvery 12-inch (30 cm) fish peaked in the 1930s. Overfishing, combined with pollution, the disruption of the food supply and predation by the non-native sea lamprey all contributed to its demise. The longjaw cisco was once thought to be another extinct species of fish, but in 2002 it was delisted. It is now believed longjaws were a distinctive population of the shortjaw ciscoes.

5. Blue Walleye—1965

The blue walleye, also known as the blue pike, was found in Lakes Ontario and Erie and in the Niagara River. Abundant and prolific, it was fished commercially from 1850 to 1956. Overfishing, combined with increased competition in the food chain with the introduction of rainbow smelts, led to the extinction of the species.

6. Banff Longnose Dace—1986

This small Alberta minnow lived only in a marsh into which the Banff hot springs drained. It was killed off when guppies, swordtails and other tropical fish were released by tourists and national park staff into the warm waters around the hot springs. The chlorine used in the nearby swimming pool and a nearby beaver dam also corrupted the longnose dace's habitat.

7. Hadley Lake Stickleback—1999

Two varieties of the Hadley Lake stickleback species (benthic and limnetic) were found in only one small lake on Lasqueti Island, British Columbia. First discovered in the late 1980s, they were preyed upon and killed off by non-native catfish that were introduced to the lake by humans.

MAXIMUM RECORDED LIFESPAN OF 58 ANIMALS

1. Tortoise   188 years
2. Lake sturgeon   152 years
3. Human   122 years, 5 months
4. Fin whale   116 years
5. Blue whale   110 years
6. Humpback whale   95 years
7. Elephant (African)   80 years
8. Turtle (eastern box)   75 years
9. Parrot (African grey)   73 years
10. Chimpanzee   71 years
11. Alligator   66 years
12. Horse   62 years
13. Orangutan   59 years
14. Eagle (eastern imperial)   56 years
15. Seal (Baikal)   56 years
16. Hippopotamus   54 years, 4 months
17. Gorilla   54 years
18. Camel   50 years
19. Dolphin   50 years
20. Grizzly bear   50 years
21. Rhinoceros (Indian)   49 years
22. Brown bear   47 years
23. Condor (California)   45 years
24. Goldfish   43 years
25. Hyena (spotted)   41 years, 1 month
26. Boa constrictor   40 years, 3 months
27. Vulture   40 years
28. Polar bear   38 years, 2 months
29. Giraffe   36 years, 4 months
30. Rhinoceros (Sumatran)   35 years
31. Cat   34 years
32. Ant (queen)   30 years
33. Kangaroo (red)   30 years
34. Panda (giant)   30 years
35. Dog   29 years, 6 months
36. Lion   29 years

37.	Porcupine (Old World)	27 years, 4 months
38.	Tiger	26 years, 4 months
39.	Wombat	26 years, 1 month
40.	Aardvark	24 years
41.	Sheep	24 years
42.	Jaguar	22 years
43.	Raccoon	20 years, 7 months
44.	Frog	20 years
45.	Koala	20 years
46.	Porcupine (normal)	20 years
47.	Vampire bat	19 years, 6 months
48.	Pigeon	18 years, 6 months
49.	Rabbit	18 years
50.	Duck-billed platypus	17 years
51.	Guinea pig	14 years, 10 months
52.	Hedgehog	14 years
53.	Shrew (non-human)	12 years
54.	Hamster	10 years
55.	Gopher (eastern pocket)	7 years, 2 months
56.	Anchovy	7 years
57.	Partridge	5 years, 2 months
58.	Mole	5 years

Primary Source: *Longevity Records: Life Spans of Mammals, Birds, Amphibians, Reptiles and Fish.* James R. Carey and Debra S. Judge. http://www.demogr.mpg.de.

8 EXTINCT ANIMALS THAT ARE NO LONGER EXTINCT

1. Cahow

This ocean-wandering bird nested exclusively on the islets of Bermuda. Also known as the Bermuda petrel, the last of the cahows was believed to have been killed during the famine of 1615, when British colonists built cook-fires into which the unwary cahows flew by the thousand. On January 8, 1951, the cahow was rediscovered by Bermuda's conservation officer, David Wingate. Under his protection, the existing 18 birds were encouraged to breed, and now number more than 150.

2. Dibbler

A marsupial mouse, the dibbler was listed as extinct in 1884. In 1967 an Australian naturalist hoping to trap live honey possums caught instead a pair of dibblers. The female of the captured pair soon produced a litter of eight, and they were then bred in captivity.

3. Dwarf Lemur

The last known dwarf lemur was reported in 1875, and the species was regarded as extinct. Then in 1966 the small tree-dwelling marsupial was seen once again, near the city of Mananara, Madagascar.

4. Ivory-Billed Woodpecker

Described by John James Audubon as the "great chieftain of the wood-pecker tribe," the ivory-billed woodpecker was, with a wingspan of 30 inches, the largest American woodpecker. Once found throughout the Southeast and in Cuba, the ivory bill began to decline as forest land disappeared. The last confirmed sighting of an ivory bill was in Louisiana in 1944. Then, on February 11, 2004, amateur birdwatcher Gene Sparling was kayaking in the Cache River National Wildlife Refuge in Arkansas, when he spotted an unusually large red-crested woodpecker flying towards him. A second sighting by professional ornithologists a mere 16 days later confirmed the discovery. Scientists kept the good news secret for a year in order to plan the protection of the bird.

5. Mountain Pygmy Possum

This small marsupial was considered to have been extinct for 20,000 years until Dr. Kenneth Shortman caught one in the kitchen of his skiing lodge, Mount Hothan, in southeast Australia in 1966. Three more of the tiny possums were discovered in 1970.

6–7. Tarpan and Aurochs

A primeval forest horse of central Asia, and long extinct, the tarpan was recreated by brothers Lutz and Heinz Heck, curators of the Berlin and Munich zoos, respectively. By selective crossbreeding of Polish primitive horses with Swedish Gotlands, Icelandic ponies and Polish Konik mares, they created a strain of wild horse identical in appearance to what we know of the mouse grey tarpan. The first colt was born on May 22, 1933.

By a similar method, the aurochs, a European wild ox that died out in Poland in 1627, has also been duplicated.

8. White-Winged Guan
A flower-eating South American bird, the guan was thought extinct for a century until sighted in September 1977. An American ornithologist and his Peruvian associate located four of the pheasant-sized birds in remote northwestern Peru.

—D.L. & Cdn. Eds.

8 "VICE-REGAL" PETS BURIED ON THE GROUNDS OF RIDEAU HALL
1. Dog, beloved companion of the Duchess of Connaught, 1914
2. "Moses," dog, friend and companion of Viscount Willingdon, April 29, 1930
3. "George," golden retriever, friend and companion of V.M. (Vincent Massey), 1953
4. "Lassie," English sheep dog belonging to Rose, Shane and Brian Alexander
5. "Tessa," English sheep dog belonging to Rose, Shane and Brian Alexander
6. "Prince," English sheep dog belonging to Rose, Shane and Brian Alexander
7. "Cachou," beagle belonging to Jules Léger's family
8. "Reggie," Irish setter belonging to Edward Schreyer's family

12 LARGE ANIMALS DISCOVERED BY WESTERN SCIENCE SINCE 1900
In 1812, the "Father of Paleontology," Baron Georges Cuvier, rashly pronounced that "there is little hope of discovering a new species" of large animal and that naturalists should concentrate on extinct fauna. In 1819 the American tapir was discovered, and since then a long list of "new" animals has disproved Cuvier's dictum.

1. Okapi

By saving a group of Congolese pygmies from a German showman who wanted to take them to the 1900 Paris Exhibition, Sir Harry Johnston gained their trust. He then began hearing stories about the okapi, a mule-sized animal with zebra stripes. In 1901 Sir Harry sent a whole skin, two skulls and a detailed description of the okapi to London, and it was found that the okapi had a close relationship to the giraffe. In 1919 the first live okapi were brought out of the Congo River basin, and in 1941 the Stanleyville Zoo witnessed the first birth of an okapi in captivity. The okapis, striking in appearance, are now rare but popular attractions at the larger, more progressive zoological parks of the world.

2. Mountain Nyala

First discovered in the high mountains of southern Ethiopia in 1910, the mountain nyala remains a relatively unknown species. The male has gently twisting horns almost 4 feet (120 cm) long and can weigh up to 450 pounds (200 kg). The coat is a majestic greyish-brown, with white vertical stripes on the back. After it was described by Richard Lydekker, the eminent British naturalist, it was ruthlessly hunted by field biologists and trophy seekers through some of the most inhospitable terrain in existence. The mountain nyala lives in the Arussi and Bale mountains at heights above 9,000 feet (2750 m), where the sun burns hotly in the day and the night temperatures fall to freezing. Its existence is presently threatened by illegal hunting.

3. Pygmy Hippopotamus

Karl Hagenbeck, a famous German animal dealer, established a zoological garden near Hamburg that was the prototype of the modern open-air zoo. In 1909 Hagenbeck sent German explorer Hans Schomburgk to Liberia to check on rumours about a "giant black pig." After two years of jungle pursuit, Schomburgk finally spotted the animal 30 feet (9 m) in front of him. It was big, shiny and black, but the animal was clearly related to the hippopotamus, not the pig. Unable to catch it, he went home to Hamburg empty-handed. In 1912 Hans Schomburgk returned to Liberia and, to the dismay of his critics, came back with five live pygmy hippos. A full-grown pygmy hippopotamus weighs only about 400 pounds (180 kg), a tenth of the weight of the average adult hippopotamus.

4. Komodo Dragon

These giant monitor lizards are named for the rugged volcanic island of Komodo, part of the Lesser Sunda Islands of Indonesia. Unknown to science until 1912, the Komodo dragon can be up to 12 feet (3.5 m) long and weigh over 350 pounds (160 kg). The discovery of the giant lizard was made by an airman who landed on Komodo and brought back incredible stories of monstrous dragons eating goats, pigs and even attacking horses. At first, no one believed him, but then the stories were confirmed by Major P.A. Ouwens, director of the Buitenzorg Botanical Gardens in Java, who offered skins and photographs as proof. Soon live specimens were caught and exhibited. The world's largest living lizard is now a popular zoo exhibit.

5. Congo Peacock

Some animal discoveries are made in museums. In 1913 the New York Zoological Society sent an unsuccessful expedition to the Congo in an attempt to bring back a live okapi. Instead, one of the team's members, Dr. James P. Chapin, brought back some native headdresses with curious long reddish-brown feathers striped with black. None of the experts could identify them. In 1934 Chapin, on another of his frequent visits to the Congo, noticed similar feathers on two stuffed birds at the Tervueren Museum. They were labelled "Young Indian Peacocks," but Chapin immediately knew that was not what they were. A mining company in the Congo had donated them to the museum and labelled them "Indian peacocks," but Chapin soon discovered that they were a new species. The following year he flew down to the Congo and brought back seven birds. Chapin confirmed them as the first new bird genus discovered in 40 years. They were not peacocks at all, but pheasants. The Congo peacock is now commonly found in European and North American zoos.

6. Kouprey

The kouprey is a large wild ox that was found along the Mekong River in Cambodia and Laos and has been the source of much controversy. It first came to the attention of Western scientists in 1936, when it showed up as a hunting trophy in the home of a French vet. The following year, the director of the Paris Vincennes Zoo, Professor Achille Urbain, went to northern Cambodia and reported that a new wild ox, unlike the gaur and the banteng, was to be seen in Cambodia. Other naturalists felt he was wrong and suggested that the kouprey might be just a hybrid of the gaur and the banteng. Finally, in 1961, a detailed anatomical study of the kouprey proved it to be so different from the area's other wild oxen that it might belong in a new genus, although many scientists continue to insist that it does not. Urbain's 1937 discovery was upheld. The Vietnam War was responsible for the death of many koupreys. A 1975 New York Zoological Society expedition was unable to capture any, although they did see a herd of 50. The kouprey has not been observed by scientists since 1988, although kouprey skulls occasionally show up at local markets. It is now considered critically endangered.

7. Coelacanth

This 5-foot (1.5 m), 127-pound (58 kg), large-scaled, steel-blue fish was brought up in a net off South Africa in December 1938. The huge fish crawled around on deck for three hours before it died. The only problem was that the coelacanth was supposed to have been extinct for 60 million years. Ms. M. Courtenay-Latimer and ichthyologist James Smith of Rhodes University, South Africa, identified the coelacanth after it was already dead and had begun to decay. Professor Smith then began years of searching for a second living coelacanth and was finally rewarded in December 1952, when a fishing trawler off the Comoro island of Anjouan, near Africa's east coast, brought up an excellent specimen. Dr. Smith was soon shocked to learn that the local inhabitants of the Comoros had been catching and eating the "living fossils" for generations.

8. Black-faced Lion Tamarin Monkey

Brazilian scientists found the black-faced lion tamarin monkey in June 1990 on the island of Superagui, along Brazil's heavily populated Atlantic coast, where less than 5% of the country's original Atlantic forest still remains. The amazing discovery led biologist Dr. Russell Mittermeier, president of Conservation International, to say, "It's almost like finding a major new species in a suburb of Los Angeles." The monkey has a lion-like head and a gold coat. Its face, forearms and tail are black. Prior to its discovery, there were only three known species of the lion tamarin monkey. It is estimated that fewer than two dozen of the new primate species exist. In 1992, two years after this species' discovery, another new species of monkey, the Maues marmoset, was found in Brazil—this time in a remote part of the Amazon rainforest. First spotted near the Maues River, a tributary of the Amazon, by Swiss biologist Marco Schwarz, the tiny monkey has a pink koala-like face and faint zebra-like stripes.

9. Sao La

According to British biologist John MacKinnon, who discovered the sao la in May 1992, the mammal "appears to be a cow that lives the life of a goat." Skulls, horns and skins of the sao la were found by MacKinnon in the Vu Quang Nature Reserve, a pristine 150,000-acre (60,000 ha) rainforest in northwestern Vietnam near the Laotian border. Known to the local Vietnamese as a "forest goat," the sao la—also called the Vu Quang ox—weighs about 220 pounds (100 kg). Smaller than a cow but larger than a goat, the mammal has a dark brown shiny coat with white markings on its face. It has dagger-like straight horns about 20 inches (50 cm) long and two-toed concave hooves that enable it to manoeuvre through slippery and rugged mountain areas. Scientists did not see a live example of the new species until June 1994, when a four-month-old female calf was captured. Unfortunately, the calf and another adolescent sao la that was subsequently captured died in October 1994, both from an infection of the digestive system. Despite the illegality of hunting and trapping sao la, by 1998 their population was estimated at just 120 to 150, and they are threatened with extinction. This is partly due to the bounties offered local hunters by TV crews and scientists trying to capture or view live specimens of this popular species.

10. Giant Muntjac Deer

Muntjacs, or barking deer, are a common food in Vietnam. But in April 1994, the World Wildlife Fund and the Vietnamese Ministry of Forestry announced that a new species of the mammal—the giant muntjac deer—had been discovered in Vu Quang Nature Reserve, the same rainforest where the sao la had been found two years earlier. One and a half times larger than other muntjacs, the deer weighs about 100 pounds (45 kg) and has 8-inch (20 cm) antlers that are bowed inward.

It has a reddish coat and large canine teeth. A live animal was captured in Laos by a team of researchers working for the Wildlife Conservation Society, and in August 1997 another muntjac, the Truong Son or dwarf muntjac, was located in the Vu Quang Nature Reserve. Weighing only 30 pounds (14 kg), it has black fur and extremely short antlers. It is expected that other new species of animals will be found in the Vu Quang Nature Reserve, which miraculously survived bombing and herbicide spraying during the Vietnam War. British biologist John MacKinnon calls the area "a corner of the world unknown to modern science" and "a biological gold mine."

11. Bondegezou

This large black and white whistling tree kangaroo was first described by zoologist Dr. Tim Flannery in 1995. The local Moni tribe in West Papua (Irian Jaya) on the island of New Guinea had long revered the bondegezou as their ancestor.

12. Highland Mangabey

A new species of monkey was discovered in 2004 by two separate research teams working in the remote mountains of southern Tanzania. Considered a relative of the baboon family, the highland mangabey is critically endangered, with an estimated population between 500 and 1,000. It has an unusual, gentle "honk bark," a black face and long brown fur that keeps it warm in the high altitudes in which it lives. Tom Butynski, one of the first scientists to spot the monkey in the wild, reported the thrill of seeing it for the first time: "Your mouth drops open and a big smile appears on your face. You say, 'Wow!'"

—L.C., C.O.M. & Cdn. Eds.

4 OF THE MOST OFT-SIGHTED LAKE AND SEA MONSTERS IN CANADA

1. Champ—The Monster of Lake Champlain

This creature apparently lives in a lake that runs from Quebec to New York state. Only a few photographs and videos of "Champ" exist. However, a 1977 photo, taken by Sandra Mansi, is considered the most impressive photo of any sea or lake "monster." Ms. Mansi was taking a leisurely drive with her family along the lake when she saw a disturbance in the water. She "saw the head come up . . . then the neck, then the back." Her fiancé began to scream, "Get the kids out of the water!" Sandra had the common sense to take a picture, which she tucked away in the family album for four years until it was published in *The New York Times*. Since then, over 130 further sightings have been reported. Books, seminars and arguments followed, and many strongly believe Ms. Mansi took a photo of a piece of driftwood. Arguing against this is her statement that "the mouth was open when it came up and water came out." Champ is most often seen in early mornings in summer.

2. Ogopogo

There are usually several sightings a year of the Ogopogo, rumoured to live in the Okanagan Lake in British Columbia. Author Mary Moon lists hundreds of sightings, beginning in the late 1700s. The creature is 30 to 50 feet long (9 to 15 m), with an undulating, serpent-like body, a long, thin neck and a rather horse-like head. It is reputed to swim extremely fast, appearing as several humps, or arches, on the surface. Native American legends tell of the Ogopogo attacking humans, and some swimmers in the lake have disappeared without a trace.

3. Cadborosaurus—"Caddy and Amy"

Cadboro Bay in British Columbia supposedly sports a pair of aquatic reptiles nicknamed "Caddy" and "Amy." Caddy's overall length is estimated at 40 to 70 feet (12 to 20 m). There have been more than 60 years of sightings, beginning in the 1940s and continuing with at least half a dozen a year. In 1946 sightings were so common that a plan developed to catch one of the creatures and put it on display in Vancouver's swimming pool; happily, Caddy and Amy's friends vetoed the idea. In 1994 Dr. Ed Bousfield published a book about Caddy—*Cadborosaurus: Survivor from the Deep*.

4. Memphre

Lake Memphremagog is a long, narrow lake that straddles the area between Magog, Quebec, and Newport, Vermont. For over 100 years, locals have insisted that a long, black sea monster with humps, which they call Memphre, lives in the lake. People who claim to have seen it describe it as a "coiling dark beast with webbed feet, tusks and horns." According to Sonja Bolduc, a researcher at the nearby University of Sherbrooke, there have been 215 known sightings of the creature.

10 MOST INTELLIGENT BREEDS OF DOG

In *The Intelligence of Dogs* (New York: The Free Press, 1994), Stanley Coren ranked breeds of dogs by working intelligence. The rankings were based on questionnaires completed by 199 obedience judges from the American and Canadian Kennel Clubs.

1. Border collie
2. Poodle
3. German shepherd
4. Golden retriever
5. Doberman pinscher
6. Shetland sheepdog
7. Labrador retriever
8. Papillon
9. Rottweiler
10. Australian cattle dog

10 LEAST INTELLIGENT BREEDS OF DOG

1. Afghan hound
2. Basenji
3. Bulldog
4. Chow chow
5. Borzoi
6. Bloodhound
7. Pekingese
8. Mastiff
9. Beagle
10. Basset hound

Source: Stanley Coren, *The Intelligence of Dogs* (New York: The Free Press, 1994).

MISTY MACDUFFEE'S TOP 5 DOS AND DON'TS WHEN ENCOUNTERING A BEAR IN THE WILD

Misty MacDuffee is a biologist with the Raincoast Conservation Society, an organization working for grizzly protection in Canada's Great Bear Rainforest on the west coast of British Columbia. Her job often requires close encounters with bears, and while she is not advocating that people seek such interactions, she believes they can occur seamlessly.

Staying safe around *Ursus* is usually about using common sense when hiking, camping or working in bear country. The number of bears killed each year in Canada for "sport" and "management" dwarfs the number of attacks on people. Bears are generally passive animals, but when frightened or threatened they can turn aggressive. While circumstances can play a large role in how human–bear encounters unfold, some basic knowledge can go a long way towards leaving both parties unscathed. If you do meet up with a bear, how you should react depends on the behaviour of the bear.

1. An unaware bear: If you come across a bear who is busy grazing or fishing, chances are he or she hasn't seen you. Try not to disturb the bear—move away quietly to a distance from which you can safely watch the bear without spooking him or her. Don't close the distance.

2. An aware bear: If a bear looks towards you, smells the air, stands up or bolts and stops, he or she has detected your presence. These are not aggressive behaviours and range in the level of surprise. Put some distance (calmly) between you and the bear if you are too close. Noise will likely frighten the bear away. If this is your objective, you can call out.

If the bear is fishing or grazing and seems unconcerned by your presence, you can usually observe him or her from a safe distance. Many people who live in bear habitat have uneventful, peaceful encounters with bears on a routine basis. Most bears are happy to go about their business and ignore you. Always treat them with respect.

3. A bear demonstrating warning behaviours: Growling, snapping and snorting are clear indications that the bear feels threatened. Speak to the bear in a calm voice as you move away and give him or her space. In close encounters, don't hold eye contact. Eye contact can be interpreted as showing dominance or aggression. Look down, be submissive, back away.

4. A bear showing aggressive behaviour: A charging bear is sending a strong message that you should get away. Hold your ground until the charge stops, then move away quickly.

5. An attacking bear: Bear attacks are rare, and I can only offer the current wisdom on how to respond. Grizzly attacks often occur suddenly, when you have no prior awareness of the bear. Playing dead or curling in a ball should be your first response, because the attack is likely coming from a bear that felt threatened. In either position, cover your neck with interlocked hands and your face with your elbows. If it's a black bear and the attack did not stem from alarm, fight back using objects or by kicking or hitting the bear, especially in the nose. Like humans, bears have sensitive noses, and aggressive black bears have been dissuaded by such a response.

AVERAGE ERECT PENIS LENGTHS FOR 10 SPECIES

Animal	Average erect penis length
1. Humpback whale	10 feet (3 m)
2. Elephant	5–6 feet (1.5–1.8 m)
3. Bull	3 feet (1 m)
4. Stallion	2.5 feet (76 cm)
5. Rhinoceros	2 feet (60 cm)
6. Pig	18–20 inches (46–50 cm)
7. Man	6 inches (15 cm)
8. Gorilla	2 inches (5 cm)
9. Cat	3/4 inch (2 cm)
10. Mosquito	1/100 inch (0.25 mm)

Note: The Argentine lake duck averages 16 inches from head to foot. However, its erect penis size is 17 inches.

Source: Leigh Rutledge, *The Gay Book of Lists* (Boston: Alyson Publications, 1987).

CHAPTER 6   **WORK AND MONEY**

ABOVE: *Striking members of the International Typographers Union
burn copies of the* Vancouver Province *in July 1946*

9 UNUSUAL CANADIAN INDUSTRIAL DISPUTES

1. A Very Thin Blue Line

In Quebec City, on June 25, 1921, 200 policemen and firemen went on strike, demanding a 25% increase in their wages. The city promptly put out a call for unemployed men who wanted to become policemen and firemen. Four days after walking off the job, the strikers were back at work.

2. Silent Nights

Before there were "talkies," theatre owners had to hire musicians to provide the musical accompaniment for silent pictures. On September 5, 1921, a couple of dozen musicians went on strike against three movie houses in Calgary. They were protesting the owners' plans to reduce their wages. A mediator from the Department of Labour was called in, and after four days, he arrived at a settlement. The musicians would continue to get the same daily rate, but a half-hour was added to their workday.

3. Time This . . .

On April 3, 1930, 50 brass workers, metal polishers and buffers in London, Ontario, walked off the job after spotting "efficiency experts" carrying stopwatches in their plant. They were worried that their boss's idea of being more "efficient" was going to mean they would be forced to work harder and faster. The employer immediately began to hire workers to replace the strikers, causing the men on the picket line to reconsider their position. On April 22, they began heading back to work.

4. Reel Trouble

On August 26, 1931, 80 projectionists were locked out of 19 movie theatres in Montreal, part of a wave of strikes and lockouts involving projectionists across the country in the 1930s. The issue in Montreal, as in most other places, was the attempt by theatre owners to reduce the number of projectionists by half. The old rules called for two projectionists to be on duty at all times. The theatre owners thought they could get by with just one. Some of the strikes were successful, and the projectionists were able to delay the inevitable. But that was not the case in Montreal. Theatre owners quickly hired replacement workers, and the striking projectionists never got their jobs back.

5. Bowling Strikes

In March 1932 six pin boys went on strike against the Bowlerdrome in Prince Albert, Saskatchewan. They were angry that they had been asked to shovel the snow in front of the building without getting paid. The boys were fired the next day. It was the first of nine strikes waged by pin boys in Canada in the 1930s.

6. Playing Around

In July 1937, 500 caddies at the Royal York Golf Club in Toronto went on strike, demanding a raise from 60 cents a round to 75 cents. The strike lasted 11 days, making it the longest of the 19 caddy strikes that hit Canadian golf courses between 1932 and 1939. The Toronto caddies were unsuccessful in getting a pay raise, but they were granted the privilege of playing one free round of golf every week.

7. Butt Seriously . . .

Twenty-nine construction workers building a road near Coboconk, Ontario, walked off the job on August 16, 1937, as a protest against a "no smoking" order. They returned victorious later that day.

8. Some Like It Hot

Forty furnace-factory workers walked off the job in Ingersoll, Ontario, on October 10, 1951, to protest a lack of heat in the furnace department. They returned the next day.

9. Safety First

Two hundred copper miners in Levack, Ontario, walked out on April 10, 1956, in a protest against wearing safety glasses. They were back two days later, wearing their glasses.

17 NAMES OF EARLY CANADIAN TRADE UNIONS

1. Wholesale Boot and Shoemakers Union
2. Cigar Makers' International Union
3. International Union of Machinists and Blacksmiths
4. International Brotherhood of Bookbinders
5. Iron Molders' International Union

6. Coopers International Union
7. Coach Builders' Union
8. Boot and Shoe Workers International Union
9. Bindery Women's Union
10. International Printing Pressmen's Union
11. Toronto Printing Press Assistants and Feeders' Union
12. Journeymen Tailors' Union
13. Female Operatives' Union
14. Brotherhood of Telegraphers
15. Amalgamated Flint Glass Blowers' Union
16. United Hatters of North America
17. The Brotherhood of Carpenters and Joiners

5 BITTER CANADIAN FAMILY FEUDS

There are more than a million family-owned businesses in Canada, and one of the most difficult challenges many of them face is succession. Seventy percent of family firms don't survive into a second generation; 90% don't make it to a third. Predictably, as the stories in this list reveal, the higher the stakes, the more bitter the fight over succession becomes.

1. The Billes Family

The fight for control over the massive Canadian Tire retail empire was one of the longest and most acrimonious in Canadian business history. It was the late 1980s when the three offspring of company founder A.J. Billes began their feud. On one side were brothers Fred and David, who had always assumed that the prize would eventually be theirs. But their middle sister, Martha, had other ideas. She believed she was being excluded because of her gender, and she had no intention of being pushed around by her brothers. After an attempt to sell the company to its dealers ended in failure in 1986, Martha sued her brothers for their shares. The brothers countersued, trying to force Martha to sell her stock to them. The stalemate lasted 10 years, during which time the two brothers saw their sister only for business reasons. The deadlock was finally broken in 1997 when David and Fred sold their shares to Martha for $45 million in cash and shares, resigned from the board and agreed that their children would never inherit the Canadian Tire mantle.

2. The Cuddy Family

Mac Cuddy spent 43 years building his company into one of the world's largest suppliers of turkeys. By the mid-1990s, Cuddy International Ltd., based in London, Ontario, was a $300-million company that controlled 45% of the Canadian processed turkey market. It should have been a nice legacy to hand off to his five sons, but instead, in the late 1990s, a pitched battle began between father and sons. The heart of the dispute was that, for Mac Cuddy, profit was thicker than blood. He was happy to welcome his sons into the business, but he was never confident that any of them had the right stuff to run the company. "You can hire better than you can sire," Mac liked to say, as he went about hiring outsiders to manage the business. His sons, however, didn't like taking orders from non–family members. Ultimately, Mac felt he had no choice but to fire two of them. A third son, Peter, who had previously held an executive position, was reassigned to the job of writing the company's corporate history. Peter responded by quitting and suing his father for misappropriating nearly $12 million of the company's money. The lawsuit was eventually dropped, and the sons went off to find other work, but the distraction caused by the bitter family feud drove the company to the brink of bankruptcy.

3. The McCain Family

Growing up together in Florenceville, New Brunswick, Wallace and Harrison McCain were about as close as two brothers could be. They even shared the same bed. In 1957 they went into business together, and by the 1990s they had both became billionaires, having created a food processing company responsible for one-third of the world's frozen french fries. That's when the issue of who would run the company after they were gone raised its ugly head. Wallace saw his son Michael as the natural heir apparent. Harrison did not want to turn the company over to Michael. The dispute over succession marked the end of the brothers' close relationship. Wallace left McCain Foods and bought Maple Leaf Foods for Michael to run. For years, Wallace and Harrison did not see each other socially. Harrison eventually turned control of McCain Foods over to another nephew after his own son died in a snowmobile accident. The cold war between Harrison and Wallace eventually began to thaw as Harrison's health deteriorated. Harrison died in March 2004.

4. The Phelan Family

Most Canadians have never heard of Cara Operations. But they have certainly heard of Swiss Chalet, Second Cup and Harvey's. Those are just three of the more visible parts of the Cara empire, a billion-dollar restaurant and food conglomerate based in Toronto. The company was founded in the 1880s by the Phelan family, but it didn't become a major player in the food industry until it was taken over by Paul J. (P.J.) Phelan in the 1950s. Thinking about succession was never high on P.J.'s list of priorities. Most people assumed that the company would be turned over to his only son, Paul Jr. But those who thought that underestimated the ambition and the tenacity of his two daughters, Gail and Rosemary, and his granddaughter, Holiday. As P.J. became increasingly incapacitated by alcoholism and dementia in the late 1990s, the three Phelan women moved to squeeze Paul Jr. out of the company by buying up his shares and taking the company private. They finally accomplished their objective in February 2004, leaving Paul Jr. on the outside looking in, bitterly reflecting on "the controlling bullies" who had deprived him of his birthright. "You wake up and you're not you anymore," he told a magazine writer after it was all over. "You're not the person you've always been."

5. The Steinberg Family

"I've had so much fun building and running this business," Sam Steinberg once said, "that I wouldn't deprive my family of running it." It is not hard to understand why the patriarch of the grocery store empire would feel that way. Starting with nothing in 1917, by the 1970s he had built Montreal-based Steinberg's into a $4.5-billion giant with 37,000 employees. Sam was determined to keep the business in the family, but out of his four daughters and their husbands, only one was qualified to take over. Rita's husband, Leo Goldfarb, was Sam's chosen successor, although the other sisters objected. After Rita and Leo's marriage broke up, Leo left the company. Rita died of cancer a year later. That left things in the unsteady hands of daughter Mitzi and her underachieving husband, Mel Dobrin. They took over after Sam's death in 1978, but succeeded mainly in alienating employees and other family members. Before long, the bitter family feud became the company's main preoccupation. Its stock and sales nosedived. In 1989 the board finally convinced the sisters to sell their shares for the sake of the company. It was the best decision they could have made. Each of them walked away with $112 million when the company was sold to the Quebec pension fund. Within a few years, Steinberg's was bankrupt, and the pension fund was out $800 million.

12 LIBRARIANS WHO BECAME FAMOUS IN OTHER FIELDS

1. David Hume (1711–76)
British philosopher, economist and historian David Hume spent the years 1752–57 as librarian at the Library of the Faculty of the Advocates at Edinburgh, where he wrote his *History of England*.

2. Casanova (Giovanni Giacomo Casanova de Seingalt, 1725–98)
At the climax of his career in 1785, the inimitable womanizer began 13 years as librarian for Count von Waldstein in the château of Dux in Bohemia.

3. August Strindberg (1849–1912)
The Swedish author of the classic drama *Miss Julie* was made assistant librarian at the Royal Library in Stockholm in 1874.

4. Pope Pius XI (Achille Ambrogio Damiano Ratti, 1857–1939)
After 19 years as a member of the College of Doctors of the Ambrosian Library in Milan, Ratti was appointed chief librarian. In 1911 he was asked to reorganize and update the Vatican Library. From 1922 until his death in 1939, the former librarian served as pope.

5. Marcel Duchamp (1887–1968)
Before launching his art career, Duchamp worked as a librarian at the Bibliothèque Sainte-Geneviève in Paris.

6. Boris Pasternak (1890–1960)
After the Russian Revolution, the future author of *Doctor Zhivago* was employed by the library of the Soviet Commisariat of Education.

7. Archibald MacLeish (1892–1982)

After a multifaceted career as a playwright, poet, lawyer, assistant secretary of state, winner of three Pulitzer prizes and a founder of the United Nations Educational, Scientific and Cultural Organization (UNESCO), in 1939 MacLeish was appointed by President Franklin D. Roosevelt as Librarian of Congress, a position he held for five years.

8. Mao Tse-tung (1893–1973)

In 1918 Mao worked as an assistant to the chief librarian of the University of Beijing. Overlooked for advancement, he decided to get ahead in another field and eventually became chairman of the Chinese Communist Party.

9. J. Edgar Hoover (1895–1972)

His first job as a young man was that of messenger and cataloguer in the Library of Congress.

10. Jorge Luis Borges (1899–1986)

After his father's death in 1938, Borges (who later became Argentina's most famous author) started his first regular job, as an assistant in a small municipal library in Buenos Aires. In 1946 he was fired for signing an anti-Perón manifesto. After Juan Perón was overthrown in 1955, Borges was named director of the National Library of Argentina.

11. Philip Larkin (1922–85)

The English poet, author of *The Whitsun Weddings* (1964) and *High Windows* (1974), spent his entire working life as a university librarian, at the University of Leicester (1946–50), Queen's University, Belfast (1950–55) and the Brynmor Jones Library in the University of Hull (1955–85).

12. Bill Richardson (1955–)

Author and CBC radio host Bill Richardson graduated from the University of British Columbia with a master's degree in library science in 1980. He subsequently worked as a children's librarian at several libraries in the province. Among his many books is *The Bachelor Brothers' Bed and Breakfast*, which won the Stephen Leacock Medal for Humour in 1994.

The name of his latest radio program, *Bunny Watson*, is a reference to the librarian played by Katharine Hepburn in the movie *Desk Set*.

—S.S. & C.F. and Cdn. Eds.

25 JOBS FOR COAL MINERS AND WHAT THEY WERE PAID, 1920

In October 1920 the Western Canada Coal Operators Association signed an agreement with District No. 18 of the United Mine Workers of America. Among other things, the pact outlined what jobs were available for coal miners and what their daily rate of pay would be. The agreement provides an interesting window into life in a Canadian coal mine in the 1920s. Here's a sample.

	Job	Daily Wage
1.	Tail rope engineers	$7.88
2.	Tipple engineer	$7.61
3.	Incline engineers	$7.61
4.	Endless rope engineers	$7.50
5.	Bottom man	$7.08
6.	Tipple dumper (man)	$7.08
7.	Breaker picker boss	$7.08
8.	Fan fireman	$6.85
9.	Screen engine tender	$6.76
10.	Tipple dumpers' helper	$6.75
11.	Top cagers	$6.75
12.	Water tender	$6.71
13.	Washer or tipple oiler	$6.71
14.	Slate pickers (men)	$6.58
15.	Fan men	$6.58
16.	Dirt bank man	$6.58
17.	Rock bank man	$6.58
18.	Wiper (man)	$6.58
19.	Breaker screen (man)	$6.58
20.	Ashman	$6.58
21.	Car oilers (men)	$6.58

22.	Car oilers (boys)	$4.40
23.	Tipple dumper (boy)	$4.40
24.	Slate pickers (boys)	$4.03
25.	Tally boys	$4.03

15 FAMOUS PEOPLE WHO WORKED IN BED

1. King Louis XI (1423–83)

This French king was ugly, fat and sickly, but also ruthless and clever, earning the title "the universal spider." He introduced the custom of the *lit de justice* ("bed of justice"), a ceremonial appearance of the monarch, in bed, before *le parlement* with the princes of the realm on stools, the greater officials standing and the lesser ones kneeling. No one is sure exactly why he began the practice, but it caught on and lasted until the French Revolution. Fontenelle, a critic of Louis XV, was asked on the eve of the Revolution, "What, sir, is a 'bed of justice'?" He replied, "It is the place where justice lies asleep."

2. Leonardo da Vinci (1452–1519)

Leonardo earned a unique fame as an artist and scientist, and according to his *Notebooks*, he spent some time each night "in bed in the dark to go over again in the imagination the main outlines of the form previously studied . . . it is useful in fixing things in the memory."

3. Cardinal de Richelieu (1585–1642)

In the last year of his life, the diabolically clever and scheming cardinal took to his bed and stayed there because of his rapidly deteriorating health. This did not prevent him from working—he directed his highly efficient secret police in exposing the treasonous machinations of the youthful royal favourite Cinq-Mars. Nor did it hinder the peripatetic cardinal from travelling—his servants carried him about in his bed, and if the door of the house he wanted to stay in was too narrow, they would break open the walls.

4. Thomas Hobbes (1588–1679)

Hobbes, the great British political philosopher, was renowned for his mathematical approach to natural philosophy and found bed a comfortable and handy place to work on his formulas. He wrote the numbers on the sheets and, when he ran out of room, on his thighs. He wrote his 1661 *Dialogue on Physics or On the Nature of Air* entirely in bed. Hobbes also sang in bed because, according to John Aubrey's *Brief Lives*, "he did believe it did his lungs good, and conduced much to prolong his life."

5. Henry Wadsworth Longfellow (1807–82)
Throughout his life Longfellow suffered from periodic bouts of severe insomnia. Out of desperation, he decided to put his sleepless nights to some good use, and he began to write poetry in bed—including his 1842 classic "The Wreck of the Hesperus."

6. Mark Twain (1835–1910)
Twain loved the luxurious comfort of writing in bed and there composed large portions of *Huckleberry Finn*, *The Adventures of Tom Sawyer* and *A Connecticut Yankee in King Arthur's Court*. He seems to have been the first person to point out that working in bed must be a very dangerous occupation, since so many deaths occur there.

7. Ignace Fantin-Latour (1836–1904)
Best known for his portrait groups, especially *Hommage à Delacroix*, this French painter worked in bed out of necessity when he could not afford wood for a fire. William Gaunt, in *The Aesthetic Adventure*, describes him propped up in bed, "Shivering, mournful, persistent . . . in a threadbare overcoat, a top hat over his eyes and a scarf round his mouth, balancing a candle on the edge of his drawing board and sketching with numbed, gloved hand."

8. Robert Louis Stevenson (1850–94)
For years Stevenson was racked by coughing spells caused by tuberculosis, and consequently he wrote most of *Kidnapped* and *A Child's Garden of Verses* in bed at his home in Bournemouth, England. Bed sometimes brought him inspiration in the form of dreams. One night his subconscious mind spun "a fine bogey tale," as he called it, based on a real-life criminal he had read about. Stevenson's dream became *Dr. Jekyll and Mr. Hyde*.

9. Edith Wharton (1862–1937)

Pulitzer Prize–winning author (*Age of Innocence*, 1920) Edith Wharton wrote primarily about the upper class into which she was born. Her perspective on the good life was no doubt sharpened by her work habits—she wrote in the mornings, finding inspiration in the comfort of her bed. So accustomed was she to this routine that she once suffered a fit of hysterics because her hotel room bed did not face the light, so she could not work.

10. Marcel Proust (1871–1922)

Bundled in sweaters, a hot-water bottle at his feet, the French author worked to refine his series of novels called *À la recherche du temps perdu* ("Remembrance of Things Past") while lying virtually flat in bed in a cork-lined room. He had all the necessities within arm's reach: more than a dozen pens (if he dropped one, he refused to pick it up because of dust); all of his notes, notebooks and manuscripts; even fumigation powder, which he believed helped his asthma. In spite of all his precautions, he died of pneumonia at the age of 51.

11. Winston Churchill (1874–1965)

Churchill loved to lie abed in comfort for several hours each morning while dictating letters and going through boxes of official state papers. Although he much preferred to write his books while standing up, declining health in his later years forced him to write and correct most of *The Second World War* and *History of the English Speaking Peoples* in bed.

12. Mae West (1892–1980)

The legendary sex queen with the hourglass figure was famous for her double entendre lines. She wrote several of her own screenplays, including *Diamond Lil*, and in 1959 she published her autobiography, *Goodness Had Nothing to Do with It*. She did all her writing in bed, she reported, noting that "Everybody knows I do my best work in bed."

13. Mamie Eisenhower (1896–1979)

While in the White House, First Lady Mamie Eisenhower did away with an office but not with the office routine. She held bedside conferences, dictated to her secretary, paid the bills and signed letters while ensconced in her pink-ruffled bed.

14. F. Scott Fitzgerald (1896–1940)

During the last two years of his life, while writing *The Last Tycoon*, Fitzgerald found that he could work longer hours by staying in bed. He'd retire to bed with a dozen Coca-Colas (which had replaced alcohol in his drinking habits) and prop himself up on pillows. Using a lapboard, he'd work for about five hours a day. A fatal heart attack prevented him from completing *The Last Tycoon*.

15. Hugh Hefner (1926–)

It seems appropriate that a man who made his fortune in sex should have done so in bed. For decades, Hefner controlled the Playboy empire from a massive bed in his Chicago mansion, where he stayed awake for 60-hour stretches, fuelled by amphetamines and Pepsi.

—R.W.S. & The Eds.

13 FAMOUS PEOPLE WHO WENT BANKRUPT

1. P.T. Barnum (1810–91)

Barnum, who made more than $2 million (U.S.) hawking freaks and wild animals and allegedly said, "There's a sucker born every minute," often played the fool himself by making embarrassingly bad investments. The final humiliation came in 1855, when he invested more than $500,000 in the Jerome Clock Co., only to find he'd been swindled again. The loss plunged him into bankruptcy and caused him to contemplate suicide briefly. It also provided a theme for countless moralistic newspaper editorials.

2. Kim Basinger (1953–)

Basinger was forced into bankruptcy in 1993 after losing a lawsuit and being ordered to pay $7.4 million (U.S.) for failing to honour a verbal contract to star in the movie *Boxing Helena*. As a result, she lost the Georgia town of Brazelton, which she had purchased in 1989 for $20 million, to her partners in the deal.

3. Lorraine Bracco (1949–)

The actress racked up more than $2 million (U.S.) in legal bills during a six-year custody battle with actor Harvey Keitel over their daughter Stella. The debts forced her to declare bankruptcy in 1999. Despite that, 1999 ended up being a good year for Bracco—she was cast in HBO's *The Sopranos*, which she described as "a big turning point. It allowed me to put myself back on my feet."

4. Gary Coleman (1968–)

When he starred in *Diff'rent Strokes* in the 1980s, Coleman earned $64,000 (U.S.) a week, making him the highest-paid child star of his day. Although he found few roles after the series went off the air, he still had $7 million as of 1990. A bitter legal battle with his adoptive parents (he accused them of stealing as much as $1 million) and ongoing medical problems (he underwent two kidney transplants) drained his bank account. In 1995 he filed for bankruptcy, unable to pay $72,000 in debts. "I can spread the blame all the way around," Coleman said, "from me to my accountants to my adoptive parents, to agents to lawyers and back to me again."

5. Francis Ford Coppola (1939–)

The Oscar-winning director observed, "As they say, cash doesn't stay in my pockets very long." In 1992 he filed for bankruptcy with assets of $53 million (U.S.) dwarfed by liabilities of $98 million. Coppola came back financially in 1993 when he earned $10 million for directing *Bram Stoker's Dracula*.

6. Walt Disney (1901–66)

In 1921 Disney started the Laugh-O-Gram Corp. in Kansas City, Missouri, with $15,000 (U.S.) from investors. But he was forced to file for bankruptcy two years later when his backers pulled out because of problems with New York distributors of his animated fairy tales. Then, in July 1923, Disney left for Hollywood with all his belongings: a pair of pants, a coat, one shirt, two sets of underwear, two pairs of socks and some salvaged drawing materials.

7. Ulysses S. Grant (1822–85)

Late in life, Grant became a partner in a banking house called Grant and Ward. In 1884 the firm went bankrupt, and the ensuing stock market crash left Grant so buried in debt that he was forced to hand over all his property, including his swords and trophies. Broke and dying of cancer, he spent his remaining days writing his memoirs to provide an income for his widow. Mark Twain published the book, and 300,000 copies were sold door to door. Twain generously offered the former president 70% of the net profits; after Grant died, his wife received $350,000 (U.S.) in royalties.

8. Dorothy Hamill (1956–)

After winning a gold medal at the 1976 Winter Olympics, figure skater Hamill became the first female athlete to sign a $1-million-per-year (U.S.) contract—with the Ice Capades. After the Ice Capades went bankrupt, Hamill bought it in 1993. She was unable to halt the skating tour's continuing slide into financial chaos. She sold the Ice Capades to televangelist Pat Robertson and filed for bankruptcy in 1996 with debts of $1.6 million.

9. Hammer (1962–)

His *Please Hammer Don't Hurt Them* (1990) remains the bestselling rap album of all time. Hammer earned $33 million (U.S.) in 1991 alone. He spent equally lavishly, buying 17 cars, a Boeing 747 and a racehorse. In 1996 Hammer filed for bankruptcy with debts of $13.7 million. He had to sell his $10-million mansion, which came with two bowling alleys and an indoor basketball court, at half its purchase price.

10. Burt Reynolds (1936–)

Reynolds was Hollywood's top star from 1978 to 1982. In 1996 he filed for bankruptcy with assets of $6.65 million (U.S.) and debts of $11.2 million. His creditors ranged from the IRS to the firm supplying his hairpieces. Reynolds blamed his financial troubles on an expensive divorce from actress Loni Anderson. "I'm paying the third-highest alimony and child support in the world," he told NBC's *Dateline*. "And the only two ahead of me are sheiks." In addition, the divorce hurt his reputation, costing him endorsement deals with Quaker State Oil and the Florida Citrus Commission.

11. Mark Twain (1835–1910)

Twain lost around half a million dollars on a wide range of inventions that included steam generators and marine telegraphs. But his downfall came when he decided not to invest $5,000 (U.S.) in Alexander Graham Bell's telephone company because he saw possibilities in the Paige typesetting machine. Ultimately, he backed its inventor with more than $250,000. The machine complicated rather than simplified the typesetting process, and in 1894 Twain's losses caused him to declare bankruptcy.

12. Mike Tyson (1966–)

The youngest heavyweight champion in boxing history, Tyson earned an estimated $300 million (U.S.) during his career. He spent extravagantly on mansions, cars, gifts for his entourage, even a pair of Bengal tigers. In 2003 he filed for bankruptcy with $23 million in debts, including $13.4 million to the IRS, $4 million to the British tax authorities, $300,000 to a limo service and $173,000 to a Las Vegas jeweller.

13. James Abbott McNeill Whistler (1834–1903)

Whistler often had to borrow money or pawn his pictures to pay his debts. When a bill collector would come and carry off one of his chairs or beds, Whistler did not get upset; he simply drew a picture of the missing piece of furniture on the floor where it had stood. A bailiff who had taken possession of Whistler's house was once joshed into dressing up as a butler and serving tea for Whistler and his friends. But such madcap antics could not prevent the inevitable, and on May 8, 1879, Whistler went bankrupt with debts of $10,000 (U.S.).

—C.F., W.A.D., A.K. & L.K.L.

5 CANADIANS WHO LOST A FORTUNE
1. Charles Bronfman
Fortune lost: $3.5 billion in six years

Poor Charles Bronfman. As odd as that might sound, it's hard not to feel a bit sorry for a guy who watched his starry-eyed nephew blow a sizable chunk of the family fortune chasing his showbiz fantasies. The Bronfman empire used to be based around two reliable money-spinners: booze and chemicals. But in the late 1990s, Charles's nephew and company president Edgar Jr. decided to sell off both Seagram's and the family's 25% ownership of DuPont to invest in the glamorous but highly unstable world of Hollywood. He bought into movies (MCA Inc.) and music (PolyGram), and struggled to make money in both. Then, in 2000, he essentially swapped about $7 billion in Seagram's shares for a stake in the French water utility company Vivendi SA, whose president, the egomaniacal Jean-Marie Messier, had showbiz aspirations that rivalled Edgar's. But the deal went horribly wrong. Vivendi sunk under a load of debt, reducing the value of the Bronfmans' stake from $6.8 billion in June 2000 to under $1 billion just two years later. As for Uncle Charles, *Canadian Business* pegged his net worth at $5.3 billion in 1999, making him the fourth-wealthiest man in Canada. By 2005 his rank had slipped to 13th, as his net worth had plummeted to a paltry $1.85 billion.

2. Robert Campeau

Fortune lost: $10 billion OPM (other people's money) in four years

In the 1970s and '80s, Robert Campeau was one of Canada's most successful developers, but between 1986 and 1988 he bit off way more of the Big Apple than he could chew. He took advantage of Wall Street's love affair with junk bonds and leveraged buyouts and managed to borrow more than $10 billion to buy two major U.S. department store chains, including New York's fabled Bloomingdale's. But simply servicing the debt would have cost over $800 million a year, and by 1990 Campeau's deck of cards had collapsed, leaving 10,000 employees without jobs and about 300,000 vendors and suppliers unpaid. Campeau himself was on the hook to the Bank of Montreal for $30 million, but he never allowed that small detail to get in the way of his opulent lifestyle.

3. Jim Cohoon

Fortune lost: $500,000 in 77 days

In September 1986, Jim Cohoon was a ship's hand on a freighter tied up in Thunder Bay, when he discovered he had won $500,000 in the lottery. What followed was a whirlwind of reckless spending and extravagant acts of charity, as Cohoon made his way back to his home in Nova Scotia. He began by giving $1,000 to a hooker in Thunder Bay. "It made her happy for one night," he remarked. Then there was the $50,000 he gave to a drifter he met outside the Salvation Army in Toronto, the $50,000 to one friend and the $100,000 to another. At that rate, it wasn't going to take long for Jim to kiss half a million dollars goodbye. Sure enough, 77 days after his spree began, Jim Cohoon was in Ginger's Tavern in Halifax with a total of $11 to his name. "I mean, it's gone and I don't have it," he remarked philosophically, adding, "I would have done it different if I hadn't been drinking so much."

4. The Eaton Brothers

Fortune lost: more than $700 million in 13 years

There was no single bad decision that led to the collapse of the Eaton retail empire. Rather, it was more than a decade of mistakes by four brothers who, in the end, were not smart enough, focused enough or motivated enough to make the difficult choices that could have prevented Canada's oldest and most established department store chain from disappearing from the landscape. There is no need to hold a tag day for George, Fred, John Craig and Thor Eaton. They are still very wealthy men. But the decline in their fortune has been precipitous. Between 1992 and 1999 their net worth dropped by more than half a billion dollars. For decades, the Eatons had been listed among Canada's richest families, but by 1999 their ranking in *Canadian Business Magazine*'s list of wealthiest Canadians had dropped to 55th, and by 2005 they were no longer even in the top hundred.

5. Sir Henry Pellatt

Fortune lost: $17 million in 13 years

At the dawn of the 20th century, Sir Henry Pellatt strode across the Toronto business world like a colossus. His companies held monopolies on the city's electricity and public transit. And he was poised to begin developing the massive hydroelectric potential of Niagara Falls. By 1911 his fortune was estimated at $17 million, or about a quarter of a billion dollars in today's money. But by 1914 Sir Henry's world was beginning to collapse. He lost his electrical monopoly when Ontario opted for public ownership. His real estate schemes floundered when war broke out, and he sunk $3.8 million into building his castle, "Casa Loma." By 1924 he was $1.7 million in debt. He had to surrender his castle to the city when he could no longer afford to pay the taxes. By the time of his death in

1939, he had almost no money left, but thousands lined the streets to watch the funeral procession of a man who had dreamed big—and fallen spectacularly.

THE CLOCKWATCHER'S 8 REASONS TO RAID THE OFFICE SUPPLY CLOSET

The Clockwatcher is a disgruntled temp who grinds it out in the nation's cube farms, where it's hard enough to get respect, let alone a steady gig. She was a regular contributor to the CBC Radio One program Workology, *on which she dispensed her unique brand of slacker activism: how to get by, not get ahead, in the corporate jungle. The Clockwatcher's secret identity is Lisa Ayuso.*

The modern workplace might be a nicer place to work than the firetraps and widget factories of yesterday, but that doesn't mean that people feel any better about working there. Low workplace morale is an epidemic. I'm here to propose an exciting and effective way to break that cycle of underappreciation. I call it the Self-Compensation Index—the SCI.

It works like this: Think of a routine task you perform that is not listed on your job description and figure out what it's worth to you in office supplies and break time. Voilà, a thankless task suddenly becomes a rewarding bit of business.

The Self-Compensation Index—A Reliable and Rational Way to Manage Your Own Benefits Plan.

1. *Action:* You are asked to pick up ointments or prescription drugs for your boss.
   Reaction: Is there anything more revolting than knowing intimate details about your boss's health? Help yourself to a stapler with refills and take the long route to the mall.

2. *Action:* Picking up any kind of food or drink order that has instructions you need to write down, e.g., fussy coffee orders such as non-fat extra-hot soymilk latte, or a toasted blueberry scone, buttered on one side only.
   Reaction: That'll cost the boss a shiny new tape dispenser and a stack of Post-it notes.

177

3. *Action:* Being asked to come early to an office party to help set up.
   Reaction: This is a big one. Net a full box of Sharpies for starters, and if you are asked to help serve food or start a conga line you must call in sick the following Monday.

4. *Action:* Boss cried in your presence.
   Reaction: Yuck. Do you have a car? Drive in to work tomorrow . . . those ink-jet printer cartridges are heavy.

5. *Action:* Boss asks you to provide an alibi, e.g., "If my wife calls, tell her I'm in a meeting."
   Reaction: Being stripped of your own personal ethics at the workplace has real human costs, but nothing a battery-operated pencil sharpener or a couple of boxes of blank CDs won't fix.

6. *Action:* Boss shares intimate details with you about his or her personal life—or even worse, sexual fantasies. It may seem odd, but it happens.
   Reaction: In this case, you might consider quitting, but if that's not an option, take anything in the supply closet that can be used for household maintenance: coffee filters, light bulbs, paper towels, or packing tape.

7. *Action:* The boss expects you to keep his or her secrets from coworkers, thus depriving you of the joy of sharing gossip with your peers.
   Reaction: Use the company courier service to send letters and candy to your friends.

8. *Action:* Your time is seen as unimportant and disposable, e.g., your vacation plans get switched, you are asked and expected to miss night classes and dog walks.
   Reaction: Did you take a toner cartridge already? What about a telephone headset?

6 STRIKES AND LOCKOUTS THAT LASTED A REALLY LONG TIME

1. Local 145 of The Communications, Energy and Paperworkers Union vs. The Montreal *Gazette*

Duration: 9 years

The newspaper employed 200 typographers in the mid-1980s, but by 1993 there were only 74 left. The company offered separation incentives to the workers. Sixty-three accepted; 11 refused and were locked out. The main issue was job protection in the face of technological change. On May 13, 2002, after being locked out for nine years, the 11 workers accepted management's offer and returned to work.

2. The International Typographical Union vs. The *Toronto Star*, *Toronto Telegram* and *Globe and Mail*

Duration: 8 years

This strike began in July 1964 as a relatively minor dispute over the issue of automation in the newspapers' composition rooms. There had been two years of negotiation before the strike was called, and most issues had been settled. But the union headquarters in the U.S. apparently wanted to make Toronto a testing ground for upcoming battles over technological change in the industry. The papers used managers and strike-breakers to continue publishing. In 1965 the workers voted to return to work, but management refused to take back 27 who had been involved in incidents on the picket line, and the other workers would not go back without them. By the time the dispute was settled in 1972, many of the striking workers had lost their life savings.

3. Local 950 of The United Steelworkers of America vs. Goldcorp Inc.

Duration: 3 years, 10 months

The longest strike in Canadian mining history proved to be a disaster for the unionized miners. One hundred and eighty-seven workers went on strike at the company's mine in Red Lake, Ontario, on June 23, 1996, over job security and safety. But after nearly four years on the picket line, the union concluded that the company was not interested in settling the dispute at the bargaining table. The settlement that was finally reached in April 2000 offered employment for only 45 miners at a neighbouring mine, and they could no longer be represented by a union. The other workers received a generous severance package.

4. The International Typographical Union vs. The Vancouver *Province*

Duration: 3 years, 6 months

Printers belonging to the International Typographical Union walked off their jobs at the Vancouver *Province* in June 1946. The action was actually part of a much larger strike against Southam papers in Hamilton, Winnipeg, Edmonton and Ottawa. In each case, the issue was the union's demand for a five-day week for all its members. The Vancouver strike was by far the most acrimonious and damaging for the company. The *Province*, the largest paper in the Southam chain, did not publish for the first six weeks of the strike.

When management then tried to put out a paper using replacement printers brought in from other Southam papers, there were mass demonstrations in Vancouver's Victory Square. Trucks were overturned, papers set on fire and replacement workers roughed up. A full-scale riot broke out on July 22, and 17 people were arrested. Eventually, management was able to get a regular daily edition of the paper published, but not before thousands of readers had deserted the paper and it had fallen into second place behind its rival, the *Sun*. In 1947 a judge declared the strike illegal and ordered the union to pay the company $10,000 in damages. But the dispute dragged on until late 1949, when the two sides finally reached a settlement and the company agreed to waive the $10,000 payment.

5. Local 6917 of The United Steelworkers of America vs. S.A. Armstrong

Duration: 2 years, 8 months

S.A. Armstrong is a major manufacturer of industrial pumps in Toronto. The strike by 76 workers began in April 1996, and the company immediately took advantage of new laws passed by Ontario's Conservative government that allowed for the use of replacement workers to keep the plant running. With little incentive to settle, the strike dragged on until 1999, when the workers eventually agreed to substantial wage cuts, as much as $3 an hour in some cases.

6. Local 4 of The Canadian Association of Smelter and Allied Workers vs. Royal Oak Mines

Duration: 1 year, 7 months

This strike/lockout at Royal Oak's Giant Mine in Yellowknife was one of the most bitter and violent in Canadian labour history. In May 1992,

234 gold miners voted to strike, but Royal Oak's president, Margaret Witte, chose to lock them out the day before the strike was to begin and bring in replacement workers to keep the mine operating. This set the stage for months of escalating violence and sabotage that culminated on September 18, 1992, with a bomb explosion in an underground mine shaft that killed nine of the replacement workers. A striking miner was eventually convicted of setting the bomb. In November 1993, the Canadian Labour Relations Board ruled that the company had been bargaining in bad faith and ordered the two sides to come to an agreement. The miners returned to work a month later.

7 BIG CBC MANAGEMENT BLUNDERS

Jane Farrow and Ira Basen had nothing to do with the compilation of this list. In all their years at the CBC, neither of them can recall a single blunder made by CBC management. Much of the information below comes from the book *The Microphone Wars: A History of Triumph and Betrayal at the CBC* by Knowlton Nash. Blame him if you must.

1. The Quebec Producers Strike (1959)

The worst strike in CBC history, and one of the most significant strikes in the history of Quebec, began on December 29, 1958, after a producer of French children's programming refused a reassignment and began organizing his fellow producers. But CBC management did not believe producers had the right to unionize, so 74 producers hit the picket lines, backed by other Quebec unions. They were expecting a quick resolution to the dispute, but the CBC dug in its heels, at one point even sending out letters of dismissal to all the producers still on the picket line. The strike became a *cause célèbre* among Quebec artists and intellectuals. In February, a full-scale riot broke out in front of the CBC building. The strike finally ended eight weeks after it began, with the producers winning the right to bargain collectively. The whole unhappy incident seriously damaged the CBC's reputation in Quebec, fuelled French-Canadian nationalism and helped set the stage for the "Quiet Revolution." It also boosted the public profile of one of the strike leaders. His name was René Lévesque.

2. Cancelling *Preview Commentary* (1959)

The CBC has always prided itself on its "arm's-length" relationship with the government. It is, after all, a public broadcaster, not a state broadcaster. But there have been times when CBC management has allowed the distance between it and its political masters to shrink to uncomfortable lengths. One such occasion was in June 1959, when the CBC came under attack over a radio program called *Preview Commentary*. Prime Minister John Diefenbaker and others in the Conservative government believed that too many of the opinions expressed on the program were critical of government policy. Word came down to acting CBC president Ernie Bushnell that "heads will roll" unless something was done about the program. All the parties involved denied that direct political pressure had been applied by the government, but the president was clearly spooked. Without consulting the programmers involved, Bushnell abruptly cancelled the program. When the CBC board endorsed the decision, several senior managers and dozens of producers resigned in protest. As the outrage spread across the country, the board reversed its position and ordered the program back on the air.

3. The *Seven Days* Firings (1966)

This Hour Has Seven Days had been a thorn in CBC management's side since it debuted on October 4, 1964. It was irreverent, unconventional, sometimes tasteless, highly opinionated and hugely popular with everyone except politicians in Ottawa. They were not fond of the show's withering "hot seat" interviews. The show's unpopularity in Ottawa caused CBC management many sleepless nights. Finally, in April 1966, Bud Walker, who ran the English TV network, met with one of the show's hosts, Patrick Watson, and fired him and his co-host, Laurier LaPierre. The decision touched off an unprecedented wave of outrage from viewers and from inside the CBC. A subsequent report by a parliamentary committee was highly critical of CBC management's conduct in the firing of the two hosts. By July 1966 Bud Walker was gone, but so too were Watson, LaPierre, their producer Douglas Leiterman and their program.

4. Cancelling Don Messer (1969)

CBC management is forever looking for ways to attract a "younger audience," and almost every time it tries, it winds up getting itself into a whole bunch of trouble. One of the most dramatic examples occurred in 1969 with the decision to cancel the popular musical program *Don Messer's Jubilee* after more than 30 years on CBC radio and television. "I am bloody well going to kill the geriatric fiddlers," boasted program director Doug Nixon, who then proceeded to notify the much-beloved Messer of his program's cancellation by sending him a telegram. And even though the popularity of *Don Messer's Jubilee* was not what it used to be, the decision, and the crude way in which it was undertaken, sparked howls of anger from loyal viewers. Demonstrations were held in front of Parliament Hill and at CBC offices in Ottawa and Toronto. MPs rallied to Messer's defence, but to no avail. Don Messer's days at the CBC had come to an end.

5. *Prime Time News* (1992)

For more than a decade, the combination of *The National* and *The Journal* had been a popular destination for Canadian TV viewers between 10:00 and 11:00 p.m. But by 1990 a new management team had taken over, led by a new president, Gérard Veilleux, and it was looking to "reposition" the TV network. Veilleux, his powerful communications chief, Robert Pattillo, and Ivan Fecan, the head of English TV, had concluded that "from a marketing point of view, *The National* and *The Journal* just don't make sense." So in 1992 they made two fateful decisions. They cancelled *The Journal* and merged the unhappy staff of that current affairs program with the people who had been producing the news. Then they changed the name of the show to *Prime Time News* and moved it to 9:00. The result was a ratings disaster. Seventeen percent fewer people watched *Prime Time News* than had watched its predecessor. By 1994 *The National* was back, and so too was its 10:00 starting time.

6. *The Valour and the Horror* (1992)

The Valour and the Horror was a series of three documentaries produced by two of Canada's leading filmmakers, Terence and Brian McKenna, and broadcast on the CBC in January 1992. The documentaries took a revisionist look at the record of Canada's military leadership during the Second World War, and found it wanting. It was predictable that Canadian war veterans were going to be unhappy with the series. The only question was, once the inevitable political firestorm began, would

CBC management stand behind the films it had partially paid for and agreed to broadcast? The answer, for the most part, was no. In November 1992 the McKennas suffered a setback when the CBC ombudsman ruled that the series was "flawed" and didn't measure up to CBC standards. President Gérard Veilleux responded by apologizing and promising that the corporation's "scrutiny of programming of this kind will be improved substantially." To many CBC journalists and members of the public, Veilleux's comments smacked of management interference in CBC journalism. *The Globe and Mail* attacked the "servile timidity of the CBC." Ultimately, the series went on to win several awards, and historians generally supported the filmmakers' interpretation of events. But the controversy dealt a serious blow to Veilleux's credibility and that of other senior managers.

7. Cancelling Regional TV News (2000)

In 2000, after years of devastating budget cuts that saw hundreds of millions of dollars lopped off the corporation's budget, CBC management decided to cancel all regional TV supper-hour newscasts and replace them with a single national supper-hour news program. Many of these newscasts were not highly rated, which may have led some managers to believe that their presence would not be greatly missed. Wrong! Two thousand people protested outside the CBC building in Charlottetown. Their anger was echoed by MPs of all parties who rose up to condemn the decision. In the face of mounting opposition, CBC management backtracked—but only a little. In May 2000, it announced that 14 half-hour regional news shows would be added to the national broadcast, but the new hybrid program failed to attract much of an audience. Nationally, the CBC lost 200,000 viewers in that time period. In some parts of the country, ratings have dropped by more than 50%.

CHAPTER 7   # SEX, LOVE AND MARRIAGE

ABOVE: *Britney and Madonna kiss on cue at the 2003 MTV Awards*

16 MEMORABLE KISSES

1. The kiss of life

It was a kiss from God that infused the "spirit of life" into man, according to the account of Genesis (2:7). God is said to have formed Adam from slime and dust and then breathed a rational soul into him. This concept of divine insufflation, which surfaces frequently in religious teachings, is often viewed through the kiss metaphor.

2. The betrayal kiss of Judas (c. AD 29)

As told in the New Testament, Judas Iscariot used the kiss as a tool of betrayal around AD 29, when he embraced Jesus Christ in the Garden of Gethsemane. Jewish leaders under the high priest Caiaphas had paid Judas 30 pieces of silver to identify Jesus. With a kiss, Judas singled him out. Jesus was arrested, charged with blasphemy and condemned to death.

3. The kiss that cost Thomas Saverland his nose (1837)

In 1837, at the dawn of the Victorian era in Great Britain, Thomas Saverland attempted to kiss Caroline Newton in a lighthearted manner. Rejecting Saverland's pass, Miss Newton not so lightheartedly bit off part of his nose. Saverland took Newton to court, but she was acquitted. "When a man kisses a woman against her will," ruled the judge, "she is fully entitled to bite his nose, if she so pleases." "And eat it up," added a barrister.

4. The first kiss recorded on film (1896)

The first kiss ever to be recorded in a film occurred in Thomas Edison's *The Kiss*, between John C. Rice and May Irwin, in April 1896. Adapted from a short scene in the Broadway comedy *The Widow Jones*, *The Kiss* was filmed by Raff and Gammon for nickelodeon audiences. Its running time was less than 30 seconds.

5. The most often kissed statue in history (late 1800s)

The figure of Guidarello Guidarelli, a fearless 16th-century Italian soldier, was sculpted in marble by Tullio Lombardo (c. 1455–1532) and displayed at the Academy of Fine Arts in Ravenna, Italy. During the late 1800s a rumour started that any woman who kissed the reclining, armour-clad statue would marry a wonderful gentleman. More than

5 million superstitious women have since kissed Guidarelli's cold marble lips. Consequently, the soldier's mouth has acquired a faint reddish glow.

6. The movie with 191 kisses (1926)

In 1926 Warner Brothers Studios cast John Barrymore in *Don Juan*. During the course of the film (2 hours, 47 minutes), the amorous adventurer bestows a total of 191 kisses on a number of beautiful señoritas—an average of one every 53 seconds.

7. The longest kiss on film (1941)

The longest kiss in movie history is between Jane Wyman and Regis Toomey in the 1941 production of *You're in the Army Now*. The Lewis Seiler comedy about two vacuum-cleaner salesmen features a scene in which Toomey and Wyman hold a single kiss for 3 minutes and 5 seconds (or 4% of the film's running time).

8. The VJ-Day kiss (1945)

When the news of Japan's surrender was announced in New York City's Times Square on August 14, 1945, *Life* photojournalist Alfred Eisenstaedt photographed a jubilant sailor clutching a nurse in a back-bending passionate kiss to vent his joy. The picture became an icon of the cathartic celebration that erupted over the end of the war. Over the years, at least three nurses and ten sailors claimed to be the people in the photo. Since Eisenstaedt had lost his notes and negatives by the time the claimants came forward, he was never able to say definitively who was in the photo.

9. The kiss at l'Hôtel de Ville (1950)

A 1950 photograph of a young couple kissing on the streets of Paris—"Le Baiser de l'Hôtel de Ville"—found itself under an international media spotlight when, four decades after the picture was taken, the photo became a commercial success, drawing out of the woodwork dozens of people who claimed to have been the photo's unidentified kissers. The black-and-white snapshot—originally taken for *Life* magazine by Robert Doisneau as part of his series on the Parisian working class—made Doisneau wealthy when, between 1986 and 1992, it became a bestseller through poster and postcard reprints. Among those who subsequently identified themselves as the kissers were Denise and Jean-Louis Lavergne, who sued Doisneau for $100,000 after he rejected their claim. They lost their case when it was determined, in 1993, that the kissers were actually two professional models (and real-life lovers), Françoise Bornet and Jacques Cartaud.

10. The first interracial kiss on U.S. television (1968)

NBC's *Star Trek* was the first program to show a white man kissing a black woman. In the episode "Plato's Children," aliens with psychic powers force Captain Kirk (William Shatner) to kiss Lt. Uhura (Nichelle Nichols).

11. The Majorca, Spain, kiss-in (1969)

In 1969 an effort was made to crack down on young lovers who were smooching in public in the town of Inca on the island of Majorca. When the police chief began handing out citations that cost offenders 500 pesetas per kiss, a group of 30 couples protested by staging a kiss-in at the harbour at Cala Figuera. Following a massive roundup by police, the amorous rebels were fined 45,000 pesetas for their defiant canoodling and then released.

12. The kiss of humility (1975)

In an unprecedented gesture of humility, Pope Paul VI kissed the feet of Metropolitan Meliton of Chalcedon, envoy of Patriarch Demetrios I, who was head of the Eastern Orthodox Church, during a Mass at the Sistine Chapel in Rome in 1975. The two men were commemorating the 10th anniversary of the lifting of excommunications that the churches of Constantinople and Rome had conferred on each other during the 11th century. Taken aback by the pontiff's dramatic action, Meliton attempted to kiss the Pope's feet in return but the Pope prevented him from doing so. Meliton instead kissed his hand.

13. Don Cherry's kiss-in on "Coach's Corner" (1990–93)

The irascible and bombastic ex-player and coach Don "Hotlips" Cherry has planted a few kisses on his favourite hockey players over the years on "Coach's Corner," his regular segment of *Hockey Night in Canada*. Many recall the Doug Gilmour kiss, which happened on May 19, 1993, during the playoffs, when the Leafs and "Dougie" were playing their hearts out.

But before that Cherry kissed two other much-admired players in 1990: Dale Hunter of the Washington Capitals on May 5 and legendary Boston Bruin Bobby Orr on December 15. Outspoken gay comedian and actor Scott Thompson, of *Kids in the Hall* and *Larry Sanders Show* fame, took it upon himself to reciprocate the warm feelings and nuzzled up to tough-guy Cherry when they were both guests on the *Friday Night with Ralph Benmergui* television show on October 30, 1992.

14. The first lesbian kiss on American commercial television (1991)

The first visible kiss between two women on an American network television series took place in 1991 on the show *L.A. Law*, when Michelle Greene kissed Amanda Donohoe. However, it was a later kiss, on the March 1, 1994, ABC-TV broadcast of the situation comedy *Roseanne* that caused a sensation. In a controversial scene well publicized in the press, guest star Mariel Hemingway kisses series star Roseanne Arnold on the mouth. The kiss occurs in a "gay bar" setting, and Hemingway portrays a lesbian stripper whose kiss causes Roseanne to question her own sensibilities. The episode (whose script originally included a second kiss between two additional women) became the subject of much high-profile bickering between ABC executives and series producers Tom and Roseanne Arnold during the weeks prior to its airing. Up to the eleventh hour, the very inclusion of the kiss appeared to remain in question, prompting protests by gay rights organizations. ABC finally let the kiss happen, but added a viewer warning at the start of the episode.

15. The sexual harassment kiss (1996)

Six-year-old Johnathan Prevette, a first-grader at Southwest Elementary School in Lexington, North Carolina, kissed a classmate on the cheek. A teacher saw the September 19, 1996, incident and reported it to the school principal, Lisa Horne, who punished Johnathan by keeping him from attending an ice cream party and ordering him to spend a day in a disciplinary program. But Johnathan's mother called a local radio talk show, word of the incident spread and within six months the U.S. Department of Education had rewritten its sexual harassment guidelines to omit kisses by first-graders. For the record, Johnathan said that the girl asked him for a kiss.

16. The MTV faux lesbian kiss (2003)

For the opening number of the 2003 MTV Video Music Awards, Britney Spears and Christina Aguilera sang Madonna's 1984 hit "Like a Virgin" while wearing white wedding gowns. As the music segued into Madonna's latest hit "Hollywood," Madonna stepped out of a wedding cake wearing a tuxedo. What followed was a drag show of sorts with Madonna playing the groom and Britney and Christina the virginal brides. The performance climaxed with a French kiss between Madonna and Britney and then between Madonna and Christina. The kisses overshadowed the awards themselves and were front-page news around the world.

—D.B. & Cdn. Eds.

4 CANADIAN POLITICIANS WHO RUSHED TO THE ALTAR

1. George Brown

Brown was already 43 years old when he first met Anne Nelson in Edinburgh in September 1862. He proposed five weeks later, and they were married on November 27.

2. Wilfrid Laurier

Wilfrid Laurier had loved Zoë Lafontaine for several years, but when she got engaged to another man, he left Montreal and moved to Athabaska to practise law. On May 12, 1868, he received a telegram requesting that he return to Montreal on "a matter of urgent importance." When he arrived the following morning, he was informed that Zoë had changed her mind about whom she wanted to marry. Wilfrid and Zoë were married at 8:00 that same evening.

3. John A. Macdonald

John A. began dating his cousin Isabella shortly after she moved to Kingston with her family in the summer of 1843. They were married on September 1, 1843.

4. William Lyon Mackenzie

The firebrand editor, reformer and first mayor of Toronto married Isabel Baxter three weeks after first meeting her.

8 CELEBRITY COUPLES MARRIED THREE WEEKS OR LESS

1. Rudolph Valentino (actor) and Jean Acker (actress)—6 Hours

Married November 5, 1919, Hollywood's smouldering Great Lover was locked out on his wedding night by his lovely bride. His first marriage lasted less than six hours.

2. Zsa Zsa Gabor (professional celebrity) and Felipe De Alba (socialite)—1 Day

After surviving her one-day marriage, Gabor commented, "I'm a wonderful housekeeper. Whenever I leave a man, I keep his house."

3. Jean Arthur (actress) and Julian Anker (nice Jewish boy)—1 Day

Before she gained fame in such films as *Mr. Deeds Goes to Town*, *Mr. Smith Goes to Washington* and *Shane*, Arthur fell in love with "a nice Jewish boy" named Julian Anker because "he looked like Abraham Lincoln." They married on a whim, but both sets of parents were horrified and the couple filed for annulment the following day.

4. Britney Spears (singer) and Jason Alexander (childhood friend)—2 Days

Pop superstar Britney Spears was married for 48 hours to an old Kentwood, Louisiana, buddy. The marriage took place in Las Vegas at the Little White Wedding Chapel. The bride wore a baseball cap and torn jeans. Both were 22 years old, and claimed they were not intoxicated at the time. Said the groom, "It was just crazy, man. We said, 'Let's do something wild. Let's get married, for the hell of it.'" Spears made no comment. Calling it "a mistake," the couple had a judge annul the marriage, which took two days.

5. M.M. and J.H. —5 Days

While not celebrities of Hollywood proportions, two Toronto lesbians have the dubious distinction of being the world's first and fastest gay divorcees. The two women got married on Friday, June 18, 2004, a week after the Ontario Court of Appeal legalized gay marriage. The two women, identified only as M.M. and J.H. (the initials of their lawyers), filed for divorce five days later on Wednesday, June 23, 2004. The women had lived together for seven years, but got cold feet immediately after getting hitched. Court documents indicate that the women believed that marriage would solve problems in their relationship.

191

6. Gloria Swanson (actress) and Wallace Beery (actor)—3 Weeks

Married in Hollywood in March 1916, Swanson and Beery separated three weeks later. Said Beery, "She wanted the fancy life—to put on airs and all of that. Me, I like huntin' and fishin' and the simple life." Said Swanson, "I wanted to have a baby and Wally didn't want that responsibility."

7. Germaine Greer (writer/feminist) and Paul Du Feu (model)—3 Weeks

The first male nude centrefold model for the London edition of *Cosmopolitan* magazine, Du Feu lured Greer into marriage in May 1968. However, in Greer's words, "the marriage lasted three weeks. Three weekends, to be precise."

8. Drew Barrymore (actress) and Jeffrey Thomas (Welsh barman)—3 Weeks

In 1994 the pair was married for three weeks. Barrymore later admitted that she was trying to help Thomas obtain a green card to stay in the U.S.

FIRST SEXUAL ENCOUNTERS OF 13 PROMINENT CANADIANS

Just about everyone can recall their first sexual experience. But even years after the event, it is one of those stories that most of us will share only with our closest confidantes. Rarely are people prepared to tell their tale to the outside world. Even rarer are those who feel compelled to include it in their memoirs or published diaries. So let's be grateful to those few brave Canadians (almost all of whom, predictably, are men) who have chosen to share their adventures with us. Without them, this rather unusual list could not exist.

1. Pierre Berton, author, journalist and broadcaster

In August 1939 Berton was a 19-year-old virgin working at a mining camp in Dawson City, Yukon. It was Discovery Day in the Yukon, a time of much drinking and debauchery. Berton was well fortified with gin when a friend suggested they visit one of the local brothels, a small log cabin rented by two enterprising women from Juneau, Alaska, in town to make some quick cash during the holiday. "I don't remember much about it because it all happened so quickly," Berton wrote in his autobiography. "One moment she was sitting on my knee, the next she was scrubbing my genitals in a china basin in the bedroom." "Not that way, sport," the woman counselled after Berton awkwardly threw himself on top of her. Two minutes later, it was all over, and Berton was back in the parlour with his buddies.

2. Earle Birney, poet
At the age of 16, Birney visited a brothel in his hometown of Banff, where he paid for the services of a young prostitute named June Nightingale. Birney later wrote, "my girl, young but motherly, seemed unaffectedly pleased to be priestess at my deflowering."

3. Toller Cranston, figure skater
In the summer of 1968, Cranston was a 19-year-old virgin, working on his skating in Lake Placid, New York. "Mrs. S." was the mother of one of his fellow skaters. She was 36, unhappily married, sexually frustrated and very interested in young Toller. He shared none of those feelings for her, but one evening Mrs. S. drove Toller home from practice, and followed him into the house. "She lunged from hand to thigh to crotch within less than a minute," he wrote in his autobiography. "She undid my fly with amazing dexterity and without a moment's hesitation, performed oral sex on me." Many years later, Toller wrote that he believed the encounter with Mrs. S. had left its mark. "My first experience was in many ways destined to repeat itself for the next thirty years in a series of clinical, physical encounters with no overtones of love and romance."

4. Hume Cronyn, actor
The location was a brothel on Ste-Catherine Street in Montreal. The girl was named Michelle. It cost $3. "She lay back on the bed, held out her arms and the whole business was completed in perhaps sixty seconds," Cronyn wrote in his autobiography. He then paid another $3 and got to do it again. "It was neither a glamorous experience nor a disgusting one. It wasn't the best way, nor was it the worst. I'm not prepared either to bless or to judge it."

5. William Lyon Mackenzie King, prime minister
It is probably only fitting that Mackenzie King's sex life would be as opaque as almost everything else about the man. Nowhere in his copious

diaries does King ever explicitly mention sex, but some historians have seized upon a particularly intriguing entry in the summer of 1894. By then, King had developed a particular interest in Toronto's prostitutes. Like the good social reformer he was, he wanted to save them from a life of degradation. Sometimes he would even pray with them. But on one night, the 20-year-old King may have been down on his knees for reasons other than prayer. He had taken a "little stroll," when something happened that deeply disturbed him. "I wish I could overcome sin in some of its most terrible forms," the future prime minister wrote, but now he realized that he was "very weak." The following night's diary entry was even more suggestive. "I feel very sorry for something I did last night. What kind of man am I to become?" We will never know what great weakness King succumbed to that evening. There are several possibilities. But historian C.P. Stacey is convinced that he knows the answer. "It can hardly be doubted," Stacey wrote, "that these 'strolls' were visits to prostitutes."

6. Margaret Laurence, author

Margaret Wemyss had been dreaming about having sex since the age of 14, but in the highly restricted rural Manitoba world where she grew up, girls simply did not engage in sex before marriage. And so it was not until she married Jack Laurence on September 13, 1947, that the opportunity presented itself. Even though Margaret and Jack had been living in the same house, she was still a virgin on her wedding night. But that didn't seem to pose a problem. "Not only did we love one another, we wanted one another," she later recalled. "Our love and our love-making were marvellous, amazing."

7. Irving Layton, poet

Layton's deflowering was supposed to occur with a $1 black prostitute at a brothel in Harlem. He had been taken there by his brother, who felt it was time young Irving expanded his range of life experiences. But nothing happened. "She was interested in poetry," Layton later recalled, "so I read her some. She liked it."

8. Ashley MacIsaac, fiddler

By the time he was 12 or 13 years old, MacIsaac had already figured out that "I wasn't exactly the same as all the other boys." While his friends were fantasizing about *Playboy* centrefolds, MacIsaac's fantasies included naked men. But growing up in a small, conservative and heavily Catholic town in Cape Breton, he had no way of knowing what it meant to be gay, and no opportunity to act out his fantasies. After he turned 16, MacIsaac got a car, and he would drive to Halifax to play music and cruise for sex. His first sexual experience was in the back seat of his Pontiac Parisienne. His partner was a clothing store clerk from a local mall. "It wasn't a real relationship, and it wasn't hard core, but it was my first real gay encounter, and I knew then that there was no going back."

9. Murray McLauchlan, folk singer
McLauchlan was just beginning his career as a folk singer when he enjoyed his first sexual tryst. The girl was a classmate from his Toronto high school. The two young lovers were playing hooky from school one afternoon when they ended up in McLauchlan's bed in his parents' home. "I was a deaf-mute in a minefield, praying for guidance," he wrote in his autobiography. "She gave it to me! She taught me the dance steps slowly, carefully, one by one. She laughed good-naturedly at my clumsiness and eased me through my nervousness." When it was over, McLauchlan and friend fell asleep in his bed, which is where they were when his sister discovered them. She never told their parents about what she saw.

10. Farley Mowat, author
Mowat's sexual awakening occurred one Saturday afternoon in the cellar of his Saskatoon home. Having recently arrived with his family from Ontario, 12-year-old Farley was taken down to the cellar by an older boy he had met. Mowat later wrote that "he introduced me to bestiality, onanism and homosexuality all in one fell swoop by first masturbating his dog, then himself, and finally me."

11. Peter C. Newman, journalist and author
Newman saved his first sexual experience for his wedding night. He was 21 years old in May 1951, when he married his first wife, Pat McKee. His best man had warned him against getting married without first discovering if he and his fiancée were sexually compatible. "Why would you buy a horse you haven't even tried to ride?" he asked Newman. But Newman

didn't listen. Pat and Peter spent their opening night at the Statler Hotel in Buffalo, New York. Pat retired to the bathroom and emerged moments later wearing an oversized nightgown that looked like "a Bedouin tent," her hair was in a net, and her face was slathered with Noxzema. "We somehow managed The Act," Newman recalled in his memoirs, "after which Pat rolled over and turned off the light."

12. Gordon Sinclair, journalist and broadcaster

Sinclair was 19 years old when he "eventually did obey the normal calls of the body." The location was Kew Beach Park in Toronto's eastern Beaches area. Unhappily for the young Mr. Sinclair, the girl, although a willing accomplice, proceeded to race home to unburden her guilt to her father. When Sinclair showed up at the girl's house for a second date the following Sunday afternoon, the father beat him up, blackening both his eyes. So shaken was he that he crashed his bicycle into a car on his way home. Although the girl called repeatedly, wanting to get together, Sinclair never saw her again.

13. Neil Young, musician

That old cliché that young men start playing rock and roll in order to get laid did not seem to apply to Winnipeg's Neil Young. "I don't think I got laid for fuckin' years after I got into rock and roll," he once lamented. "I think I was in Fort William when I got laid. Me and a nice little Indian and a deejay. The first time was not really that great . . . at least I didn't get any diseases. So it was good."

6 POSITIONS FOR SEXUAL INTERCOURSE—IN ORDER OF POPULARITY

Gershon Legman, an American who wrote about sex, calculated that there are more than 4 million possible ways for men and women to have sexual intercourse with each other. Most of these "postures," as he called them, are probably variations on the six main positions that Alfred C. Kinsey used as categories in the questionnaires on sexual habits that were the basis for his Kinsey Reports in 1948 and 1953.

The *Kama Sutra*, a Hindu love manual written sometime between AD 300 and 540, lists many imaginative and acrobatic variations on these positions—for example, the Bamboo Cleft, the Crab, the Wild Boar;

some *Kama Sutra* experts suggest that people try out difficult positions in the water first. Chinese pillow books, written more than 400 years ago, show more feasible positions with such as like "Two Dragons Exhausted by Battle" and name the parts of the body equally poetically—the penis is called the "jade stem" and the clitoris, the "pearl on the jade step."

According to these sources, interpretations of ancient art and anthropological studies, humans have changed their preference rankings of sexual positions—the "missionary" (man-on-top) position, overwhelmingly the number one choice of the Americans Kinsey studied, was not that high on the lists of ancient Greeks and Romans, primitive tribes or many other groups.

The advantages and disadvantages of each position are taken from Albert Ellis's *The Art and Science of Love* (Secaucus, NJ: L. Stuart, 1960) and from *Human Sexual Inadequacy* by William H. Masters and Virginia E. Johnson (New York: Little, Brown & Co., 1970).

1. Man on top

To many people, this is the only position considered biologically "natural," though other primates use the rear-entry position almost exclusively. Called the "missionary" position because it was introduced to native converts—who liked to make fun of it—by Christian missionaries, who regarded other positions as sinful.

Advantages: Allows face-to-face intimacy, deep thrusting by male, pace setting by male.

Disadvantages: Does not allow good control for the premature ejaculator or freedom of movement for the woman.

Chances for conception: Good.

2. Woman on top

Shown in ancient art as the most common position in Ur, Greece, Rome, Peru, India, China and Japan. Roman poet Martial portrayed Hector and Andromache in this position. Generally avoided by those at lower educational levels, according to Kinsey, because it *seems* to make the man less masculine, the woman less feminine.

Advantages: Allows freedom of movement for women, control for premature ejaculators, caressing of female by male. Most often results in orgasm for women. Good when the man is tired.

Disadvantage: Too acrobatic for some women.

Chances for conception: Not good.

3. Side by side

From Ovid, a poet of ancient Rome: "Of love's thousand ways, a simple way and with the least labour, this is: to lie on the right side, and half supine withal."

Advantages: Allows manipulation of clitoris, freedom of movement for man and woman. Good for tired or convalescent people and premature ejaculators, as well as pregnant women.

Disadvantage: Does not allow easy entry.

Chances for conception: Okay.

4. Rear entry

Frequently used by 15% of married women. Favoured by primates and early Greeks. Rejected by many Americans because of its "animal origins" and lack of face-to-face intimacy.

Advantages: Allows manual stimulation of clitoris. Exciting for men who are turned on by female buttocks. Good for pregnant women, males with small penises, women with large vaginas.

Disadvantages: Does not allow easy entry or face-to-face intimacy. Penis tends to fall out.

Chances for conception: Good.

5. Sitting

According to Kinsey, learned by many while "making out" in back seats of cars.

Advantages: Allows clitoral contact with male body, free movement, intimacy. Good for males who want to hold off orgasm and pregnant women.

Disadvantages: Does not allow vigorous thrusting. Sometimes tiring. Penetration may be too deep.

Chances for conception: Poor.

6. Standing

Has echoes of a "quickie" against an alley wall with a prostitute, therefore exciting. Indian lotus position: each stands on one leg, wraps other around partner.

Advantages: Allows caressing. Exciting, can flow from dancing, taking shower.

Disadvantages: Does not allow much thrusting. Entry difficult, particularly when one partner is taller than the other. Tiring. Not good for pregnant women.

Chances for conception: Poor.

—A.E.

ROMANTIC MUSINGS OF 4 CANADIAN PRIME MINISTERS

1. Sir John Thompson (prime minister, 1892–94)

"Now your ugly coward boy that nobody likes but Annie and that nobody ever did like but Annie, is far away. . . . I wish I could give you a kiss now and get a box on my ears and then a hug and a kiss and be called your darling."

—24-year-old Thompson to his future wife, Annie Affleck (December 3, 1869)

2. Sir Wilfrid Laurier (prime minister, 1896–1911)

"I love you so much. You have no idea. My love is not flashy or noisy, but it is deep. My mouth says little, but my heart feels greatly. I do not know how to define the effect you have on me. When I am close to you, I feel happy, serene, calm. . . . You have been my good angel, indeed, you have made me do all that you wanted me to do, you have led me and it goes without saying, you have always led me in the right path."

—Written to his wife, Zoë (1867)

3. William Lyon Mackenzie King (prime minister, 1921–26, 1926–30, 1935–48)

"She is, I think, the purest and sweetest soul that God ever made. She is all tenderness and love, all devotion, knows nothing of selfishness and thinks only of others. . . . The more I think and see of her the more I love her and the greater I do believe her to be. She is young too in heart and feeling as a girl of 15, in beauty she is wonderfully fair. Everyone looks with admiration on her."

—Writing about his mother, Isabel King (1900)

4. R.B. Bennett (prime minister, 1930–35)

"I shall think tonight as I journey west of a week ago and the sunlight. . . . And I will be sad and pity myself and be thankful that I know you and grateful for all you have meant to me . . . it would so please me to see your handwriting and have a few words from you. . . . I miss you beyond all words and I am lonesome beyond cure without your presence and so I go on with all my love."

—To Hazel Kemp Colville, a young, wealthy, attractive widow whom Bennett courted in 1932–33. She refused his offer of marriage, and he remained a bachelor for the rest of his life.

8 UNLIKELY COUPLES

1. Jim Brown and Gloria Steinem

Brown, football hero and actor, claims in one of his memoirs to have had a fling with feminist Steinem. They met in 1968, when she interviewed him for a magazine profile. The affair caused Brown's then girlfriend, Eva Bohn-Chin, to become jealous, which in turn led to a quarrel during which Brown was arrested for allegedly throwing Bohn-Chin off a balcony.

2. Marlene Dietrich and General George S. Patton

During the Second World War, Dietrich devoted herself wholeheartedly to entertaining the Allied troops at the front. Travelling together, Patton and Dietrich began an intense affair. This unlikely passion was eventually replaced by an even hotter liaison—that between Dietrich and the handsome General James A. Gavin.

3. Errol Flynn and Truman Capote

In 1947 Flynn visited Capote at his tiny walk-up apartment. The two had a one-night stand while they were both drunk. "If it hadn't been Errol Flynn," Capote later noted, "I wouldn't have remembered."

4. Janis Joplin and William Bennett

When he was a graduate student at the University of Texas, future U.S. anti-drug czar and self-appointed arbiter of virtue Bennett was set up on a blind date for a barbecue with Janis Joplin, who was then at the height of her career. Although Bennett and the uninhibited rock singer may not seem to have had anything in common, Bennett was a bit wilder in his youth. At his fraternity he earned the nickname "Ram" by head-butting down a door that his girlfriend had locked on him. When asked what he and Janis did on their date, Bennett responded, "Hey, that is really none of your business." On another occasion, he said that they "sat under the Texas sky, talked and had a couple of beers."

5. Danny Kaye and Laurence Olivier

Kaye met Olivier and his wife, Vivien Leigh, at a Hollywood party in 1940. From then on, he visited and entertained them constantly, lavishing attention on his new friend, whom he nicknamed "Lally." Kaye was married, but apparently had an arrangement with his wife. The Olivier–Leigh marriage was more volatile, with Olivier finding his wife too sexually demanding. When the men began an affair, according to biographer Donald Spoto, it was no secret to Leigh. Nevertheless, the Oliviers continued to socialize with Kaye. On one occasion, Kaye disguised himself as a customs inspector in order to strip-search Olivier when he entered the U.S. on a 1953 trip. Their liaison lasted 10 years, until Olivier's next wife, Joan Plowright, strongly objected to it.

6. Gypsy Rose Lee and Otto Preminger

Lee, the famous stripper, instigated an affair with the Hollywood film-maker in order to have a child by him. She selected him over the other men "in spite of his reputation" for being a brute. She "sensed he was a good man" and admired his mind. Once she was pregnant, she brushed him off. Their son, Erik, did not know who his real father was until he was an adult. After Lee's death, Preminger legally adopted Erik, and the two became close friends.

7. Imelda Marcos and Benigno Aquino, Jr.

When she won the Miss Manila beauty contest in 1953, Imelda Romualdez attracted several suitors. Among them was the young journalist Benigno Aquino, whom she dated for a time. But it was another of her suitors, politician Ferdinand Marcos, whom she married. Nearly 30 years later, the assassination of Aquino brought down the Marcos government and swept the widowed Corazón Aquino into power.

8. Aimee Semple McPherson and Milton Berle

In 1930, four years after her infamous "kidnapping," the flamboyant evangelist met Berle—then a rising young comic—at a charity show. The two had a brief affair. Berle found her a worldly, passionate woman who enjoyed making love in her apartment in front of a homemade altar, complete with candles and crucifix.

6 INCESTUOUS COUPLES OF THE BIBLE

1–2. Lot and His Daughters

After the destruction of Sodom and Gomorrah, the only survivors, Lot and his two virgin daughters, lived in a cave. One night the daughters plied their father with wine, and the elder daughter seduced Lot in order to "preserve the seed of [their] father." The following night they got him drunk again, and the younger daughter took her turn. Lot apparently had no memory of the events, although nine months later his daughters gave birth to two sons, Moab and Ben-ammi. (Gen. 19:30–38)

3. Abraham and Sarah

Abraham and Sarah had the same father but different mothers. Sarah married her half-brother in Ur, and they remained together until she died, at the age of 127. (Gen. 20:12)

4. Nahor and Milcah

Abraham's brother, Nahor, married his niece, the daughter of his dead brother Haran and the sister of Lot. (Gen. 11:27, 29)

5. Amram and Jochebed

Amram married his father's sister, and Aunt Jochebed bore him two sons, Aaron and Moses. (Exod. 6:20)

6. Amnon and Tamar

Amnon raped his half-sister Tamar and was murdered in revenge two years later by Tamar's full brother Absalom. (II Sam. 13:2, 14, 28–29)

HOW 14 FAMOUS PEOPLE MET THEIR MATES

1. Pamela Anderson and Tommy Lee

Baywatch actress Anderson met the Mötley Crüe drummer at a New Year's party. "He sat with me and kept licking my face," she recalled. "When I left, he was begging me for my phone number. I said no way. But then I gave him my number because he was interesting." After a five-day courtship at a resort in Cancún, Mexico, the couple was wed on the beach.

2. Julie Andrews and Blake Edwards

Their romance began after Andrews heard that movie director Edwards had described her as "so sweet she probably has violets between her legs." Amused by this remark, she sent him a bunch of violets and a note. They soon began dating and were married in 1969.

3. Samuel Beckett and Suzanne Deschevaux-Dumesnil

Avant-garde playwright Beckett had been stabbed by a pimp and was discovered bleeding in the street by Deschevaux-Dumesnil. She found help and visited him in the hospital. After his release, they moved in together, married and were together 28 years, until his death in 1989.

4. Conrad Black and Barbara Amiel

The first couple of Canadian conservatism first met at media tycoon John Bassett's house in 1979. In the years after that, they continued to run into each other at parties and other occasions. In his memoirs, Conrad Black recalls that since they were among the few conservative voices on the Canadian political landscape, "we always found our fairly frequent encounters convivial." But things changed when Black's first marriage fell apart towards the end of 1991. Amiel went from being a "cordial acquaintance" to "the summit of my most ardent and uncompromising desires." One day, before they attended the opera together, Black informed Amiel of his amorous intentions. She responded by suggesting he see a psychiatrist. After he was pronounced sane, the relationship was consummated.

5. Tina Brown and Harold Evans

Brown, the future editor of *Vanity Fair* and *The New Yorker*, was a 22-year-old Oxford co-ed when she decided to meet Evans, the 47-year-old editor of the venerable *Times* of London. Brown camped outside Evans's door and refused to move until he agreed to see her. Four years later, Evans divorced his wife and married Brown.

6. Hume Cronyn and Jessica Tandy

The odds were definitely stacked against Hume Cronyn the first time he met a young English actress named Jessica Tandy in October 1940. She was performing in a play called *Jupiter Laughs* in New York. Cronyn was in the audience because a friend and fellow Canadian actor was also in the cast. After the show, the three of them went out to dinner, but things didn't go well. After listening to Cronyn carry on about the English and their idiosyncrasies, Tandy turned to him and declared, "You are a fool." Of course, since Cronyn was engaged to be married, and Tandy was already married with a six-year-old daughter, neither was really in the market for a new partner. Two years later, they were married to each other.

7. Edward VIII and Wallis Simpson

The future Duke of Windsor was introduced to Mrs. Wallis Simpson—the woman for whom he eventually gave up the throne—at a house party. He asked whether she missed American central heating. She replied, "I'm sorry, sir, but you disappoint me. . . . Every American woman that comes to your country is always asked the same question. I had hoped for something more original from the Prince of Wales."

8. Oliver Hardy and Virginia Lucille Jones

Jones was a script girl on *The Flying Deuces*, starring Laurel and Hardy. One day on the set, she tripped over a rolled-up carpet, struck her head on the arc light and was taken to the hospital. While she was unconscious, Hardy was struck by her beauty. He courted her by sending flowers and notes to the hospital. They were married in 1940.

9. John Lennon and Yoko Ono

According to biographers, avant-garde artist Ono pursued Lennon relentlessly. At the time they met, she was showing her work at London's Indica Gallery. Lennon saw the show, which impressed him, but did not respond immediately to her advances, which included pleas for sponsorship of her art, hanging around outside his door and bombarding him with notes. Eventually, the couple divorced their respective spouses and married in 1969 on the Rock of Gibraltar.

10. Peter C. Newman and Christina McCall

Peter C. Newman was a rising star in Canadian journalism when he began working with Christina McCall at *Maclean's* magazine in 1957. He was also still married (albeit unhappily) to his wife, Pat, and working on his first book. McCall was six years younger and starting to make her way up the magazine's journalistic ladder. She had, Newman later recalled, "long black hair, the eyes of a nightingale, a zaftig figure, and smooth, alabaster skin." More importantly, she had "a lust for life, literature, learning, and an appreciation of Peter C. Newman." Within a few months, he had informed his now-pregnant wife that their marriage was over, and in 1959, Newman and McCall were married.

11. Ozzy Osbourne and Sharon Arden

Heavy-metal rocker Osbourne met his wife-to-be when she was working as a receptionist for her father, a London music agent. He walked into her office barefoot, with a faucet dangling from his neck, and sat on the floor. "I was terrified," she recalled. The couple wed two years later, in 1981, and had three children together. The Osbournes subsequently became beloved MTV stars as the world watched their vivid family life unfolding on the small screen.

12. Dolly Parton and Carl Dean

On her first day in Nashville in 1964, Parton took a suitcase of dirty clothes to a launderette. Dean drove by and honked his truck's horn at the pretty blonde. Parton cheerfully waved back, and he stopped. They chatted, began dating and fell in love. After Dean got out of the army two years later, he and Parton married.

13. Lester B. Pearson and Maryon Moody

Maryon Moody was a fourth-year history student at the University of Toronto in the winter of 1924. Her European history professor was a young Oxford graduate named Lester Pearson. In his *Memoirs*, the future prime minister described Maryon as a "pretty dark-haired girl with a clear and enquiring mind (which, as a professor, was what I was supposed to be solely concerned with)." In March, just before final exams were about to start, the student and the professor became engaged. In order to avoid controversy, they kept their news secret until after the term.

14. Ruth Westheimer and Manfred "Fred" Westheimer

The diminutive sex therapist met her third husband on a ski trip in the Catskills in 1966. Her boyfriend, Hans, was 6 feet (183 cm) tall, and an uncomfortable match on the ski-lift T-bar. At the top she told Hans, "I'm going up with that short man," pointing to the 5-foot (152 cm) Westheimer. They married less than a year later. Westheimer sometimes called his wife "my skiing accident."

—The Eds. and C.F.

MEMBERS OF SOCIETY: PRESERVED SEX ORGANS OF 4 FAMOUS MEN

1. Napoleon Bonaparte

When the exiled former emperor of France died of stomach cancer on May 5, 1821, on the remote island of St. Helena, a post-mortem was held. According to Dr. C. MacLaurin, "his reproductive organs were small and apparently atrophied. He is said to have been impotent for some time before he died." A priest in attendance obtained Napoleon's penis. After a secret odyssey of 150 years, the severed penis turned up at Christie's Fine Art Auctioneers in London around 1971. The 1-inch (2.5 cm) penis, resembling a tiny sea horse, an attendant said, was described by the auction house as "a small dried-up object." It was put on sale for £13,300, then withdrawn from bidding. Shortly thereafter, the emperor's sex organ (along with bits of his hair and beard) was offered for sale in Flayderman's Mail Order Catalogue. There were no buyers. In 1977 Napoleon's penis was sold to an American urologist for about \$3,800. Today, Napoleon's body rests in the crypt at the Hôtel des Invalides, Paris—sans penis.

2. John Dillinger

One of the controversial legends of the 20th century concerns the disposition of bank robber and bad man John Dillinger's private parts. When Dillinger was shot to death by the FBI in front of a Chicago cinema in 1934, his corpse was taken to the morgue for dissection by forensic pathologists. The gangster's penis—reported as 14 inches (36 cm) long when flaccid, 20 inches (50 cm) long when erect—was supposedly amputated by an overenthusiastic pathologist. After that, many people heard that the penis had been seen (always by someone else) preserved in a showcase at the Smithsonian Institution. Since the initial publication of *The Book of Lists*, the authors have received a great number of letters asking if the story of Dillinger's pickled penis is true. The editors called the Smithsonian, and museum curators denied any knowledge of such an exhibit. Tour guides at the museum believe that, years ago, many people mistakenly entered the building next door to the Smithsonian, thinking it was part of the same complex; it was, however, a different museum altogether—the Medical Museum of the Armed Forces Institute of Pathology—and it housed gruesome displays of diseased and oversized body parts, including penises and testes, as well as pictures of victims of gunshot wounds. It was here that some visitors claimed they had seen Dillinger's giant penis. The collection has since been moved to the Walter Reed Army Medical Center, but its operators deny that Dillinger's organ has ever been one of its displays.

3. Ishida Kichizo

Kichizo, a well-known Tokyo gangster, and his mistress, a young Japanese geisha named Abe Sada, were involved in a long, passionate sadomasochistic love affair. He enjoyed having her try to strangle him with a sash cord as she mounted him. Kichizo could make love to Abe Sada only at intervals, because he was married and had children. She hated their separations and suggested they run away or commit suicide together. On the night of May 18, 1936, fearing he was going to leave her forever, she started to play their strangling game, then really strangled him to death. Taking a butcher knife, she cut off Kichizo's penis and testicles, wrapped them in his jacket, and placed the bundle in a loin-cloth she tied around her kimono. Abe Sada fled her geisha house, but the police eventually caught her and confiscated the penis. She was tried for her crime, found guilty and sentenced to jail. She languished in prison for eight years, all through the Second World War, until the American army of occupation moved into Tokyo. The Americans released all Japanese political prisoners—including Abe Sada, by mistake. In 1947 an "aging but vivacious" Abe Sada owned a bar near Tokyo's Sumida River. A sensational film, *In the Realm of the Senses*, was made about the affair, which made dear Abe and dead Kichizo—and his penis—legendary in Japan.

4. Grigori Rasputin

In 1968, in the St-Denis section of Paris, an elderly White Russian female émigré, a former maid in czarist St. Petersburg and later a follower and lover of the Russian holy man Rasputin, kept a polished wooden box, 18 inches (46 cm) by 6 inches (15 cm) in size, atop her bedroom bureau. Inside the box lay Rasputin's penis. It "looked like a blackened, overripe banana, about a foot long, and resting on a velvet cloth," reported Rasputin biographer Patte Barham. In life, this penis, wrote Rasputin's daughter Maria, measured "a good 13 inches when fully erect." According to Maria's account, in 1916, when Prince Felix Yussupov and his fellow assassins attacked Rasputin, Yussupov first raped him, then fired a bullet into his head, wounding him. As Rasputin fell, another young nobleman pulled out a dagger and "castrated Grigori Rasputin, flinging the severed penis across the room." One of Yussupov's servants, a relative of Rasputin's lover, recovered the penis and turned the severed organ over to the maid. She fled to Paris with it.

—I.W.

CHAPTER 8

CRIME

ABOVE: *Sabrina the Flying Squirrel: nutty hero of an unusual Canadian lawsuit*

10 AMERICAN UNDERWORLD NICKNAMES

1. Frank "The Dasher" Abbandando

A prolific hit man for Murder, Inc.—organized crime's enforcement arm in the 1930s—and with some 50 killings to his credit, Frank Abbandando once approached a longshoreman on whom there was a "contract." Abbandando fired directly into his victim's face, only to have the weapon misfire. The chagrined executioner dashed off, circling the block so fast that he came up behind his slowly pursuing target, and this time Abbandando managed to shoot him dead, picking up his moniker in the process.

2. Israel "Ice Pick Willie" Alderman

This Minneapolis gangster liked to brag about the grotesque murder method that earned him his nickname. Israel Alderman (also known as "Little Auldie" and "Izzy Lump Lump") ran a second-storey speakeasy, where he claimed to have committed 11 murders. In each case he deftly pressed an ice pick through his victim's eardrum into the brain; his quick technique made it appear that the dead man had merely slumped in a drunken heap on the bar. "Ice Pick Willie" would laughingly chide the corpse as he dragged it to a back room, where he dumped the body down a coal chute leading to a truck in the alley below.

3. Louis "Pretty" Amberg

Louis Amberg, the underworld terror of Brooklyn from the 1920s to 1935—when he was finally rubbed out—was called "Pretty" because he may well have been the ugliest gangster who ever lived. Immortalized by Damon Runyon in several stories as the gangster who stuffed his victims into laundry bags, Amberg was approached when he was 20 by Ringling Brothers Circus, which wanted him to appear as the missing link. "Pretty" turned the job down but often bragged about the offer afterwards.

4. "Scarface" Al Capone

Al Capone claimed that the huge scar on his cheek was from a WWI wound suffered while fighting with the lost battalion in France, but he was never actually in the armed service. He had been knifed while working as a bouncer in a Brooklyn saloon and brothel by a hoodlum named

Frank Galluccio during a dispute over a woman. Capone once visited the editorial offices of William Randolph Hearst's Chicago *American* and convinced the paper to stop referring to him as "Scarface Al."

5. Vincent "Mad Dog" Coll

Vincent "Mad Dog" Coll was feared by police and rival gangsters alike in the early 1930s because of his utter disregard for human life. Once he shot down several children at play while trying to get an underworld foe. When he was trapped in a phone booth and riddled with bullets in 1932, no one cried over his death, and police made little effort to solve the crime.

6. Charles "Pretty Boy" Floyd

Public enemy Charles Arthur Floyd hated his nickname, which was used by prostitutes of the Midwest whorehouses he patronized; in fact, he killed at least two gangsters for repeatedly calling him "Pretty Boy." When he was shot down by FBI agents in 1934, he refused to identify himself as "Pretty Boy" Floyd. With his dying breath, he snarled, "I'm Charles Arthur Floyd!"

7. Jake "Greasy Thumb" Guzik

A long-time devoted aide to Al Capone, Jake Guzik continued until his death in 1956 to be the payoff man to the politicians and police for the Chicago mob. He often complained that he handled so much money he could not get the inky grease off his thumb. This explanation of the "Greasy Thumb" sobriquet was such an embarrassment to the police that they concocted their own story, maintaining that Jake had once worked as a waiter and gained his nickname because he constantly stuck his thumb in the soup bowls.

8. "Golf Bag" Sam Hunt

Notorious Capone mob enforcer "Golf Bag" Sam Hunt was so called because he lugged automatic weapons about in his golf bag to conceal them when on murder missions.

9. Alvin "Kreepy" Karpis

Bank robber Alvin Karpis was tabbed "Kreepy" by fellow prison inmates in the 1920s because of his sallow, dour-faced looks. By the time he became public enemy No. I in 1935, Karpis's face had become even creepier thanks to a botched plastic surgery job that was supposed to alter his appearance.

10. Charles "Lucky" Luciano

Charles Luciano earned his "Lucky" when he was taken for a ride and came back alive, although a knife wound gave him a permanently drooping right eye. Luciano told many stories over the years about the identity of his abductors—two different criminal gangs were mentioned, as well as the police, who were trying to find out about an impending drug shipment—but the most likely version is that he was tortured and mutilated by the family of a cop whose daughter he had seduced. Luciano parlayed his misfortune into a public relations coup, since he was the one and only underworld figure lucky enough to return alive after being taken for a one-way ride.

—C.S.

5 CANADIAN MOB HITS (AND 1 MESSAGE SENT)

Canadian mobsters may not have the colourful nicknames of their counterparts south of the border, but they can be every bit as nasty when crossed. This list is largely based on information contained in two books: *The Enforcer: Johnny Pops Papalia; A Life and Death in the Mafia* by Adrian Humphreys (1999) and *King of the Mob: Rocco Perri and the Women Who Ran His Rackets* by James Dubro (1987).

1. Bessie Perri (Hamilton, August 30, 1930)

Bessie Perri was the wife of Hamilton mobster Rocco Perri, but she was no stay-at-home pasta-cooking mob mamma. Bessi was heavily involved in the family business, which in this case mostly meant drugs and bootlegging. On the evening of August 30, 1930, Bessie and Rocco were returning home from an evening on the town. They had pulled into the garage of their 17-room Hamilton mansion. Bessie got out of the car and was heading towards the front door when she was ambushed by two hit men. She died instantly from several gunshot wounds. Ten thousand people attended her funeral. Bessie's killers were never found. Some people suspected Chicago mobsters who were upset because Bessie was refusing to pay for a drug shipment. Others thought it might be Hamilton's Papalia family, who wanted to get a piece of Rocco and Bessie's action. Rocco Perri disappeared on April 23, 1944. His remains were never discovered.

2. Paolo Violi (Montreal, January 22, 1978)

There simply wasn't enough room in Montreal in the 1970s for both Paolo Violi and Nick Rizutto. One of them was going to have to go. Violi, a Calabrian, became the leader of the Cotroni mob family in the early '70s, a development that did not sit well with some of the city's Sicilian mobsters, most notably Nick Rizutto. Several peace conferences were organized by New York mob leaders throughout the 1970s, but the gap between the two sides proved to be too wide to bridge.

Meanwhile, the situation in Montreal continued to deteriorate. Frank Cotroni was serving time in the U.S. for drug running. Vic Cotroni and Paolo Violi were both sent to jail for refusing to cooperate with a Quebec inquiry into organized crime. Finally, in 1977, Nick Rizutto and Paolo Violi had one last face-to-face meeting, but the talks failed to resolve their differences. It was just a matter of time before one of them would have to die.

On January 22, 1978, Violi was invited to a card game at his old café in the north end of Montreal. According to reports, he was given a traditional *bacio della morte*, the "kiss of death," by one of the men at the table. Then, someone pushed a shotgun behind his ear and squeezed the trigger. He was 46 years old. Three people with ties to Rizutto were eventually convicted of the murder.

3. Domenic Racco (Milton, Ontario, December 1983)

Domenic Racco was a Mafia purebred. His father, Mike, was the leader of Toronto's Calabrian mob, and Domenic was being groomed to take over the reins. But Domenic had two problems. First, he was a bit of a hothead. In the 1970s he had served time in prison for attempted murder after he shot and injured three men at a shopping plaza. Domenic thought they were being rude to him. Second, he had a major cocaine habit. Mike Racco knew his son needed someone to look after him. He asked Johnny Papalia to keep an eye on the kid, even though Johnny was

CRIME

not a Calabrian. Johnny had served time with Domenic and he liked him. But Domenic's coke habit had got him deeply in debt, and he was probably too proud to ask Johnny for help. In December 1983, Domenic's body was found stretched across a railroad track in Milton, Ontario, halfway between Hamilton and Toronto, a .38-calibre bullet in his head. He was 32 years old. "He was killed for no good reason," Johnny lamented. "They could have come to me [for the money]; it was really a lack of respect." Police ultimately linked the murder to Johnny's great rivals, the Musitano brothers.

4. Paul Volpe (Toronto, 1983)

Paul Volpe was a man who got to be too big for his own good, and he paid the price for it. Volpe was first introduced to crime through his family's bootlegging business in Toronto. In 1961, at the age of 34, he was initiated into the Mafia, and he rose to become one of the city's leading crime bosses. But he became restless and wanted to extend his influence. He decided Atlantic City would be fertile ground for his various illegal activities. In the 1970s he started moving his operation there. But the New Jersey city was already controlled by mobsters from Philadelphia, who felt the Canadian interloper did not pay them proper respect or provide them with adequate compensation.

What happened next is speculation, since Volpe's killers have never been caught. It is believed that the boys from Philly hired two gangsters from Hamilton who knew Volpe well enough to get close to him. They got so close that they were able to fire a few shots into the back of his head. Volpe's body was eventually discovered in the trunk of his wife's leased BMW in the parking lot at Toronto's Pearson Airport. Some Mafia observers have interpreted this to mean that the Philadelphia mob wanted to send a signal that Volpe's fate would await others who tried to move their business out of town.

5. Johnny Papalia (Hamilton, May 31, 1997)

Johnny "Pops" Papalia was the long-time boss of all of southern Ontario, but by the late 1990s his iron grip was starting to weaken. Other families were chafing under Johnny's autocratic rule, and he had not put any succession plans in place. Hamilton's Musitano brothers thought they saw an opportunity to extend their power if only Johnny were out of the way.

They approached a local hit man by the name of Ken Murdock, who agreed to do the hit in exchange for $2,000 and 40 grams of cocaine. On May 31, 1997, Murdock visited Johnny at the Papalia family headquarters on Railway Street in Hamilton. The two men went for a walk in the parking lot, and just as Johnny started to walk back inside, Murdock pulled out his .38-calibre revolver and shot the mob boss in the head. Johnny was 73 years old when he died. Murdock was eventually caught and convicted for the crime, but not before he fingered the Musitano brothers as the people who had ordered the hit.

+1. Max Bluestein (Toronto, March 21, 1961)

Johnny Papalia didn't want to kill Maxie Bluestein. He just wanted to send him a message. Maxie controlled the Toronto gambling scene in the 1950s. According to some estimates, he took in about $13 million a year. Johnny Papalia was the boss in Hamilton, and he wanted to extend his reach into Toronto. The problem was that Max Bluestein stood in his way, and Max was not a guy who could be pushed around—not by Papalia, not by anyone. So when Johnny asked Max for a piece of the action, Max said no. Nobody said no to Johnny Pops. It was the immovable object meeting the irresistible force.

On the night of March 21, 1961, Max, Johnny and three of Johnny's goons were at the Town Tavern at Queen and Yonge. When Max got up to leave, Johnny and his friends met him near the exit and proceeded to beat him over the head with an iron bar and brass knuckles. Then, for good measure, they ground a broken bottle into his mouth. Miraculously, Max survived, and he refused to finger Johnny for the hit. So did the hundreds of people at the bar that night who witnessed the beating. Columnist Pierre Berton called it "the most remarkable case of mass blindness in scientific history." Eventually, the police were able to gather enough evidence to convict Johnny Papalia and his buddies. Johnny spent 18 months in jail for the beating, but he had succeeded in delivering his message—you don't mess with "the Enforcer."

STEPHEN REID'S 10 TOUGHEST PRISONS IN NORTH AMERICA

Stephen Reid has spent nearly two decades in more than 20 different prisons in Canada and the U.S., making daring escapes at least three times. In the 1970s, Reid and two cohorts made up the "Stopwatch Gang," so named for their ability to rob banks and armoured cars in less than two minutes. In more than 100 robberies, the gang netted roughly $15 million. Reid is also an accomplished writer of fiction and non-fiction. Reid was paroled in 1987, but in 1999 he was convicted of bank robbery and attempted murder and sentenced to 18 years in jail. He is currently serving his sentence at William Head, a minimum-security prison on Vancouver Island.

1. Alcatraz (Northern California)

Any list of tough prisons has to begin with the Granddaddy of them all—The Rock. I did time with the last man to escape from Alcatraz. He made it to shore, but was so exhausted from swimming the treacherous channel that he passed out on the rocks and was reported to the local sheriff's deputies by a young boy who thought he had found a drowned body. The prison was mostly closed down by 1960, but Alcatraz remains the original supermax and a true American legend.

2. USP Marion (Illinois)

Located in the bottom lands of Illinois, in the middle of an insect sanctuary, Marion took the place of Alcatraz as America's toughest pen. The tower guards wear helmets and flak jackets and carry handheld rocket launchers to combat helicopter escapes. In the mid-'70s, a Canadian was the last to successfully escape, by devising a remote control that opened all the electronic barriers up to and including the front gate. I spent four years there in the early '80s after it became a lockdown joint, a place where we went to the showers wearing handcuffs. The mainline numbered less than 200, and I never once heard a heated argument between two prisoners—because an argument didn't have time to develop before someone was stabbed. Two guards were killed in H Unit on the same day in 1984, and one of the killers, Tommy Silverstein, lives to this day with a no-human-contact order, inside a Plexiglas cage in the basement of Leavenworth. Marion remains locked down.

3. Kingston Penitentiary (Ontario)

Built in 1835, Kingston Pen is one of the oldest penitentiaries in North America, but the bloody riot of April 1971 forever altered the course of KP. After the riot, it became a reception centre for the Ontario Region, then in 1978 it was transformed into a protective custody institute. Before the riot, old Kingston at times housed up to 1,000 of the toughest cons in the country. The last escape from the old pen was in 1954, when Nick Minelli and Mickey MacDonald climbed the wall behind the East Cell Block. Nick was recaptured days later in Ottawa, but Mickey MacDonald's name is still on the count board in the Keepers Hall, next to the words "At Large." Kingston Penitentiary was known for its harsh environment and strict discipline. Cramped cells, rats in the toilet, steel trays, tin cups, mailbag repair workshops, 4:30 smoke-ups, the silent system and the strap stayed legal and in regular use until 1970. It was a place feared and revered by crooks far and wide. I once got talking with an old swamp convict in Pensecola, Florida, and he went all wide-eyed at the mention of Kingston Penitentiary, saying to me, "You did time in that place?"

4. The Haven (Kingston, Ontario)

Millhaven Institution opened prematurely in 1971 to accommodate the aftermath of the KP riot. The guards formed a gauntlet all the way down T-Passage, and as each busload of prisoners arrived they were beaten with oak batons all the way to their cells. No one was spared. The joint went in the crapper on opening day and stayed there. A Native prisoner from the nearby area told me that the prison was built on an Indian burial ground and was therefore cursed to forever remain a place of deep and abiding human misery. I did nine years in Millhaven, and nothing in my experience ever contradicted that theory.

5. Maricopa County Jail (Arizona)

I didn't know there were this many ugly people in Arizona. I slept on a concrete floor for 11 days in a bullpen with one open toilet for 60 people. We were given a white bread pimento sandwich and a warm Tetra Pak of milk twice a day. I wanted to hang myself, but I never saw a sheet or blanket for my whole time there.

6. Terre Haute (Indiana)

I spent a record-hot summer locked down in what is known as I-Up, a long range of cells in a tin-roofed building well segregated from the mainline. I-Up houses all the bad actors and potential escape risks in transit from all over America. Three men to a cell, walking up and down in the yard every second day for 30 minutes in a dog run with a rusted corrugated cover. Indiana in the summertime, inside an airless concrete box. It didn't surprise me that Terre Haute is where they eventually built a death house and sent Timothy McVeigh to his own hell.

7. San Quentin (California)

Never been there, but I've walked the big yard with too many who have. Quentin has to be mentioned because any joint with a death row is a tough joint, and plenty of state joints have them. But San Quentin is the West Coast Big House, and the birthplace of the dominant prison gangs that have spread into the federal system. Quentin in the '70s was famous for the phrase "DA Rejects," which meant that the State Attorney's Office refused to prosecute cases of prisoner-on-prisoner homicides. Imagine how that policy played out in the gang-ridden, racially divided 2 acres of dirt and concrete that held 5,000 of the most violent men in the state of California.

8. McAllister (Oklahoma)

Corn cereal, corn mush, cornmeal, cornbread, corn on the cob, corn ad nauseam. Who knew you could make so many dishes from the golden kernel? And all shoved through our food slots by a shift of blond giants who looked like the practice squad for the University of Oklahoma Sooners football team. These Oklahoma farm boys moonlighting as prison guards made it abundantly clear they didn't like us come-from-away city types. If you didn't like corn, they didn't want to see the left-overs. I learned to speak in a drawl and never to deign to rise above two syllables in the same word.

9. Angola (Louisiana)

The Louisiana State Prison has to be named because it has a death house and an annual rodeo in which prisoners are routinely injured and killed for the pleasure of the spectators. It is where you can find the best prison magazine in the U.S., where the solitary confinement huts are known as the Red Hats for the colour of their little roofs, and where the warden for some 30 years is named Burl Cain. Both he and his institution look like stereotypes from a bad prison movie.

10. Florence ADX (Colorado), Pelican Bay (California), Tamms (Illinois) et al.

These are the new breed of supermax prisons. Hundreds are being built by federal and state governments at breakneck speeds across the length and breadth of America. Canada has not yet been caught up in the frenzy of prison building and privatization of the industry that is taking place south of the 49th parallel. The new supermax model is a bloodless, antiseptic and remote-monitored environment. The cells are prefab, the furnishings fixed, moulded and as cold and lifeless as their designers. Many of the newer prisons are literally buried beneath the ground, saving the prisoner the imaginative leap to understanding the metaphor. A farmer standing within the vicinity of Tamms, Illinois, describes the bone-chilling cries he hears coming across his fields on some nights. Perhaps, when a more compassionate age dawns upon us, the new supermaxes will be kept as museums of man's inhumanity to man. Until then, the unfortunate souls who remain imprisoned inside these sterile tombs will continue to howl as they descend into their madness, void of witnesses, void of human contact.

4 NOTORIOUS CANADIAN "KIDNAPPINGS"
1. John Labatt

August 14, 1934, started out like any other day for beer mogul John Labatt, but it certainly didn't end that way. Labatt was driving on a deserted country road from his summer home on Lake Huron to his office in London, Ontario, when he was pulled over by three gunmen. They ordered him to write a note to his brother, Hugh, informing him that he had been kidnapped. They then drove Labatt north towards Muskoka cottage country. The three men were American rum runners who had fallen on hard times with the repeal of Prohibition in 1933. But they were clearly amateurs when it came to kidnapping. They took their hostage to a well-populated area of Muskoka, where their American accents and city-slicker clothes made their neighbours suspicious. Three days after seizing Labatt, the kidnappers concluded they were probably in over their heads. They drove their hostage back to Toronto and released him unharmed. But the story doesn't end there. Having only got a brief glimpse of his kidnappers, Labatt incorrectly identified an innocent man, David Meisner. Labatt's testimony helped convict Meisner, who spent months in jail before the real kidnappers were picked up the following summer.

2. Marilyn Lastman

Was she or wasn't she? That's the question many people still ask about the "kidnapping" of Marilyn Lastman, more than 30 years after the event. Lastman was the flashy blonde wife of the flamboyant millionaire appliance salesman turned politician, Mel Lastman. On January 15, 1973, the day her husband chaired his first council meeting as mayor of the Toronto borough of North York, Marilyn Lastman disappeared. She returned home in a taxi nine hours later, shaken and confused. She claimed she had been kidnapped by two men who told her they had injected her with a poison that would kill her within 48 hours. They would give her the antidote only if she paid them $800,000 the following day. They allegedly told her "there was a big revolution coming" and they needed the money. In her statement to police, Marilyn said she was able to negotiate her release by turning over two diamond rings worth $92,000, and by promising to give the kidnappers $1 million. But the kidnappers demurred. "It doesn't have to be that high," they apparently told her.

Right from the beginning, there were doubts raised about Marilyn's story. The rings turned up in her drawer under her pyjamas, there was no evidence of any injection, no ransom note or other contact from the kidnappers was ever received, and no arrests were ever made. Despite the fact that Marilyn Lastman passed a lie detector test, many believe that the true story of what happened that afternoon has yet to be told.

3. Signy Eaton

June 15, 1976, could have been a very bad day for 14-year-old Signy Eaton, daughter of retailing mogul John Craig Eaton. Instead, thanks to a sharp-eyed neighbour, and a bungling would-be kidnapper, Signy's unfortunate adventure lasted only a few scary moments. The intruder had broken into the family's Toronto home in the middle of the night. He seized the young girl at gunpoint, but despite several tries, he never succeeded in tying a bag over her head to conceal his identity from her. Signy was struck by how slightly built the man was. Her original impulse was simply to push him over. But that proved to be unnecessary. A neighbour had spotted the intruder scurrying across the Eatons' front lawn and had called for help. When the police arrived, Signy broke free and ran upstairs to rejoin her family. The hapless kidnapper managed to escape, but he was discovered a couple of hours later in a trench he had dug not far from the Eatons' home. He turned out to be a 47-year-old Frenchman with an extensive criminal record who had already been deported twice from Canada. He was convicted and sentenced to life in prison.

4. Dar Heatherington

On May 3, 2003, Lethbridge, Alberta, alderman Dar Heatherington disappeared in Great Falls, Montana. Three days later, she was found at the Treasure Island Hotel and Casino in Las Vegas. What happened in between depends on whom you talk to. Heatherington's story was that she had been kidnapped, taken to Las Vegas and possibly drugged and sexually assaulted. But police in Great Falls weren't buying it. They proclaimed that Heatherington's story was "not credible," and charged her with making false statements. After questioning by police, Heatherington dropped the claim that she had been kidnapped. She later recanted, arguing that police had coerced her to change her story. She continued to insist that a man she had met while riding along a bike path in Great Falls had indeed abducted her and taken her to Las Vegas, where she was forced to do things that were "very disturbing." In July 2004 Dar Heatherington was convicted of public mischief in Calgary. Not only had her kidnapping story been proven unfounded, but so too had more than a year of complaints to police about being stalked and threatened. The court concluded that Heatherington had been writing sexually explicit letters to herself.

11 CASES OF ANIMALS AND INSECTS BROUGHT BEFORE THE LAW

There has been a long and shocking tradition of punishing, excommunicating and killing animals for real or supposed crimes. In medieval times, animals were even put on the rack to extort confessions of guilt. Cases have been recorded and documented involving such unlikely creatures as flies, locusts, snakes, mosquitoes, caterpillars, eels, snails, beetles, grasshoppers, dolphins and most larger mammals. In 17th-century Russia, a goat was banished to Siberia. The belief that animals are morally culpable is happily out of fashion—but not completely, for even now, these travesties and comedies occasionally occur.

1. What's a mayor to do?

In Ansbach, Germany, in 1685, it was reported that a vicious wolf was ravaging herds and devouring women and children. The beast was believed to be none other than the town's deceased mayor, who had turned into a werewolf. A typical politician, the wolf/mayor was hard to pin down, but was finally captured and killed. The animal's carcass was then dressed in a flesh-coloured suit, a brown wig and a long grey-white beard. Its snout was cut off and replaced with a mask of the mayor. By court order, the creature was hanged from a windmill. The weremayor's pelt was then stuffed and displayed in a town official's cabinet, to serve forever as proof of the existence of werewolves.

2. Putting the bite on the landlord

In the 1700s, an order of Franciscan friars in Brazil was driven to despair by the termites that were devouring not only the food and furniture, but also the very walls of the monastery. The monks pleaded with the bishop for an act of excommunication, and an ecclesiastical trial was held. When the accused defiantly failed to appear in court, they were appointed a lawyer. He made the usual speech about how all God's creatures deserved to eat, and he praised his clients' industry, which he said was far greater than that of the friars. Further, he argued that the termites had occupied the land long before the monks. The lengthy trial overflowed with complicated legal speeches and much passionate quoting of authorities. In the end, it was decided that the monks should give the termites their own plot of land. The judge's order was read aloud to the termite hills. According to a monk's document dated January 1713, the termites promptly came out of the hills and marched in columns to their new home. Woodn't you know it?

3. I'm not that kind of girl

In Vanvres, France, in 1750, Jacques Ferron was caught in the act of love with a she-ass and sentenced to hang. Normally, his partner would have died as well—but members of the community took an unprecedented step. They signed a petition that stated they had known the she-ass for four years, that she had always been well behaved at home and abroad and had never caused a scandal of any kind. She was, they concluded, "in all her habits of life a most honest creature." As the result of this intervention, Ferron was hanged for sodomy and the she-ass was acquitted.

4. A happy tail

In 1877 in New York City, Mary Shea, a woman of Celtic origin, was bitten on the finger by Jimmy, an organ-grinder's monkey. Mary demanded retribution, but the judge said he could not commit an animal. Miffed, Mary stormed out of the courtroom, snarling, "This is a nice country for justice!" The monkey, who was dressed in a scarlet coat and velvet cap, showed his appreciation: he curled his tail around the gas fixture on the judge's desk and tried to shake hands with him. The police blotter gave this record of the event: "*Name:* Jimmy Dillio. *Occupation:* Monkey. *Disposition:* Discharged."

5. Canine convict no. C2559

Rarely in American history has an animal served a prison term. Incredibly, it happened as recently as 1924, in Pike County, Pennsylvania. Pep, a male Labrador retriever, belonged to neighbours of Governor and Mrs. Gifford Pinchot. A friendly dog, Pep unaccountably went wild one hot summer day and killed Mrs. Pinchot's cat. An enraged Governor Pinchot presided over an immediate hearing and then a trial. Poor Pep had no legal counsel, and the evidence against him was damning. Pinchot sentenced him to life imprisonment. The no doubt bewildered beast was taken to the state penitentiary in Philadelphia. The warden, also bewildered, wondered whether he should assign the mutt an ID number like the rest of the cons. Tradition won out, and Pep became No. C2559. The story has a happy ending: Pep's fellow inmates lavished affection on him, and he was allowed to switch cellmates at will. The prisoners were building a new penitentiary in Graterford, Pennsylvania, and every morning the enthusiastic dog boarded the bus for work upon hearing his number called. When the prison was completed, Pep was one of the first to move in. In 1930, after six years in prison (42 dog years), Pep died of old age.

6. Monkeying around

As recently as January 23, 1962, an animal was called into the court-room. Makao, a young cercopithecoid monkey, escaped from his master's apartment in Paris and wandered into an empty studio nearby. He bit into a tube of lipstick, destroyed some expensive knick-knacks and "stole" a box that was later recovered—empty. The victims of Makao's pranks filed a complaint stating that the box had contained a valuable ring. The monkey's owner contended before the judge that his pet could not possibly have opened such a box. Makao was ordered to appear in court, where he deftly opened a series of boxes. His defence ruined, Makao's master was held liable for full damages.

7. The rising cost of air travel

In Tripoli in 1963, 75 carrier pigeons received the death sentence. A gang of smugglers had trained the birds to carry banknotes from Italy, Greece and Egypt into Libya. The court ordered the pigeons to be killed because "They were too well trained and dangerous to be let loose." The humans were merely fined.

8. Free speech

Carl Miles exhibited Blackie, his "talking" cat, on street corners in Augusta, Georgia, and collected "contributions." Blackie could say two phrases: "I love you" and "I want my momma." In 1981 the city of Augusta said the enterprise required a business licence and a fee, which Miles refused to pay. He sued the city council, arguing that the fee impinged on the cat's right to free speech. The judge actually heard Blackie say "I love you" in court. However, he ruled that the case was not a free speech issue. Since Blackie was charging money for his speech, the city was entitled to their fee. Miles paid $50 for the licence and Blackie went back to work. He died in 1992 at the age of 18.

9. Last-minute escape

On September 30, 1982, Tucker, a 140-pound (64 kg) bull mastiff, ran into a neighbour's yard and attacked the neighbour's black miniature poodle, Bonnie. Tucker's owner, Eric Leonard, freed the poodle from Tucker's mouth, but the poodle had received critical injuries and died. A district court in Augusta, Maine, ruled that Tucker was a danger to other dogs and should be killed by intravenous injection. Leonard appealed to the Maine Supreme Court, but it upheld the lower court's ruling. In 1984, two days before his scheduled execution, the "National Doggie Liberation Front" removed Tucker from the shelter where he was being held. What happened to Tucker is unknown.

10. Death-row dog

The long arm of the law almost took the life of a 110-pound (50 kg) Akita named Taro, who got into trouble on Christmas Day, 1990. Owned by Lonnie and Sandy Lehrer of Haworth, New Jersey, Taro injured the Lehrers' 10-year-old niece, but how the injury occurred was in dispute. Police and doctors who inspected the injury said the dog bit the girl's lower lip. The Lehrers said the child provoked the dog and that, while protecting himself, Taro scratched her lip. Taro had never before hurt a human being, but he had been in three dogfights and had killed a dog during one of the fights. A panel of local authorities ruled that Taro fell under the state's vicious-dog law and sentenced the Akita to death. A three-year legal nightmare ensued as the Lehrers fought their way through municipal court, superior court, a state appeals court and finally the New Jersey Supreme Court.

While the legal battle raged on, Taro remained on death row at Bergen County Jail in Hackensack, where he was kept in a climate-controlled cell and was allowed two exercise walks a day. By the time his execution day neared, the dog had become an international celebrity. Animal rights activist and former actress Brigitte Bardot pleaded for clemency; a businessman from Kenya raised money to save the dog. Thousands of animal lovers wrote to the Lehrers and offered to adopt the dog. Even the dog's jailer and the assemblyman behind the vicious-dog law interceded on behalf of Taro. But when the courts failed to free the dog, the final verdict fell to Governor Christine Todd Whitman. Although the governor did not exactly pardon the Akita, she agreed to release him on three conditions:

Taro would be exiled from New Jersey; Taro must have new owners; and Taro's new owners, or the Lehrers, must assume all financial liability for the dog's future actions. The Lehrers agreed, and the dog was released in February 1994, after spending three years in jail. The Lehrers subsequently found a new home for Taro in Pleasantville, New York. When all the costs of the canine death-row case were added up, the total exceeded $100,000. Taro died of natural causes in 1999.

11. Flying squirrel in limbo

Sabrina the Flying Squirrel of Mississauga, Ontario, had a lawyer, a devoted owner, a legal defence fund and an MP all working on her behalf. Her owner, Steve Patterson, knew that it was illegal to capture these small rodents, which roam free in the forests of Canada, but also knew that it was legal to buy them for $200 in the U.S. Teacher and naturalist Patterson wanted to use Sabrina for educational work in the preservation of the species, so he drove to Indiana, bought a flying squirrel, filled out the paperwork at the border and brought her home. Not long afterwards, the Canadian Food Inspection Agency contacted him and told him he couldn't keep the rodent due to the health risks—humans might contract monkeypox from Sabrina. Patterson got her tested, and she came back clear, but the agency still insisted that the squirrel be deported. Patterson refused and hired noted defence attorney Clayton Ruby to defend Sabrina. His local MP, Carolyn Parrish, got on the bandwagon and an online petition and defence fund was established. When the case went before the Federal Court of Canada in October 2004, the judge ruled that there was no serious issue, and Sabrina could stay. Sabrina was granted "permanent residency status" in Canada in March 2005.

—A.W., C.O.M. & Cdn. Eds.

8 TRIAL VERDICTS THAT CAUSED RIOTS
1. The Dreyfus Affair (1894–1906)

The conviction of a Jewish army officer for high treason in 1894 unleashed a tidal wave of anti-Semitism and popular unrest in France. Alfred Dreyfus, the son of a manufacturer who lived in Alsace, a region annexed by Germany in 1871, had achieved the rank of captain and was the only Jew on the general staff when he was accused of selling military secrets to the Germans. On the basis of forged and falsified evidence, he was court-martialled and sentenced to life imprisonment on Devil's Island, the notorious prison of French Guiana. His trial polarized French society into two groups—the "revisionists" (liberals and anti-clericals) and the "nationalists" (the army and the Catholic Church). Friendship and family ties were broken over the case, duels were fought, strikes occurred, and street fights broke out, bringing France to the verge of civil war. Novelist Émile Zola was convicted of criminal libel for writing a newspaper article that accused the authorities of framing Dreyfus. Retried in 1899—and again found guilty by the army—Dreyfus was pardoned by the president of France that year, but he was not restored to his former rank until 1906.

2. Mme Caillaux (July 28, 1914)

In July 1914 the wife of France's minister of finance was tried for the murder of Gaston Calmette, the editor of Le Figaro. Lacking any legal means to stop Calmette's personal and professional attacks upon her husband, Henriette Caillaux had purchased a pistol, presented herself at the editor's office and shot him to death. During her nine-day trial she wept copiously and was subject to fainting spells, especially when her prenuptial love letters from the then-married Caillaux were read in open court. After the verdict of acquittal was announced on July 28, pandemonium broke out in the courtroom and in the streets of Paris, reflecting the widespread feeling that power and wealth had subverted justice. Coincidentally, that very day, Austria-Hungary declared war on Serbia, swallowing up the Caillaux verdict in the general onrush towards the First World War.

3. Sacco and Vanzetti (1921–27)

In 1921 two Italian-born anarchists were convicted, on the basis of disputed evidence, of murdering a guard and a paymaster in a South Braintree, Massachusetts, payroll robbery. The six-year legal battle for the lives of shoemaker Nicola Sacco and his friend Bartolomeo Vanzetti, a fishmonger, became an international *cause célèbre*. There were general strikes in South America, massive demonstrations in Europe and protest meetings in Asia and Africa to affirm a worldwide belief in their innocence. Despite new evidence, the trial judge refused to reopen the case, sending Sacco and Vanzetti to the electric chair on August 23, 1927, and sparking a new wave of riots all over the world. In the U.S., important people and public facilities were placed under armed guard as a precaution, while thousands of mourners conducted the martyrs to their final resting place.

4. The Scottsboro Boys (1931–50)

Nine black youths, aged 13 to 19, were charged with the "rape" of two white prostitutes who had been riding the rails with them. Hurriedly tried and convicted in the Alabama town of Scottsboro, all but the youngest boy received a death sentence in 1931. The case attracted the attention of the Communist Party, and workers throughout the U.S. soon demonstrated—at Communist instigation—against the convictions of the "Scottsboro boys." In Dresden, Germany, the U.S. consulate was stoned by a crowd of Communist youths. In New York City's Harlem, 1,500 protestors led by Communists left so many signs and banners after their march that two dump trucks were needed to haul the refuse away. The U.S. Supreme Court twice ordered retrials, citing the inadequacy of defence counsel and the exclusion of black citizens from Southern juries. The Scottsboro boys were retried three times in all. It was 1950 before the last one—middle-aged by then—was released.

5. The Maria Hertogh Custody Case (December 11, 1950)

Maria Hertogh was born in 1937 in Indonesia to Dutch Roman Catholic parents. When the Japanese invaded in the Second World War, they interned Maria's parents. During this time, Che Amirah and her husband looked after Maria. She was renamed Nadra and raised as a Muslim. Later, the Amirahs moved to the British colony of Malaysia. After the war, Maria's parents tried to find her, but were unable to locate her until 1949. Adeline Hertogh went to court to claim custody of Maria. A Singapore court ruled that Maria should be returned to her natural parents. After the verdict was announced, Maria cried, "Amirah is my mother. She has loved me, cared for me and brought me up." Che Amirah then appealed, and the verdict was reversed in July 1950. In August, 13-year-old Maria married a 22-year-old teacher in a Muslim ceremony. Meanwhile, the custody case was again appealed. The court ruled that Maria's father had never consented to have the Amirahs raise the girl and that the Hertoghs should therefore have custody. The court also annulled Maria's marriage. While Che Amirah appealed this latest verdict, authorities decided to place Maria in the care of a convent. Newspaper pictures of Maria in a Christian convent aroused the antipathy of Singapore's Muslim population. On December 11 the court rendered its final decision, dismissing Amirah's appeal and confirming the Hertoghs' custody of Maria. After the verdict was announced, crowds of Muslims outside the courthouse started rioting. By the time British military police regained control of the streets three days later, 18 people had been killed and 173 injured.

6. The Chicago Seven (1969–70)

The case of the Chicago Seven, spawned in street rioting during the 1968 Democratic national convention in Chicago, triggered a renewed round of protest after the jury verdict was delivered in 1970. The trial itself was chaotic: Black Panther leader Bobby Seale had to be bound and gagged to keep him quiet, and the wife of Yippie leader Abbie Hoffman warned the judge that she would dance on his grave. The seven defendants were acquitted of conspiracy, but five of them received maximum sentences (five years plus fines and court costs) for their intent to incite a riot. The "jury of the streets" registered its immediate disapproval: some 5,000 marchers protested the verdict in Boston; 3,000 assembled in Chicago; and in Washington, D.C., more than 500 demonstrators convened in front of the Watergate residence of U.S. attorney general John Mitchell. Students at the University of California in Santa Barbara burned down a local bank in protest, prompting Governor Ronald Reagan to threaten further anti-riot prosecutions.

7. The Dan White Case (1979)

At his trial for the murders of San Francisco mayor George Moscone and supervisor Harvey Milk, Dan White claimed as a mitigating circumstance that he ate too much junk food. A former policeman and a member of the city's board of supervisors (he was elected with the slogan, "Crime is number one with me"), White had resigned from the board, then changed his mind. Angered by the mayor's refusal to reappoint him, he shot Moscone and Milk, leader of the city's large gay population, on November 27, 1978. White had suffered from depressions that were compounded by his overconsumption of Twinkies, his attorney argued. On May 21, 1979, when the jury returned a verdict of involuntary manslaughter due to "diminished capacity"—which meant the possibility of parole in five years—the huge gay community and their supporters rioted in the streets of San Francisco, torching 12 police cars and causing $1 million (U.S.) worth of property damage. As one gay leader announced, "Society is going to have to deal with us not as nice little fairies, who have hairdressing salons, but as people capable of violence." White committed suicide in 1985.

8. The Rodney King Beating Trial (April 29–30, 1992)

In the early morning hours of March 3, 1991, motorist Rodney King was stopped by Los Angeles police officers following a three-mile (5 km) high-speed chase. According to the arrest reports filed later, King refused orders to exit the car, then put up such a struggle that officers had to use batons and stun guns to subdue him. However, unknown to the police, the entire incident had been filmed by a nearby resident, and the video told a different story. On the tape, King appeared to offer little resistance as several officers kicked and beat him to the ground, while a dozen of their colleagues looked on. Public outrage led to a grand jury investigation that indicted four officers—Theodore J. Briseno, Stacey C. Koons, Laurence M. Powell and Timothy E. Wind—for assault and the use of excessive force. Because of the massive publicity, when the trial opened on March 4, 1992, it had been moved from L.A. to suburban Simi Valley. The prosecution presented several witnesses who testified that the officers—particularly Powell—were "out of control." However, defence attorney Michael Stone insisted, "We do not see an example of unprovoked police brutality. We see, rather, a controlled application of baton strikes for the very obvious reason of getting this man into custody." The jury clearly agreed. On April 29 they returned not-guilty verdicts for all the defendants. The verdict rocked L.A. Within hours, the city erupted in rioting that left 58 people dead and caused $1 billion (U.S.) in damages.

—C.D. & C.F.

WITTICISMS OF 9 CONDEMNED CRIMINALS

1. George Appel (electrocuted in 1928)

As he was being strapped into the electric chair, Appel quipped, "Well, folks, you'll soon see a baked Appel."

2. Jesse Walter Bishop (gassed in 1979)

The last man to die in Nevada's gas chamber, Bishop's final words were, "I've always wanted to try everything once . . . Let's go!"

3. Guy Clark (hanged in 1832)

On the way to the gallows, the sheriff told Clark to pick up the pace. Clark replied, "Nothing will happen until I get there."

4. James Donald French (electrocuted in 1966)

Turning to a newsman on his way to the electric chair, French helpfully suggested, "I have a terrific headline for you in the morning: 'French Fries.'"

5. Robert Alton Harris (gassed in 1992)

The last person to die in the gas chamber at San Quentin, Harris issued a final statement through the prison warden that stated, "You can be a king or a street-sweeper, but everybody dances with the Grim Reaper." The quote was inspired by a line from the film *Bill and Ted's Bogus Journey*.

6. William Palmer (hanged in 1856)

As he stepped onto the gallows, Palmer looked at the trap door and exclaimed, "Are you sure it's safe?"

7. Sir Walter Raleigh (beheaded in 1618)

Feeling the edge of the axe soon to be used on him, Raleigh said, "'Tis a sharp remedy but a sure one for all ills."

8. James W. Rodgers (shot in 1960)

Asked if he had a last request, Rodgers stated, "Why yes—a bulletproof vest."

9. Frederick Charles Wood (electrocuted in 1963)

Sitting down in the electric chair, Wood said, "Gentlemen, you are about to see the effects of electricity upon wood."

11 UNUSUAL LAWSUITS

1. "Miss Babe"

In April 1918, a Toronto bachelor named William John Wright went into a vaudeville theatre in Fort Wayne, Indiana, to watch a burlesque show. In the show was a young girl, about five years old, who appeared onstage with her parents as "Miss Babe." She obviously made quite an impact on Mr. Wright, because when he died 20 years later, the young girl showed up in his will. Mr. Wright offered a small but not insignificant amount of money to this mystery girl "provided my executors are able to or shall locate her within three years after my decease." The executors took out an ad in *Variety*, and, not surprisingly, several eager young women came forward claiming they were the "Miss Babe" who appeared in Fort Wayne in 1918. Meanwhile, members of Mr. Wright's family challenged the will, arguing that he could not possibly have been in his right mind when he wrote it. The case finally went to trial in Toronto in 1941. Three American showgirls presented evidence purporting to show that they were the long-lost "Miss Babe." In the absence of any conclusive proof, the judge decided to split half the estate among them and divide the other half between Mr. Wright's family and his church.

2. A Cable Car Named Desire

The case of Gloria Sykes caused a sensation in San Francisco throughout the month of April 1970. A devout Lutheran and college graduate from Dearborn Heights, Michigan, the 23-year-old Sykes had been involved in a cable car accident. The Hyde Street cable car lost its grip and plunged backwards, throwing Sykes against a pole. She suffered two black eyes and several bruises, but worst of all, claimed her lawyer, she was transformed into a nymphomaniac. Although she had had sex back in Michigan, she became insatiable after the accident and once engaged in sexual intercourse 50 times in five days. This inconvenience caused her to sue the Municipal Railway for $500,000 (U.S.) for physical and emotional injuries. The jury of eight women and four men was basically sympathetic and awarded Sykes a judgment of $50,000.

3. The Louisiana Purchase Rip-Off

In 1976 Cecilia M. Pizzo filed suit in New Orleans to nullify the Louisiana Purchase, which had doubled the size of the U.S. in 1803.

Pizzo claimed that neither Napoleon nor Thomas Jefferson had the authority to make the deal and that the 8-million-acre parcel still belonged to Spain. Judge Jack M. Gordon ruled that, although it might be true that only the French Parliament and the U.S. Congress had had the legal right to engage in negotiations, the fact was that Pizzo had filed her suit 167 years too late, since the statute of limitations on such cases is only six years.

4. Extrasensory Pain

Martha Burke's twin sister, Margaret Fox, was one of 580 people killed in the plane disaster at Tenerife in the Canary Islands on March 27, 1977. Consequently, Mrs. Burke sued Pan American—not for the wrongful death of her sister, but for her own injuries, which she sustained because of the "extrasensory empathy" that is common among identical twins. At the moment of the collision, Mrs. Burke, sitting at her home in Fremont, California, suffered burning sensations in her chest and stomach and a feeling of being split. On February 21, 1980, Federal Court judge Robert Ward ruled against Burke, explaining that legally she had to be physically present at the accident to collect damages.

5. Coke Isn't It

Amanda Blake of Northampton, Massachusetts, had been working for Coca-Cola Bottling Company for eight years when, in 1985, Coca-Cola discovered that she had fallen in love with and become engaged to David Cronin, who worked for Pepsi. Blake was ordered to break off her engagement, persuade Cronin to quit his job or quit herself. She refused, and was fired for "conflict of interest." Black sued Coca-Cola for damages and won a settlement worth several hundred thousand dollars (U.S.).

6. The Big Spin

On December 30, 1985, Doris Barnett of Los Angeles appeared on television to try her luck at the California lottery's Big Spin. Barnett spun the lottery wheel and watched as her ball settled into the $3 million (U.S.) slot. Show host Geoff Edwards threw his hands in the air and shouted, "Three million dollars!" Barnett's children rushed out of the audience and joined her in celebration, whooping and jumping for joy.

Then Edwards tapped Barnett on the shoulder and turned her attention back to the wheel. The ball had slipped out of the $3 million slot and into the $10,000 slot. Edwards explained that lottery rules required the ball to stay in the slot for five seconds. Barnett was hustled offstage, but she did not go meekly. She sued the California lottery. In 1989, after watching endless videos of other contestants being declared winners in less than five seconds, a jury awarded Barnett the $3 million, as well as an extra $400,000 in damages for emotional trauma. But the California lottery didn't go meekly either: they refused to pay. Eventually, though, "a mutually satisfactory settlement" was reached, with the agreement that the amount not be made public.

7. False Pregnancy

"World's Oldest Newspaper Carrier, 101, Quits Because She's Pregnant," read the headline in a 1990 edition of the *Sun*, a supermarket tabloid. The accompanying article, complete with a photograph of the sexually active senior, told the story of a newspaper carrier in Stirling, Australia, who had to give up her job when a millionaire on her route impregnated her. The story was totally false. Stirling, Australia, didn't even exist. But, as it turned out, the photo was of a real, living person— Nellie Mitchell, who had delivered the Arkansas *Gazette* for 50 years. Mitchell wasn't really 101 years old—she was only 96, young enough to be humiliated when friends and neighbours asked her when her baby was due. Mitchell sued the *Sun*, charging invasion of privacy and extreme emotional distress. John Vader, the editor of the *Sun*, admitted in court that he had chosen the picture of Mitchell because he assumed she was dead. Dead people cannot sue. A jury awarded Mitchell $850,000 (U.S.) in punitive damages and $650,000 in compensatory damages. In 1993 a federal district court judge reduced the amount of compensatory damages to $150,000.

8. A Hard Case

On the surface, *Plaster Caster* v. *Cohen* was just another lawsuit concerning disputed property. What made the case unusual was the nature of the property. In 1966 Cynthia Albritton was, in her own words, "a teenage virgin dying to meet rock stars." She was also a student at the University of Illinois. When her art teacher gave her an assignment to make a plaster cast of "something hard," she got an idea. She began approaching visiting rock groups and asking if she could make plaster casts of their penises. She had no problem finding girlfriends to help her prepare her models. At first she used plaster of Paris, then a combination of tinfoil and hot wax, before settling on an alginate product used for tooth and jaw moulds. Her project gained underground notoriety and she changed her name to Cynthia Plaster Caster. In 1970 her home in Los Angeles was burgled, so she gave 23 of her rock members to music publisher Herb Cohen for safe-keeping. Cohen refused to return them, claiming they were a payoff for a business debt owed him by Frank Zappa, who had employed Plaster Caster. In 1991 Plaster Caster filed suit against Cohen, who countersued. Two years later an L.A. superior court ruled in favour of Cynthia Plaster Caster, who regained control of her "babies," including casts of Jimi Hendrix, Anthony Newley, Eric Burdon and Eddie Brigati.

9. Martian v. Humans

Thirty-four-year-old Rene Joly made legal history on May 17, 1999, when he filed a lawsuit in the Ontario Superior Court alleging that Canadian defence minister Art Eggleton, Citibank and several drug-store chains were out to kill him because he is a Martian. The college-educated sales manager claimed that Shopper's Drug Mart poisoned his medication, Citibank defrauded him and Canadian soldiers in Germany implanted a microchip in his brain as part of an international conspir-acy to capture his Martian body and use it for research purposes. Joly insists he is cloned from debris NASA dug up on Mars in the 1960s. Joly represented himself against a team of 13 lawyers who argued to dismiss the case. The judge agreed, reasoning that Mr. Joly was not human and therefore had no business in a court that dealt exclusively with earthlings.

10. Politician Found Guilty of Lying

History was made in March 2000 in the small town of McBride, British Columbia. For the first time in Canadian history, a politician was convicted of not telling the truth. B.C. election law stipulates that a candidate cannot use "fraudulent means" to win votes. It defines "fraudulent means" as "misrepresentations of material fact which were intended to, and did, lead voters to vote for a candidate or party for whom the voter would not otherwise have voted." In March 2000 a

B.C. court overturned the results of a mayoralty election in McBride, ruling that the successful candidate had knowingly included incorrect information about his opponent's position on a tax measure in his campaign literature. It was the first time that a sitting politician had been removed for not telling the truth during a campaign, and the decision sent chills through many B.C. politicians. "We all colour things to a certain degree to further distinguish ourselves from our opponents," argued a city councillor from Surrey, before going on to declare he would never "lie" to get elected. The court ordered the election be run again, and the deposed mayor was handily re-elected.

11. Master of His Own Domain

On the evening of October 28, 2000, Daryl Clark of Nanaimo, British Columbia, was in his living room masturbating. He thought no one was watching, but he was wrong. A couple living in a house about 130 feet (40 m) away were watching television with their two young daughters when they noticed "some movement" in Mr. Clark's house. Concerned for the welfare of their daughters, the couple went up to their bedroom, where they spent the next 15 minutes observing Mr. Clark, using binoculars and a telescope. They also attempted to videotape him in action. Once they became convinced that Mr. Clark was indeed masturbating, they called the police. Mr. Clark was charged and convicted of committing an indecent act "in a public place, in the presence of one or more persons." He served four months in jail. In January 2005 the Supreme Court of Canada overturned Mr. Clark's conviction. In a unanimous decision, the court ruled that lower courts had erred in considering Mr. Clark's living room to be a "public place," simply because he could be seen through his living-room window.

11 LOW POINTS IN CANADIAN LAW

1. The Female Refuges Act of Ontario, 1896–1964

This statute made it legal for the courts and police to arrest and detain women, ages 16 to 35, who were deemed "unmanageable" and suspected of "immoral behaviour." The law was applied to women who had stepped outside the strict sexual and social norms of the day by dating men not of their own race. In 2004, 84-year-old Velma Demerson wrote about her experience of being incarcerated for a year in 1939 for dating and having a baby with her Chinese fiancé, Harry Yip. In 2002 the government of Ontario formally apologized to her.

2. The *Komagata Maru* Incident, 1914

The *Komagata Maru*, a chartered boat carrying 376 Sikhs from Punjab, India, arrived in Vancouver on May 23, 1914. Twenty returning passengers were allowed to disembark, but the Canadian government would not permit anyone else to come ashore. A legal battle ensued, and while the case churned through the immigration courts, the passengers languished with minimal amounts of food, water and medical supplies. Two months passed, culminating in the government's refusal to allow the Sikhs to enter the country, even though they were considered loyal subjects of the British Empire. The Canadian navy pointed guns at the *Komagata Maru* and told the Sikhs to leave Vancouver harbour and sail back to Asia. The Sikhs had to plead for adequate provisions for the long return trip, which they eventually received. The *Komagata Maru* eventually returned to India, but it remains a shameful low point in exclusionary immigration policy.

3. The Persons Case, 1928

On April 24, 1928, the Supreme Court of Canada unanimously found that "persons," as referred to in the British North America Act of 1867, did not apply to women. As a result, women in Canada were not eligible to become members of the Senate. The five Canadian women who had brought the action, Emily Murphy, Henrietta Muir Edwards, Louise McKinney, Irene Parlby and Nellie McClung, took the case to the British Privy Council for a final ruling. The Lordships overturned the Supreme Court decision on October 18, 1929, granting women the status of "persons." The decision went on to say that political exclusion on the basis of gender "was a relic of days more barbarous than ours."

4. The Sexual Sterilization Act, 1928–72

In 1928, Alberta passed the Sexual Sterilization Act, which allowed doctors to sterilize patients and inmates of mental hospitals without their consent. Based on the principles of eugenics popular at the time, the government promoted the law as reducing crime, poverty, alcoholism and other common vices. Almost 3,000 people were sterilized under the act. In 1972 it was repealed when 55 sterilizations were performed on the basis that the patients being sterilized were "incapable of intelligent parenthood." Since then, more than 1,200 forcibly sterilized former patients have sued the Alberta government for their losses and suffering. The province's initial attempt to limit the amount they would pay victims as compensation was halted in 1998. A more conciliatory approach has since been adopted.

5. "The Padlock Act" of Quebec, 1937–57

On March 24, 1937, the Union Nationale government of Premier Duplessis passed a law that empowered the attorney general to close for up to a year any building that was shown to be used for the propagation of Communism. The onus was on the owner of the building to prove that it was not being used as such before a judge would consent to removing the padlock. This law was declared unconstitutional in 1957 by the Supreme Court of Canada.

6. Japanese-Canadian Internment, 1942

The Japanese attack on Pearl Harbor occasioned an intensely xenophobic response from Canadian officials, who felt threatened by the presence of Japanese-Canadians on the West Coast. On February 26, 1942, Minister of Justice Louis St. Laurent used the War Measures Act to order the confinement of all Japanese-Canadians living within 100 miles (160 km) of the Pacific Coast. Their homes, property, fishing boats and possessions were liquidated, with the proceeds going in part towards the cost of maintaining the internment camps. In all, some 22,000 Japanese-Canadians were forcibly confined in concentration camps in the interior of British Columbia. Of those interned, 13,309 were born in Canada, while most of the older Japanese-Canadians had lived in Canada for 20 to 40 years. The last of the restrictions on them was lifted in 1949, when Japanese-Canadians were allowed to vote. In 1988 the Canadian government issued a formal apology, but internees were not compensated for the full value of the property and freedom that was taken from them.

7. Lavell v. Attorney General of Canada, 1971

Jeanette Vivian Corbière Lavell was a member of the Nishnawbe Peoples of Manitoulin Island, Ontario. When she married David Lavell, a non-

Native, she was stripped of her Indian status and treaty rights. Native men, on the other hand, did not lose their status when they married non-Natives; indeed, they conferred it on their spouse. After Lavell married in 1970, she challenged the inequity in the federal Court of Appeal, but lost. The court found that it was not discriminatory under the 1960 Bill of Rights to treat women differently than men because women and men are different. The Canadian Indian Act was scrutinized by the United Nations Human Rights Commission when Sandra Lovelace filed a complaint about its gender inequity in 1977. They eventually found it discriminatory, and in 1985 the Indian Act was changed to allow Native women to maintain their status after marrying non-Natives.

8. *Murdoch* v. *Murdoch*, 1973

Irene Murdoch of Nanton, Alberta, walked away from her abusive husband with a broken jaw and collarbone in 1968 after 25 years of marriage. This set in motion a legal process to deal with their property that culminated in 1971 with the Alberta Supreme Court stripping her of all claims to their family assets even though she had contributed to them with both her finances and her labour. This decision was upheld in 1973 by the Supreme Court of Canada. It wasn't until the provincial legislature reformed the divorce laws that matrimonial property law changed. Irene's courage to challenge the laws greatly contributed to their eventual reform, but her perseverance was never rewarded with a piece of the family ranch she helped build over decades.

9. *Bliss* v. *Attorney General of Canada*, 1979

In 1979, the Supreme Court of Canada ruled that discrimination on the basis of pregnancy was not sexual discrimination because not all women become pregnant. In 1989 the court overturned this ruling in the case of *Brooks* v. *Safeway Canada*. Invoking the new Charter of Rights, the court found that denying workplace rights and benefits on the basis of pregnancy is sexual discrimination and illegal. This landmark court ruling established the legal precedent that childbearing benefits society as a whole and that women should not be economically or socially disadvantaged due to their ability to bear children.

10. *Regina* v. *Daviault,* 1992

A partially paralyzed 65-year-old woman wheeled herself to her wash-room in the middle of the night and was attacked by Henri Daviault, the husband of a friend, who had dropped by earlier in the evening for a drink. He took her into her own bedroom and sexually assaulted her. He claimed he woke up naked in her bed an hour later and had no idea how he got there or what had happened. The complainant pressed charges, and in court Daviault admitted that he was a chronic alcoholic. On the day the assault occurred, he had drunk approximately 40 ounces of brandy and eight beers. He denied assaulting the woman, and a pharma-cologist testified that a person who had consumed that much alcohol would suffer a blackout and become dissociated from his actions. The judge found that Daviault had committed the assault but that he was not responsible for his actions—he was so intoxicated that he was incapable of formulating the necessary intent to commit the crime. The Supreme Court reversed the verdict a year later and plugged the loophole that would have permitted the criminal defence of self-induced intoxication resulting in a state of mind equal or akin to automatism or insanity.

11. *Regina* v. *Ewanchuk,* 1994

In 1994, the Alberta Court of Appeal acquitted 49-year-old Steve Ewanchuk of sexually assaulting a 17-year-old girl during a job interview in his trailer. Judge John McClung ruled that even though the woman said "no" three times to his groping, there was "implied consent," in part because she had dressed in shorts and a T-shirt. The judge reasoned that Ewanchuk's advances were "less criminal than hormonal," implying that the girl was in some way culpable for the assault because she had "not pre-sented herself . . . in a bonnet and crinolines." Finally, McClung sug-gested that "a well-chosen expletive, a slap in the face or, if necessary, a well-directed knee" would have been a better way of dealing with the situ-ation than bringing the matter into a courtroom. In 1999 the Supreme Court of Canada overturned this decision, affirming the notion that "no means no." Ewanchuk, who had three previous rape convictions, was sentenced to two years in prison. In the summer of 2004 he was again charged with sexual assault; this time, the victim was an eight-year-old girl and the assaults took place over a period of several months.

10 UNUSUAL STOLEN OBJECTS

1. Gene Kelly's lamppost

Bryan Goetzinger was part of the labour crew that cleared out the Metro-Goldwyn-Mayer film company vaults when MGM ceded its Culver City, California, lot to Lorimar Telepictures, in 1986. Among the items scheduled to be dumped was the lamppost that Gene Kelly swung on in the Hollywood musical classic *Singin' in the Rain*. Goetzinger took the lamppost home and installed it in the front yard of his Hermosa Beach home. Four years later it was stolen. It was never recovered.

2. Bull semen

In October 1989, $10,000 (U.S.) worth of frozen bull semen and embryos was taken from the dairy building at California Polytechnic University in San Luis Obispo, California. The embryos were later found, but despite a $1,500 reward, the semen was never recovered.

3. 20-foot inflatable chicken

To mark the March 1990 debut of a new franchise in Sherman Oaks, California, the El Pollo Loco fast-food chain installed a 20-foot (6 m) inflatable rubber chicken in front of the restaurant. Two weeks later, it was stolen. "Don't ask me what someone would do with it," said Joe Masiello, director of operations for Chicken Enterprises, Ltd. "If you put it in your yard, someone would notice it." The restaurant's owners offered a reward of 12 free chicken combos for its return, but the thieves didn't bite.

4. 15-ton building

In August 1990 businessman Andy Barrett of Pembroke, New Hampshire, reported the unexpected loss of an unassembled 15-ton pre-fabricated structure, complete with steel girders and beams 35 feet (11 m) long and 3 feet (1 m) thick.

5. Vintage airplane

Israeli air force reserve major Ishmael Yitzhaki was convicted in February 1992 of stealing a WWII Mustang fighter plane and flying it to Sweden, where he sold it for $331,000 (U.S.). He had managed to remove the plane from the air force museum by saying it needed painting.

6. Buttons

Felicidad Noriega, the wife of Panamanian dictator Manuel Noriega, was arrested in a Miami-area shopping mall in March 1992. She and a companion eventually pleaded guilty to stealing $305 (U.S.) worth of buttons, which they had removed from clothes in a department store.

7. Half a human head

Jason Paluck, a pre-med student at Adelphi University, was arrested in May 1992 after his landlord discovered half a human head in a plastic bag while evicting Paluck from his Mineola, New York, apartment. Paluck admitted that he had taken the head from one of his classes.

8. Fake bison testicles

In celebration of the 2001 World Championships in Athletics, the host city of Edmonton, Alberta, erected statues of bison, painted in colours representing the competing nations. Twenty of the statues were vandalized, with thieves removing the testicles from the bison. Although two vandals were caught red-handed in August, police considered the remaining cases unsolved. Ric Dolphin, chairman of the project that erected the statues, suggested that if the vandals were caught, "Let the punishment fit the crime."

9. Cabin

Kay Kugler and her husband, B.J. Miller, bought 40 acres in California's El Dorado County and erected a 10-by-20-foot (3 by 6 m) prefabricated cabin on the property, which they used as a vacation home. In July 2003 they arrived at their property to discover that the cabin was gone. In their absence, someone had stolen the cabin, a shed, a generator, an antique bed, a well pump and a 2,600-gallon (9,842 L) water tank.

10. Wedding dresses

Hundreds of wedding dresses worth more than $250,000 were stolen from Lisange Wedding World in Vancouver, British Columbia, on the evening of August 29, 2004. The thieves breached the security system, smashed the front door and made off with 300 brand new wedding gowns, 150 bridesmaids' dresses and 150 nightgowns. The store also rented gowns, but none of these were stolen. So far, none of the dresses has been recovered, nor has anyone been charged.

10 STUPID THIEVES AND 2 DISHONOURABLE MENTIONS

1. Checking out

Eighteen-year-old Charles A. Meriweather broke into a home in north-west Baltimore on the night of November 22–23, 1978, raped the woman who lived there, then ransacked the house. When he discovered she had only $11.50 (U.S.) in cash, he asked her, "How do you pay your bills?"

She replied, "By cheque," and he ordered her to write out a cheque for $30. Then he changed his mind and upped it to $50.

"Who shall I make it out to?" asked the woman, a 34-year-old government employee.

"Charles A. Meriweather," said Charles A. Meriweather, adding, "It better not bounce or I'll be back."

Meriweather was arrested several hours later.

2. Burglary by the number

Terry Johnson had no trouble identifying the two men who burgled her Chicago apartment at 2:30 a.m. on August 17, 1981. All she had to do was write down the number on the police badge that one of them was wearing and the identity number on the fender of their squad car. The two officers—Stephen Webster, 33, and Tyrone Pickens, 32—had actually committed the crime in full uniform, while on duty, using police department tools.

3. The worst lawyer

Twenty-five-year-old Marshall George Cummings Jr. of Tulsa, Oklahoma, was charged with attempted robbery in connection with a purse-snatching at a shopping centre on October 14, 1976. During the trial the following January, Cummings chose to act as his own attorney. While cross-examining the victim, Cummings asked, "Did you get a good look at my face when I took your purse?" Cummings later decided to turn over his defence to a public defender, but it was too late. He was convicted and sentenced to 10 years in prison.

4. Safe at last

On the night of June 12, 1991, John Meacham, Joseph Plante and Joe Laattsch were burgling a soon-to-be-demolished bank building in West Covina, California, when Meacham came upon an empty vault. He called over his accomplices and invited them inside to check out the acoustics. Then he closed the vault door so they could appreciate the full effect. Unfortunately, the door locked. Meacham spent 40 minutes trying to open it, without success. Finally he called the fire department, who called the police. After seven hours, a concrete-sawing firm was able to free the locked-up robbers, after which they were transported to another building they could not get out of.

5. Big mouth

Dennis Newton was on trial in 1985 for armed robbery in Oklahoma City. Assistant District Attorney Larry Jones asked one of the witnesses, the supervisor of the store that had been robbed, to identify the robber. When she pointed to the defendant, Newton jumped to his feet, accused the witness of lying, and said, "I should have blown your ——ing head off!" After a moment of stunned silence, he added, "If I'd been the one that was there." The jury sentenced Jones to 30 years in prison.

6. Inconvenience store

In December 1989 three 15-year-old boys stole a car in Prairie Village, Kansas, and stopped at the nearest convenience store to ask for directions back to Missouri. Except that it wasn't a convenience store—it was a police station. At the same moment, a description of the stolen vehicle was broadcast over the police station public address system. The car thieves tried to escape, but were quickly apprehended.

7. Wrong fence

Stephen Le and two juvenile companions tried to break into a parked pickup truck in Larkspur, California, on the night of September 27, 1989. But the owner caught them in the act, chased them and hailed a police car. Le and one of his friends climbed a fence and ran. It soon became apparent that they had chosen the wrong fence—this one surrounded the property of San Quentin prison. The suspects were booked for investigation of auto burglary and trespassing on state property, although charges were never filed. "Nothing like this has ever happened here before," said Lieutenant Cal White. "People just don't break into prison every day."

8. Returning to the scene of the crime

While training to become a military police officer, U.S. Army private Daniel Bowden was taught how criminals commit bank robberies. As it turned out, Bowden was not a very good student. In May 1997 he robbed a federal credit union in Fort Belvoir, Virginia, making away with $4,759 (U.S.) in cash. The following week, Bowden, who had not worn a mask during the commission of his crime, returned to the same bank and tried to deposit the money into his personal account. He was immediately recognized by a teller, who alerted the military police.

9. Shooting himself in the foot

In February 2004 Carlos Henrique Auad of Petrópolis, Brazil, broke into a bar near his home and stole a television set. A few nights later, Auad tried to break into the same bar through the roof. This time, carrying a gun, he slipped, fell and shot himself in the right foot. Auad went straight home, but failed to notice that he left a trail of blood that led right to his door. He was arrested by police, who found the television set.

10. Shrek always gets his man

On the night before Halloween, October 30, 2004, a 20-year-old man walked into a liquor store and shoplifted a couple of bottles of alcohol. On his way out the door, he was accosted by an alert 6-foot 3-inch (191 cm), 260-pound (118 kg) green ogre, a.k.a. off-duty Lethbridge, Alberta, police officer Mark Smallbones, dressed up as Shrek. Smallbones quickly gave chase, yelling "Stop, Police!" When the suspect turned around and saw what was chasing him, he panicked and ran faster, only to realize he was heading directly into an isolated area. He said later that he was so afraid of what Shrek would do to him if he caught him, he decided to double back to the store and turn himself in. Two more off-duty officers were waiting there, including Constable Smallbones's wife, Roberta, who got the collar.

Dishonourable Mentions

1. Stupid drug dealer

Alfred Acree Jr. was sitting in a van in Charles City, Virginia, on April 7, 1993, with three friends and at least 30 small bags of cocaine. When sheriff's deputies surrounded the van, Acree raced into a dark, wooded area by the side of the road. He weaved in and out of the trees in an attempt to evade his pursuers. He thought he had done a pretty good job—and was amazed when the deputies caught him (and found $800 worth of cocaine in his pockets). What Acree had forgotten was that he was wearing LA Tech sneakers that sent out a red light every time they struck the ground. While Acree was tiring himself zigzagging through the forest, the deputies were calmly following the blinking red lights.

2. Stupid terrorist

In early 1994 an Islamic fundamentalist group in Jordan launched a terrorist campaign that included attacks against secular sites such as video stores and supermarkets that sold liquor. During the late morning of February 1, Eid Saleh al Jahaleen, a 31-year-old plumber, entered the Salwa Cinema in the city of Zarqa. The cinema was showing soft-core pornographic films from Turkey. Jahaleen, who was apparently paid $50 (U.S.) to plant a bomb, had never seen soft-core porn and became entranced. When the bomb went off, he was still in his seat. Jahaleen lost both legs in the explosion.

CHAPTER 9 **POLITICS AND WORLD AFFAIRS**

ABOVE: *Marine Corps colour guard causes cross-border*
embarrassment at the 1992 World Series game in Atlanta

247

11 CANADIAN FLAG FLAPS (PLUS ONE NON-EVENT)

The history of flag flaps in Canada is intriguing because our national colours have not produced the type of patriotic fervour and drama that can be found in other countries. In true Canadian fashion, we have been comparatively civil in our adoption and treatment of the flag. That said, there have been some high-profile incidents involving the Maple Leaf. For the full story on our national symbol, consult Rick Archbold's excellent history *I Stand for Canada: The Story of the Maple Leaf Flag* (2002), which is our source for several of these stories.

1. Grand designs (1964–65)

Until 1965, when the current version of the flag was adopted, the Union Jack or Red Ensign stood in as our national flag. William Lyon Mackenzie King first raised the idea of getting our own flag in 1919, but it went nowhere with Canadians. He tried again during the next world war, with the same result. But in 1964 Prime Minister Lester B. Pearson proposed a bold new flag, designed by graphic artist Alan Beddoe, which featured three red maple leaves floating on a white background, framed by two blue vertical stripes. Opposition leader John Diefenbaker led the charge to stop the design from being adopted, and he was joined by an unusual alliance of loyalists, Quebec separatists, and veterans. But popular support for the cheerful design grew, and after six months of debate and dramatics, a modified design that dropped the blue bar and featured a lone maple leaf was adopted. The red and white Canadian flag was first hoisted on February 15, 1965. According to Pearson's wife, Maryon, "The flag was the achievement he prized the most." (See "11 Men Who Cried in Public" in Chapter 1 for Diefenbaker's reaction.)

2. Burning anger (1987–95)

In the years between the Meech Lake Accord in 1987 and the 1995 Quebec referendum, the Quebec fleur-de-lys and the Canadian flag became targets for Anglo/Franco anger and hostility. In Brockville, Ontario, a few men stomped, spit on and burned a Quebec flag. In retaliation, a few Canadian flags were burned in Quebec.

3. Banned in Quebec City (1990–98)
Following the failure of the Meech Lake Accord in 1990, Jean-Paul L'Allier, the mayor of Quebec City, ordered the Canadian flag removed from the roof of City Hall. It returned in 1998.

4. Costly giveaway (1996)
In 1996 Heritage Minister Sheila Copps announced a program to give away 1 million Canadian flags to promote national unity. The total cost was $23 million. The program drew criticism from all sides of the political spectrum.

5. Flag-waving in the House (1998)
On March 11, 1998, a group of Reform MPs raised a ruckus in the House of Commons by waving Canadian flags while singing "O Canada." Their hijinks were a response to comments made by Bloc Québécois MP Suzanne Tremblay, who had suggested that there were too many Canadian flags being waved at the Nagano Winter Olympics. The flag-waving disruption in the House dragged on for weeks, culminating when the Speaker, Gilbert Parent, declared that the Canadian flag was a "prop" and as such could not be brought into the House "except to quietly adorn individual desks."

6. Burning in protest (1999)
In 1999 a group of students at the University of Brandon burned the Canadian flag to protest against the presence of Canada's troops in East Timor.

7. Flaming homophobia (1999)
In 1999 a small group of protestors from Topeka, Kansas, burned a Canadian flag in front of Ottawa's Supreme Court building after the court ruled in favour of granting spousal benefits to same-sex partners. They called it "the fag flag."

8. Patriotic eyesore? (2001)
In 2001 Chris Hollingworth of St. Albert, Alberta, got into a dispute with the building manager of his condo over a Canadian flag in his window. Craig said he put it there after the September 11 terrorist attacks

against the U.S., but the building manager insisted he take it down because it was "aesthetically unpleasing."

9. The red rag (2001)

In 2001 Quebec premier Bernard Landry referred to the Canadian flag as "*le chiffon rouge,*" a red rag. Ottawa voiced its displeasure, and he quickly backtracked, saying he was referring only to bits of red rag used to provoke bulls.

10. Remembrance Day flag (2004)

In November 2004 André Bellavance, a rookie Bloc Québécois MP, refused to provide a Canadian flag to veterans marking Remembrance Day in his riding. Bellavance said he was a separatist and did not feel obligated to provide the flag. Conservative leader Stephen Harper sent the veterans 10 flags from his own stash, but Prime Minister Paul Martin quickly devised a way to appear even more patriotic: he gave them the flag that flew on Parliament Hill.

11. Newfoundland furls its flags (2004)

On December 23, 2004, Danny Williams, premier of Newfoundland, ordered that all Canadian flags on provincial government buildings be pulled off their official flagpoles to pressure Ottawa for a new offshore oil deal. Ottawa refused to budge, saying there would be no further talks until the flags went back up. Williams caved, but not before the debate whipped up considerable anti-Newfoundland sentiment in mainlanders.

+1. No hard feelings (1992)

October 18, 1992. During Game 2 of baseball's World Series in Georgia, between the Toronto Blue Jays and the Atlanta Braves, the U.S. Marines colour guard flew the Canadian flag upside down. It could have become an international incident; instead, the mix-up became a source of amusement. Fans at the next game displayed hand-painted signs with both flags and an upside-down caption that said "no hard feelings." To make up for their mistake, the colour guard flew to Toronto for the next game and flew the Maple Leaf right side up. Toronto ended up winning that game and the World Series.

14 DEPOSED DICTATORS . . . AFTER THE FALL

1. Idi Amin, Uganda

Amin seized power in 1971 and launched a reign of terror that led to the deaths of an estimated 300,000 people. Deposed in 1979, Amin was offered asylum in Saudi Arabia, with all living expenses paid. In 1989 he tried to return to Uganda, using a false passport. He got as far as the Congo, where he was recognized and arrested, then sent back to Saudi Arabia. Amin died in 2003 at the age of 80. Ugandan president Yoweri Museveni vetoed a suggestion to give Amin a state funeral in order to win votes in his home region: "I would not bury Amin. I will never touch Amin. Never. Not even with a long spoon."

2. Jean-Bédel Bokassa, Central African Republic

Bokassa seized power in 1965. In 1976 he declared himself emperor and a year later staged an elaborate coronation celebration that used up a quarter of the nation's annual earnings. He was overthrown in 1979, but not before he had committed a series of horrible outrages, including ordering the massacre of schoolchildren who refused to buy uniforms made in a factory owned by Bokassa's wife. After he was ousted, he lived lavishly in Paris and the Ivory Coast. Then, incredibly, in 1986 he returned to the CAR, where he was arrested upon arrival and charged with murder and cannibalism. He was convicted of the former charge and was kept in "comfortable confinement" in the capital city of Bangui. Bokassa was set free in 1993, when General André Kolingba, the country's dictator at the time, ordered all the nation's convicts released. He died in 1996.

3. Jean-Claude Duvalier, Haiti

When long-time Haitian dictator François "Papa Doc" Duvalier died in 1971, the mantle of power passed to his 19-year-old son, Jean-Claude, better known as "Baby Doc," who also inherited the dreaded Tonton Macoutes secret police. Baby Doc was finally forced out of office in 1986 after widespread protest and was flown out of the country on a U.S. Air Force plane. Baby Doc and his wife, Michelle, not content with stuffing an Air Haiti cargo plane with plunder, bumped 11 passengers off their escape flight—including Michelle's grandparents—to make room for more loot. The Duvaliers settled on the French Riviera and spent millions of dollars a year before divorcing in 1990. Because of his costly divorce and extravagant lifestyle, Baby Doc has fallen on hard times. He now lives in a small apartment in Paris with his girlfriend. In light of the recent political unrest in Haiti, Baby Doc has recently announced his intention to return and restore order to the politically troubled country.

4. Hissène Habré, Chad

Hissène Habré, sometimes known as the "African Pinochet," ruled the former French colony of Chad from 1982 until he was deposed in 1990. Both his rise to power and his murderous reign were supported by the U.S. government, which saw Habré as a bulwark against Muammar Khaddafi of Libya, Chad's northern neighbour. The U.S. military operated a clandestine base in Chad to train both Habré's dreaded secret police and captured Libyan soldiers, whom it was organizing into an anti-Khaddafi force. Habre's one-party regime was marked by widespread atrocities. The exact number of his victims is not known, but a 1992 Truth Commission accused Habré's government of tens of thousands of political murders and systematic torture. After his fall, Habré fled to Senegal, where he still lives. Meanwhile, back in Chad, his victims and their families are working hard to bring the former dictator to justice. They are attempting to have Habré extradited to Belgium, where he could stand trial for his crimes.

5. Erich Honecker, East Germany

As head of East German security, Honecker supervised the construction of the Berlin Wall in 1961. Ten years later he assumed leadership of the Communist Party. Among his more odious acts was ordering all border areas to be mined and equipped with automatic shooting devices. With the fall of Communism in 1989, Honecker was put under house arrest. In 1991 he was flown from a Soviet military hospital near Berlin to Moscow itself. However, on July 29, 1992, the 79-year-old Honecker was expelled from the Chilean embassy where he had sought refuge and was flown back to Berlin to face charges of corruption and manslaughter. Because he was diagnosed as dying from liver cancer, Honecker was allowed to leave for Chile in January 1993. He died on May 29, 1994.

6. Saddam Hussein, Iraq

Saddam Hussein took power in 1979. A ruthless dictator, he used poison gas during his eight-year war with neighbouring Iran and to suppress rebellions by his country's Kurdish minority. He managed to survive despite losing the first Gulf War against a U.S.-led coalition in 1991. In 2003 the U.S. led a "pre-emptive" war against Iraq. As Baghdad swiftly fell, Saddam disappeared. He remained elusive until December 13, 2003, when U.S. forces found Saddam in a 6-foot-deep (1.8 m) hole on a farm outside his hometown of Tikrit. He offered no resistance, telling the American soldiers in English, "My name is Saddam Hussein. I am the president of Iraq and I want to negotiate." At the time of writing, Saddam is being held in Baghdad, awaiting trial on war crimes and other charges.

7. Mengistu Haile-Mariam, Ethiopia

Mengistu was a member of the military junta that ousted Haile Selassie in 1974. By 1977 Mengistu had consolidated his personal power. While the Ethiopian people were suffering through a series of droughts and famines, Mengistu concentrated on brutally suppressing his opponents. Tens of thousands were killed as a result of forced relocations. Bodies of political prisoners who had been tortured to death were displayed in public and shown on television. Mengistu's ability to beat back various secessionist armies finally failed, and on May 21, 1991, he resigned and fled the country. He settled in Zimbabwe, where he was welcomed by that country's dictator, Robert Mugabe. In 2001 he was granted permanent resident status.

8. Mobutu Sese Seko, Congo

After taking power in 1965, Mobutu amassed a huge fortune through economic exploitation and corruption, leading some observers to dub the government a "kleptocracy." He stole more than half of the $12 billion (U.S.) in aid that Congo (formerly Zaire) received from the International Monetary Fund during his 32-year reign, saddling the country with a crippling debt. On May 18, 1997, Mobutu fled the country as rebel forces led by Laurent Kabila seized the capital. For his exile, Mobutu could choose between luxury residences in Morocco, South Africa, France, Belgium, Spain and Portugal. The wine collection at his castle in Portugal was worth an estimated $23 million. Mobutu didn't have much time to enjoy his ill-gotten luxuries: he died on September 7, 1997, of prostate cancer in the Moroccan capital of Rabat.

9. Manuel Noriega, Panama

Noriega was raised in a poor family of Colombian background. Something of an ugly duckling, he found his place in the military. He rose rapidly to become head of Panama's intelligence service. In 1983 he took command of the national army and, with it, the nation. A devious manipulator who played all sides, Noriega cooperated with the U.S. government and the CIA while at the same time making huge profits from drug trafficking, money laundering and racketeering, for which he was indicted in Florida in 1988. When Noriega refused to abide by the results of the 1989 free election, President George H.W. Bush ordered the invasion of Panama. In 1990 troops seized Noriega and brought him back to Miami to stand trial. He was convicted and sentenced to 40 years in prison. In December 1992 U.S. district court judge William Hoeveler declared Noriega a prisoner of war, entitled to the rights guaranteed by the third Geneva Convention. In 1999 his sentence was reduced to 30 years, making him eligible for parole in 2006, although the Panamanian government has sought his extradition because in 1995 he was tried *in absentia* and found guilty of murder. On December 4, 2004, he was taken to a hospital in Miami after suffering a minor stroke.

10. Augusto Pinochet, Chile

As commander-in-chief of Chile's armed forces, Pinochet led the 1973 coup that overthrew the elected government of Salvador Allende. For the next 17 years he ruled Chile with an iron fist, dissolving Congress and ordering the abduction and murder of 2,000 political opponents. He did, however, agree to democratic elections in 1988, which he lost. In 1990 he stepped down as president, but retained control of the armed forces, a position he held until 1998, when he entered the Senate. Pinochet was arrested in Great Britain in 1998 and held under house arrest while the British government considered extradition requests from four countries. During his house arrest, he lived at Wentworth, an exclusive estate outside London, at a cost of $10,000 (U.S.) per month. In May 2000 he was returned to Chile on medical grounds. He was then arrested in Chile, with more than 200 charges filed against him. In 2001 the Chilean Supreme Court declared Pinochet unfit to stand trial. He resigned from the Senate in 2002. To this day, Pinochet deals with new charges, with his immunity from prosecution and his fitness to stand trial continually being contested. On December 18, 2004, he suffered a minor stroke. As of January 12, 2005, he was free on bail, awaiting trial for kidnapping and murder.

11. Pol Pot, Cambodia

Pol Pot was one of the few modern dictators whose genocidal policies were so horrible they rivalled those of Adolf Hitler. As leader of the notorious Khmer Rouge, Pol Pot launched a four-year reign of terror (1975–79) that turned Cambodia into one large forced-labour camp and led to the deaths of an estimated 1 million people. When Vietnamese forces finally drove the Khmer Rouge from power in 1979, Pol Pot and his followers set up shop in Thailand and northern Cambodia, where, with the encouragement of the government of the U.S., he continued to be supported by the governments of China and Thailand. As late as 1996, Pol Pot was still executing Khmer Rouge opponents. He finally died of heart failure on April 15, 1998.

12. Alfredo Stroessner, Paraguay

Stroessner seized power in a 1954 military coup and held on for over 34 years, thus setting a record as the longest-ruling head of state in the western hemisphere, a record since broken by Castro. He was finally deposed in February 1989. He flew to exile in Brazil with one of his sons, while the rest of his family moved to Miami and later joined him in Brazil. In April 2004 the Paraguayan government paid compensation to 34 victims of Stroessner's repression.

13. Suharto, Indonesia

Shortly after he forced the incumbent president from office in 1967 and was declared president in 1968, Suharto launched an anti-Communist and anti-Chinese campaign that killed at least 500,000 people. In 1975 the Indonesian army invaded the former Portuguese colony of East Timor and killed 200,000 people—more than a quarter of the island's population. Despite these genocides, the U.S. supported Suharto as an anti-Communist throughout the Cold War. The recession that hit East Asia in 1997 sent the Indonesian economy into free fall. As increasing numbers of demonstrators took to the streets, Suharto was forced out of office in May 1998. In April 2000 Suharto was put on trial for misappropriating $571 million (U.S.) from various charities that he controlled. However, in September, a panel of judges dismissed the charges, concluding that Suharto, who had suffered several strokes, was medically unfit to stand trial. They also lifted a house arrest that had been imposed on him. The decisions led to rioting in the streets. (Unable to prosecute Suharto himself, Indonesian authorities arrested his son Tommy and, in 2000, convicted him of corruption and sentenced him to 18 months in jail. He fled the country and, while he was gone, the judge who sentenced him was murdered. He was recaptured in November 2001 and in 2002 was convicted of having the judge killed.)

14. Charles Taylor, Liberia

In 1989 Taylor launched a revolt against the Liberian government, beginning 14 years of near-constant civil war. In 1997 Taylor was elected president, drawing 75% of the vote from a populace hoping his election would end the warfare. Taylor's regime became increasingly repressive and brutal. He was notorious for using child soldiers, organized into "Small Boy Units." Even as civil war resumed in Liberia, Taylor participated in conflicts in nearby Guinea, Ivory Coast and Sierra Leone. His soldiers were repeatedly accused by human rights groups of widespread looting, rape, torture, forced labour and summary killings. By 2003 Taylor controlled little but the downtown of the Liberian capital, referred to derisively by rebels as the "Federal Republic of Central Monrovia." On August 11, 2003, Taylor accepted an asylum offer from Nigeria and fled Liberia, taking along $1 billion (U.S.), which emptied the national treasury. As Taylor settled into a luxury villa in the Nigerian city of Calabar, a United Nations tribunal indicted him on charges of committing war crimes in Sierra Leone. Although the Nigerian journalists' union and bar association have both called for Taylor to be handed over to Sierra Leone, Nigerian president Olusegun Obasanjo has said he will not extradite the former warlord.

—D.W., C.F. & Cdn. Eds.

5 CANADIAN GOVERNMENTS THAT FELL FROM GRACE (BIG TIME)

1. The Conservative Government of Ontario (1934)

The 1930s were not a good time to be in government. Voters were suffering during the Great Depression, and they took out their frustrations on whoever was in office. In Ontario, the recipient of their anger was the Conservative government of Premier George Henry. The Tories had won 90 seats in the 1929 vote, but had only 17 when the election of 1934 was over.

2. The Conservative Government of Prince Edward Island (1935)

Political fortunes can shift quickly in Canada's smallest province. In the provincial election of 1931, the Conservatives won 18 of 30 seats. Four years later, the government of Premier William MacMillan met the same fate as many Depression-era governments. The Tories lost all 30 seats to the Liberals. It was the first time in the British Commonwealth that a government would face no opposition in the House.

3. The Progressive Conservative Government of New Brunswick (1987)

The New Brunswick Tories, led by Richard Hatfield, had been in power since 1970. In the 1982 election, they had won 39 of the province's 58 seats. But in 1987, they lost every single seat to Frank McKenna and the Liberals.

4. The Progressive Conservative Government of Canada (1993)

The federal Tories had 151 seats and were completing their second majority mandate when Prime Minister Kim Campbell called an election for October 25, 1993. On voting day, the Conservatives were reduced to just two seats and went from being the party with the most seats in the House to fifth place. Kim Campbell lost in her own riding and lost her seat in Parliament.

5. The NDP Government of British Columbia (2001)

The NDP held 39 of the province's 75 seats when the legislature was dissolved by Premier Ujjal Dosanjh. But after the votes were counted on May 16, 2001, the governing party had been reduced to just two seats, as Gordon Campbell and the Liberals swept the province. Like Kim Campbell, Dosanjh lost his own seat.

WHAT 11 U.S. PRESIDENTS SAID ABOUT CANADA

There's a joke that circulated recently in which a Canadian and an American are asked what distinguishes Canada from the U.S. The Canadian struggles valiantly to come up with a long and thoughtful reply. The American merely shrugs and says, "Only the Canadian cares what the answer is." We share a 6,800-mile (11,000 km) border (if you include Alaska), the largest trade relationship in the world and a whole lot of culture, but somehow it's still hard to get noticed by the elephant that's sleeping beside us. But once in a while they do acknowledge our existence. Here's what a few presidents have had to say about their northern neighbour.

1. John Adams

"The Unanimous Voice of the Continent is 'Canada must be ours; Quebec must be taken.'" —1776, while a delegate to the Continental Congress

2. Thomas Jefferson

"The acquisition of Canada this year, as far as the neighbourhood of Quebec, will be a mere matter of marching, and will give us experience for the attack of Halifax the next, and the final expulsion of England from the American continent." —1812, letter to Colonel William Duane

3. Franklin Roosevelt

"The Dominion of Canada is part of the sisterhood of the British Empire. I give my assurance that the people of the U.S. will not stand idly by if domination of Canadian soil is threatened by any other empire. We can assure each other that this hemisphere, at least, shall remain a strong citadel wherein civilization can flourish unimpaired." —1938, during a convocation speech at Queen's University in Kingston, Ontario

4. Harry S. Truman

"Canadian-American relations for many years did not develop spontaneously. The example of accord provided by our two countries did not come about merely through the happy circumstance of geography. It is compounded of one part proximity and nine parts good will and common sense. . . . We think of each other as friends, as peaceful and cooperative neighbours on a spacious and fruitful continent." —1947, address to Parliament

5. Dwight Eisenhower

"Our forms of government—though both cast in the democratic pattern—are greatly different. Indeed, sometimes it appears that many of our misunderstandings spring from an imperfect knowledge on the part of both of us of the dissimilarities in our forms of government." —1958, address to Parliament

6. John F. Kennedy

"Geography has made us neighbours. History has made us friends. Economics has made us partners. And necessity has made us allies. Those whom nature hath so joined together, let no man put asunder. What unites us is far greater than what divides us." —1961, address to Parliament

7. Lyndon B. Johnson

"We of the United States consider ourselves blessed. We have much to give thanks for. But the gift of Providence that we really cherish is that we were given as our neighbours on this great, wonderful continent, the people and the nation of Canada." —1967, address at Expo 67, Montreal

8. Richard Nixon

"I would say quite candidly that we have had very little success to date in our negotiations with our Canadian friends, which shows, incidentally, that sometimes you have more problems negotiating with your friends than you do with your adversaries." —1972, press conference in Washington, D.C.

9. Ronald Reagan

"We are happy to be your neighbour. We want to remain your friend. We are determined to be your partner and we are intent on working closely with you in a spirit of cooperation." —1981, address to Parliament.

10. Bill Clinton

"In a world darkened by ethnic conflicts that tear nations apart, Canada stands as a model of how people of different cultures can live and work together in peace, prosperity, and mutual respect." —1995, address to Parliament

11. George W. Bush

"I want to thank all the Canadians who came out today to wave to me—with all five fingers!" —2004, during his first visit to Canada

11 COMMANDERS KILLED BY THEIR OWN TROOPS

1. Col. John Finnis (1804–57), English

On the morning of May 10, 1857, in Meerut, India, Colonel Finnis, commander of the 11th Native Regiment of the British Indian Army, was informed that his troops had occupied the parade grounds and were in a state of mutiny. He mounted his horse, rode to the parade ground and began lecturing his troops on insubordination. The inflamed Indian soldiers—known as sepoys—promptly fired a volley at Finnis and killed him. This violent action triggered the Sepoy (or Indian) Mutiny.

2. Capt. Yevgeny Golikov (d. 1905), Russian

On June 13, 1905, the crew of the Russian cruiser *Potemkin* mutinied after an unsuccessful protest challenging the quality of meat served on the ship. Captain Golikov, the ship's commander, was seized by the mutineers and flung overboard. This incident was dramatized in the classic film *Battleship Potemkin* (1925), directed by Sergei Eisenstein.

3. King Gustavus II (1594–1632), Swedish

In 1632, at the Battle of Lützen during the Thirty Years' War, King Gustavus Adolphus was shot in the back while leading his cavalry in a charge against the Catholic armies of the Holy Roman Empire. Who actually killed him remains an unanswered question. However, many historical authorities insist that Gustavus must have been killed by one of his own men, if not accidentally, then intentionally by a traitor.

4–5. Lt. Richard Harlan and Lt. Thomas Dellwo (d. 1971), American

In the early morning hours of March 16, 1971, an enlisted man at the U.S. Army base in Bienhoa, Vietnam, cut a hole through the screen covering a window in the officers' quarters and threw a fragmentation grenade inside. Two lieutenants—Richard Harlan and Thomas Dellwo—were killed. Private Billy Dean Smith was arrested and court-martialled for the crime but was later declared innocent. The real murderer was never found.

6. Gen. Thomas "Stonewall" Jackson (1824–63), American (Confederate)

On the night of May 2, 1863, at the Battle of Chancellorsville during the American Civil War, Confederate general Thomas "Stonewall" Jackson went on a scouting mission ahead of his lines in order to find a way to attack the rear of the Union forces. When he returned, Jackson was fired upon by a North Carolina Confederate regiment that thought he and his staff were Yankee cavalrymen. He died eight days later.

7. Capt. Lashkevitch (d. 1917), Russian

On March 12, 1917, in Petrograd (now St. Petersburg), Russian soldiers of the Volynsky Regiment refused to fire on street demonstrators and, instead, shot their commanding officer, Captain Lashkevitch. This marked a major turning point in the Russian Revolution, because after killing Lashkevitch, the Volynsky Regiment—the first Russian unit to mutiny—joined the revolutionary forces.

8. Col. David Marcus (1901–48), American

In 1948 U.S. Army colonel David Marcus resigned his post at the Pentagon and enlisted in the newly formed Israeli army. On the night of June 10, 1948, after overseeing the construction of a relief road from Tel Aviv to besieged Jerusalem during the Israeli war for independence, Marcus was shot and killed while urinating in a field. One of his own sentries had mistaken him for an Arab because he had a bedsheet wrapped around him.

9. Nadir Shah (1688–1747), Persian

A Turkish tribesman who became a Persian general and then head of the Persian Empire, Nadir Shah was a highly successful conqueror who defeated the Afghans, Mongols, Indians and Turks. In 1747 Nadir's own military bodyguard murdered him. His death met with widespread approval in Persia because of the harshness and cruelty of his rule.

10. Cpl. Pat Tillman (d. 2004), American

Tillman, a member of the Arizona Cardinals football team, gave up a lucrative contract extension to join the U.S. Army in 2002. On April 22, 2004, Tillman was killed while leading a team of army rangers up a hill in southeastern Afghanistan to knock out enemy fire that had pinned down other soldiers. The army posthumously awarded him the Silver Star, its third-highest honour. One month later, the army announced that Tillman had been killed by fellow Americans in a "friendly fire" accident.

11. Capt. Pedro de Urzúa (d. 1561), Spanish

In 1559 Captain Pedro de Urzúa led an expedition of Spanish soldiers from coastal Peru across the Andes to the Amazon Basin in search of El Dorado. Two years later, while still searching unsuccessfully for gold, de Urzúa was killed by his own men when they mutinied under the leadership of Lope de Aguirre. De Urzúa's death and the fate of the mutineers was depicted in the 1973 movie *Aguirre, Wrath of God*.

—R.J.F.

"IS IT SOMETHING I SAID?" JOHN DUFFY'S 10 ELECTION-LOSING ZINGERS

Liberal strategist John Duffy is the author of Fights of Our Lives: Elections, Leadership, and the Making of Canada. *This bestselling account of Canada's five greatest federal elections was selected as Canada's political book of the year in 2003 by the Writer's Trust of Canada.*

Elections are a national conversation held at 120 decibels in an over-lit echo chamber. In an intense campaign, or in the nail-biting run-up to one, a perfectly intelligent, thoughtful politician can incinerate a life-long dream with a single ill-judged remark. But today's gaffes are just part of a long tradition of howlers.

1. Randy White, MP (2004)

"Well the heck with the courts, eh?"
In the final see-saw days of Campaign 2004, backbench B.C. Conservative MP White declares on video that he doesn't care for gays' human rights, he doesn't think the courts should uphold them, and he will trash the

Charter of Rights to thwart the courts. In so doing, White proves every single scare about Stephen Harper's Conservatives that Paul Martin's Liberals have been trying to monger. Conservatives skid in the final week; Liberals retain a reduced hold on power.

2. Stockwell Day (2000)

"No Two-Tier Health Care"

The newly minted Canadian Alliance under rookie leader Day sallies smartly in the campaign's run-up against a tired Liberal government under Jean Chrétien. Then, in week two, a CA backbencher wrong-foots himself on private health care. Against the unanimous advice of his handlers, Day decides that the TV debate will feature a stupid little hand-drawn sign that draws attention to this misstep, the CA's greatest vulnerability, when the whole country is watching. Day's "Kick Me Hard" sign entices all four other leaders to join in the fun. Chrétien romps to third majority.

3. Kim Campbell (1993)

"An election is no time for a serious discussion of policy."

After nine years of chafing under the increasingly remote and arrogant rule of Prime Minister Brian Mulroney, Canadians welcome his successor, our first female PM, as a breath of fresh air. A wicked case of halitosis intervenes when Campbell makes it clear she has no more time for the views and impulses of Canadians than did her loathed predecessor. Stumbling from one gaffe to another, Campbell takes the PCs from 151 seats on dissolution to 2 on election night.

4. John Turner (1984)

"I had no option."

After years of chafing under the increasingly remote and arrogant rule of Prime Minister Trudeau, Canadians welcome John Turner as something different. First, Turner erases his differentiation from Trudeau by appointing 13 of his predecessor's buddies to patronage posts. Then, in the campaign's TV debate, he lamely defends the move, arguing he "had no option." Turner transforms himself into same-old same-old—only weaker! Mulroney poleaxes Turner on TV and wins massive majority three weeks later.

5. Joe Clark (1979)

"Short-Term Pain for Long-Term Gain"

Less a matter of wording than of the dreadful strategy behind it. With a shaky minority in a four-party Parliament, Clark and his finance minister, John Crosbie, decide to tackle the country's fiscal woes with a get-tough budget that includes a whopping 18-cents-a-gallon hike to the gas tax. They figure the Liberals, leaderless since Trudeau's exit the previous month, will fold in the budget vote. Wrong. The three opposition parties bring down the government; Trudeau rescinds his resignation; the Grits storm home to a majority; and Clark loses his leadership three years later. "Short-term pain for long-term pain" is more like it.

6. Lester Pearson (1958)

"His Excellency's advisers should . . . submit their resignation forthwith . . ."

Having suffered a shocking upset defeat in '57 to John Diefenbaker's Tories, the Liberals, under rookie leader Pearson, show that they have utterly failed to grasp the public's rejection of their arrogant ways while in power. On his first day in the House as leader, Pearson calls for the PC minority government to resign and let the Liberals return to power without an election. Dief goes ape: he trashes the entire smug Liberal mindset, dissolves Parliament and barnstorms the country to bag the largest majority in history.

7. William Lyon Mackenzie King (1930)

"[For] these alleged unemployment purposes, with these governments situated as they are today . . . I would not give them a five-cent piece."

A government nears the end of its mandate. A devastating global depression threatens our entire way of life. All eyes turn to Ottawa. There, Prime Minister King rises in the House to explain—he was windy even when making a gaffe—that dealing with the Great Depression . . . is a *provincial* responsibility! And he won't give any money to Conservative provincial governments! Niiiiice. Bennett's Tories cream King's Liberals in the campaign four months later.

8. Arthur Meighen (1925)

"Before there was anything in the way of participation involving the despatch of troops, the will of the people of Canada should first be obtained."

This one's complicated. In an extremely dicey minority situation, Opposition Leader Meighen struggles to lift from his neck the albatross he had donned when he imposed conscription in Quebec. This he does by telling hard-core Anglo Conservatives in Hamilton, Ontario, that if war broke out, what he'd do this time is conscript the army, send it overseas, then hold an election, and if he lost, bring the army back. This absurd position both fails to convince Quebecers and infuriates his Ontario base. Thanks to the "Heresy in Hamilton," when the vote happens 10 months later, his core stays home, he loses Ontario, and King sneaks back into power.

9. Wilfrid Laurier (1891)

"Commercial Union"

Rookie Liberal Laurier is up against the old Tory pro, Macdonald. Laurier chooses to invigorate his troops by boldly repackaging his party's support for free trade with the U.S. as "commercial union." Oooopsie. Macdonald calls an election, ignores the policy substance and goes for the Liberals on two fronts. In English Canada, he paints Grit pro-Americanism as treason to Britain. In Quebec, it's depicted as anti-Catholic heresy. Old pro: 1; Rookie: 0.

10. John A. Macdonald (1873)

"I must have another ten thousand . . . Do not fail me. Answer today."

These words were not, of course, meant for anyone to actually hear. This mid-campaign plea for political lubricant was sent in a secret telegram from PM Macdonald to Sir Hugh Allan, a Montreal businessman. In return, Allan was promised the contract to build the Canadian Pacific Railway. Macdonald got his money and actually won the election. But the telegram leaked and, two years later, Macdonald was forced to resign in disgrace.

7 HIGHS AND LOWS IN CANADIAN FEDERAL ELECTION HISTORY

1. Highest number of election victories: 13

Both John Diefenbaker and Herb Gray were elected to Parliament 13 times. Diefenbaker also lost twice.

2. Highest number of election defeats (without ever winning): 22

This dubious distinction belongs to John C. Turmel, who lost 7 general elections and 15 by-elections running as an independent candidate between 1979 and 2000. H. Georges Grenier, of "Esprit Social," and two Communist candidates, William Kashtan and William C. Ross, hold the record for losing in nine general elections.

3. Highest voter turnout in a general election: 93.91%

The politically active voters in the Quebec riding of Îles-de-la-Madeleine set this record in the general election of 1965. They broke their own record of 93.69% set in 1949.

4. Lowest voter turnout in a general election: 23.71%

The voters of Toronto South set this record for apathy in the general election of 1921.

5. Lowest number of candidates running in a single constituency: 1

Over the years, several candidates have won federal seats by acclamation. But the last one to do it in a general election was a Liberal, Chelsey William Carter, who was all alone in the Newfoundland riding of Burin–Burgeo in 1957.

6. Highest number of candidates running in a single constituency: 13

The general election of 1993 saw the city of Vancouver caught up in an electoral frenzy. Three of the city's ridings, Vancouver East, Centre and Quadra, each had 13 candidates vying for the big prize. The Liberals wound up prevailing in all three ridings. One of the defeated candidates was Prime Minister Kim Campbell, who lost her seat in Vancouver Centre.

7. Margins of victory in recent general elections:

Highest

Year	Candidate	Riding	% of votes cast
1993	Sheila Finestone (L)	Mont-Royal	82.94
2000	Irwin Cotler (L)	Mont-Royal	81.24
1988	Brian Mulroney (PC)	Charlevoix	80.04
1997	Derek Lee (L)	Scarborough–Rouge River	74.80

Lowest

Year	Candidate	Riding	% of votes cast
1997	Howard Hilstrom (Reform)	Selkirk–Interlake	28.30
1993	Paul E. Forseth (Reform)	New Westminster–Burnaby	29.33
2000	Larry Bagnell (L)	Yukon	32.48
1998	Thomas Suluk (PC)	Nunatsiaq	32.49

Source: Centre for Election Studies, Department of Political Science, University of Waterloo.

THE 10 MEN WHO CONQUERED THE MOST AREA

1. Genghis Khan (1162–1227)

From 1206 to 1227 Mongol chieftain Genghis Khan conquered approximately 4,860,000 square miles (7,821,000 sq. km). Stretching from the Pacific Ocean to the Caspian Sea, his empire included northern China, Mongolia, southern Siberia and central Asia.

2. Alexander The Great (356–323 BC)

From 334 to 326 BC Macedonian king Alexander the Great conquered approximately 2,180,000 square miles (3,508,000 sq. km). His empire included the southern Balkan peninsula, Asia Minor, Egypt and the entire Near East, as far as the Indus River.

3. Tamerlane (1336?–1405)

From 1370 to 1402 Islamic Turkicized Mongol chieftain Tamerlane conquered approximately 2,145,000 square miles (3,452,000 sq. km). His empire included most of the Near East, from the Indus River to the Mediterranean Sea, and from the Indian Ocean north to the Aral Sea.

267

4. Cyrus the Great (600?–529 BC)

From 559 to 539 BC Persian king Cyrus the Great conquered approximately 2,090,000 square miles (3,364,000 sq. km). He conquered the Median Empire, Babylonia, Assyria, Syria, Palestine, the Indus Valley and southern Turkestan.

5. Attila (AD 406?–453)

From 433 to 453 Attila, the king of the Huns and the Scourge of God, conquered approximately 1,450,000 square miles (2,334,000 sq. km). Although he failed in his attempt to conquer Gaul, Attila ruled an empire encompassing central and eastern Europe and the western Russian plain.

6. Adolf Hitler (1889–1945)

From 1933 to the autumn of 1942 Nazi dictator Adolf Hitler conquered 1,370,000 square miles (2,205,000 sq. km), all of which he lost within three years. Hitler's Third Reich included most of continental Europe and extended from the English Channel to the outskirts of Moscow, and from North Africa to Norway.

7. Napoleon Bonaparte (1769–1821)

From 1796 to the height of his power in 1810 Napoleon Bonaparte conquered approximately 720,000 square miles (1,159,000 sq. km). Napoleon's Grand Empire included France, Belgium, Holland, Germany, Poland, Switzerland and Spain.

8. Mahmud of Ghazni (971?–1030)

From 997 to 1030 Mahmud, the Muslim sultan and Afghan king of Ghazni, conquered 680,000 square miles (1,094,000 sq. km). His Near Eastern empire extended from the Indian Ocean north to the Amu Darya River, and from the Tigris River east to the Ganges River in India.

9. Francisco Pizarro (1470?–1541)

From 1531 to 1541 Spanish adventurer Francisco Pizarro conquered 480,000 square miles (772,500 sq. km). Employing treachery and assassination, and taking advantage of internal discord, he subjugated the Inca Empire, which extended from Ecuador south through the Andes to Bolivia.

10. Hernando Cortés (1485–1547)

From 1519 to 1526 Hernando Cortes, commanding a small Spanish military expedition, conquered 315,000 square miles (506,900 sq. km). Defeating the Aztecs, he seized central and southern Mexico and later subjugated Guatemala and Honduras to Spanish rule.

—R.J.F.

AISLIN'S 10 FAVOURITE FACES FOR POLITICAL CARTOONS

Aislin is the nom de plume *of Canada's most famous political cartoonist, Terry Mosher. Over the course of his 33-year career with the Montreal* Gazette, *he has skewered virtually every Canadian newsmaker, earning himself a devoted readership and not a few un-amused targets of his artistic fulminations.*

1. Brian Mulroney: His hat size was 8½ (true).
2. Richard Nixon: He had five o'clock stubble before it was cool.
3. René Lévesque: The second-craftiest politician in Canadian history.
4. Pierre Trudeau: The craftiest.
5. Brian Mulroney: He had a huge chin, a tiny mouth and no neck.
6. Jean Chrétien: Almost *too* easy to caricature.
7. Joe Clark: He walked the talk and talked the walk, straight into bayonets and things.
8. Louise Beaudoin: Everyone's favourite dominatrix.
9. Jean Drapeau: Without him around, Montreal hasn't been the same.

And, finally . . .

10. Brian Mulroney: I miss drawing his face most of all.

9 ORDINARY MEN WHO PLAYED KING

1. Giuseppe Bartoleoni (1780?–1848?), King of Tavolara

One day in 1833, Carlo Alberto (1798–1849), King of Sardinia, instructed the captain of his ship to leave him on the island of Tavolara—located off the coast of Sardinia—for a few hours of solitary hunting. After a short time, the king was approached by a huge man more than

7 feet (213 cm) tall. The man was the sole inhabitant of the island, and the king was so impressed with his harmonious lifestyle that he declared him King of Tavolara. The hermit identified himself as Giuseppe Bartoleoni, a shepherd from Maddalena—an island north of Sardinia. Carlo Alberto found this hard to believe. Most people of the time—especially peasants—were illiterate, but Giuseppe was fluent in several languages and extremely well educated. He was also the head of two families: one wife and children lived on another island, while a second wife and children lived on yet a third island. He sent for both to live with him in his new kingdom and, because he was sovereign, the Italian government failed in its attempt to prosecute him for bigamy. Paolo, his eldest son, was named his successor upon his father's death in the late 1840s. When Paolo died 50 years later, the inhabitants of Tavolara proclaimed a republic.

2. Patrick Watkins (*fl. c.* 1810), King of the Galapagos

Watkins, a redheaded Irish seaman, left his British whaling ship for the isolation of the Galapagos Islands off the coast of Ecuador. Crowning himself king, Patrick grew potatoes and pumpkins, which he sold to ships that stopped at the islands. He considered all of the Galapagos his domain and even pressed some unsuspecting sailors into slavery. To share his throne, he picked up a "queen" in Payta, Peru. Unfortunately, local police there found Patrick hiding on board a ship and put him in prison, where he eventually died.

3. Orélie-Antoine de Tounens (1825–78), King of Araucanía and Patagonia

De Tounens, an adventurous French lawyer, succeeded in winning the favour of the Araucanían Indians, a belligerent agrarian people of southern Chile. He was crowned Orélie-Antoine I. After a time, de Tounens was arrested and chased back to France. Upon his death, Antoine left the throne to his secretary, Gustave Achille Laviarde, who took the name Achille I and "ruled in exile" from Paris, where he became known as "Achille the Jovial."

4. David O'Keefe (d. 1901), King of Yap

In 1871 O'Keefe, an Irish immigrant who had settled in Savannah, Georgia, said goodbye to his wife and daughter and left for China. En route, he was shipwrecked on Yap, an island in the West Pacific Ocean, southwest of Guam. Adjusting well to island life, he acquired land from local chiefs and, in a few short years, became king. He even designed a royal emblem (an American flag waving over the letters "OK") and erected a mansion on a small island in the harbour. Not forgetting Mrs. O'Keefe, he sent money home to Savannah twice a year. His tranquil reign was upset one day when the tribal chiefs presented him with a suitable queen. Ever mindful of Mrs. O'Keefe, he tried to sidestep this bigamous marriage. But the chiefs were insistent. Reluctantly, King David accepted Queen Dollyboy—reluctantly at first, that is, since the royal couple eventually produced seven children. In 1901 O'Keefe sent word to wife number one that he was coming home. With two of his Yapese sons, he boarded the ship *Santa Cruz*. It was lost at sea.

5. Baron James A. Harden-Hickey (1854–98), King of Trinidad

"I propose to take possession of the Island of Trinidad under a maxim of international law which declares that anybody may seize and hold waste land that is not claimed by anybody else." So declared Baron Harden-Hickey—a Francophile American novelist, Catholic-turned-Buddhist/ Theosophist and author of a how-to book on suicide—in 1893 as he prepared to assume the throne as King James I. Although his kingdom was not *the* Trinidad in the West Indies, but rather a small uninhabited island 700 miles (1127 km) off the coast of Brazil, Harden-Hickey fully expected to be welcomed into the family of nations. But it was not to be. While Harden-Hickey recruited suitable subjects and issued fancy postage stamps and 1,000-franc bonds from a Manhattan office, Great Britain and Brazil haggled over possession of the South Atlantic rock. In 1896 Great Britain abandoned its claim. Brazil, assured of no further British occupation, left the island to the turtles. And lost in the shuffle was the would-be king, his crown gathering dust in a trunk. Two years later, Baron Harden-Hickey, taking a leaf from his own book, committed suicide in El Paso, Texas.

6. John Davis Murray (c. 1870–?), King of Christmas Island

In 1891 Murray, a mechanical engineer who graduated from Purdue University, went to work for the British-owned Phosphate Mining and Shipping Company. They first dispatched him to Christmas Island, southwest of Java, to oversee its phosphate mines. Since most of the miners were native islanders, it was decided that the surest way to get things done was to make Murray king, complete with full executive and judicial powers. In 1910, while in London, he met a young woman and decided to marry. The prospect of royal life on a remote island held little appeal for the bride, so King John dutifully relinquished his throne.

7. Carl Haffke (*fl.* 1900), King of the Ilocanos

A German immigrant, Haffke first found work as a Western Union messenger in Omaha, Nebraska. He later joined the navy and, serving under Admiral Dewey during the Spanish-American War, ended up in the Philippines, where he was a court stenographer. In due time, he became acquainted with various Ilocano chieftains. When a cholera epidemic wiped out the royal family, Haffke was offered the crown. He accepted, but not before making sure that the venture would turn a profit: he demanded up front a one-time six-figure tribute from the tribe, a 5% cut of all tribal profits and the customary royal perks, including servants. In exchange for this, he agreed to serve as sovereign, purchase farm machinery and teach the natives modern agricultural techniques. After a year on the throne, King Carlos I, longing for the Cornhusker State, visited his home. He looked up an old girlfriend while there and, failing to convince her of the charms of the Philippines, abdicated to practise law in Nebraska.

8. Edward Thompson (d. *c.* 1910), King of Naikeva

Dumped by his girlfriend in his hometown of Albion, Illinois, Thompson sought solace at sea and wound up in the Fijis. On Naikeva Island, he rebounded into the arms of Princess Lakanita, the king's daughter. Still, Thompson pressed on to other adventures on other islands. Then one day a messenger from Naikeva brought him word that insurgents on the island were threatening to topple the monarchy. Thompson hastily returned to Naikeva and joined the battle. Although the king died in action and Thompson was wounded, loyalists managed to put down the rebellion. While convalescing, Thompson rekindled his romance with Princess Lakanita and decided, after all, to settle down. Assuming the throne, he ruled Naikeva until his death 25 years later.

9. Faustin E. Wirkus (1897–1948), King of La Gonave

In 1925 Wirkus, a 28-year-old U.S. Marine Corps sergeant stationed in Haiti, volunteered for the post of district commander on the island of La Gonave, just 40 miles (64 km) from the mainland. The position entailed supervising the collection of taxes to be paid to the capital of Port-au-Prince. He was warned that his job would be complicated by the islanders' occult customs—including voodoo—but Wirkus was intent on his mission. When he landed, by an incredible coincidence, the people opened their hearts to him and proclaimed him King Faustin II. (It appeared that in 1849 a black man named Soulouque had become emperor of Haiti and its surrounding islands. He had declared himself King Faustin I. Why he chose the name Faustin, no one knows.) When Wirkus arrived on La Gonave, he learned from Queen Ti Memenne the legend that Faustin I would return. Even though Wirkus was white, the natives believed him to be the fulfillment of the prophecy and crowned him King Faustin II a few weeks later. Wirkus retained his post of district commander and his title of king for four years, until his duty was officially terminated in 1929. He returned to a hero's welcome in the U.S. in the early 1930s, lived in New York for a brief time, lecturing and writing about voodoo, and then rejoined the Marines when the Second World War began. He died of cancer in a New York military hospital.

—W.A.D. & L.O.

11 POSSIBLE ALTERNATIVE GUNMEN IN THE ASSASSINATION OF JOHN F. KENNEDY

According to the Warren Commission, Lee Harvey Oswald was the lone assassin in the killing of President Kennedy. However, a large majority of the public believes that the assassination was the result of a conspiracy. The CIA, the FBI, the Mafia, the military, pro-Castro Cubans and anti-Castro Cubans have all been cited as possible forces behind the scenes. Among the people accused of doing the actual shooting are the following.

1. Lucien Sarti and two Corsican hit men

According to jailed French mobster Christian David, Kennedy was shot by three Corsican assassins. David named the deceased Sarti as one of the gunmen and offered to reveal the identities of the others if he was given his freedom. According to David, the two unnamed assassins were in buildings to the rear of the president, while Sarti fired from the grassy knoll in front of the motorcade. The British television documentary *The Men Who Killed Kennedy* identified Sarti as the man in a police uniform apparently firing a rifle on the grassy knoll, visible in a computer-enhanced enlargement of a photo taken by Mary Moorman at the moment of the fatal shot.

2. Charles V. Harrelson

Harrelson—the father of actor Woody Harrelson—has been serving a life sentence since 1979 for murdering federal judge John H. Wood Jr. During a six-hour standoff before his arrest, Harrelson held a gun to his head and confessed to shooting Kennedy. He later retracted the statement, saying he had been high on cocaine at the time.

3. "Carlos" and others

Minister Raymond Broshears reported that David Ferrie—a bizarre individual often suspected of involvement in the assassination who had ties to Oswald, the CIA and the Mafia—would, after getting drunk, often talk about his role in the conspiracy. Ferrie reportedly said his job was to wait in Houston for two gunmen, one of them a Cuban exile Ferrie referred to as Carlos, and then fly them on the second leg of an escape route that was to take the assassins to South Africa via South America. Ferrie told Broshears the plan fell apart when the assassins, flying in a light plane, decided to skip the stop in Houston and press on to Mexico. They allegedly died when their plane crashed near Corpus Christi, Texas.

4. Luis Angel Castillo

According to assassination researcher Penn Jones, Castillo has stated under hypnosis that "he was on the parade route with a rifle that day . . . [with] instructions to shoot at a man in a car with red roses." Jackie Kennedy was the only person in the motorcade with red roses; all the other women had been given yellow Texas roses.

5. Eladio del Valle and Loran Hall

According to "Harry Dean" (the "war name" of a man who claims to be a former CIA agent), as quoted by W.B. Morris and R.B. Cutler in *Alias*

Oswald, the assassins were anti-Castro activists Hall and del Valle, who were hired by the John Birch Society. Although Hall says he was at his home in California on November 22, 1963, he allegedly told the *Dallas Morning News* in 1978 that, a month before the assassination, right-wing activists working with the CIA tried to recruit him for a plot to kill Kennedy. As for del Valle, he died under suspicious circumstances in 1967. Del Valle, who was being searched for as a possible witness in the Clay Shaw conspiracy trial, was discovered shot through the heart and with his head split open by a machete.

6. "Brother-in-Law" and "Slim"

In 1992 Kerry Thornley appeared on the television show *A Current Affair* and said he had been part of a conspiracy to kill President Kennedy. His co-conspirators were two men he called "Brother-in-Law" and "Slim." Thornley also denied having been responsible for framing Oswald, whom Thornley had befriended in the Marines: "I would gladly have killed Kennedy, but I would never have betrayed Oswald." He added, "I wanted [Kennedy] dead. I would have shot him myself." Thornley has also claimed that he and Oswald were the products of a genetic engineering experiment carried out by a secret neo-Nazi sect of eugenicists called the Vril Society, and that the two of them had been manipulated since childhood by Vril overlords.

7. Jean Rene Soutre

Soutre, a terrorist in the French Secret Army organization, is believed by some researchers to have been recruited by the CIA to serve as an assassin. According to CIA documents obtained under the Freedom of Information Act by researcher Mary Ferrell, French intelligence reported that Soutre was in Fort Worth on the morning of November 22, 1963, and in Dallas that afternoon. Soutre was picked up by U.S. authorities in Texas within 48 hours of the assassination and expelled from the country.

8. Roscoe White, "Saul" and "Lebanon"

In 1990 Ricky White claimed that his father Roscoe, a Dallas police officer, had been one of President Kennedy's assassins. According to Ricky, a detailed description of the conspiracy could be found in Roscoe's diary, which had disappeared after it was taken by the FBI for inspection. Two other gunmen, referred to in the diary only by the code names "Saul" and "Lebanon," were also involved. In addition, Roscoe's widow, Geneva, told journalist Ron Laytner that she had overheard Roscoe and Jack Ruby plotting to kill Kennedy, adding, "We at first thought the assassination was more Mob [but later realized] it was more CIA." Fifteen years before Ricky and Geneva White went public, Hugh McDonald, in *Appointment in Dallas*, identified one of the killers as a professional assassin known as Saul. McDonald claimed to have tracked down Saul, who admitted to having been paid $50,000 (U.S.) to shoot the president. Saul claimed to have fired from the Dallas County Records Building— which was also described in Roscoe White's diary as one of the locations the assassins had shot from. Despite these similarities, there are some inconsistencies in the plots described by McDonald and Ricky White. Most notably, Roscoe White in his diary and Saul in his meeting with McDonald each allegedly claimed to have fired the fatal shot.

9. George Hickey Jr.

According to Bonar Menninger's book *Mortal Error*—based on 25 years of research by ballistics expert Howard Donahue—Kennedy was accidentally killed by Hickey, a secret service agent in the car behind the presidential limo. According to this theory, when Oswald began shooting, Hickey reached for his rifle and slipped off the safety. As he tried to stand in the back seat of the car to return fire, he lost his balance and accidentally pulled the trigger, firing the shot that killed the president. Hickey himself told the Warren Commission that he did not even pick up his rifle until after the fatal shot.

10. Frank Sturgis and Operation 40

Marita Lorenz, a CIA operative who had been Fidel Castro's mistress, told the *New York Daily News* in 1977 that she had accompanied Lee Harvey Oswald and an assassination squad to Dallas a few days before Kennedy was killed. She identified her companions on the trip as CIA operative (and future Watergate burglar) Frank Sturgis and four Cuban exiles: Orlando Bosch, Pedro Diaz Lang and two brothers named Novis. The men were members of "Operation 40," a group of about 30 anti-Castro Cubans and their American advisers originally formed by the CIA in

1960 for the Bay of Pigs invasion. Lorenz later stated that Sturgis had been one of the actual gunmen and that he told her after the assassination, "You could have been part of it—you know, part of history. You should have stayed. It was safe. Everything was covered in advance. No arrests, no real newspaper investigation. It was all covered, very professional." Sturgis denies that there is any truth to Lorenz's story. However, he once said that the FBI questioned him about the assassination right after it happened, because, the agents said, "Frank, if there's anybody capable of killing the President of the United States, you're the guy who can do it."

11. James Files and Charles Nicoletti

In 1996 Files claimed that he and Nicoletti, a Mafia hit man, had been on the grassy knoll at Dealey Plaza and that they had both shot President Kennedy at the same time. Files said that he was paid $30,000 (U.S.) and had orders not to hit Jacqueline Kennedy. He added that Nicoletti took his order from Sam "Momo" Giancana, who in turn answered to Anthony "Big Tuna" Accardo. Since all three mobsters were murdered between 1975 and 1977, there was no one to corroborate Files's story. The FBI dismissed the story, noting that Files is now serving a 50-year sentence in Illinois for murdering a policeman and thus had little to lose by "confessing," while gaining his 15 minutes of fame.

—C.F.

WHAT 13 ASSASSINATION VICTIMS HAD PLANNED FOR THE REST OF THE DAY

1. Gaius Julius Caesar (100–44 BC)

Roman statesman and soldier Julius Caesar was assassinated in a hall of Pompey's Theatre in Rome by a group of 60 conspirators led by Marcus Junius Brutus and Gaius Cassius Longinus on March 15, 44 BC. In the street a few minutes earlier, a Greek logic teacher named Artemidorus had handed Caesar a note, warning him that it should be read immediately. But Caesar had put it aside. The unread note cautioned him that assassins planned to attack him as he entered the hall. At the theatre, Caesar had expected to attend a meeting of the Roman senate, where he and his followers were to speak in favour of his being crowned king of Rome.

2. Abraham Lincoln (1809–65)

President Lincoln was shot at Ford's Theater in Washington, D.C., by John Wilkes Booth at 10:15 p.m. on Good Friday, April 14, 1865; he died the next day. Lincoln had intended to watch the play *Our American Cousin* and then be introduced to the cast. From the theatre, he and Mrs. Lincoln, accompanied by two young friends—Major Henry Rathbone and the major's fiancée, Clara Harris—were to return to the White House for a small party, at which refreshments would be served as the president had missed supper that evening.

3. Thomas D'Arcy McGee (1825–68)

Thomas D'Arcy McGee was shot and killed in the early hours of Tuesday, April 7, 1868, in front of his rooming house on Sparks Street in downtown Ottawa. Earlier that evening, McGee had delivered a rousing speech in the House of Commons in defence of Confederation. It had been well received by his colleagues in the chamber and the roughly 500 spectators who had witnessed it in the gallery. McGee left Parliament that evening feeling tired, but exhilarated. He was looking forward to a good night's sleep. In a few days it would be his 43rd birthday, and he was planning to travel to Montreal to celebrate with family and friends.

4. James Garfield (1831–81)

President Garfield was shot at the Baltimore and Potomac train depot in Washington, D.C., by Charles J. Guiteau at 9:30 a.m. on July 2, 1881; he died on September 19. Shot while preparing to leave the capital for the Fourth of July holidays, President Garfield had arranged to take the 9:30 train to Elberon, New Jersey, where his wife, Lucretia, and their sons Harry and James were to join him before he proceeded to Williams College in Williamstown, Massachusetts. Garfield was to observe the 25th anniversary of his graduation and enrol his sons in the college's freshman class, after which he expected to spend the evening as an overnight guest at the home of Cyrus Field, the entrepreneur who developed the first transatlantic cable.

5. William McKinley (1843–1901)

President McKinley was shot at the Temple of Music at the Pan-American Exposition in Buffalo, New York, by Leon Czolgosz at 4:07 p.m. on

September 6, 1901; he died on September 14. Shot during a public handshaking reception, President McKinley had intended to leave three minutes later and take his private carriage to the John Milburn mansion, where he was staying while in Buffalo. That night, McKinley was looking forward to one of those rarities in a president's life, an unscheduled evening of privacy with his wife and a few friends. Before retiring that night, he would have done some packing, since he was returning to his family home in Canton, Ohio, the next morning.

6. Emiliano Zapata (1877–1919)

The Mexican revolutionary leader was assassinated at Chinameca hacienda near Cuautla, Mexico, by soldiers commanded by Colonel Jesús Guajardo, at 2:10 p.m. on April 10, 1919. Zapata, who was ambushed while riding into the hacienda, had planned to share a dinner of tacos and beer with the treacherous Colonel Guajardo, who, with his 50th Regiment, had tricked Zapata into believing he was defecting from the Mexican federal government. (Actually, Guajardo's sole purpose was to lure Zapata into a trap.) After dinner, Zapata had intended to negotiate the final details of the new alliance and to obtain 12,000 rounds of ammunition for his men. After officially announcing the new partnership, Zapata would have returned to his guerrilla camp at Sauces, 2 miles (3 km) to the south.

7. Leon Trotsky (1877–1940)

The exiled Russian revolutionary leader was attacked at his home in Mexico City by Jaime Ramón Mercader just before 6:00 p.m. on August 20, 1940. Trotsky was reading an article that Mercader had written. Trotsky died the next day. He had expected to have dinner with his wife, Natalia, and possibly would have invited Mercader to join them. After dinner, Trotsky would have studied some recently published French economic statistics and written a few pages of an article on Stalin that was to be published in *Harper's Magazine*.

8. Mohandas K. Gandhi (1869–1948)

Indian independence leader Mahatma Gandhi was assassinated in New Delhi, India, by Hindu fanatic Nathuram Godse at 5:13 p.m. on January 30, 1948. Gandhi was killed upon arriving in the Birla House gardens, where he was supposed to lead a prayer meeting attended by several hundred of his followers. After the religious ceremonies, he was to return to the home of Ghanshyam Das Birla, his host in New Delhi. That evening, Gandhi had intended to follow his usual evening routine, which consisted of talking to his relatives and followers for a short time before a session of reading and writing. At about 9:00 p.m., he would have had his nightly enema before going to bed.

9. Rafael Leonidas Trujillo Molina (1891–1961)

The dictator of the Dominican Republic was assassinated on the highway between Ciudad Trujillo and San Cristóbal by seven men in two automobiles at approximately 10:15 p.m. on May 30, 1961. When hit by machine-gun bullets, Trujillo was on his way to one of his immense ranches, Estancia Fundación, where he was to spend the night. Awaiting his arrival was at least one of his mistresses. In fact, he may well have been looking forward to an orgy that night. These frequently involved as many as 40 women, who were supplied by a government official whose fee was 10% of all funds allocated for public works.

10. John F. Kennedy (1917–63)

President Kennedy was assassinated in Dealey Plaza in Dallas, Texas, at 12:30 p.m. on November 22, 1963. After the motorcade—during which he was shot—Kennedy was scheduled to speak at the new Trade Mart building and then to fly to Bergstrom Air Force Base near Austin, Texas, where the coach of the University of Texas Longhorns was to present him with a team-autographed football. In Austin, a second motorcade was planned, to be followed by a Democratic fundraising banquet for which 8,000 steaks had been prepared. Presidential advance man Bill Moyers had found out too late that the menu featured steaks—a highly inappropriate selection for a Catholic president's Friday night dinner. Kennedy had agreed to take a helicopter from Austin to the LBJ Ranch, near Johnson City, Texas, where he was to spend the night. To entertain Kennedy that evening, Vice President Lyndon Johnson had organized a whip-cracking and sheepherding demonstration.

11. Martin Luther King Jr. (1929–68)

Dr. King was assassinated at the Lorraine Motel in Memphis, Tennessee, by James Earl Ray just after 6:00 p.m. on April 4, 1968. When he was shot, King was leaving his room on his way to a soul-food dinner at the home of the Reverend Samuel (Billy) Kyles. Accompanying King were his friends and supporters, including Dr. Ralph Abernathy, the Reverend Jesse Jackson, the Reverend Andrew Young and lawyer Chauncey Eskridge. King had also promised to attend an evening rally in support of the striking garbage collectors of Local 1733. He had requested that Ben Branch, the lead singer of the Breadbasket Band, which was providing the evening's entertainment, sing "Precious Lord" at the rally.

12. Robert F. Kennedy (1925–68)
The Democratic presidential candidate was shot at the Ambassador Hotel in Los Angeles, California, by Sirhan Sirhan and possibly a second gunman at 12:15 a.m. on June 5, 1968; he died the following day. Kennedy was shot while walking through a corridor off the kitchen on his way to the hotel's Colonial Room for a press conference following his victory in the California Democratic primary election. After that, he had planned to return to his room, suite 511, where several dozen celebrities were awaiting him. Once freshened up, he would have gone with his friends and supporters—including Roosevelt "Rosie" Grier, Rafer Johnson and Pierre Salinger—to the Factory, an exclusive and very chic Los Angeles discotheque.

13. Faisal ibn Abd al-Aziz ibn Saud (1905–75)
King Faisal was assassinated before noon on March 25, 1975, in the Ri'Assa Palace in Riyadh, Saudi Arabia. The assassin was his nephew, ibn Musad Abd al-Aziz. At the time, the king was preparing to meet with a Kuwaiti delegation, which included that nation's oil minister. Matters concerning both nations—such as a territorial dispute over a tract of oil-rich desert—were to be discussed. Also, since it was the birthday of the Prophet Mohammed, Faisal had planned to hold the traditional *majlis*, an open court in which any Saudi Arabian, aristocrat or peasant, could have an audience with the king and ask a personal favour of him.

—R.J.F. & Cdn. Eds.

10 LITTLE-KNOWN FACTS ABOUT R.B. BENNETT

Richard Bedford Bennett (1870–1947) was Canada's prime minister between 1930 and 1935, during the darkest days of the Great Depression. It is hard to imagine that any leader could have achieved much success navigating the ship of state through those dangerous waters, but R.B. Bennett was a singularly unlikable politician. By the time he left office, he was as unpopular as any prime minister before or since. In public, Bennett was widely viewed as uncompromising, unfeeling, imperious, arrogant and rude. The private R.B. Bennett was a kinder, gentler man than his public image would suggest, but he was still, by all accounts, a very unusual man. How unusual? Well, unlike his great political rival and fellow oddball William Lyon Mackenzie King, Bennett did not keep copious diaries, so we do not know as much about his eccentricities as we do about King's. But while R.B. Bennett may not have conducted séances with the dead, he was unquestionably a strange duck in his own unique way. Here's a glimpse inside the hidden world of R.B. Bennett.

1. He promised his mother when he was a child that he would never drink alcohol or smoke, and he never did. Later in life, he would allow sherry to be included in his consommé because he believed that the heat had burned off the alcohol.

2. He had no interest in games, sports, athletics, dancing, hobbies or amusements of any kind.

3. He never went to sleep without first reading a chapter from the Bible.

4. He never married and as a youth showed little interest in sex. According to a document found in the archives of the Conservative Party, it appears he may have suffered from a condition called "phimosis," which caused his foreskin to be wrapped so tightly around his penis that it was painful for him to have an erection. He may have had this condition treated in later life.

5. He preferred to live in expensive hotels rather than houses or apartments. After moving to Calgary in 1897, he checked into the Alberta Hotel and stayed there until 1923, when he moved into suite 759 of the

Palliser Hotel. He maintained that suite until he left for England in 1939. When he entered federal politics and moved to Ottawa, he took up permanent residence at the Château Laurier hotel.

6. Despite his reputation for not caring about the poor, he was actually very generous and gave away lots of money to people who wrote him seeking help. He also gave each of the 178 employees of the Palliser Hotel a box of chocolates at Christmastime.

7. In 1937 he fell madly in love with the widowed mother of future prime minister John Turner. He sent her a dozen roses every day and unsuccessfully tried to convince her to marry him.

8. He was very self-conscious about his clothes. He dressed like a turn-of-the-century banker, favouring a top hat, striped pants and morning coat. He purposely gained weight so as to better fill out his clothes and more closely conform to his carefully cultivated image of a stuffed shirt.

9. He was obsessed with negative press coverage and intensely disliked the ink-stained wretches of the parliamentary press gallery. In 1928, concerned about his lack of favourable coverage in Saskatchewan, he quietly arranged for the purchase of the *Regina Daily Star* to provide a pro-Conservative voice for the province. But the paper was a financial disaster, and Bennett occasionally wound up having to meet the payroll out of his own pocket.

10. He carried on a rather public flirtation with Agnes Macphail, the only female member of the House of Commons. "You have very nice ankles, Agnes," he once said *sotto voce* as she walked past him. For her part, Macphail much preferred Bennett to Mackenzie King, whom she described as a "fat man full of words." And although it is undeniably true that politics makes strange bedfellows, the ultra-conservative prime minister from the country clubs of Calgary and the CCF member from rural Ontario would have made an unlikely couple indeed.

10 SECRET ARMIES OF THE CIA

1. Peruvian Regiment

Unable to quell guerrilla forces in its eastern Amazonian provinces, Peru called on the U.S. for help in the mid-1960s. The CIA responded by establishing a fortified camp in the area and hiring local Peruvians, who were trained by Green Beret personnel on loan from the U.S. Army. After crushing the guerrillas, the elite unit was disbanded because of fears it might stage a coup against the government.

2. Congo Mercenary Force

In 1964, during the Congolese Civil War, the CIA established an army in the Congo to back pro-Western leaders Cyril Adoula and Joseph Mobutu. The CIA imported European mercenaries and Cuban pilots—exiles from Cuba—to pilot the CIA air force, composed of transports and B-26 bombers.

3. The Cambodian Coup

For over 15 years the CIA had tried various unsuccessful means of deposing Cambodia's left-leaning Prince Norodom Sihanouk, including assassination attempts. However, in March 1970 a CIA-backed coup finally did the job. Funded by U.S. tax dollars, armed with U.S. weapons and trained by American Green Berets, anti-Sihanouk forces called Kampuchea Khmer Krom (KKK) overran the capital of Phnom Penh and took control of the government. With the blessing of the CIA and the Nixon administration, control of Cambodia was placed in the hands of Lon Nol, who would later distinguish himself by dispatching soldiers to butcher tens of thousands of civilians.

4. Kurd Rebels

During the early 1970s the CIA moved into eastern Iraq to organize and supply the Kurds of that area, who were rebelling against the pro-Soviet Iraqi government. The real purpose behind this action was to help the Shah of Iran settle a border dispute with Iraq favourably. After an Iran–Iraq settlement was reached, the CIA withdrew its support from the Kurds, who were then crushed by the Iraqi army.

5. Angola Mercenary Force

In 1975, after years of bloody fighting and civil unrest in Angola, Portugal resolved to relinquish its hold on the last of its African colonies. The transition was to take place on November 11, with control of the country going to whichever political faction controlled the capital city of Luanda on that date. In the months preceding the change, three groups vied for power: the Popular Movement for the Liberation of Angola (MPLA), the National Front for the Liberation of Angola (FNLA) and the National Union for the Total Independence of Angola (UNITA). By July 1975 the Marxist MPLA had ousted the moderate FNLA and UNITA from Luanda, so the CIA decided to intervene covertly. Over $30 million (U.S.) was spent on the Angolan operation, the bulk of the money going to buy arms and pay French and South African mercenaries, who aided the FNLA and UNITA in their fight. Despite overwhelming evidence to the contrary, U.S. officials categorically denied any involvement in the Angolan conflict. In the end, it was a fruitless military adventure, for the MPLA assumed power and controls Angola to this day.

6. Afghan Mujahedin

Covert support for the groups fighting against the Soviet invasion of Afghanistan began under President Jimmy Carter in 1979, and was stepped up during the administration of Ronald Reagan. The operation succeeded in its initial goal, as the Soviets were forced to begin withdrawing their forces in 1987. Unfortunately, once the Soviets left, the U.S. essentially ignored Afghanistan as it collapsed into a five-year civil war followed by the rise of the ultra-fundamentalist Taliban. The Taliban provided a haven for Osama bin Laden and al-Qaeda, the perpetrators of the 9/11 terrorist attacks in 2001.

7. Salvadoran Death Squads

As far back as 1964 the CIA helped form ORDEN and ANSESAL, two paramilitary intelligence networks that developed into the Salvadoran death squads. The CIA trained ORDEN leaders in the use of automatic weapons and surveillance techniques, and placed several leaders on the CIA payroll. The CIA also provided detailed intelligence on Salvadoran individuals later murdered by the death squads. During the civil war in El Salvador from 1980 to 1992, the death squads were responsible for

40,000 killings. Even after a public outcry forced President Reagan to denounce the death squads in 1984, CIA support continued.

8. Nicaraguan Contras

On November 23, 1981, President Ronald Reagan signed a top secret National Security Directive authorizing the CIA to spend $19 million (U.S.) to recruit and support the Contras, opponents of Nicaragua's Sandinista government. In supporting the Contras, the CIA carried out several acts of sabotage without the Congressional intelligence committees giving consent—or even being informed beforehand. In response, Congress passed the Boland Amendment, prohibiting the CIA from providing aid to the Contras. Attempts to find alternate sources of funds led to the Iran-Contra scandal. It may also have led the CIA and the Contras to become actively involved in drug smuggling. In 1988 the Senate Subcommittee on Narcotics, Terrorism, and International Operations concluded that individuals in the Contra movement engaged in drug trafficking; that known drug traffickers provided assistance to the Contras; and that "there are some serious questions as to whether or not U.S. officials involved in Central America failed to address the drug issue for fear of jeopardizing the war effort against Nicaragua."

9. Haitian Coups

In 1988 the CIA attempted to intervene in Haiti's elections with a "covert action program" to undermine the campaign of the eventual winner, Jean-Bertrand Aristide. Three years later, Aristide was overthrown in a bloody coup that killed more than 4,000 civilians. Many of the leaders of the coup had been on the CIA payroll since the mid-1980s. For example, Emmanuel "Toto" Constant, the head of FRAPH, a brutal gang of thugs known for murder, torture and beatings, admitted to being a paid agent of the CIA. Similarly, the CIA-created Haitian National Intelligence Service (NIS), supposedly created to combat drugs, functioned during the coup as a "political intimidation and assassination squad." In 1994 an American force of 20,000 was sent to Haiti to allow Aristide to return. Ironically, even after this, the CIA continued working with FRAPH and the NIS. In 2004 Aristide was overthrown once again, with Aristide claiming that U.S. forces had kidnapped him.

10. Venezuelan Coup Attempt

On April 11, 2002, Venezuelan military leaders attempted to overthrow the country's democratically elected left-wing president, Hugo Chávez. The coup collapsed after two days, as hundreds of thousands of people took to the streets and as units of the military joined with the protestors. The administration of George W. Bush was the only democracy in the western hemisphere not to condemn the coup attempt. According to intelligence analyst Wayne Madsen, the CIA had actively organized the coup: "The CIA provided Special Operations Group personnel, headed by a lieutenant colonel on loan from the U.S. Special Operations Command at Fort Bragg, North Carolina, to help organize the coup against Chávez."

—R.J.F. & C.F.

MARGARET MACMILLAN'S 12 FAVOURITE 20TH-CENTURY DIPLOMATIC INCIDENTS

Margaret MacMillan's *Paris 1919* won the Samuel Johnson Prize, the PEN Hessell Tiltman Prize and the 2003 Governor General's Literary Award for Non-Fiction. She is provost of Trinity College and professor of history at the University of Toronto, and is currently at work on a book about Richard Nixon in China.

1. Nikita Khrushchev's shoe

At the United Nations in the fall of 1960, Krushchev heckled and jeered and leapt to his feet at every opportunity to rail against the West. When the representative from the Philippines suggested that the Soviet Union was scarcely in a position to talk about imperialism, given its own record in Eastern Europe, the shoe came off and an enraged Khrushchev banged the desk in front of him. Khrushchev, who actually turned out to be a reasonable man, looked like everyone's image of the brutish Soviet leader.

2. Mussolini's boat

As the European statesmen gathered in Locarno in 1925 to sign a far-reaching agreement to bring peace to Europe, Mussolini astonished them all by arriving in Locarno at the wheel of a fast speedboat, splashing many of the onlookers. His aim was to show the virility and modernity of the new Fascist movement and its leader. In the 1920s, though, Mussolini was still prepared to work with the European democracies. In the 1930s his grandiose ambitions to shine on the world stage and to build a second Roman Empire led him and his unfortunate country into the arms of Nazi Germany.

3. Arafat's choice

In November 1974, over the objections of the United States, Israel and their allies, Yasser Arafat, the chairman of the Palestinian Liberation Organization, was invited to speak to the UN's General Assembly. With his head covered by his checked keffiyeh, wearing his usual dark glasses and a gun holster, he asked the world to decide whether it wanted an olive branch or a freedom fighter's gun. Arafat had wanted to bring the gun as well, but that was not allowed in the UN so he had to make do with the holster.

4. Stalin's toast

The German-Soviet non-aggression pact of 1939 signalled the start of another European war. Its secret clauses, which only became public after the war, divided up the centre of Europe between the two totalitarian regimes. Hitler now had a free hand to turn on Poland, which Britain and France had promised to defend. After Joachim von Ribbentrop, a smooth-talking former champagne salesman turned German foreign minister, and Vyacheslav Molotov, his dour Russian counterpart, had signed the pact, Stalin held a late night celebration dinner in the Kremlin. Ribbentrop congratulated the Soviet dictator on his 60th birthday. Stalin replied with a toast to Hitler, and spoke warmly of the friendship between the Germans and the Russians, "forged," as he put it, "in blood."

5. De Gaulle's mischief

In 1967, the French president, Charles de Gaulle, came to Canada, ostensibly to share in the nation's centenary celebrations. As he entered the Hôtel de Ville in Montreal, he told the mayor, Jean Drapeau, that he wished to address the crowd from the balcony. None of his party, including the French ambassador to Canada, knew that the old man intended to declaim the separatist slogan, "Vive le Québec libre." The Liberal government of Lester Pearson, in an un-Canadian display of anger, declared de Gaulle's statement "unacceptable."

6. Chamberlain's piece of paper

In September 1938, Neville Chamberlain flew to Munich in a last-ditch effort to dissuade Hitler from invading Czechoslovakia. Britain and France, both of which still hoped that appeasing Hitler would prevent a general European war, persuaded a reluctant Czech government to hand over the Sudetenland, where the German minority lived. Hitler, who had already swallowed up Austria, now acquired a valuable strategic territory and many of Czechoslovakia's industrial plants. The British prime minister got Hitler to sign a declaration stating that both countries intended to avoid war with each other and to settle their differences peacefully. When Chamberlain landed in England, he waved the piece of paper at the waiting reporters. He was bringing back, so he hoped, "peace in our time." He was wrong, of course. Hitler had no intention of keeping his promise. Nor did he intend, in spite of what he had said, to leave what was left of Czechoslovakia in peace. A year later, Europe was at war.

7. The Yalta photograph

The last time the three great Allied leaders of the Second World War met was in the Crimean resort town of Yalta. The photograph shows a gaunt Roosevelt (he was dead two months later) between Churchill and Stalin. All three men are smiling, but in reality the conference was a difficult one that foreshadowed the breakup of the Grand Alliance and the beginning of the Cold War. While Roosevelt talked hopefully of the new United Nations, Churchill did his best to plead for independence for the countries in the centre of Europe. Stalin gave vague and, in the end, worthless assurances. With his armies occupying the centre of Europe, the Soviet Union started to consolidate its grip on countries such as Poland and Czechoslovakia.

8. Kennedy's visit to West Berlin

The East Germans took the West by surprise when they threw up the wall between East and West Berlin one night in August 1961. Although the United States and its allies considered a military response, they did nothing. President Kennedy, though, went to West Berlin the following year and told the enthusiastic crowds, "Ich bin ein Berliner." The "ein" was a mistake, and his carefully memorized sentence translated as "I am a jelly doughnut."

9. Dulles's snub

The Geneva conference of 1954, which was supposed to wrap up the Korean War and settle the fate of French Indochina, was one of the first times that representatives of the new People's Republic of China appeared on the international stage. As Chou Enlai, the urbane Chinese foreign minister, advanced towards John Foster Dulles with his hand outstretched, the American secretary of state cut him off. The Chinese did not forget the snub; when President Nixon went to Beijing in 1972, he had to assure the Chinese that this time there would be a handshake.

10. The ambassador's tears

On August 2, 1914, Count Friedrich von Pourtalès, the German ambassador in St. Petersburg, delivered Germany's declaration of war on Russia. German troops were already moving towards Belgium and France; Austria-Hungary was preparing to invade Serbia; and the British were under intense pressure to support France and Russia. The general European war, which had threatened to explode for so long, was under way. Pourtalès, who had never believed that Russia and Germany would go to war, wept as he handed over the declaration to the Russian foreign minister.

11. Sadat's trip

In 1977, the Egyptian president, Anwar Sadat, stunned his fellow Arabs and the world when he declared that he was ready to go to the ends of the earth, even to Israel itself, in the cause of peace. That November, he flew to Ben Gurion Airport, the first Arab statesman to pay an official visit to the Jewish state. At the Knesset, Sadat pleaded for an end to the bloodshed that had destroyed so many Arab and Jewish lives. Israel had a right to exist, he affirmed, at peace with its neighbours, as a state in the Middle East. Two years later Egypt and Israel signed a peace treaty. In 1981 Sadat paid the ultimate price for his courage: an Islamic fundamentalist assassinated him.

12. Clemenceau's revenge

The great Hall of Mirrors in Louis XIVs palace at Versailles has seen many events in the long struggle between Germans and French for control of Europe. In 1871, in the aftermath of a French defeat, the new

German Reich was proclaimed there and the King of Prussia crowned as the German emperor. In 1919, at the end of the First World War, Georges Clemenceau arranged for German delegates to come to the Hall of Mirrors to sign the Treaty of Versailles, which marked, for a time, Germany's defeat by France and its allies.

CHAPTER 10   PLACES

ABOVE: *The giant horse ankle bone of Macklin, Saskatchewan*

DAVE PHILLIPS'S 14 MOST UNBELIEVABLE CANADIAN WEATHER EVENTS OF ALL TIME

Dave Phillips is the go-to guy in this country when it comes to talking about the weather. A long-time employee of Environment Canada, Phillips is a tireless and devoted collector of anecdotes and data.

1. The power of storm surge

Two days after a severe storm that struck the Maritimes in January 2000, it was discovered that two cottages at Tatamagouche Bay, Nova Scotia, had been lifted from their foundations, turned around and deposited hundreds of yards down the beach. One cottage owner said, "We had bottles on a shelf over the kitchen cabinets. None of the bottles had fallen off. They were still sitting there."

2. Seeing is believing

Frigid weather persisted across the Prairies in January 1996. Near Stavely, Alberta, a farmer used duct tape on the ears of his newborn calves so their ears wouldn't fall off. In Vanscoy, Saskatchewan, Pepper the dog got his tongue stuck to an electric frying pan as he gobbled up food. He was spotted running home with the pan hanging from his tongue.

3. Is it cold enough for you?

Snag, Yukon Territory, recorded the lowest temperature ever observed in Canada, −81°F (−63°C), on February 2, 1947. In fact, it was the coldest moment in North America. It was so cold that axes bounced off ice, metal snapped in half and wood became petrified. The freezing of one's breath produced hissing, and dental fillings popped out. A layer of fog hovered above the dog teams. If you ventured outside, your nose hairs became icicles, and any deep breathing scaled your throat and lungs. It was so cold that a pan of warm water, when thrown in the air, made a hissing sound and froze into wheat-sized kernels of ice before it hit the ground.

4. Is it wet enough for you?

On May 30, 1961, the most intense rainstorm ever in Canada, 10 inches (250 mm) in under one hour, occurred at Buffalo Gap, Saskatchewan. Accompanied by heavy hail and strong winds, the torrents of water washed out roads, eroded fields and even peeled bark from several large trees. The land was stripped clean of soil and vegetation. Strong winds moved an empty boxcar upgrade 180 feet (55 m).

5. Is it snowy enough for you?
Two days before Canada Day in 1963, a remarkable one-day snowfall of 44 inches (111.8 cm) occurred at Livingston Ranger Station, Alberta. For several years this stood as the greatest all-time one-day snowfall ever recorded in Canada.

6. End-of-the-world weather
As a result of a wind-driven ice jam near Buffalo, Niagara Falls ran dry in late March 1848. The sudden silence startled hundreds from their sleep and filled churches with those who feared the end of the world. Others walked out onto the riverbed to hunt for artifacts. By April 1 the river and the falls had returned to normal.

7. A dog changes his spots
A lightning bolt played an unkind prank on a collie dog owned by a resident near Burnt River, Ontario. The lightning hit the house chimney, ripped apart the rafters, bulged a metal ceiling, tore off plaster, then followed a telephone wire to the woodshed, where the owner was splitting wood—his dog at his side. The bolt then circled near the dog and flipped him on his back. The white dog was scorched a dark brown.

8. Weather survivor
A farmer about 50 miles (80 km) north of Edmonton, Alberta, lost a market-sized hog during a January 1956 blizzard. While trying to locate a hog trough, the farmer thought he saw the snow move near a mound of hay. He dug into the snowbank and the long-lost pig finally wiggled clear. Its weight had dropped from about 243 pounds (110 kg) to 75 pounds (34 kg) during its 93-day imprisonment, but it did manage to make its own way to the pig shed.

9. Back from the dead
On August 3, 1916, a tornado levelled crops and destroyed several large barns near Wynyard, Saskatchewan. One farmer was caught under his barn when a huge beam fell on his chest. Neighbours rescued him, but

the local doctor pronounced him dead. His obituary appeared in the next edition of the local newspaper. However, 13 hours later, he regained consciousness and eventually lived to be almost 80 years old.

10. Tornado prank
A powerful wind and driving rainstorm on June 7, 1933, played queer pranks in southern Ontario. In Woodstock, a farmer was trying to close his barn's double doors when the wind suddenly slammed them shut, cutting off his ear. Another resident found the linoleum from his kitchen floor in the next lot, despite it having been beneath a heavy stove. The wind carried a veranda from one house to the front lawn of another, whose owner lost a garage.

11. Tornado prank 2
A tornado struck Aubigny, Manitoba, on June 19, 1978. One town resident lost her freezer. It ended up in the basement of another house—without the meat. Another resident reported, "The last time I saw our outhouse it was going down the front street as fast as you please."

12. Raining wild ducks
It didn't rain "cats and dogs" in Banff, Alberta, on June 5, 1932—it rained wild ducks. During a brief but heavy rainstorm, a night flight of wild ducks was forced down, and they mistook the illuminated asphalt and oiled roads for streams. Many birds crashed, breaking their necks. The next morning, children reaped a harvest of dimes by collecting and selling the dead birds to a local taxidermist.

13. Wrong place at the wrong time
On July 9, 1926, lightning struck the chimney of the Orange Hall in Rednersville, Ontario, instantly killing a father and son and injuring 30 others. The son had just been initiated into the Orange Lodge when the terrific bolt of lightning hit. Remarkably, father and son were sitting on opposite sides of the room, 33 feet (10 m) apart, when they were struck simultaneously. Not a mark of any kind was found on them.

14. The year without summer

Following a summer of snow, ice and killing frost in eastern North America, the first two weeks of September 1816 turned warm. But by mid-month cold weather returned. Many people believed the sun had cooled and the end of the world was near. One man near Stanstead, Quebec, killed his livestock and hanged himself rather than wait for "a slow death by freezing."

10 UNUSUAL CANADIAN PLACE NAMES THAT START WITH THE LETTER "B"

1. Blow Me Down, Newfoundland
2. Bummers' Roost, Ontario
3. Buzwah, Ontario
4. Birdtail, Manitoba
5. Biggar, Saskatchewan
6. Buffalo Head Prairie, Alberta
7. Baldy Hughes, British Columbia
8. Bella Bella, British Columbia
9. Blubber Bay, British Columbia
10. Burnt Flat, British Columbia

YANN MARTEL'S 15 SHIPWRECK SURVIVAL TIPS

This list is from Yann Martel's Man Booker Prize—winning novel, *Life of Pi*.

1. Always read instructions carefully.
2. Do not drink urine. Or sea water. Or bird blood.
3. Do not eat jellyfish. Or fish that are armed with spikes. Or that have parrot-like beaks. Or that puff up like balloons.
4. Pressing the eyes of fish will paralyze them.
5. The body can be a hero in battle. If a castaway is injured, beware of well-meaning but ill-founded medical treatment. Ignorance is the worst doctor, while rest and sleep are the best nurses.
6. Put up your feet at least five minutes every hour.
7. Unnecessary exertion should be avoided. But an idle mind tends to sink, so the mind should be kept occupied with whatever light

distraction may suggest itself. Playing card games, Twenty Questions and I Spy with My Little Eye are excellent forms of simple recreation. Community singing is another surefire way to lift the spirits. Yarn spinning is also highly recommended.

8. Green water is shallower than blue water.

9. Beware of far-off clouds that look like mountains. Look for green. Ultimately, a foot is the only good judge of land.

10. Do not go swimming. It wastes energy. Besides, a survival craft may drift faster than you can swim. Not to mention the danger of sea life. If you are hot, wet your clothes instead.

11. Do not urinate in your clothes. The momentary warmth is not worth the nappy rash.

12. Shelter yourself. Exposure can kill faster than thirst or hunger.

13. So long as no excessive water is lost through perspiration, the body can survive up to 14 days without water. If you feel thirsty, suck a button.

14. Turtles are an easy catch and make for excellent meals. Their blood is a good, nutritious, salt-free drink; their flesh is tasty and filling; their fat has many uses; and the castaway will find turtle eggs a real treat. Mind the beak and the claws.

15. Don't let your morale flag. Be daunted, but not defeated. Remember: the spirit, above all else, counts. If you have the will to live, you will. Good luck!

(Note that urine has on occasion been found to have positive health properties in emergency situations. —The Eds.)

28 FAILED NAMES FOR CANADA

Canada comes from the Huron-Iroquois word *kanata*, which means "village" or "settlement." Jacques Cartier first heard it in reference to Quebec City, but it was soon used to refer to the whole region. Looking back, *Canada* seems like an obvious pick for our country, but that was not the case in 1867, when the Fathers of Confederation went looking for a name. Many suggestions were made, but fiery Member of Parliament Thomas D'Arcy McGee made the case for adopting *Canada* on February 9, 1865, when he pointed out that the alternatives were absurd: "Now I would ask any Hon. Member of the House how he would feel if he woke up some fine morning and found himself, instead of a Canadian, a Tuponian or Hochelagander?" His words rang true, evidently, and on July 1, 1867, when the British North America Act was declared, the name Canada was formally adopted. Here is a list of the names for Canada that were suggested and rejected:

1.	Acadia	15.	Laurentia
2.	Albertland	16.	Mesopelagia
3.	Albionara	17.	New Albion
4.	Albona	18.	Niagarentia
5.	Alexandrina	19.	Norland
6.	Aquilonia	20.	Superior
7.	Borealia	21.	Transatlantia
8.	British North America	22.	Transatlantica
9.	Brittanica	23.	Transylvania
10.	Cabotia	24.	Tuponia
11.	Canadensia	25.	Ursulia
12.	Colonia	26.	Vesperia
13.	Efisga	27.	Victorialand
14.	Hochelaga	28.	Victorialia

5 EXPEDITIONS IN THE CANADIAN NORTH THAT ENDED BADLY

1. Eating Shoe Leather and Each Other, Part 1

Sir John Franklin could be on this list twice. In 1819 he led an expedition to map part of what is now the Canadian Arctic coastline. On a desperate return journey overland, several of Franklin's men ran out of food. They attempted to subsist on *trip de roche* (a black and nearly nutritionless lichen) and boiled shoe leather. In the end, nine of them died of starvation and exposure. Another man was killed because he was thought to have resorted to cannibalism. But the biggest disaster was yet to come. In 1845 the famous explorer set sail from England in search of the Northwest Passage. With well over 100 men on board his two ships, and enough food to last several years (including 8,000 cans of meat, vegetables and soup), Franklin's was the best-equipped expedition ever. Unfortunately, they were never heard from again. Both ships became trapped in the Arctic ice and were finally abandoned in the spring of 1848. By then, Franklin and 23 others had died. The 105 survivors trudged south across the mainland; some apparently resorted to cannibalism along the way. None of them was ever found alive. The most commonly held theory is that either scurvy or lead poisoning from badly soldered tins killed the majority of the men.

2. Eating Shoe Leather and Each Other, Part 2

American lieutenant Adolphus Greely didn't pack lightly either. In the summer of 1881, when his supply ship sailed away, Greely and his 25 men were left in the remote Canadian High Arctic with 350 tons of gear and food. It wasn't enough. The men built a base camp on Ellesmere Island. From there they planned to trek farther north than the record-setting English had gone six years before. Greely's men achieved the goal and then waited to be picked up. They waited for three years before giving up hope that a ship would reach them. On August 9, 1883, the men abandoned their camp and made a desperate attempt to reach a known rendezvous point. Along the way, there was mutiny, starvation, suicide, more consumption of shoe leather and cannibalism. By the time a ship finally did reach the expedition in June 1884, only seven of Greely's 25 men were still alive, and one of them died shortly thereafter. A subsequent investigation cleared Greely of any wrongdoing. He went on to write a book about his adventures.

3. The Leonidas Hubbard Expedition

Leonidas Hubbard was an American writer who wanted to make a name for himself as an explorer. So, in 1903, along with two companions, he embarked on a canoe trip to explore the interior of Labrador. However, almost immediately after leaving civilization, the three men made a critical blunder: they read their map incorrectly and turned up the wrong river. For months the explorers paddled and portaged deeper and deeper into the wilderness, becoming more and more lost. Finally, with their food supplies dwindling and winter upon them, they turned back. Nearing the end of their strength, and with Hubbard deathly ill, his companions left him behind and made a dash for help. Hubbard wrote in his diary, ". . . acute pangs of hunger have given way to indifference. I am sleepy. But let no one suppose that I expect it. I am prepared, that is all. I think the boys will be able with the Lord's help to save me." In fact, they couldn't. Hubbard died of starvation, alone in his tent. Two years later, his wife, Mina, embarked on the same trip. She completed it without a problem.

4. Starvation on the Thelon River

There is a point along the Thelon River in northern Canada where the barren tundra gives way to an oasis of spruce trees. It was there in 1926 that legendary trapper John Hornby planned to spend the winter with his 17-year-old nephew Edgar Christian and another young man named Harold Adlard. Hornby's theory was that, because of the trees, some of the migrating caribou would stick around for the winter. Hornby was wrong. By mid-winter the group's meagre food supply was almost gone. By early spring Hornby and Adlard had both starved to death. Christian, too weak to hunt, subsisted on the fur and bones the group had thrown out earlier in the year. He lay in his bed and wrote a diary as he slowly wasted away. When spring arrived and the animals returned to the area, Christian was too weak to pick up the loaded gun he kept by the door. His final journal entry was on June 1, 1927: "Got out too weak and all in now. Left Things Late." The three bodies weren't recovered until more than two years after Christian's death. The story of the three men starving in the Canadian wilderness became an international media sensation.

5. Tragedy on the Barrens

It was supposed to be the trip of a lifetime. In 1955 Arthur Moffat, an experienced canoeist, led a group of five young men down the remote Dubawnt River in northern Canada. The trip was badly planned, and by late summer the group was running out of food. Then it began to snow. The young men suffered from a kind of insanity brought on by hunger and fatigue, and instead of quickening their pace at this point, they slowed down. They took rest days and went hiking. Then, on September 14, two of the three canoes dumped in a set of rapids. The water was almost freezing. The young men managed to drag their leader to shore, but Moffat died of exposure. The five younger men barely survived. One of them, George Grinnell, wrote a book about the experience, *A Death on the Barrens*. In 1984 disaster struck Grinnell again when two of his sons went missing on James Bay after a canoe trip down the Albany River. They were never found.

—N.P.

THE 15 LEAST POPULOUS INDEPENDENT NATIONS

		Population
1.	Tuvalu	11,636
2.	Nauru	13,048
3.	Palau	20,303
4.	San Marino	28,880
5.	Monaco	32,409
6.	Liechtenstein	33,717
7.	Saint Kitts and Nevis	38,958
8.	Marshall Islands	59,071
9.	Antigua and Barbuda	68,722
10.	Dominica	69,029
11.	Andorra	70,549
12.	Seychelles	81,188
13.	Grenada	89,802
14.	Kiribati	103,092
15.	Federated States of Micronesia	108,105

Source: U.S. Census Bureau, International Data Base, April 26, 2005.

8 SECRET OR ABANDONED TUNNELS IN CANADA

1. Calgary City Hall

There's a tunnel under the CP rail tracks south of 9th Avenue in downtown Calgary that is in use, but a stub that veers west under City Hall has been sealed off. The tunnel was originally intended as a possible subway system, begun in Calgary in the 1980s. There is also a network of tunnels under the sidewalks in certain parts of the downtown core.

2. Diefenbunker

Built to withstand a 5-megaton nuclear blast, the Central Emergency Government Headquarters was constructed under an old gravel pit in Carp, a small town west of Ottawa. Dubbed the Diefenbunker because it was commissioned by the prime minister in 1959, it is a sprawling 100,000-square-foot (30,480 sq. m) facility that was supposed to function as the seat of government in the event of a nuclear attack. Designed to shelter and sustain 535 people for 30 days, it has its own hospital, a vault for Canada's gold reserve, a kitchen and cafeteria, dormitories, and bedrooms for the prime minister and governor general. Downplayed by officials as a small "communications hub," the project was too large to keep under wraps. One journalist flew over the site and counted the toilets that were still in the packing cases. There were 78, which he speculated seemed like a lot more toilets than the proposed 150 military personnel would actually need, much to the chagrin of Diefenbaker. The facility was obsolete before it began functioning in 1961 because nuclear bombs had become much bigger and more powerful. Still, it was maintained for 33 years at great expense, until it was decommissioned in 1994.

3. Dunsmuir Tunnel, Vancouver
The SkyTrain in downtown Vancouver travels through an old stretch of CPR line called the Dunsmuir Tunnel. One part of it, however, is not used and has been sealed up. Mouldy and abandoned, it is now owned by Concord Pacific, who occasionally rent it out as a film set.

4. Lower Bay Station
The original plan for Toronto's subway system included a second station at Bay Street that would allow downtown trains to loop around. This plan was abandoned when it was found to cause numerous delays. Decrepit and decaying since being shut down in 1966, Lower Bay is now used for storage, training drivers and occasionally as a movie set. Films that have been shot there include *Johnny Mnemonic*, *Bulletproof Monk* and *Don't Say a Word*.

5. NORAD North Bay
The task of maintaining surveillance for North American airspace is shared between three NORAD regions—Alaska, Canada and the Continental United States. Canadian radar and sensor data is collected and processed in a complex of tunnels, labs and offices underneath the Canadian Forces Base in North Bay, Ontario. This information is forwarded to Canadian NORAD Region Headquarters at CFB Winnipeg and on to NORAD Command and Control Center in Colorado.

6. Steam Tunnels

Many large government buildings, hospitals and educational facilities have extensive steam tunnels and mechanical rooms that run underneath and between buildings. "Urban Explorers" are an ethical subculture of people who like to wander through these tunnels, without stealing or vandalizing property. Websites and blogs document their "missions" in these off-limits buildings and tunnels, some of which are abandoned and decaying. Others are "active," but hard to access. Some of the postings include explorations of the tunnels of Parliament Hill, Toronto General Hospital, York University, University of British Columbia, University of Calgary, Union Station in Toronto, University of Toronto, the Palliser Hotel of Calgary, Vancouver's Woodlands Hospital (originally the Provincial Lunatic Asylum, built in 1878) and the old Whitby Psychiatric Hospital.

7. Tranquille Asylum, near Kamloops

British Columbia built this medical facility in 1907 during the tuberculosis epidemic. The complex was joined by an underground network of service tunnels. Although the locals objected to its location, officials deemed the sunny skies and cool, dry mountain air ideal for tuberculosis patients. It expanded over the years to 51 buildings, including cafeterias, gyms, offices, hospitals and a central laundry. From 1958 to 1984 Tranquille was a home for the mentally handicapped. The site now sits dormant and decaying.

8. Tunnels of Moose Jaw

Moose Jaw is home to a subterranean maze of tunnels under its main street. They were carved out during Prohibition, when Moose Jaw became the thriving hub of an illegal trade in bootleg alcohol. American gangsters would come north to cool their heels and live it up in the underground complex of speakeasies, card gaming parlours and brothels. One tunnel ran right under the train tracks into the yard and was used to load and unload whisky directly into the tunnels, where it was warehoused. The local police, led by Chief Walter Johnson, were thoroughly corrupt, and the mayor refused or was afraid to step in and change anything. Rumours still circulate that crime boss Al Capone came to the Moose Jaw tunnels on several occasions. The tunnels have recently been overhauled and turned into a tourist attraction. Contrary to popularly held belief, the tunnels did not function as living quarters for Chinese families attempting to avoid the racist violence of the head tax at the turn of the century.

8 CANADIAN CASTLES

1. Brownie Castle

Palmer Cox, the Canadian writer and illustrator who invented the Brownies, built a castellated wood frame house in Granby, Quebec, which still stands today. Cox designed the 17-room castle himself, giving it grandiose touches such as an octagonal tower, battlements and a Brownie-adorned stained glass window and weather vane. In 1905 Cox hoisted a Brownie flag up the flagpole and moved into the house. He died in Brownie Castle 19 years later. His tombstone reads "In creating the Brownies he bestowed a priceless heritage on childhood."

2. Canadian Railway Castles

The dream of a national railway carried with it the idea that Canadians would want to explore their own country. CPR president and visionary William Cornelius Van Horne declared, "If we can't export the scenery, we'll import the tourists." Between 1887 and 1939 a string of grand hotels were designed and built from east to west in homage to European styles of palatial architecture, with turrets, spires, archways and ramparts. The interiors were equally impressive, with vaulted ceilings, marble floors and staircases, mosaics and gold-leaf details. The "Château style" became a symbol of Canada's national aspirations, and it was adapted in the design of many government buildings. Built by both the Canadian Pacific Railway and the Canadian National Railways, the original castellated railway hotels are Victoria's Empress Hotel, Hotel Vancouver, the Banff Springs Hotel, Château Lake Louise, Calgary's Palliser Hotel, Edmonton's Hotel Macdonald, Saskatoon's Bessborough, Regina's Radisson Plaza Hotel Saskatchewan, Winnipeg's Hotel Fort Garry, Toronto's Royal York, Ottawa's Château Laurier, Quebec City's Château Frontenac, the Algonquin Hotel in St. Andrews, New Brunswick, and the Hotel Charlottetown.

3. Casa Loma

Casa Loma, the famous "house on the hill," was built by multi-millionaire Henry Pellatt, businessman, financier, military officer and ambitious homeowner. Started in 1911 and finished three years later, Pellatt's spectacular European-style castle had 95 rooms and all the modern conveniences: electrical wiring, phones and central vacuuming. With a $3.5-million price tag, the building materials and design details were first rate. When it was finished, he and his wife, Lady Pellatt, added another $1.5 million in furnishings. They entertained lavishly, but when the First World War started their financial fortunes turned and they lost everything. The Pellatts had lived in Casa Loma for only nine years when the building was sold for back taxes and they moved to their farm in King township. Lady Pellatt died shortly afterwards; Sir Henry soldiered on until 1939. Widely considered an eyesore at the time, Casa Loma was boarded up for years, but was spared from the wrecking ball because it would have cost an exorbitant amount to tear it down and cart it down to the lake as landfill. The Kiwanis Club eventually secured it and have run it as a tourist attraction and event hall ever since.

4. Dundurn Castle

This sprawling 72-room Italianate mansion overlooking Lake Ontario was built between 1832 and 1835 by Allan MacNab, a lawyer, soldier, land speculator, railway man and Tory member of the Legislative Assembly of Canada for Hamilton for 16 years. MacNab poured his fortune into his dream home, which he called Dundurn to honour his Scottish roots—the locals added the nickname "castle." He decorated it lavishly with oak panelling, crystal chandeliers and imported tiles and had it fitted out with the latest high-tech luxuries, such as running water, gas lighting and a "dumb waiter." A big spender who invested recklessly and had a taste for the good life, MacNab was eventually hobbled by gout and died, penniless, in 1862. Dundurn Castle was subsequently bought and sold several times, suffering neglect and deterioration, before being purchased by the city of Hamilton in 1899. Since then it has served as a museum and cultural centre, with periodic breaks for renovations and restoration work.

5. The Glass House

Funeral director David Brown retired from the business in 1952 and built himself a home made entirely of empty embalming fluid bottles—half a million of them. The Glass House of Boswell, British Columbia, overlooking Kootenay Lake, is a fully functional six-room castle, complete with turrets and archways. Once Brown had collected enough embalming fluid empties, he laid the square-bottomed bottles in rows, like bricks. He finished construction of the house two years later, in 1954, but continued to add to the structure over the next 16 years until he died on July 13, 1970, at the age of 70. Today, his relatives live there during the winter, and offer tours and operate a gift shop during the summer.

6. Henry Hoet Castle

Cardston, Alberta, woodworker Henry Hoet took 16 years to build an elaborate and luxurious cobblestone castle for his sweetheart, whom he had left behind in Belgium. Convinced that she would join him in Canada if he had a grand enough home for her to live in, he began constructing a glorious mansion using salvaged materials and wood scraps from the area. When he finished it in 1929, he waited a full year before the news arrived from Belgium—his sweetheart would not be coming to Cardston, ever. Heartbroken, he began acting strangely. Within a couple of years the locals had him committed to a mental institution, where he died soon afterwards. His castle was sold to the Mormon Church for $1,200, a fraction of its worth. It currently serves as a restaurant, the Cobblestone Manor.

7. Snow Castle of Yellowknife

Every March, Anthony Foliot, a.k.a. the Snow King of Yellowknife, builds a life-size snow castle on the frozen surface of Great Slave Lake. He's been performing this feat every year since 1995. Using heavy machinery, wood saws, shovels and chisels, the Snow King and his dedicated team of volunteers carve out massive bricks and windows of hard-packed snow and ice to make the enormous castle structure and courtyard, complete with turrets and archways. Ice sculptures of dragons and loyal Snowvillians dot the compound. In previous years the Snow King's Castle has come alive with performances by bands, fireworks, skating at the "royal rink" and puppet shows for kids.

8. White Otter Castle

The legend of Jimmy McQuat lives on through the three-storey log castle he built on the shores of White Otter Lake, north of Atikokan, Ontario, and accessible only by snowmobile, plane or boat. At the turn of the century he single-handedly constructed the castle from red pine logs that he cut, hauled and interlocked. The story goes that he was haunted by a childhood incident in which he was scolded and told he would never amount to anything and would die, alone, in a shack. Indeed, he did become reclusive and died alone, drowned in his own fishing nets, but he did not live in a shack. The castle has recently been restored through the efforts of the Friends of White Otter Castle.

11 VANCOUVER STREET NAMES DERIVED FROM THE WORKS OF SIR WALTER SCOTT

1. Dinmont Avenue
2. Durward Avenue
3. Ivanhoe Street
4. Marmion Avenue
5. Midlothian Avenue
6. Nigel Avenue
7. Glengyle Street
8. Peveril Avenue
9. Talisman Avenue
10. Waverley Avenue
11. Woodstock Avenue

13 POSSIBLE SITES FOR THE GARDEN OF EDEN

"And the Lord God planted a garden eastward in Eden . . . And a river went out of Eden to water the garden; and from thence it was parted and became into four heads. The name of the first is Pison: that is it which compasseth the whole land of Havilah, where there is gold; And the gold of that land is good: there is bdellium and the onyx stone. And the name of the second river is Gihon: the same is it that compasseth the whole land of Ethiopia. And the name of the third river is Kiddekel: that is it which goeth toward the east of Assyria. And the fourth river is Euphrates." (Gen. 2:8–14)

1. Southern Iraq

Many biblical scholars believe that the Garden of Eden, the original home of Adam and Eve, was located in Sumer, at the confluence of the Euphrates and Tigris (or Hiddekel) rivers in present-day Iraq. They presume that the geographical references in Genesis relate to the situation from the ninth to the fifth centuries BC and that the Pison and Gihon were tributaries of the Euphrates and Tigris that have since disappeared. In fact, they may have been ancient canals.

2. Eastern Turkey

Other students of the Bible reason that if the four major rivers flowed *out* of the garden, then the garden itself must have been located far north of the Tigris–Euphrates civilization. They place the site in the mysterious northland of Armenia, in present-day Turkey. This theory presumes that Gihon and Pison may not have been precise geographical designations, but rather vague descriptions of faraway places.

3. Northern Iran

British archaeologist David Rohl claims that Eden is a lush valley in Iran, located about 10 miles (16 km) from the modern city of Tabriz. Rohl suggests that the Gihon and Pison are the Iranian rivers Araxes and Uizhun. He also identifies nearby Mount Sahand, a snow-capped extinct volcano, as the prophet Ezekiel's Mountain of God.

4. Israel

There are those who say that the garden of God must have been in the Holy Land and that the original river that flowed into the garden *before* it split into four separate rivers must have been the Jordan, which was longer in the days of Genesis. The Gihon would be the Nile, and Havilah would be the Arabian Peninsula. Some supporters of this theory go further, stating that Mount Moriah in Jerusalem was the heart of the Garden of Eden and that the entire garden included all of Jerusalem, Bethlehem and Mount Olivet.

5. Egypt

Supporters of Egypt as the site of the Garden of Eden claim that only the Nile region meets the Genesis description of a land watered not by rain but by a mist rising from the ground, in that the Nile ran partially underground before surfacing in spring holes below the first cataract. The four rivers, including the Tigris and Euphrates, are explained away as beginning far, far beyond the actual site of Paradise.

6–7. East Africa and Java

Since Adam and Eve were the first humans, and since the oldest human remains have been found in East Africa, many people conclude that the Garden of Eden must have been in Africa. Likewise, when archaeologists discovered the remains of *Pithecanthropus* in Java in 1891, they guessed that Java was the location of the Garden of Eden.

8. Sinkiang, China

Tse Tsan Tai, in his work *The Creation, the Real Situation of Eden, and the Origin of the Chinese* (1914), presents a case for the garden being in Chinese Turkestan in the plateau of eastern Asia. He claims that the river that flowed through the garden was the Tarim, which has four tributaries flowing eastward.

9. Lemuria

In the mid-19th century a theory developed that a vast continent once occupied much of what is now the Indian Ocean. The name Lemuria was created by British zoologist P.L. Sclater in honour of the lemur family of animals, which has a somewhat unusual range of distribution in Africa, southern India and Malaysia. Other scientists suggested that Lemuria was the cradle of the human race; thus it must have been the site of the Garden of Eden.

10. Praslin Island, Seychelles

General Charles "Chinese" Gordon supported the theory that Africa and India used to be part of one massive continent. While on a survey expedition for the British government in the Indian Ocean, he came upon Praslin Island in the Seychelles group. So enchanted was he by this island, and by its Vallée de Mai in particular, that he became convinced that this was the location of the original Garden of Eden. The clincher for Gordon was the existence on Praslin of the coco-de-mer, a rare and exotic tree, which is native to only one other island of the

Seychelles and which Gordon concluded was the tree of the knowledge of good and evil.

11. Mars

In his book *The Sky People*, Brinsley Le Poer Trench argues that not only Adam and Eve but Noah lived on Mars. He states that the biblical description of a river watering the garden and then parting into four heads is inconsistent with nature. Only canals can be made to flow that way, and Mars, supposedly, had canals. So the Garden of Eden was created on Mars as an experiment by Space People. Eventually, the north polar ice cap on Mars melted, and the descendants of Adam and Eve were forced to take refuge on Earth.

12. Galesville, Wisconsin

In 1886 the Reverend D.O. Van Slyke published a small pamphlet that expounded his belief that Eden was the area stretching from the Allegheny Mountains to the Rocky Mountains and that the Garden of Eden was located on the east bank of the Mississippi River between La Crosse, Wisconsin, and Winona, Minnesota. When the Deluge began, Noah was living in present-day Wisconsin, and the flood carried his ark eastward until it landed on Mount Ararat.

13. Jackson County, Missouri

While travelling through Davies County, Missouri, Mormon Church founder Joseph Smith found a stone slab that he declared was an altar that Adam built shortly after being driven from the Garden of Eden. Declaring, "This is the valley of God in which Adam blessed his children," Smith made plans to build a city called Adam-ondi-Ahram at the site. The Garden of Eden itself, Smith determined, was located 40 miles (64 km) south, near the modern-day city of Independence.

BECKY MASON'S 12 FAVOURITE RIVERS TO CANOE

Becky Mason is a canoeist, artist and environmentalist, who acquired her paddling skills and her fondness for canoes from her father, Bill Mason, the National Film Board filmmaker and author of Path of the Paddle. *In 2000 she wrote, directed and produced the award-winning DVD* Classic Solo Canoeing, *profiling her course and her love of paddling.*

1. South Nahanni River (Northwest Territories)

From top to bottom, perhaps the greatest combination of wild white-water, eye-popping scenery, wildlife and a fascinating history of murder, mystery and hidden gold. All this and the fact that it is protected within the confines of a national park and includes the incomparable Virginia Falls, a UNESCO World Heritage Site. Even if I never return to the Nahanni, I am pleased to know it is protected, not for me, or even for future generations, but for the sake of the river itself.

2. French River (Georgian Bay, Ontario)

This is the river I learned all about swimming in rapids on. I had many formative moments here as a kid, canoeing with my family. To this day I can still feel the sun-warmed rocks, taste the mists of Blue Chute and hear the lazy humming of cicadas as I revisit in my mind the seemingly endless lazy days of childhood summers gone.

3. Rivière Saguenay (Quebec)

Perhaps not the safest place for a canoe (here I must concede that sea kayaks do have their advantages!), but where else can you paddle in such spectacular fjords and share the water with seals, belugas and blue whales?

4–7. Rivers of the North Shore (Lake Superior, Ontario)

The best part of all of the North Shore rivers is . . . Lake Superior itself. This is such a unique, awe-inspiring and powerful place that at times it leaves me speechless. I have had more spiritual, strange and downright unsettling experiences here than anywhere else in my travels, and that's one of the reasons I continue to return. A few of my favourite North Shore rivers are:

a. Dog River. It doesn't get much more rugged than this. No developed campsites, no marked portages, unreliable map information on the rapids; this is canoe tripping at its best. You have to be tough as nails to get through this trip. The portage around Denison Falls was once listed by *Paddler Magazine* as one of the top 10 worst portages on the planet. But it's all worth it, and nothing beats the thrill of descending this rarely canoed river down to the lake.

b. Pukaskwa River. I think the blackflies carried us down most of the Puk, but the section of Superior coastline we paddled is unparalleled anywhere. Firing up a trapper's old sod sauna we found one cold evening at Oiseau Bay is a memory and a luxurious feeling I'll not soon forget.

c. White River. Although I was once windbound at the mouth for a week and had to hike out, this river still has some great memories. Tragically, with the inevitable damming of Umbata Falls, starting in 2005, the White will be changed forever.

d. Sand River. Getting dropped off by a train in the middle of nowhere with your canoe and packs to start a trip has to be the most romantic and hopelessly clichéd Canadian experience one can have. And it feels fantastic!

8. Rivière du Lièvre (Quebec)

It seems like way too much fun to fit into one weekend. A challenging stretch of turbulent river that includes chutes, ledges, a "can't scout" white-knuckle canyon run and a half-mile-long (1 km) continuous roller-coaster ride that, trust me, you don't want your friends to swim through . . .

9. Petawawa River (Ontario)

Though it's famous for its thrilling whitewater, what really moves me about the Petawawa is its natural beauty and how it fuels my creative side. Tom Thomson popularized Algonquin Park and the Petawawa River through his paintings, and you can't help but feel his presence in the early morning mist and cool river currents. My dad and I paddled here many times, but the most memorable was a painting trip we took together after I graduated from art college. Although we did some paintings, it was then that I learned it was just as important to take the time to stop and experience the land with *all* your senses.

10. Red Deer River (Alberta)

Okay, I have yet to paddle the Red Deer, but I have hiked parts of the river valley badlands and splashed about in it, and it's about as far from my idea of stereotypical Canadian canoe country as I can imagine. But wow! Fossils, rattlesnakes, hoodoos . . . way cool.

11. Missinaibi River (Ontario)

One of the great things about canoeing in Canada is the immediacy of our history. Much of this country was explored and mapped by canoe, a watercraft that has remained virtually unchanged in design for millennia. Even today, with a few skills and a lot of determination, one can go into the bush with nothing but a crooked knife and build a craft that could cross the continent. The Missinaibi was a highway for Natives and voyageurs, and evidence of their presence can be found everywhere. When on rivers like this one, it is well worth it to read the old explorers' trip journals and marvel at their exploits while revelling in the history of the land.

12. Berens River (Ontario, Manitoba)

Canada's boreal forest is an awe-inspiring place to be. Stretching from coast to coast across the north, it is like a vast green halo of virtually pristine forests, lakes and rivers. The Berens is a thin blue ribbon of water winding through some spectacular boreal scenery. As I paddled, I marvelled at the jet-black spruces sculpting the skyline, feasted on fresh pickerel sushi, trembled at the roar of the falls and admired the thick green moss that cushioned the forest floor. Not only is it stunning scenery, but our Canadian boreal lands are unique and important filters for the entire planet. And what better way to journey through this wild and rugged land and see the amazing beauty of this last true wilderness than by canoe.

"ROSIE" ROWBOTHAM'S 8 FAVOURITE SOURCES FOR HASHISH

In the 1960s and early '70s Robert "Rosie" Rowbotham was one of Canada's leading importers of marijuana and hashish. He supplied a substantial portion of the soft drugs that fuelled the infamous drug scene at Toronto's Rochdale College. But federal authorities did not appreciate Rosie's entrepreneurial spirit. He spent most of the years between 1977 and 1997 locked up in various federal institutions. After his release, Rosie worked as a journalist for CBC radio. During his years of incarceration, Rosie never lost his appreciation for fine-quality hashish. Here are the sources of eight of his road-tested favourites.

1. Mazar-e Sharif, Afghanistan

In the northwest frontier region is the timeless hub of hashish production steeped in centuries of tradition and pride. The bulk of Afghani commercial hash production is derived by beating cannabis plants over a series of screens and collecting the consequent pollen. This crude pollen is then pounded into kilo blocks, with animal fat or milk added for adhesion and as a preservative, by ancient presses, usually made of stone. But with primo Afghani hashish, the pollen is hand-pressed with only water. Buddha Bob, from Timothy Leary's brotherhood, introduced me to Afghani "surfboards," which the hippies brought into California through Mexico. Each plate was 4 by 10 inches (10 by 25 cm) long and ¼ inch (0.5 cm) thick, and weighed about 7 ounces (200 g). Black outside and a smooth, creamy brown inside. Kneads up easily and burns with a clear white ash. Strong, smooth, sweet taste and pungent smoke. Kick-ass buzz!

2. Chitral, Pakistan

This frontier area between Pakistan and Afghanistan is adjacent to the ancient Silk Road and, although claimed by Pakistan, is controlled by a loose association of over 20 tribes. Marijuana cultivation and hashish production dates back centuries in this area. It's the world's oldest and ultimate free trade zone, dating back before Marco Polo. Commercial "Chitrali" hashish is shaken and pounded by ancient presses and is known for average or below-average quality. However, if you look far enough, you'll find a farmer who hand-presses for his own personal stash. If you can get your hands on a couple of kilos of this, you'll find the texture, smell and quality is of a primo variety. Black on the outside, more greenish than brown on the inside. Superb high.

3. Kashmir

You're wondering what rubbed hashish is? On massive plantations of marijuana fields, women run naked through the fields, and mature cannabis plant resin sticks to their bodies. Men wear wetsuits, because of body hair. Resins and pollen are collected and rubbed with goat's milk or butter "ghee." Hashish has a coarse, crude, grainy texture, with the odd seed, stalk or stem. Excellent high.

4. Minali, Kulu Valley, India

Unlike Kashmir hashish, Minali is smooth outside, but with a grainy blackish brown inside. Don't be surprised if you find a yak hair or two, sticks and stems. Fine cross between taste and texture—between Nepalese and Kashmir. White willowy smoke definitely knocks your socks off.

5. Nepal

Soft, distinct smell, grainy texture, kneads up easily. Like Minali, Nepal hashish needs to be wrapped airtight or it will turn brittle and mould. Long slabs called Nepalese fingers or hand patties usually give a kilo weight. Don't be fooled by temple balls—they're not rolled by Buddhist monks. Nepalese are the true connoisseurs. Kick-ass.

6. Bekáa Valley, Lebanon

Could I be the Rose of Lebanon?—sorry, I wander. This is one of the least expensive yet most consistent when it comes to quality and packaging. You always know what you're getting. Blond, brown Lebanese hashish is commercial and low quality. Moist, red Lebanese is as good as any hashish in the world. Shaken and heated before being pressed into 1-kilo cheesecloth sacks. Smokes beautifully, primo taste and nice buzz.

7. Atlas Mountains, Morocco

If you follow the mountains from Lebanon westward towards Morocco, you reach the Atlas Mountains and the last decent hash of the Middle East. "00" Moroccan is the prize. Special aged pollen, shaken and carefully screened. Brownish green colouring and distinct flavour. Not top shelf, but often a nice surprise. Don't be a tourist and get fooled by the green, powdery, low-rider "keef." It's garbage, like Turkish, Israeli and less mentionable hashish.

8. Western Hemisphere

North American hash is a relatively new phenomenon. Resins from the more potent *Cannabis sativa* strain—not Middle Eastern *Cannabis indica* plants—are collected and rubbed. The most popular is the Jamaican "rub." More recently, North American bubble and ice hashish have rewritten potency levels. Fine crystalline particles are flash-frozen and collected with ice hashish, or shaken screened with water, for hashish looking like keef, but don't let the colour fool you. Extremely potent— nice buzz, but irritates the throat.

7 CONTROVERSIAL CANADIAN PLACE NAMES

The intriguing people, anecdotes and geography behind Canada's place names have provided the raw material for plenty of books and articles. Writer and geographer Alan Rayburn has managed to dig deeper than most, delving into the rich history and evolution of Canada's toponyms. He wrote a regular column on the subject for *Canadian Geographic* between 1983 and 1996 and adapted the columns for his book *Naming Canada: Stories about Canadian Place Names*, which is the source of several of these anecdotes.

1. Bastard Township

This area of Ontario, in Leeds County, was named in 1796 at a time when the surname Bastard was not uncommon in England. Locals seem quite content with the name, but every once in a while someone makes a motion to change it and gets rejected. The most recent proposal was put forward in 1994 by a real estate developer, who suggested calling the area Beverly Hills. The name Bastard Township prevailed.

2. Berlin/Kitchener

The majority of the residents in the southern Ontario town of Berlin had German roots, and as the First World War dragged on, the town council thought it a good idea to change the name to something "more patriotic." A plebiscite was held on the issue, and it was decided by a narrow 81-vote margin to change the name. Another poll was held to choose the new name from a list that included Adanac, Benton, Brook, Corona, Keotwana and Kitchener. The name was changed to Kitchener on September 1, 1916, in honour of a British military leader who had drowned earlier that year.

3. Castle Mountain/Mount Eisenhower

Just outside Banff there is a spectacular castellated mountain, 7 miles (11 km) long, that rises from the Bow River Valley. Geologist James Hector did the obvious on August 17, 1858, and christened it Castle Mountain. Many years later, on the eve of a presidential visit from Dwight Eisenhower, Mackenzie King made a snap decision to rename the mountain in honour of his guest. Locals were outraged that the prime minister could make such arbitrary decisions and fought the name change over the next three decades. Prime Minister Joe Clark eventually changed the name back in 1979, but allowed for the renaming of one part of the mountain to Eisenhower Peak.

4. Mount Logan/Mount Trudeau

The Kluane National Park and Reserve in the Yukon is home to the highest mountain in Canada, Mount Logan. Rising 19,550 feet (5,959 m), it was named after Sir William Edmond Logan (1798–1875), founder of the Geological Survey of Canada in 1842. Prime Minister Jean Chrétien sparked a storm of protest in 2000 when he proposed changing the name to Mount Trudeau, in honour of the former prime minister. Since then, the village of Valemount, British Columbia, has offered an unnamed peak in the nearby Premier Range of the Cariboo Mountains as Mount Pierre Elliott Trudeau. It will likely take its place alongside its neighbours, Mount Arthur Meighen, Mount Lester Pearson, Mount Sir Wilfrid Laurier and so on, after an official review process. In the meantime, Dorval Airport, outside Montreal, has been renamed Pierre Elliott Trudeau International Airport.

5. Squaw

The word "squaw" is a phonetic rendering of an Algonquian word that was traditionally meant to signify the totality of being female, but early settlers and traders came to use it as a pejorative reference to a woman's private parts. Since then, Native groups have deemed it offensive, and have asked that it be removed from local place names. Since this issue was first raised in the 1980s, all the "squaw" place names have been changed in British Columbia, Saskatchewan, Alberta, Prince Edward Island and the Yukon.

6. Swastika

Swastika is a small town near Kirkland Lake in northern Ontario named in 1906 by two miners, Bill and Jim Dusty. While looking for silver, they found gold, the first such strike in Ontario. To honour their windfall, they called the spot Swastika, a Sanskrit word for "good luck." During the Second World War various attempts were made by government officials to change the name to Winston, as in Churchill. But the locals resisted, tearing down new signs and replacing them with another: "To Hell with Hitler: We Had the Swastika First." The town is still called Swastika.

7. Wawa

The name of this Ontario town, established as a fur trading outpost in the 1700s, derives from an Ojibwa word for "wild goose." In 1947 bureaucrats took it upon themselves to change the name from Wawa to Jamestown, in honour of Sir James Dunn. Locals resisted all the way, playing pranks with the new signage. "Jamestown Post Office" became "town Post Office," then "own Post Office" and finally "own Post Of ice." Eventually, the bureaucrats bowed to local pressure and changed the name back to Wawa in 1960.

THE 7 WONDERS OF THE ANCIENT WORLD

Who created one of the earliest and most enduring of all lists, a list that arbitrarily named the seven most spectacular sights existing in the world 150 years before the birth of Jesus Christ? The list was created by a most respected Byzantine mathematician and traveller named Philon. In a series of arduous trips, Philon saw all of the Western civilized world there was to see in his time, and then he sat down and wrote a short but widely circulated paper entitled *"De Septem Orbis Spectaculis"* ("The Seven Wonders of the World").

1. The Great Pyramid of Cheops (Egypt)

Begun as a royal tomb around 2600 BC, and standing in splendour for 2,000 years before any of the other seven wonders were built, this largest of Egypt's 80-odd pyramids is the only wonder to have survived to this day. Located outside Cairo, near Giza, the burial tomb of King Cheops was made up of 2.3 million blocks of stone, some of them 2½ tons in weight. With a height of 481 feet (147 m), and a base width of 755 feet (230 m) on each side, it's large enough to enclose London's Westminster Abbey, Rome's St. Peter's and Milan's and Florence's main cathedrals.

2. The Hanging Gardens of Babylon (Iraq)

When Nebuchadnezzar brought home his new wife, a princess from Medes, she pined for the mountains and lush growth of her native land. To please her, in 600 BC the king started to build a man-made mountain with exotic growths. Actually, it was a square climbing upward, each balcony or terrace densely planted with grass, flowers and fruit trees, irrigated from below by pumps manned by slaves or oxen. Inside and beneath the gardens, the queen held court amid the vegetation and artificial rain. Due to the erosion of time and the influx of conquerors, the Hanging Gardens had been levelled and reduced to wilderness when Pliny the Elder visited them before his death in AD 79.

3. The Statue of Zeus at Olympia (Greece)

The multicoloured Temple of Zeus, in the area where the Greek Olympic Games were held every fourth year, contained the magnificent statue of Zeus, king of the gods. Sculpted by Phidias (who had done Athena for the Parthenon) sometime after 432 BC, the statue was 40 feet (12 m) high, made of ivory and gold plates set on wood. Zeus, with jewels for eyes, sat on a golden throne, feet resting on a footstool of gold. Ancients came from afar to worship at the god's feet. A Greek writer, Pausanias, saw the statue intact as late as the second century AD. After that, it disappeared from history, probably the victim of looting armies and fire.

4. The Temple of Diana at Ephesus (Turkey)

Summing up his seven wonders, Philon chose his favourite: "But when I saw the temple at Ephesus rising to the clouds, all these other wonders were put in the shade." The temple, a religious shrine built after 350 BC, housed a statue of Diana, goddess of hunting, symbol of fertility. The kings of many Asian states contributed to the construction. The temple, 225 feet (69 m) wide and 525 feet (160 m) long, was supported by 127 marble columns 60 feet (18 m) high. As quoted in the New Testament, St. Paul railed against it, saying, "the temple of the great goddess Diana should be despised, and her magnificence should be destroyed, whom all Asia and the world worshippeth." The craftsmen of the temple disagreed: "And when they heard these sayings, they were full of wrath, and cried out, saying, 'Great is Diana of the Ephesians.'" Ravaged and brought down by invaders, the temple was rebuilt three times before the Goths permanently destroyed it in AD 262. In 1874, after 11 years of digging, the English archaeologist J.T. Wood unearthed fragments of the original columns.

5. The Tomb of King Mausolus at Halicarnassus (Turkey)

King Mausolus, conqueror of Rhodes, ruled over the Persian province of Caria. His queen, Artemisia, was also his sister. When he died in

353 BC, he was cremated and his grieving widow drank his ashes in wine. As a memorial to him, she determined to build the most beautiful tomb in the world at Halicarnassus, now called Bodrum. She sent to Greece for the greatest architects and sculptors, and by 350 BC the memorial was complete. There was a rectangular sculpted marble tomb on a platform, then 36 golden-white Ionic columns upon which sat an architrave, which in turn held a pyramid topped by a bronzed chariot with statues of Mausolus and Artemisia. The monument survived for 1,900 years, only to tumble down in an earthquake. What remains of it today is the word "mausoleum."

6. The Colossus of Rhodes on the Isle of Rhodes (in the Aegean Sea)

To celebrate being saved from a Macedonian siege by Ptolemy I, the Rhodians, between 292 and 280 BC, erected a mammoth statue to their heavenly protector, the sun god Apollo. Chares, who had studied under a favourite of Alexander the Great, fashioned the statue. The nude Colossus was 120 feet (37 m) tall, with its chest and back 60 feet (18 m) around, built of stone blocks and iron and plated with thin bronze. It did not stand astride the harbour, with room for ships to pass between the legs, but stood with feet together on a promontory at the entrance to the harbour. In 224 BC it was felled by an earthquake. It lay in ruins for almost 900 years. In AD 667 the Arabs, who controlled Rhodes, sold the 720,900 pounds (327,000 kg) of broken statue for scrap metal to a Jewish merchant. When the merchant hauled his purchase to Alexandria, he found that it required 900 camel loads.

7. The Lighthouse on the Isle of Pharos (off Alexandria, Egypt)

On the orders of Ptolemy Philadelphus, in 200 BC the architect Sostratus of Cnidus constructed a pharos, or lighthouse, such as the world had not seen before. Built on a small island off Alexandria, the tiers of the marble tower—first square, then round, each with a balcony—rose to a height of 400 feet (122 m). At the summit, a huge brazier with an eternal flame was amplified by a great glass mirror so that the fire could be seen 300 miles (483 km) out at sea. Half of the lighthouse was torn down by occupying Arabs, who hoped to find gold inside. The rest of the structure crashed to the ground when an earthquake struck in 1375.

—I.W.

WILL FERGUSON'S 15 FAVOURITE CANADIAN ROADSIDE ATTRACTIONS

Will Ferguson, a connoisseur of Giant Objects Beside the Road, is the author of Beauty Tips from Moose Jaw: Travels in Search of Canada, *which won the 2005 Leacock Medal for Humour, and* Hitching Rides with Buddha: A Journey Across Japan. *His debut novel,* Happiness™, *also won the Leacock Medal for Humour and has been published in 26 languages around the world.*

1. World's Largest Hockey Stick in Duncan, British Columbia

The community of Duncan, north of Victoria on Vancouver Island, is a "City of Totem Poles," with dozens of examples on display downtown and throughout the area. It is also home of the World's Largest Hockey Stick, which comes complete with the World's Largest Puck and is located out-side the local rec centre. At night it is outlined in prima donna lights.

2. The Airplane Weather Vane of Whitehorse, Yukon

You can find aircraft on display across Canada, pinned like butterflies, usually outside military or aeronautical museums. But the historic Canadian Pacific DC-3 at the Whitehorse Airport is also "the world's largest wind gauge." Turning smoothly on its pivot, this beautifully restored passenger plane always faces into the wind.

3. The Giant Ukrainian Easter Egg in Vegreville, Alberta

The famed *pysanka* of Vegreville, made of interconnecting aluminum patterns, also turns on the wind like a weather vane. Created in celebra-tion of the RCMP's 100th anniversary in 1974, the pysanka honours the city's staunch Ukrainian heritage. Add the Giant Pyrogy in Glendon and the Ukrainian Sausage of Mundare, and you can complete a full-course meal in a single drive through Alberta.

4. The Leaning Coffee Pot of Davidson, Saskatchewan

On the long highway between Saskatoon and Regina, the coffee shops of Davidson are a welcome sight. Situated at the halfway point between the two cities, Davidson is a natural travel break and meeting place. Hence a gigantic, welcoming pot of coffee, leaning towards an equally gigantic mug.

5. The Giant Horse Ankle Bone of Macklin, Saskatchewan

One of the oddest, by far. The town of Macklin hosts the World Bunnock Championships—bunnock being an old Russian game that involves the throwing of horse ankle bones. And so, a mighty ankle bone rises majestically from the prairie at Macklin, confounding travellers who slow down with an inevitable "What the . . ."

6. The Huge Mosquito of Komarno, Manitoba

Most of Canada's Giant Objects Beside the Road were erected as tourist attractions. Which makes you wonder about the evil-looking weather vane mosquito of Komarno. The community of Inwood, also in Manitoba, boasts giant snakes. And Kenaston, over in Saskatchewan, has a giant fibreglass snowman to mark the town's title of "Blizzard Capital." Snakes, blizzards, mosquitoes—it all sounds so enticing.

7. The Happy Rock of Gladstone, Manitoba

Giant Objects Beside the Road are often visual puns. The town of Pincher Creek, Alberta, for example, has a giant pair of "pincers." Indian Head, Saskatchewan, has, well, an Indian head—complete with Native headdress. But the single most groan-inducing of them all is Gladstone's smiling "Happy Rock" (glad *stone*, happy *rock* . . . yeah, you get it).

8. The Enormous Viking of Gimli, Manitoba

Gimli, on the shores of Lake Winnipeg, is home to the largest Icelandic community in Canada, and a towering statue of a Viking with a suitably sombre expression stands guard over the town. (The community of Erickson, also in Manitoba, has a competing claim on the title "Land of the Vikings," and they have a replica Norse ship with fibreglass Vikings to prove it.)

9. The Big Nickel of Sudbury, Ontario

Built more than 40 years ago as the centrepiece of a proposed "numismatic" theme park (dedicated to coin collecting), Sudbury's famous Big Nickel is now owned by Science North. Heading west on the Trans-Canada, you will also find the Giant Loonie of Echo Bay. (Indeed, spare change is scattered across the country: another giant loonie in Churchbridge, Saskatchewan; a giant toonie in Campbellford, Ontario;

and a gigantic replica of Canada's first gold coin in Virginiatown, Ontario.)

10. "Ms. Claybelt," New Liskeard, Ontario

Giant cows can be found grazing in many areas of Canada—most notably, the statue to the "Snow Countess" in Woodstock, Ontario, which was built back in the 1930s. What sets the giant fibreglass Holstein of New Liskeard apart is (a) its name (that's right, *Ms.* Claybelt) and (b) the fact that said cow is situated in front of a McDonald's.

11. Jumbo the Elephant, St. Thomas, Ontario

Why Jumbo? Good question. The beloved star of the P.T. Barnum Circus was not born in St. Thomas. Nor did he ever perform in St. Thomas. Jumbo was, however, killed in St. Thomas—and of that the good townspeople are inordinately proud. The elephant was hit by a train while crossing rail tracks outside of town in 1885, and a life-sized statue was erected to mark the centennial of this event. Morbid? Perhaps. Worth a detour? Absolutely.

12. The Edible Ferns of Plaster Rock, New Brunswick

Fiddlehead ferns, named for the shape of their tightly curled tops, are a local delicacy in this corner of northern New Brunswick, and a chainsaw sculpture has been erected in the village of Plaster Rock in their honour, along with a sign that reads: "World's Largest Fiddleheads!" (Now, I'm going to go out on a limb here and say that not only is the sculpture the world's largest monument to edible ferns, it is also the world's *only* monument to edible ferns.)

13. The Giant Lobster of Shediac, New Brunswick

More regional cuisine. The Acadian community of Shediac is Atlantic Canada's "Lobster Capital" (a title, it should be noted, that is hotly contested), and the gigantic crustacean was built to promote this. When my wife and I moved to New Brunswick from Japan, one of our first trips was out to Shediac to see the Giant Lobster. That's the type of sophisticated travellers we are.

14. The O'Leary Potato of Prince Edward Island

True, there is another, more venerable giant potato in Maugerville, New Brunswick. But the one in O'Leary, P.E.I., has the added appeal of standing in front of Canada's only "Potato Museum." That's right, an entire museum dedicated to the humble spud. (Note to purists: This isn't just some generic potato, mind. It's a *Russet Burbank*.)

15. The Mastodon of Stewiacke, Nova Scotia

Looking like Jumbo's rougher, rowdier twin, this replica of a prehistoric mastodon was built to mark the discovery of the skeletal remains of one such creature in a nearby quarry. (A statue of a woolly mammoth, meanwhile, stands in Kyle, Saskatchewan, to commemorate a similar find.)

14 STREETS IN SASKATOON NAMED AFTER GOVERNORS GENERAL

1. Aberdeen Place
2. Byng Avenue
3. Connaught Place
4. Devonshire Crescent
5. Dufferin Avenue
6. Hnatyshyn Avenue
7. Lansdowne Avenue
8. Lisgar Avenue
9. Lorne Avenue
10. Massey Drive
11. Michener Crescent
12. Stanley Place
13. Vanier Crescent
14. Willingdon Place

PLACES

MIKE MYERS'S 10 BEST THINGS TO DO IN TORONTO

To most people, Mike Myers is Austin Powers, Goldmember, Dr. Evil, Fat Bastard, Wayne Campbell, Dieter, the Cat in the Hat and Shrek. But Canadians know and love Mike for more than his screen roles. He is a diehard hockey fan, a rabid Scarborough booster and a consummate rock 'n' roller. He may live in Los Angeles now, with his wife, Robin Ruzan, and their three dogs, but he hasn't forgotten how great it is to come back to his hometown, Toronto.

1. Watching *Hockey Night in Canada* at a friend's house, knowing that after the game I'm going to hook up with an even bigger group of friends I haven't seen in a long time.
2. Taking the TTC subway to the hockey game and standing at the window of the front car, putting my face against it and imagining I'm flying through the tunnel.
3. Gouging out the corner of a Lowney's Cherry-Blossom with my teeth and watching it bleed.
4. Eating a Swiss Chalet quarter-chicken white meat dinner, salting up the fries and dunking them into that mysterious sauce, while watching the game (see #1). I save the Toblerone that comes with the dinner for the streetcar ride along Queen Street.
5. Trick-or-treating in Cabbagetown on Halloween.
6. Listening to the ice sheets collide by the Toronto Police Boat station on Lake Ontario at 3:00 in the morning in the dead of winter with a Tim Hortons double-double and a raised maple doughnut.
7. Eating ketchup-flavoured chips while walking through Kensington Market in late May.
8. Playing shinny on a bright, sunny afternoon between Christmas and New Year's at the outdoor rink in Ramsden Park, across from Rosedale subway station.
9. Eating a hot dog from Licks in the Beaches while walking through Kew Gardens in October, trying to figure out if the Leafs have a chance this year.
10. Sitting on the front bench on the top deck of the Centre Island Ferry at 4:00 in the afternoon in late August.

19 POSSIBLE EXPLORERS OF AMERICA BEFORE COLUMBUS

1–2. Hsi and Ho (c. 2640 BC), Chinese

Based on evidence derived from the geography text *Shan Hai Ching T'sang-chu* and the chronicle *Shan Hai Jing*, it is argued that the Chinese imperial astronomers Hsi and Ho were the first explorers of America in the 27th century BC. Ordered by the emperor Huang Ti to make astronomical observations in the land of Fu Sang—the territories to the east of China—the two men sailed north to the Bering Strait and then south along the North American coastline. They settled for a while with the "Yao people," ancestors of the Pueblo Indians living near the Grand Canyon, but eventually journeyed on to Mexico and Guatemala. Returning to China, they reported their astronomical studies and geographic discoveries to the emperor. However, a short time later, they were both executed for failing to predict a solar eclipse accurately.

3–6. Votan, Wixepecocha, Sume and Bochia (c. 800–400 BC), Indian

According to Hindu legends and to Central American tribal legends, seafaring Hindu missionaries reached the Americas more than 2,000 years before Columbus. Sailing from India to Southeast Asia, they voyaged to the Melanesian and Polynesian islands and then across the Pacific to South and Central America. Votan was a trader from India who lived among the Mayans as a historian and chieftain, while his contemporary, Wixepecocha, was a Hindu priest who settled with the Zapotecs of Mexico. Two more Hindu emigrants were Sume, who reached Brazil and introduced agriculture to the Cabocle Indians, and Bochia, who lived with the Muycas Indians and became the codifier of their laws.

7. Hui Shun (AD 458), Chinese

Using official Chinese imperial documents and maps from the Liang dynasty, scholars have reconstructed the travels of the Chinese explorer and Buddhist priest Hui Shun and proposed that he arrived in North America in the 5th century. Sailing from China to Alaska in 458, Hui—accompanied by four Afghan disciples—continued his journey on foot down the North American Pacific coast. Reaching Mexico, he taught and preached Buddhism to the Indians of central Mexico and to the Mayans of the Yucatán. He allegedly named Guatemala in honour of Gautama Buddha. After more than 40 years in America, he returned to

China, where he reported his adventures to Lord Yu Kie and Emperor Wu in 502.

8. St. Brendan (*c.* AD 550), Irish

Two medieval manuscripts, *The Voyage of Saint Brendan the Abbot* and the *Book of Lismore*, tell of an Irish priest who, with 17 other monks, sailed west from Ireland and reached the "Land Promised to the Saints." Employing a curragh—a leather-hulled boat still in use in Ireland—Brendan and his companions made a sea pilgrimage that lasted seven years during the sixth century AD. They travelled to Iceland, Greenland and Newfoundland, and one authority asserts that Brendan reached the Caribbean island of Grand Cayman, which he called the Island of Strong Men. Brendan returned safely to his Irish monastery and reported on his travels, but died soon after. In 1977 Timothy Severin, sailing a modern curragh, retraced Brendan's voyage to America.

9. Bjarni Herjulfson (AD 986), Norse

According to two medieval Icelandic narratives, *Flateyjarbok* and *Hauksbok*, a young Norse merchant named Bjarni Herjulfson sailed from Iceland towards Greenland to visit his father, who lived there, but was blown off course by a gale. When the storm ended, Bjarni sighted a hilly, forested land, which is now thought to have been Cape Cod. Wanting to reach the Norse settlements on Greenland before winter, he did not drop anchor and send men ashore to explore. Instead, he sailed north to Greenland. He was criticized by the Greenlanders for not investigating the new land, and his discoveries stimulated further exploration of North America.

10. Leif Ericson (1003), Norse

In 1003 Ericson bought Bjarni Herjulfson's ship and, with a 35-man crew, sailed for North America. While most scholars agree that Ericson did land in North America, there is disagreement about where he landed. The only Viking site ever found in the New World is L'Anse aux Meadows in Newfoundland, which was discovered in 1960 and excavated for the next eight years by Helge Ingstad, a Norwegian explorer. According to Ingstad, Ericson's first landing was on Baffin Island, which he named Helluland; his second was in Labrador, which he called Markland; and his third was in Newfoundland, which he christened

Vinland. To Leif and his companions, Vinland was an abundant country, rich in game, wild wheat and timber, and its climate was mild compared with that of Iceland and Greenland. The explorers spent the winter in Vinland, where they constructed a village of "big houses." In 1004 Leif returned to Greenland, where he was given the honorary name "Leif the Lucky."

11. Thorvald Ericson (1004), Norse

The Icelandic sagas record that, soon after Leif Ericson returned to Greenland, he gave his ship to his brother Thorvald. In the autumn of 1004, Thorvald sailed to Leif's Vinland settlement and wintered there. The next summer, while exploring the St. Lawrence region, Thorvald and his crew attacked a band of Indians, killing eight of them. In retaliation, the Indians ambushed the Norsemen, and Thorvald was killed in the ensuing battle. In 1007 the expedition's survivors returned to Greenland and took with them Thorvald's body, which was delivered to Leif for burial.

12. Thorfinn Karlsefni (1010), Norse

The Greenlanders' Saga and Karlsefni's Saga are the two medieval sources that give accounts of the Icelander Thorfinn Karlsefni's attempt to establish the first permanent European settlement in America. In 1010, with 60 men and 5 women, Thorfinn—who was Leif Ericson's brother-in-law—sailed to Leif's Vinland camp, which he planned to colonize. In Vinland, Thorfinn's wife gave birth to a son—the first European child born in America—who was named Snorri. Thorfinn explored extensively, travelling as far south as Long Island and the Hudson River and, possibly, Chesapeake Bay. Four years later, Thorfinn and the Norse settlers returned to Greenland because of Indian attacks and violent internal discord caused by the shortage of women.

13. Prince Madog Ab Owain Gwynedd (1170, 1190), Welsh

The Atlantic voyages of this Welsh prince were recorded by the medieval historian Gymoric ap Grono Guntyn Owen and by the 17th-century chroniclers Thomas Herbert and Richard Hakluyt. Because of political conflicts with his brothers, Prince Madog sailed from Abergwili, Wales, in 1170. He voyaged westward across the Atlantic and landed somewhere in the Americas, where he built and fortified a settlement. After several years, Madog returned to Wales, leaving 120 men behind in the new colony. In 1190 he again crossed the Atlantic to discover that most of his men had been annihilated, presumably by Indians. Madog himself died in the New World a short time later. The actual site of Madog's settlement is disputed. Possible locations are the Florida peninsula; Mobile, Alabama; and the West Indies.

14. King Abubakari II (1311), Malian

According to medieval Arab historical and geographical documents and Malian oral epics, King Abubakari II of Mali, a Black Muslim, sailed from West Africa to northeastern South America. After learning from Arab scholars that there was land on the west side of the Atlantic, King Abubakari became obsessed with the idea of extending his kingdom into these as yet unclaimed lands. He mobilized the resources of his empire to hire Arab shipbuilders from Lake Chad to build a fleet. (Their descendants were employed by Thor Heyerdahl to construct his reed boat, *Ra I*.) In 1311 the king and his crew sailed down the Senegal River and across the Atlantic. It is believed that, while he sighted the north coast of South America, he made his first landfall in Panama. From there, King Abubakari and his entourage supposedly travelled south and settled in the Inca Empire.

15. Paul Knutson (1356), Norwegian

In a letter dated 1354, King Magnus of Norway and Sweden ordered the Norwegian sea captain Paul Knutson to journey to Greenland to restore the Christian faith to the Norsemen still living there. Knutson sailed to Greenland in 1355 and, the next year, to Vinland, where he established a camp on the North American coast. Knutson's camp was probably at Newport, Rhode Island, where a tower believed to have been constructed by his party still stands. One group of Knutson's men, who explored Hudson Bay and the territory to the south of it, are thought to be responsible for the Kensington Stone, a rock with possible Norse runes carved on its surface that was found in central Minnesota. Most of the members of the expedition, including Knutson, died in America. A few survivors returned to Norway in 1364.

16. Henry St. Clair (1398), Scottish

The voyage of St. Clair, the Prince of Orkney and Earl of Rosslyn, is described in the 15th-century *Zeno Narrative*, allegedly written by the grandnephew of St. Clair's Venetian navigator, Antonio Zeno. During a trip to Iceland and Greenland in 1393, St. Clair reportedly learned of a land to the west. Five years later, he led an expedition consisting of 13 ships and 200 to 300 men that landed in Nova Scotia. He left behind a group of settlers, who may have travelled as far south as New England. St. Clair died in a battle at Kirkwall in August 1400, just after his return from America. His sudden death severed all links with the colony in the New World.

17–18. Johannes Scolp and João Vaz Corte Real (1476), Danish and Portuguese

In 1475 King Alfonso of Portugal and King Christian I of Denmark arranged a joint expedition to North America to find a sea route to China. Danish sea captain Johannes Scolp and a Portuguese nobleman named João Vaz Corte Real were appointed as commanders of the combined fleet. Sailing from Denmark across the North Atlantic to the Labrador coast, they explored Hudson Bay, the Gulf of St. Lawrence and the St. Lawrence River. Failing to find a sea passage to Asia, they returned to Denmark, where their discoveries were largely ignored.

19. Alonso Sanchez de Huelva (1481), Spanish

De Huelva reportedly landed in the West Indies at Santo Domingo after being blown off course by a tempest. He returned to Madeira with a handful of survivors. According to some, Columbus learned about the New World from de Huelva. Martin Alonzo Pinzon, Columbus's second-in-command, had earlier been de Huelva's first mate.

—R.J.F.

12 MUSEUMS OF LIMITED APPEAL

1. American Academy of Otolaryngology Museum (One Prince Street, Alexandria, Virginia; http://www.entnet.org/museum/index.cfm)

Devoted to the world of head and neck surgery, the museum displays special exhibits dealing with such topics as the history of the hearing aid and the evolution of tracheotomies. The diseases of famous people are examined, including Oscar Wilde's ear infections and Johannes Brahms's sleep apnea. The gift shop sells holiday decorations in the shape of ear trumpets.

2. Antique Vibrator Museum (603 Valencia, San Francisco, California; http://www.goodvibes.com/museum.html)

The museum has collected more than 100 vibrators going back to 1869. Antique models include a handcrafted wooden vibrator that works like an egg beater and another that advertises "Health, Vigor and Beauty" to users. The museum's collection is displayed in Good Vibrations, a sex-toy emporium.

3. British Lawnmower Museum (106–114 Shakespeare Street, Southport, Lancashire, U.K.)

The museum includes 400 vintage and experimental lawn mowers, highlighting the best of British technological ingenuity. Of particular interest are the 1921 ATCO Standard 9 Blade, a solar-powered robot mower, and unusually fast or expensive mowers.

4. Dog Collar Museum (Leeds Castle, Maidstone, Kent, U.K.; http://www.leeds-castle.com/content/visiting_the_castle/dog_collar_museum/.html)

Housed in the Gate Tower of Leeds Castle, the museum features medieval and ornamental dog collars spanning four centuries. Included are numerous spiked collars designed for dogs used in hunting and bull- and bear-baiting.

5. Icelandic Phallological Museum (Hedinsbraut 3a, 640 Husavik, Iceland)

The world's only museum for genitalia, the Icelandic Phallological Museum contains 218 preserved penises, as well as specimens that have been pressed into service as purses, walking sticks and pepper pots. The museum's holdings represent nearly all of Iceland's land and sea mammals, with the 47 whale specimens making for the most impressive viewing. As yet, the museum has no human specimen, but an elderly man has pledged his privates in a legally binding letter of donation.

6. Kim Il Sung Gift Museum (Mount Myohyang, North Korea)

Housed in a 120-room, 6-storey temple north of Pyongyang, the museum is home to 90,000 gifts that have been given to Kim Il Sung, the late dictator of Communist North Korea, and to his son, Kim Jong Il, the current dictator. Included are Nicolae Ceausescu's gift of a bear's head mounted on a blood-red cushion, a Polish machine gun and a rubber ashtray from China's Hwabei Tyre factory. Twenty rooms are devoted to gifts given to Kim Jong Il, including an inlaid pearl and abalone box from the Ayatollah Khomeini and a pen set from the chairman of the Journalist Association of Kuwait.

7. Marikina City Footwear Museum (Manila, Philippines)

Former Philippine first lady Imelda Marcos, the world's most notorious shoe collector, donated the collection that made possible the opening of this footwear museum on February 16, 2001. The displays at the museum include several hundred pairs of shoes left behind at the presidential palace when Imelda and her husband, Ferdinand, fled the country in disgrace in 1986. Other shoes at the museum were donated by local politicians and film stars.

8. Museum of Bad Art (580 High Street, Dedham, Massachusetts; www.glyphs.com/moba/)

Founded in 1993, the MOBA is located in the basement of the Dedham Community Theater, 8 miles (13 km) south of Boston. Its motto is "Art too bad to be ignored." Although the bulk of the collection has been acquired at thrift shops, many of the finest pieces were fished out of rubbish bins.

9. Museum of Computers, Videogames and Robots (302 St. George Street, Annapolis Royal, Nova Scotia; http://www.computermuseum.20m.com)

Housed in a few rooms is a good-sized collection of "vintage" computers from the '70s and early '80s. Displays include the earliest personal computers, such as the clunky Commodore Chicklet and the "super-rare" Kenbak-1, complete with manuals and training films. The first portable computers are also featured, some of which weigh as much as 33 pounds (15 kg) and were toted around in massive plastic suitcases. And, of course, geeks and nerds from every walk of life can relive their glory days on the museum's vintage computer game display of Pong and Pacman.

PLACES

10. Mütter Museum (College of Physicians of Philadelphia, 19 South 22nd Street, Philadelphia, Pennsylvania; www.collphyphil.org/muttpg1.shtml)

This stunning collection of medical oddities and instruments includes the Chevalier Jackson collection of foreign bodies removed from the lungs and bronchi, the Sappey collection of mercury-filled lymphaticus, the B.C. Hirot pelvis collection, and medical tools from Pompeii. Individual items include Florence Nightingale's sewing kit; the joined liver of Chang and Eng, the original Siamese twins; bladder stones removed from U.S. chief justice John Marshall; a piece of John Wilkes Booth's thorax; a wax model of a 6-inch (15 cm) horn projecting from a woman's forehead; and a cheek retractor used in a secret operation on President Grover Cleveland, as well as the cancerous tumour that was removed from his left upper jaw.

11. Striptease Museum (29053 Wild Road, Helendale, California; www.exoticworldusa.org/)

Officially titled Exotic World Burlesque Hall of Fame and Museum, it is the domain of former exotic dancer Dixie Evans, whose specialty was imitating Marilyn Monroe. Items on display include breakaway sequinned gowns, tasselled panties and Gypsy Rose Lee's black velvet shoulder cape.

12. Sulabh International Museum of Toilets (Mahavir Enclave, Palm Dabri Marg, New Delhi, India; www.sulabhtoiletmuseum.org)

The Sulabh International Social Service Organization was created to bring inexpensive but environmentally safe sanitation to poor rural areas. On the grounds of their headquarters, they have built an indoor and outdoor museum that presents the history of toilets around the world. One panel reprints poetry relating to toilets and another gives examples of toilet humour.

15 THINGS MIRIAM TOEWS LIKES JUST FINE ABOUT WINNIPEG

Miriam Toews is the author of Summer of My Amazing Luck, A Boy of Good Breeding, Swing Low: A Life *and* A Complicated Kindness.

1. Esplanade Riel, the new bridge
Because it's beautiful, especially at night.

2. The beer tent at the Fringe Festival

Because it's fun, especially at night.

3. The heartbreaking scent of fall in late August, early September

Because it reminds me of my stern Russian forebears saying: "Now smarten up, summer's over, stop dreaming, pay attention, get serious, or soon you will die from exposure."

4. Our neighbour Barry's front lawn

Because it's a strange and beautiful, meticulously arranged garden of junk and interesting monuments and what sometimes look like open graves. And it's always changing; there's a new surprise every day. It's a welcome relief from the typical grass, shrub and flower look everyone's going for these days.

5. Rae and Jerry's lounge

Because it hasn't changed since the '50s and it's all red and vinyl and they have great pens.

6. Dancing Gabe

Because at every sporting event in the city I see him dancing and smiling and his enthusiasm is completely infectious.

7. VJ's drive-in

Because it's a tiny little ramshackle building across from the train station with a great slamming screen door. It's a Winnipeg institution. Nothing about it ever changes and it's very comforting. You can get a Fat Boy with chili and fries and a chocolate shake for something like seven bucks. You can sit at a picnic table outside the little shack and eat your food or you can sit in your car by yourself and watch the trains leave the station.

8. Independent Fish Company

I really like the name, and the images it conjures up in my mind of a bunch of anarchic fish stickin' it to the Man.

PLACES

335

9. Black Pearl Coffee

A store that sells nothing but coffee, run by one guy who really knows his stuff, in this building on Dufferin under the Salter Street bridge.

10. Oscar's Deli

Because it's downtown on Hargrave and the food is delicious and fresh, and the place is always packed at lunch. A long time ago, when I was twenty or something, Larry Brown, the ever-gracious owner, gave me the best job I've ever had driving the delivery car for the North End Oscar's deli (that one isn't there anymore) delivering lox and bagels and smoked meat and borscht to hungry bikers who lived in "club houses" with reinforced steel doors and who tipped really, really well.

11. The Weakerthans

Great band. And what's not to love about a band capable of inspiring a bar full of rowdy German concertgoers to chant "I hate Vinnipeg"?

12. Ladies' Day at the racetrack

My friend Carol and I like to make a lot of two- or five-dollar bets. We check the horses out before each race, in that corral by the track, and we try to make eye contact with them. Those are the ones we bet on. We really admire their beauty, and it's fun to be able to do that without our husbands getting jealous. And we are also trying to figure out whether it's very calm, cool horses who race better, or the kind of wild ones that are sidestepping and bucking and pissing off their jockeys. We're not sure, although the old guys at the track usually say it's the calm ones that are the deadliest.

13. Blake the butcher's blood-covered apron

Because he's a guy who takes meat seriously and always has time to give out tips and recipes. And it's just interesting to have a polite, friendly conversation with a man who is covered in blood.

14. Storytime at the Cornish library

Because Evelyn, the storytime lady who has been there for something like 30 years, is very cool and funny and all the kids love her and remember her all their lives.

15. Mosquito death squad late night fogging trucks .

Because they're very sinister and toxic—it's malathion or Agent Orange or something bad, and they operate secretly at night and if you happen to have your windows open when they drive by, you'll get all sick and choked up. On the other hand, I hate mosquitoes so intensely that I also love it when the trucks roll by my house. The next morning there's this horrible, chemically smell hanging over the whole block, but everyone (except for anti-fogging activists) is out rejoicing.

CHAPTER 11   LITERATURE

ABOVE: *Canadian literary lions at play*, circa 1988 *(from left: Pierre Berton, Jack McClelland, Margaret Atwood, Leonard Cohen and W.O. Mitchell)*

17 BEGINNINGS TO CANADIAN NOVELS

1. "Philip has thrown himself across the bed and fallen asleep, his clothes on still, one of his long legs dangling on the floor." —*As for Me and My House*, Sinclair Ross

2. "He had been walking around Halifax all day, as though by moving through familiar streets he would test whether he belonged here and had at last reached home." —*Barometer Rising*, Hugh MacLennan

3. "Catherine Tekakwitha, who are you?" —*Beautiful Losers*, Leonard Cohen

4. "I am a Newfoundlander." —*The Colony of Unrequited Dreams*, Wayne Johnston

5. "The cure for death by lightning was handwritten in thick, messy blue ink in my mother's scrapbook, under the recipe for my father's favourite oatcakes: Dunk the dead by lightning in a cold water bath for two hours and if still dead, add vinegar and soak for an hour more." —*The Cure for Death by Lightning*, by Gail Anderson-Dargatz

6. "She stands up in the garden where she has been working and looks into the distance." —*The English Patient*, Michael Ondaatje

7. "My lifelong involvement with Mrs. Dempster began at 5:58 p.m. on 27 December 1908, at which time I was ten years and seven months old." —*Fifth Business*, Robertson Davies

8. "In 1981, during the interval between the AA speakers at the meeting in the prison, a man was led in late." —*For Those Who Hunt the Wounded Down*, David Adams Richards

9. "I was driving you up to Prince George to the home of your grandfather, the golf wino." —*Life after God*, Douglas Coupland

10. "For the last couple of decades, there has been a museum in Walley, dedicated to preserving photos and butter churns and horse harnesses and an old dentist's chair and a cumbersome apple peeler and such

curiosities as the pretty little porcelain-and-glass insulators that were used on telegraph poles." —*The Love of a Good Woman*, Alice Munro

11. "Snowman wakes before dawn." —*Oryx and Crake*, Margaret Atwood

12. "It's really embarrassing to admit, but I forget why I killed my husband." —*Seduction*, Catherine Gildiner

13. "One morning—during the record cold spell of 1851—a big menacing black bird, the likes of which had never been seen before, soared over the crude mill town of Magog, swooping low again and again." —*Solomon Gursky Was Here*, Mordecai Richler

14. "Above the town, on the hill brow, the stone angel used to stand." —*The Stone Angel*, Margaret Laurence

15. "It happens that I am going through a period of great unhappiness and loss right now." —*Unless*, Carol Shields

16. "All day there are glaring omens that go undetected." —*The White Bone*, Barbara Gowdy

17. "Here was the least common denominator of nature, the skeleton requirements simply, of land and sky—Saskatchewan prairie." —*Who Has Seen the Wind*, W.O. Mitchell

ANN-MARIE MACDONALD'S 5 FORMATIVE FICTIONAL CHARACTERS

Ann-Marie MacDonald is an arts pentathlete—she's an author, playwright, actor and host of CBC-TV's Life and Times *biography series. Okay, that's only four, but she has won the gold in every event: a Commonwealth Writers' Prize, the Governor General's Award, the Chalmers Award, several Dora Mavor Moore Awards and a Gemini. Her debut novel,* Fall on Your Knees *(1997), was an international sensation. Her second novel,* The Way the Crow Flies *(2003), is also a bestseller.*

1. Bugs Bunny

Wise guy and eternal optimist, jaundiced but never jaded, savvy but never cynical, Bugs has an inquiring mind and extraordinary insight into the desires, the fears and the self-deceptions of others. Never malicious, he embodies, rather, the martial arts principal of catching incoming energy, turning it around and sending it back: thus, Yosemite Sam is continually hoisted on his own petard—"Of course, you know, this means war"—but Bugsy never starts it. In fact, he's willing to believe the best of others until he has no choice but to take them on, be they a belligerent opera singer, a rampaging bull or an evil scientist. His ruses are almost compassionate, as when he dolls himself up in drag to seduce Elmer Fudd or the Tasmanian Devil; for one brief moment, Elmer and Tas are really living. This early modelling of gender transgression was formative. Bugsy's irreverence coupled with tolerance, his open mind together with his healthy skepticism, make him the most enduring Enlightenment hero the 20th century produced.

2. Nancy Drew

These books aroused the shopper in me. They were disposable. No sooner had you cracked the spine on Number 39, *The Clue of the Dancing Puppet*, than you were getting all lathered up for Number 40, *The Moonstone Castle Mystery*. You had to have it. The narrative quality control and consistency meant that you chased the dream from one book to the next with the empty promise of fulfillment that ignites every shopping spree/gambling binge/streak of tawdry sex, only to wind up with a tepid shame and emptiness that would leave you prey to fresh cravings. Nancy was ungettable. She lured you in with the powder-blue roadster, but never failed to observe the speed limit. She had no meddlesome mother, just a terrific, trusting, pipe-smoking father, and if her white-bread world with its "swarthy" villains and perfectly preserved footprints in flowerbeds was a lie, it was a shiny one, as if the world had been taken over by cool, mean, successful kids who had suddenly turned nice; thus, the eerie Stepford quality. The only real texture was provided by George, the proto-lesbian, and the only girl one suspected of getting her period was plump Bess, who had the discomfiting whiff of fertility about her. Otherwise, each book left me feeling a little sick and dirty. And hungry for the next one.

3. Jane Eyre

The eponymous book has everything: outrageous 19th-century narrative coincidence, injustice, vindication and a heroine whose humility is sustained by a covert but towering ego. I first read it at age 11 and, bereft at having finished it, promptly decorated my room in a facsimile of 19th-century genteel poverty: I hung a chenille toilet-seat cover on my wall as a tapestry and, from the depths of the basement, fished out the old enamel basin that my mother had used to bathe us in and set that up on a doily on my dresser, along with a chipped milk pitcher and a floor rag for a washcloth. I vowed privately not to use running water, and each morning I imagined that the water in the pitcher had turned to ice. I longed for chilblains, though I had no clear idea of what they were; so, too, did I crave that enigmatic Victorian delicacy, "Blanc Mange." Jane slept with her only friend, Helen Burns, at a merciless boarding school, and one morning awoke to find the erudite, remote yet loving Helen dead at her side of TB. That is still the high romantic water mark for me. Jane was the ultimate underdog; the mouse who, eventually, roars; the virtuous virgin who is aflame with desire, and whose desire is finally fulfilled with no compromise. The boss. Jane. By Charlotte Brontë, who, along with her magnificent siblings, wrote and published (under a man's name) against staggering odds. I have since read it four or five more times.

4. Harriet the Spy

Harriet's circumstances were foreign, even a little intimidating to me: she was urban, had a nanny, remote cocktail-drinking parents and a friend, Sport, who lived with his divorced dad. But her odd intelligence, her acerbic (I didn't have a word for it then) mini–Dorothy Parker wit combined with tomboyish independence were irresistible. She was an obsessive observer and recorder and, like me, a kid who was neither positively outcast nor embraced by any clique at school. I also responded to the outlines of classic tragedy in her hubristic love of judging others mercilessly and entertainingly in the privacy of her own notebook. Literature is powerful, and that is what Harriet learns when her notebook is read, not only by despised individuals who could use a good skewering, but by a beloved friend whose wound might heal but never disappear. Harriet is humbled before her own gifts; they are not to be trifled with, especially not by her. It is a very adult story in terms of love, loneliness and the chilling effect of Harriet's notebook. By the end, the world has changed. The stakes are higher, but not in a "thrilling" way; rather, in a grey real-world grown-up kind of way. We are mended, perhaps; never quite healed.

5. Casey from *Mr. Dressup*

Casey was of indeterminate gender. S/he was probably referred to at some point as "he," but that was lost on me. His/her voice was ambiguous to say the least—even somewhat repulsive—and oddly addictive. S/he was fussy, a bit of a know-it-all and, while not exactly endearing, s/he was compelling. For example, Casey was the only one who could hear, or at least translate, what Finnigan was saying. Casey's intimate relationship with this silent but nonetheless opinionated dog added to his/her strange cachet, and Finnigan's sunny disposition provided an effective foil to Casey's prickly manner. Casey was a bit of a child-tyrant for whom Mr. Dressup had endless patience. I sometimes worried about Mr. Dressup because Casey seemed smarter and not always well-intentioned. Mr. Dressup, though he was the adult, was more innocent than the wily Casey, and I think that, although this was not altogether reassuring, it reflected my view of the world.

12 POETS AND HOW THEY EARNED A LIVING

1. William Blake (1757–1827), English poet and artist

Trained as an engraver, Blake studied art at the Royal Academy but left to earn a living engraving for booksellers. For a few years he was a partner in a print-selling and engraving business. He then worked as an illustrator, graphic designer and drawing teacher. It became increasingly hard for Blake to earn a living. He had a patron but lived essentially in poverty and obscurity, occasionally receiving an art commission. Blake was later recognized as one of England's finest engravers and its most remarkable poet.

2. Robert Burns (1759–96), Scottish poet

Raised on a farm in Ayrshire, Burns was a full-time labourer on the land at the age of 15. He tried to become a surveyor, but ill health forced him to give up. Next he lived with relatives who ran a flax-dressing business, until their shop burned down. Farming barely paid his bills, so Burns published *Poems, Chiefly in the Scottish Dialect* in 1786 to get money for passage to Jamaica, where he had a job offer as an overseer. The book was so successful that he used the money to visit Edinburgh instead. Returning to the farm, Burns took a job as a tax inspector, trying unsuccessfully to juggle three occupations. He lost the farm, but moved to Dumfries and continued as a tax inspector and poet.

3. John Keats (1795–1821), English poet

Keats was trained as a surgeon and apothecary in Edmonton, and later moved to London to work as a dresser in a hospital. For a year or so, Keats had his own surgeon/apothecary practice, and at the same time began publishing his poetry. His first major work, *Poems*, appeared in 1817, and that year he gave up medicine for the literary life. Charles Armitage Brown became his patron, providing him with a house in Hampstead, outside London.

4. Walt Whitman (1819–92), American poet

Whitman had a checkered career in newspaper work, starting as a printer's assistant and eventually becoming an editor in New York throughout the 1840s. After 10 years he gave up journalism for carpentry and verse. During the Civil War, Whitman moved to Washington, D.C., took a job in the paymaster's office and spent his spare time nursing the wounded. In 1865 he became a clerk at the Department of the Interior's Bureau of Indian Affairs, but was soon fired for being the author of the scandalous *Leaves of Grass*. He then clerked in the attorney general's office until a paralytic stroke forced him to retire in 1873.

5. Arthur Rimbaud (1854–91), French poet

Rimbaud's lover Paul Verlaine supported him for a while in Paris; after their separation, Rimbaud lived in London, working at various menial jobs until poverty or ill health or both caused him to return to France. In 1876 he joined the Dutch colonial army and went to Indonesia, but deserted and again returned to France. From there he joined a circus en route to Scandinavia; went to Cyprus as a labourer and later as a builder's foreman; and finally gave up his wandering in Harar, Ethiopia. There he worked for a coffee exporter, and later tried (unsuccessfully) to become an independent arms dealer. In 1888 he was managing a trading post, dealing in coffee, ivory, arms and possibly slaves.

6. Wallace Stevens (1879–1955), American poet

After leaving Harvard University without a degree, Stevens was a reporter for the *New York Herald Tribune* for a year. He then attended New York University Law School, passed the bar in 1904 and for the next 12 years practised law in New York. In 1916 he joined the legal department of the Hartford Accident and Indemnity Company in Connecticut; by 1934 he was vice-president of the company.

7. William Carlos Williams (1883–1963), American poet

Williams earned a medical degree from the University of Pennsylvania in 1906, interned at a hospital in New York City and for a year did post-graduate work in pediatrics at the University of Leipzig in Germany. He established a medical practice in his hometown of Rutherford, New Jersey, in 1910, and until the mid-1950s maintained both a medical and a literary career. An appointment to the chair of poetry at the Library of Congress in 1952 was withdrawn because of Williams's radical politics. He spent his last 10 years lecturing at many American universities.

8. Pablo Neruda (1904–73), Chilean poet

In recognition of his poetic skills, the Chilean government awarded Neruda a non-paying position as Chile's consul in Burma in 1927. Eventually he graduated to a salaried office, serving in Ceylon, the Dutch East Indies, Argentina and Spain. With the outbreak of the Spanish Civil War in 1936, Neruda, without waiting for orders, declared Chile on the side of the Spanish Republic. He was recalled by the Chilean government and later reassigned to Mexico. In 1944 he was elected to the national Senate as a member of the Communist Party. He later served as a member of the central committee of the Chilean Communist Party and as a member of the faculty of the University of Chile.

9. Irving Layton (1912–), Canadian poet

Layton was a devout Communist as a young man, and his main ambition was to further the revolution by working for the Co-operative Commonwealth Federation (CCF). He even went to work on his brother's farm in New York State, hoping the Party would be impressed by his agrarian roots. Alas, Layton proved to be a bit too far to the left for the CCF, and in 1939, while trying to figure out what to do with his life, he became a Fuller Brush man in Halifax. He proved to be spectacularly unsuccessful at peddling brushes door to door. But then, by all accounts, he never really tried very hard, preferring to spend most of his day stretched out under a tree on the Dalhousie University campus, smoking a pipe and reading. After six months of doing that, he embarked on an equally unsuccessful attempt at selling insurance for Confederation Life. Recalling that period in a letter written later in life, Layton admitted, "I broke no Olympic records in either enterprise."

10. Allen Ginsberg (1921–97), American poet

In 1945, while suspended from Columbia University for a year, Ginsberg worked as a dishwasher in a Times Square, New York, restaurant, as a merchant seaman and as a reporter for a newspaper in New Jersey. He returned to Columbia and graduated with a BA in literature in 1948. Far more influential was his off-campus friendship with a number of figures in the future Beat movement, including Jack Kerouac, Neal Cassady and William S. Burroughs. In 1949 Ginsberg was arrested for letting one of the friends, Herbert Huncke, use his apartment to store stolen property. For his sentence, Ginsberg was committed to a psychiatric hospital for eight months. Upon his release, he went home to Patterson, New Jersey, to live with his father. After a few years, Ginsberg completely changed his lifestyle. He moved to San Francisco and led a life of middle-class respectability. He had a high-paying job in market research, a live-in girlfriend and an upscale apartment. He was also miserable and began seeing a therapist. "The doctor kept asking me, 'What do you want to do?' Finally I told him—quit. Quit the job, my tie and suit, the apartment on Nob Hill. Quit it and go off and do what I wanted, which was to get a room with Peter [Orlovsky], and devote myself to writing and contemplation, to Blake and smoking pot, and doing whatever I wanted." Ginsberg wrote a memo to his boss explaining how his position could be eliminated and then he left. In 1955, shortly after devoting himself to poetry, he created a sensation with the first public reading of his poem "Howl," an event considered the birth of the Beat revolution. Ginsberg and his partner, Orlovsky, were able to live off

Ginsberg's royalties, money Ginsberg earned at poetry readings and disability cheques Orlovsky received as a Korean War veteran.

11. Milton Acorn (1923–86), Canadian poet

For a man who billed himself as "the people's poet," and who was accustomed to hearing himself described as a working-class hero, Milton Acorn's employment history was decidedly un-proletarian. Although later in his life he liked to speak about his days working as a union carpenter in Prince Edward Island, it appears that those days were actually few and far between. Acorn's family was decidedly middle-class and white-collar, and young Milton followed firmly in that path. He started working as a clerk with the New Brunswick Unemployment Insurance Commission in Moncton in July 1944, and he stayed there for three years. Indeed, he spent more of his time working as a civil servant than doing anything else, apart from writing.

12. Maya Angelou (1928–), American poet and memoirist

In her youth, Angelou worked as a cook and a waitress, and as the first black female fare-collector with the San Francisco Streetcar Company. In the 1950s she became a nightclub performer, specializing in calypso songs and dances. She also performed in *Porgy and Bess* on a 22-country tour of Europe and Africa organized by the U.S. State Department in 1954 and 1955. During the 1960s Angelou was northern coordinator of Dr. Martin Luther King Jr.'s Southern Christian Leadership Council, associate editor of an English-language newspaper in Cairo, features editor of a paper in Ghana and assistant administrator at the University of Ghana. She acted in Jean Genet's play *The Blacks*, wrote songs for B.B. King, wrote and produced educational television series, and acted on Broadway (for one night in 1973) and on television (as Kunta Kinte's grandmother in *Roots*, in 1977). In 1972 she wrote the script for *Georgia, Georgia*, the first original screenplay by a black woman to be produced. She continues to be a popular lecturer, as well as a university professor.

—The Eds.

MARGARET ATWOOD'S 10 ANNOYING THINGS TO SAY TO WRITERS

Margaret Atwood was born in Ottawa in 1939 and grew up in northern Quebec and Ontario, and later in Toronto. She is the author of more than 30 books, including novels, collections of short stories, poetry, literary criticism, social histories and children's books. Her most recent novel is Oryx and Crake (2003). *She recently published* The Penelopiad, *the first in a worldwide series of books in which prominent authors reinterpret the great myths.*

a)   What to say
b)   *What the writer hears*

1.   a) "I always wait for your books to come in at the library."
     b) *I wouldn't pay money for that trash.*

2.   a) "I had to take your stuff in school."
     b) *Against my will.*
        Or: *And I certainly haven't read any of it since!*
        Or: *So why aren't you dead?*

3.   a) "You don't look at all like your pictures!"
     b) *Much worse.*

4.   a) "You're so prolific!"
     b) *You write too much, and are repetitive and sloppy.*

5.   a) "I'm going to write a book too, when I can find the time."
     b) *What you do is trivial, and can be done by any idiot.*

6.   a) "I only read the classics."
     b) *And you aren't one of them.*

7.   a) "Why don't you write about ____?"
     b) *Unlike the boring stuff you do write about.*

8.   a) "That book by ____ (add name of other writer) is selling like hot cakes!"
     b) *Unlike yours.*

9. a) "So, do you teach?"

   b) *Because writing isn't real work, and you can't possibly be supporting yourself at it.*

10. a) "The story of *my* life—now *that* would make a good novel!"

    b) *Unlike yours.*

8 UNLIKELY HOW-TO BOOKS

1. *How to Be Happy Though Married* by "A Graduate in the University of Matrimony" (1895)

2. *How to Be Pretty Though Plain* by Mrs. Humphry (1899)

3. *How to Speak with the Dead: A Practical Handbook* by "Sciens" (1918). The author is identified as also having written "recognized scientific textbooks."

4. *How to Rob Banks without Violence* by Roderic Knowles (1972)

5. *How to Avoid Huge Ships* by Captain John W. Trimmer (1983)

6. *How to Start Your Own Country* by Erwin S. Strauss (1984)

7. *How to Shit in the Woods* by Kathleen Meyer (1989)

8. *How to Become a Schizophrenic* by John Modrow (1992)

30 CURIOUS HISTORIES AND ESOTERIC STUDIES FROM THE LIBRARY OF *THE PEOPLE'S ALMANAC*

1. *Manuale di Conversazione: Italiano-Groenlandese* by Ciro Sozio and Mario Fantin (1962)

One of the least-used dictionaries in the world, this slim 62-page booklet translates Italian into the language of the Greenland Eskimos. Collectors of obscure dictionaries will also appreciate Vladimir Marku's seminal work *Fjalori I Naftës* (1995), which translates 25,000 oil industry—related terms from English into Albanian.

2. Sturgeon Hooks of Eurasia by Géza de Rohan-Csermak (1963)

An important contribution to the history of fish hooks. Here are some of the chapter titles: "The Character of Sturgeon Hooks"; "Hooks in Eastern Europe"; and "Life Story of Hooks of the Samolov Type."

3. The Evoked Vocal Response of the Bullfrog: A Study of Communication by Sound by Robert R. Capranica (1965)

This monograph details the responses of caged bullfrogs to the recorded sound of mating calls of 34 kinds of frogs and toads. The author's academic career was made possible by a fellowship awarded by Bell Telephone Laboratories.

4. Why Bring That Up? by Dr. J.F. Montague (1936)

A guide to and from seasickness by the medical director of the New York Intestinal Sanitarium.

5. Cluck!: The True Story of Chickens in the Cinema by Jon-Stephen Fink (1981)

At last, a fully illustrated filmography of every movie in which a chicken—living, dead or cooked—appears. Films in which the words "chicken," "hen" or "rooster" are mentioned are also included.

6. On the Skull and Portraits of George Buchanan by Karl Pearson (1926)

Buchanan, one of Scotland's greatest scholars and historians, died in poverty in 1582. This publication was part of a series that included *Phrenological Studies of the Skull and Endocranial Cast of Sir Thomas Browne of Norwich* by Sir Arthur Keith and *The Relations of Shoulder Blade Types to Problems of Mental and Physical Adaptability* by William Washington Graves.

7. Communism, Hypnotism, and the Beatles by David A. Noebel (1979)

This 15-page diatribe contends that the Beatles were agents of Communism, sent to America to subvert its youth through mass hypnosis. "The Beatles' ability to make teenagers take off their clothes and riot is laboratory tested and approved," states Noebel. He supports his theory with no fewer than 168 footnotes.

8. *Camel Brands and Graffiti from Iraq, Syria, Jordan, Iran, and Arabia* by Henry Field (1952)

The publication of this study was made possible by the generosity of an anonymous donor.

9. *Ice Carving Professionally* by George P. Weising (1954)

An excellent textbook by a master ice sculptor. Weising gives instructions for carving such items as Tablets of the Ten Commandments Delivered by Moses (for bar mitzvahs); Rudolph, the Red-Nosed Reindeer; and the Travellers Insurance Company Tower in Hartford, Connecticut.

10. *The One-Leg Resting Position (Nilotenstellung) in Africa and Elsewhere* by Gerhard Lindblom (1949)

A survey of cultures in which people commonly rest while standing by placing one foot on or near the knee of the other leg. Contains 15 photographs from Africa, Sri Lanka, Romania, Australia and Bolivia, as well as a fold-out locator map of Africa.

11. *Dirt: A Social History as Seen through the Uses and Abuses of Dirt* by Terence McLaughlin (1971)

Readers who are drawn to dirty books might also enjoy *Smut: An Anatomy of Dirt* by Christian Engnensberger (1972); *The Kingdom of Dust* by J. Gordon Ogden (1912); and *All about Mud* by Oliver R. Selfrige (1978).

12. *Birds Asleep* by Alexander F. Skutch (1989)

A detailed and surprisingly readable study by an ornithologist resident in Costa Rica. A 12-page bibliography is included for serious students. Less pacific readers might prefer *Birds Fighting* by Stuart Smith and Erik Hosking (1955), which includes numerous photos of real birds attacking stuffed birds.

13. *How to Conduct a Magnetic Healing Business* by A.C. Murphy (1902)

A nuts-and-bolts account including advertising tips and postal rules and regulations, as well as discussion of such difficult topics as "Should a lady healer employ a gentleman assistant?"

14. *I Dream of Woody* by Dee Burton (1984)

Burton presents the cases of 70 people from New York and Los Angeles who have dreamed about Woody Allen. Fans of books on people who dream about famous people will also want to track down *Dreams about H.M. the Queen* by Brian Masters (1973), a collection of dreams about Queen Elizabeth II and other members of the British royal family; *I Dream of Madonna* by Kay Turner (1993); *Dreams of Bill* by Judith Anderson-Miller and Bruce Joshua Miller (1994), a collection of dreams about Bill Clinton; and *Dreaming of Diana: Dreams of Diana, Princess of Wales, from Around the World*, compiled by Rita Frances (1998).

15. *Little-Known Sisters of Well-Known Men* by Sarah G. Pomeroy (1912)

A review of the lives of eight little-known sisters, including Sarianna Browning, Sarah Disraeli and Sophia Thoreau, as well as two known sisters of English writers, Dorothy Wordsworth and Mary Lamb.

16. *The Royal Touch: Sacred Monarchy and Scrofula in England and France* by Mark Bloch (1973)

This book, written in 1923, examines the unusual custom of curing the disease of scrofula, a form of tuberculosis, by being touched by the King of France or the King of England. The practice died out after 1825.

17. *Lust for Fame: The Stage Career of John Wilkes Booth* by Gordon Samples (1982)

A biography that ignores Booth's assassination of Abraham Lincoln and deals instead, for 234 pages, with his career as an actor, which continued until four weeks before he killed the president of the United States.

18. *The History and Romance of Elastic Webbing* by Clifford A. Richmond (1946)

A lively account of the birth and growth of the elastic webbing industry in the 19th century. In the words of the author, once a man has "got the smell of rubber in his nostrils . . . he either stays with rubber or is thereafter ever homesick to get back into the rubber industry."

19. *Canadian National Egg Laying Contests* by F.C. Elford and A.G. Taylor (1924)

A report of the first three years of the Canadian national egg laying contests, from 1919 to 1922, as well as a preliminary contest held on Prince Edward Island in 1918–19. The work consists almost entirely of charts comparing production and costs by owner, bird and year. In 1921–22 one of the birds belonging to Lewis N. Clark of Port Hope, Ontario, produced 294 eggs.

20. *The Direction of Hair in Animals and Man* by Walter Kidd (1903)
In his preface, Dr. Kidd states, "No doubt many of the phenomena here described are intrinsically uninteresting and unimportant." However, if you have ever yearned for a book that analyzes the direction in which hair grows on lions, oxen, dogs, apes, tapirs, humans, asses, anteaters, sloths and other animals, you won't be disappointed.

21. *A Study of Splashes* by A.M. Worthington (1908)
This pioneering classic makes use of 197 photographs to help answer the question, "What actually happens when a drop falls and splashes?" Worthington's book was considered so valuable to students of physics that it was reissued as recently as 1963.

22. *Paintings and Drawings on the Backs of National Gallery Pictures* by Martin Davies (1946)
A rare opportunity to view the flip side of 42 famous works of art.

23. *Early United States Barbed Wire Patents* by Jesse S. James (1966)
A definitive listing of 401 barbed wire patents filed between the years 1867 and 1897.

24. *Movie Stars in Bathtubs* by Jack Scagnetti (1975)
One hundred and fifty-six photographs of movie stars in bathtubs. There are also numerous shots of actors, actresses and animals in showers and steam baths.

25. *America in Wax* by Gene Gurney (1977)
A complete guidebook to wax museums in the U.S., with 678 illustrations, including Brigitte Bardot, Nikita Khrushchev and the Battle of Yorktown.

26. *The Gender Trap* by Chris Johnson and Cathy Brown with Wendy Nelson (1982)
The autobiography of the world's first transsexual parents. Chris and Cathy began life as Anne and Eugene. Anne was a social worker who wished she was a man; Eugene was a kung fu instructor who wished he was a woman. They fell in love, Anne gave birth to a baby girl, Emma, and

then Anne and Eugene switched sexes. Anne, now Chris, became Emma's father and Eugene, now Cathy, took over the role of mother.

27. Sell Yourself to Science by Jim Hogshire (1992)

The subtitle says it all: *The Complete Guide to Selling Your Organs, Body Fluids, Bodily Functions, and Being a Human Guinea Pig*. If you are reasonably healthy but have no job skills, this is the book for you. Hogshire explains how to earn $100 (U.S.) a day as a subject for drug studies and other scientific experiments, and how to sell your blood, sperm, hair, breast milk and bone marrow.

28. The Life and Cuisine of Elvis Presley by David Adler (1993)

In exquisite detail, Adler traces the evolution of what Elvis ate from the time he was a baby (cornbread soaked in buttermilk) through his years in the army, Las Vegas, Hollywood and Graceland, and finally the bingeing that weakened his health. Elvis gobbled a dozen honey doughnuts in a cab before a visit to the White House and once ate five chocolate sundaes for breakfast before passing out. Included are recipes for fried squirrel, peanut butter and American cheese sandwich, and Elvis's last supper, which was ice cream and cookies.

29. The Alien Abduction Survival Guide: How to Cope with Your ET Experience by Michelle LaVigne (1995)

Unlike most books that deal with alien abduction, LaVigne's treatise is a practical guide that helps abductees control their fear and "take control" of the experience. The author smashes various myths, such as "the ETs have no lips, and do not open their mouths," "all ETs who are called greys are grey" and "the ETs have long tentacle-like fingers covered with suction cups, similar to those found on an octopus."

30. Pie Any Means Necessary: The Biotic Baking Brigade Cookbook (2004)

The BBB presents the history of pie-throwing as a political act and includes several recipes for easy-to-throw pies. Also included are photographs of such celebrities as Bill Gates and U.K. cabinet minister Clare Short being pied.

DAVID YOUNG'S 5 ESSENTIAL COLD-LIT CLASSICS

David Young is a Canadian playwright best known for Glenn *(1992), his theatrical portrait of Glenn Gould, and* Inexpressible Island *(1998), a history-based play about six Royal Navy officers and men who overwintered in an Antarctic snow cave in 1912.*

Cold-lit classics, the great stories about cold as a crucible of suffering, are found in the literature of exploration—particularly in books written by and about the English. Rotting gums, blackened toes, dog brains for breakfast, the literature of the Heroic Age is without question in the "stinky cheese" category, an acquired taste that offers many shadings and nuances to the true connoisseur.

1. *The Worst Journey in the World* by Apsley Cherry-Garrard (1922)

This is thought by many to be the greatest cold-lit book of all time. Cherry-Garrard, an English gentleman explorer, accompanied Robert Falcon Scott on his fateful voyage south in 1910. Cherry, as he was called, was not only a hero, he was also a writer of great clarity and feeling who was particularly attuned to the metaphysical pings and pangs of the Antarctic landscape. His book—brimming equally with elegiac melancholy and lyric understatement—conjures those days of epic, crucifying hardship at the bottom of the world better than any other.

The cheerful threesome pulled their sledges over the hump of Ross Island, enduring temperatures (−80°F/−62°C) that literally shattered their teeth. All the while, "we did not forget the please and the thank you and we kept our tempers, even with God." The epic peaks when their tent blows away in a hurricane, leaving them in "darkness and cold such as had never been experienced by human beings." After an unimaginable night in the open, they found their tent snagged on the rocky shore and survived. "Our lives had been taken away and given back to us. We were so thankful we said nothing."

2. *The Endurance: Shackleton's Incredible Voyage* by Caroline Alexander (1998)

Sir Ernest Shackleton obviously belongs in Cherry's company. There are many accounts of his legendary Antarctic expedition in 1914; my favourite version is Alexander's, which is also the most recent. Alexander weaves her finely written tale in and around 135 duotone reproductions of Frank Hurley's expeditionary photographs.

In 1914 Shackleton sailed from England with a crew of 27 and a plan to cross Antarctica on foot. Why? Because nobody else had done it and, from a sentimental point of view, it was the last great polar journey. The *Endurance* sailed into the Weddell Sea and was promptly frozen into the pack ice. Shackleton and his crew overwintered there. Then things went seriously pear-shaped: their ship was smashed to kindling by ice pressure. Shackleton and his men retrieved what they could from the wreck and lived rough on a vast ice floe for four months, drifting far to the north. Inevitably, their ice floe started to break up, forcing them into lifeboats for six days. They went sleepless for 100 horrific hours, weathering a full gale; the open boats almost sank. "At least half the party were insane," according to Frank Wild, Shackleton's second-in-command. The worst was still to come. Shacks parked his crew on Elephant Island and set off with five men in a crudely rigged lifeboat to sail 800 miles (1,297 km) of open ocean to South Georgia Island. This is where the survival saga soars into myth and miracle. Alexander's rendering of the sea voyage is flawless, her voice calm and transparent as she takes us inside the precise human detail of an unimaginably extreme experience.

3. *The Home of the Blizzard: A True Story of Antarctic Survival* by Sir Douglas Mawson (1915)

This is my last nominee for the cold-lit pantheon of the Heroic Age. In 1912 Mawson set off from Cape Denison with his colleagues Xavier Mertz and Belgrave Ninnis to do a bit of summer sledging. They travelled east, mapping the coastline and collecting geological samples. Three hundred miles (500 km) from base camp, Ninnis disappeared down a deep crevasse with a sledge, a team of six dogs, the tent and most of the food and spare clothing. Mawson and Mertz turned around and headed back over dangerous ground in very bad conditions on a five-week return journey. They had nothing to eat but their dogs. Soon Mertz became ill (poisoned by toxic levels of vitamin A from the dog livers). Mawson dragged Mertz under the tent fly and stood by in utter helplessness for a period of days while his friend came unstuck, spun out of control, bit off his own finger and died a raving lunatic. And the nightmare was only beginning. Mawson was alone and without supplies in the middle of a vast crevasse field. A hundred miles (160 km) of dangerous ground separated him from the safety of the hut at base camp. Mawson arrived at Aladdin's Cave, a depot on the ice cap above Cape Denison, a month after Mertz's death and was trapped there for a week by a raging blizzard. He finally staggered back to the hut on the same day his expedition supply ship sailed for home.

4. *The Shining Mountain: Two Men on Changabang's West Wall* by Peter Boardman (1984)

After books about the Heroic Age, the next best source for armchair travel to hell frozen over is books by mountaineers. Peter Boardman and Joe Tasker were best friends and, in the late 1970s, two of the boldest young climbers in the world. They died roped together while attempting the unclimbed northeast ridge of Everest in 1982. *The Shining Mountain* is Boardman's classic account of their 1976 two-man winter assault on the unclimbed west face of Changabang (23,000 feet/7,000 m). It was the most difficult climb ever attempted in the Himalayas. The horrifyingly exposed route required sleeping in "bat bags" suspended from pegs hammered into the sheer granite face. Boardman and Tasker designed their own gear and tested it by sleeping in a meat locker in Manchester for three nights. *The Shining Mountain* provides a sustained blast of adrenalin that will leave your ears ringing. Here's Boardman contemplating life as he hangs by his fingernails 6,000 feet (1,800 m) off the deck: "My mind was working quickly, absorbing all the tiny details around me, bringing movements into slow motion. In the white granite in front of my eyes were particles of clear quartz, silver muscovite and jet black tourmaline. My attention floated to them, they emphasized my insignificance—the fact that I was fragile, warm blooded and living, clinging to the side of this inhospitable world."

5. *I May Be Some Time: Ice and the English Imagination* by Francis Spufford (1996)

The last required read in the pantheon of cold-lit classics is Spufford's magisterial and deeply felt work. Named in honour of Captain Oates's famous last laconicism, spoken over his shoulder as he staggered away from Scott's tent to perish in the drift, this wonderful book is a learned and elegant historical overview of the way British society built fantasies about the polar regions into the cozy domestic interior of 19th-century life—an ice-cold wing appended to the great house of Empire, a place for the long-term storage of romance, heroism and the boyish pleasures of death by frost in a tent. And what an astonishing reliquary it is! There are chapters devoted to the notion of the sublime, to Lady Franklin's hold on the English imagination, to the naming of the features in the Canadian Arctic and the managed vision of "Eskimos" in the literature of various Victorian nitwits.

In the final chapter, Spufford "channels the tent" and gives us an intimate portrait of Scott's final hours, when, knowing his life was lost, he composed those famous letters to the English people: "It is forty below in the tent. The cold comes into him . . . a spearing and dreadful presence turning the cavities of him to blue glass . . . at its tip the cold moves inside him like a key searching for a lock."

THE ORIGINAL TITLES OF 20 FAMOUS BOOKS

1. Original title: *Seven Seas and the Thirteen Rivers*
   Final title: *Brick Lane* (2003)
   Author: Monica Ali

2. Original title: *Blood Road*
   Final title: *The Cure for Death by Lightning* (1996)
   Author: Gail Anderson-Dargatz

3. Original title: *First Impressions*
   Final title: *Pride and Prejudice* (1813)
   Author: Jane Austen

4. Original title: *Interzone*
   Final title: *Naked Lunch* (1959)
   Author: William S. Burroughs

5. Original title: *Bar-B-Q*
   Final title: *The Postman Always Rings Twice* (1934)
   Author: James M. Cain

6. Original title: *Twilight*
   Final title: *The Sound and the Fury* (1929)
   Author: William Faulkner

7. Original title: *Generica*
   Final title: *Happiness*^{TM} (2001)
   Author: Will Ferguson

8.   Original title: *Before This Anger*
     Final title: *Roots: The Saga of an American Family* (1976)
     Author: Alex Haley

9.   Original title: *Catch-18*
     Final title: *Catch-22* (1961)
     Author: Joseph Heller

10. Original title: *Landfall*
     Final title: *The Colony of Unrequited Dreams* (1998)
     Author: Wayne Johnston

11. Original title: *The Shine*
     Final title: *The Shining* (1977). Altered when King learned that "shine" was a derogatory term for African-Americans as they were often employed shining shoes; a black man is a central character in the novel.
     Author: Stephen King

12. Original title: *Hagar*; also *Old Lady Shipley*
     Final title: *The Stone Angel* (1964)
     Author: Margaret Laurence

13. Original title: *Tenderness*
     Final title: *Lady Chatterley's Lover* (1928)
     Author: D.H. Lawrence

14. Original title: *Barney Like a Player Piano*
     Final title: *Barney's Version* (1997)
     Author: Mordecai Richler

15. Original title: *A Jewish Patient Begins His Analysis*
     Final title: *Portnoy's Complaint* (1969)
     Author: Philip Roth

16. Original title: *Harry Potter and the Doomspell Tournament*
     Final title: *Harry Potter and the Goblet of Fire* (2000)
     Author: J.K. Rowling

17. Original title: *The Sea-Cook*
Final title: *Treasure Island* (1883)
Author: Robert Louis Stevenson

18. Original title: *Swivelhead*
Final title: *A Complicated Kindness* (2004)
Author: Miriam Toews

19. Original title: *All's Well That Ends Well*
Final title: *War and Peace* (1866)
Author: Leo Tolstoy

20. Original title: *The Chronic Argonauts*
Final title: *The Time Machine* (1895)
Author: H.G. Wells

—R.J.F., Cdn. Eds.

MICHAEL ONDAATJE'S 12 20TH-CENTURY CLASSICS IN TRANSLATION

Michael Ondaatje is an internationally acclaimed novelist and poet. His novels include Anil's Ghost, The English Patient, Coming Through Slaughter, *and* In the Skin of a Lion. *He has written a memoir,* Running in the Family, *and his books of poetry include* Handwriting *and* The Cinnamon Peeler.

1. *Le Grand Meaulnes* by Henri Alain-Fournier (France, 1913)
2. *My Mother's House* by Colette (France, 1922)
3. *The Man Without Qualities* by Robert Musil (Austria, 1930)
4. *The Radetzky March* by Joseph Roth (Austria, 1932)
5. *The Street of Crocodiles* by Bruno Schulz (Poland, 1934)
6. *The Master and Margarita* by Mikhail Bulgakov (Russia, 1939)
7. *Pedro Pàramo* by Juan Rulfo (Mexico, 1955)
8. *Collected Stories* by Isaac Babel (Russia, 1955)
9. *The Devil to Pay in the Backlands* by João Guimarães Rosa (Brazil, 1956)
10. *The Baron in the Trees* by Italo Calvino (Italy, 1957)
11. *Beauty and Sadness* by Yasunari Kawabata (Japan, 1965)
12. *The Rings of Saturn* by W.G. Sebald (Germany, 1995)

MICHAEL ONDAATJE'S 12 20TH-CENTURY CLASSICS IN ENGLISH

1. *Kim* by Rudyard Kipling (England, 1901)
2. *Victory* by Joseph Conrad (England, 1915)
3. *The Professor's House* by Willa Cather (U.S., 1925)
4. *To the Lighthouse* by Virginia Woolf (England, 1927)
5. *Wolf Solent* by John Cowper Powys (England, 1929)
6. *Light in August* by William Faulkner (U.S., 1932)
7. *Call it Sleep* by Henry Roth (U.S., 1934)
8. *An Imaginary Life* by David Malouf (Australia, 1978)
9. "The Three Lives of Lucy Cabrol" from *Pig Earth* by John Berger (England, 1979)
10. *So Long, See You Tomorrow* by William Maxwell (U.S., 1980)
11. *Blood Meridian* by Cormac McCarthy (U.S., 1985)
12. *The Selected Stories of Mavis Gallant* by Mavis Gallant (Canada, 1996)

12 RECENT CASES OF ATTEMPTED BOOK BANNING IN CANADA

Sections dealing with "sexual perversion" were actually removed from an earlier edition of the book you are presently reading. The rest of the best-seller by David Wallechinsky, Irving Wallace and Amy Wallace was allowed to remain intact on the library shelf at Glen Rose High School in Arkansas. In 1981, Saudi Arabia dealt more severely with *The Book of Lists 2*. The entire book was banned because it contained critical comments about the Saudi government.

Canadians like to believe that these sorts of things would never happen in Canada. This list, adapted from PEN Canada's Freedom to Read campaign, demonstrates that there have been many instances in which books have been under attack in Canada for moral or politically motivated reasons.

1. *The Diviners* by Margaret Laurence (1976–94)

This book was repeatedly challenged, even in Laurence's own community. In a letter to Gabrielle Roy, Laurence writes, "A local school trustee, who is a fundamentalist, has got into the act and stated in the *Peterborough Examiner* that only 'true' Christians have the right to choose material for English courses (this would, I suspect, exclude not only those of the Jewish faith, but also Roman Catholics, Anglicans, etc etc!) . . . He has not read *The Diviners*, because 'one does not have to wade in the muck to know what it is all about.'"

2. *Lives of Girls and Women* by Alice Munro (1982)
In 1982 a group of Toronto parents petitioned, without success, to remove the book from the high school curriculum. Parents objected to the "language and philosophy of the book."

3. *The Apprenticeship of Duddy Kravitz* by Mordecai Richler (1982)
In Ontario, the Etobicoke Board of Education was asked to ban this book from the high school curriculum. The motion was defeated.

4. *The Satanic Verses* by Salman Rushdie (1988)
On February 17, 1989, Canada became the only Western nation to detain *The Satanic Verses*. Ottawa blocked shipments of the book after a Canadian Muslim group complained that the book was blasphemous to Islam. Two days later, Canada Customs reversed the ban, saying the book was not hate literature. The book had already been on sale in Canadian stores for six months. The book was also banned in India, Pakistan, Saudi Arabia, Egypt, Somalia, Sudan, Malaysia, Qatar, Indonesia and South Africa for allegedly blaspheming Islam and the Koran. In Iran, Ayatollah Khomeini sentenced to death author Salman Rushdie and anyone else involved in the publication of the book. Khomeini also offered a substantial cash reward to whoever assassinated Rushdie.

5. *The Handmaid's Tale* by Margaret Atwood (1990s)
Although there are no cases of Margaret Atwood's novel being banned in Canada, it ranks 37th on the American Library Association's list of the 100 most frequently challenged books of the 1990s. The book is regularly accused of being anti-Christian and pornographic.

6. *Huckleberry Finn* by Mark Twain (1991)
In New Brunswick, the Saint John school division attempted to have this book removed from recommended reading lists because of perceived racism in characterization and language.

7. *Suffer Little Children* by Dereck O'Brien (1991)

This autobiographical account by Dereck O'Brien of child abuse at the Mount Cashel orphanage in St. John's, Newfoundland, was banned in that city during the trials of the eight Christian Brothers for abusing boys at Mount Cashel. People interested in reading it had no trouble getting it sent to them from other Canadian centres during that time, and it is now available in St. John's.

8. *Different Seasons* by Stephen King (1995)

This collection of novellas by Stephen King was deemed "unsuitable due to language and sexual content" by the Lanark County School Board in Ontario. One of the board members had not even read the book. A local bookseller helped recruit the author himself to fight the ban: Stephen King sent 600 free copies of the book to interested readers in the community. As a result of these actions, the board backed down and promised it would no longer make arbitrary decisions about book choices.

9. *Asha's Mums* by Rosamund Elwin (1997)

Rosamund Elwin's children's book was one of three banned by the Surrey Public School Board in British Columbia. The others were *Belinda's Bouquet* by Leslea Newman and *One Dad, Two Dads, Brown Dad, Blue Dads* by Johnny Valentine. Some parents felt the books promoted a homosexual lifestyle. The books did not contain the words "lesbian," "gay" or "homosexual," but did portray same-sex parents in a positive light. The Supreme Court of Canada repealed the ban in December 2002, stating that public schools should be secular, pluralistic and respectful of diversity.

10. *Underground to Canada* by Barbara Smucker (1998)

Following a complaint from a concerned mother in Winnipeg, the mayor brought the book before the city's race relations committee. The committee recommended that the book be withdrawn from provincial lists of materials approved for classroom use. The novel, which describes the underground railroad that brought slaves escaping from the American South to Canada during the 1850s and '60s, employs the word "nigger" 20 times.

11. *Harry Potter and the Philosopher's Stone* **by J.K. Rowling (2000)**
In 2000 three Harry Potter books were banned by the Durham, Ontario, Board of Education in response to parental contentions that the books promoted Wicca, wizardry and violence. Similar challenges to the popular Potter books have occurred in Corner Brook, Newfoundland, in Pembroke, Ontario, and in the Niagara district of Ontario.

12. *Of Mice and Men* **by John Steinbeck (2000)**
Terry Lewis, a member of the Reform Party's national executive council, complained about this novel's inclusion on Winnipeg's River East School Division's reading lists. Lewis distributed 10,000 pamphlets saying that Steinbeck's frequent use of "God," "God-damned" and "Jesus" in profane and blasphemous ways offended Christians and couldn't possibly have any educational benefit. No action was taken by the school division.

—Cdn. Eds.

MICHELE LANDSBERG'S 14 FAVOURITE CHILDREN'S BOOKS

Michele Landsberg was a columnist for the Toronto Star *for almost 25 years, and has been a member of CBC Radio One's Children's Book Panel for almost as long. Her* Guide to Children's Books, *published in the mid-1980s, was a bestseller. She hates making lists of her favourites because she then lies awake at night feeling guilty about all the beloved books she had to leave out. These are the children's books that "went straight into my heart and stayed there."*

1. *Stella, Star of the Sea* by Marie-Louise Gay (1999)
Stella, with a blazing mane of red hair, is the wildly imaginative big sister of timid toddler Sam. In scintillating watercolours that sparkle with summer joy, Gay shows how Stella uses poetic licence to interpret the world to Sam. Starfish, she explains breezily, are "stars that fell in love with the sea." I'm in love with Stella and Sam.

2. *Alfie Gets In First* by Shirley Hughes (1982)
When a toddler accidentally locks himself in, Hughes's marvellously warm and humane drawings of a working-class English family show us

every flicker of the tension, tears and eventual triumph. It's a celebration of resilience and neighbourhood friendship, a tiny domestic drama that rings utterly true.

3. *Cannonball Simp* by John Burningham (1966)

There is no more heart-rending illustration in all of children's literature than the opening panorama of ugly, unloved, stumpy little dog Simp being cast into the vast darkness of the garbage dump. When Simp finds light and love at last—as a circus performer—the glow of redemption is unforgettable.

4. *The Story of the Amulet* by Edith Nesbit (1907)

The first great fantasist for children, Nesbit sent her young Victorian characters on magical journeys to ancient Egypt and into a Fabian utopia of a future London. Deliciously funny and poignant, with an undercurrent of yearning imagination.

5. *Tom's Midnight Garden* by Philippa Pearce (1958)

A brilliant, complex and subtle fantasy of an unlikely friendship caught in a mysterious time warp. A powerfully moving, even thrilling, story that became an instant classic.

6. *Bilgewater* by Jane Gardam (1977)

It's impossible to choose among Gardam's painfully hilarious and sharp-witted literary novels of adolescence. This one, about a clumsy but gifted Yorkshire girl and her romantic entanglements, makes recent "chick lit" seem as hopelessly leaden as Dick and Jane.

7. *Bud, Not Buddy* by Christopher Paul Curtis (1999)

Orphaned Bud is only 10, on the road alone in Depression-era Flint, Michigan, looking for his unknown father. Bud is a black Huck Finn, all innocent heart and wily intelligence, battling an unjust world—and winning. The evocation of jazz-era music alone is worth the price of admission.

8. *A Year and a Day* by William Mayne (1976)

A haunting story about two little village girls in Cornwall and the changeling child they find in the woods, who will stay with them but "a year and a day." Mayne's delicacy of perception and vigorously poetic prose are unsurpassed; emotion is always conveyed obliquely, to powerful effect, and physical sensation is captured with laser accuracy.

9. *Wingman* by Daniel Pinkwater (1991)

A lonely, comics-loving Chinese boy called Donald plays hooky to climb the George Washington Bridge—and meets a Chinese superhero named Wingman. It's a touching family story, as well as a bracing evocation of transcending life's gritty realities through art.

10. *Demeter and Persephone* by Penelope Proddow, illustrated by Barbara Cooney (1972)

Proddow translates the Homeric hymn with superb force and clarity—the most lucid telling ever of this familiar myth—and Cooney's Botticelli-like paintings are ravishing in their tenderness and beauty.

11. *Goldie the Dollmaker* by M.B. Goffstein (1985)

Goffstein uses precise, fable-like language and line drawings of extreme simplicity to tell this affecting tale of an independent young woman who spurns false love for the enduring consolations of an artist's life. And she has a Jewish name.

12. *Swallows and Amazons* by Arthur Ransome (1930)

Not just the famous series of books about children's sailing holidays on the English lakes, but charters of independence, scripts of playful adventure, maps of bravery and ingenuity, dreams of freedom for its sheltered young readers in pre-war England—and Canada. With hot tea around the campfire at the end.

13. *The Seeing Stone* (Book 1 of the Arthur Trilogy) by Kevin Crossley-Holland (2001)

A stunningly vigorous and enthralling tale of a boy of the Middle Ages in the Welsh marches, whose own life as a young knight strangely parallels the story of King Arthur as he sees it unfold mysteriously in a "seeing stone." The characters are alive, the prose pungent, the pace dazzling, the story complex and rich.

14. *Black Hearts in Battersea* by Joan Aiken (1964)

The late Joan Aiken was one of the most prolific and comically gifted language-spinners in children's literature. Dido Twite, her sharp-tongued

Cockney heroine in the "Wolves of Willoughby Chase" series about a fictional "Hanoverian" England, is unforgettable—as fizzily unpredictable and fascinating as a sparkler. Hair-raising adventures, delicious language, hilarious dialogue and lovable protagonists: could anyone ask for more?

12 BAD REVIEWS OF FAMOUS WORKS

1. *Anna Karenina* by Leo Tolstoy (1877)

"Sentimental rubbish . . . Show me one page that contains an idea."
—*The Odessa Courier*

2. *The Apprenticeship of Duddy Kravitz* by Mordecai Richler (1959)

"The book seems to be an authentic description of a Jewish area in Montreal. As a satire on the money-maker, however, it is too contrived, too bitter, and too simple in its approach. Mr. Richler does not convince us that he is describing the situation which actually exists; rather we feel he is approaching his material with certain preconceptions derived from a type of fiction which happens to be fashionable. Its unconventionality, in other words, is too conventional." —D.J. Dooley, *Dalhousie Review*, Spring 1960

3. *Beautiful Losers* by Leonard Cohen (1966)

"For Cohen, tumescence is all, and the book is a talented, perverse, often badly-written, and always undisciplined and in the end, unsuccessful hymn to Onan who, like Cohen, spilled his substance rather than guiding it to where it might have given new life to an old form." —Arnold Edinborough, *Saturday Night* magazine, May 1966

4. *Breakfast of Champions* by Kurt Vonnegut (1973)

"From time to time it's nice to have a book you can hate—it clears the pipes—and I hate this book." —Peter Prescott, *Newsweek*

5. *Coming Through Slaughter* by Michael Ondaatje (1976)

"*Coming Through Slaughter* is written in several voices, none of them satisfactory. Far too many sentences float between cliché and bombast."
—Anatole Broyard, *New York Times Book Review*, April 24, 1977

6. *The Edible Woman* by Margaret Atwood (1969)

"*The Edible Woman*, as is to be expected from a poet like Margaret Atwood, is chock-full of startling images, superbly and classically crafted, but it is superficial and unimpassioned. . . . If you're used to writing poems, I suppose it is some wrench to wrap your mind and passions around a full-length novel, first go. But she's so excellent a stylist I hope she tries again." —Anne Montagnes, *Saturday Night* magazine, November 1969

7. *Finnegans Wake* by James Joyce (1939)

"As one tortures one's way through *Finnegans Wake* an impression grows that Joyce has lost his hold on human life." —Alfred Kazin, *New York Herald Tribune*

8. *For Whom the Bell Tolls* by Ernest Hemingway (1940)

"This book offers not pleasure but mounting pain . . ." —*Catholic World*

9. *Gulliver's Travels* by Jonathan Swift (1726)

". . . evidence of a diseased mind and lacerated heart." —John Dunlop, *The History of Fiction*, 1814

10. *Paradise Lost* by John Milton

"*Paradise Lost* is one of the books which the reader admires and lays down, and forgets to take up again. Its perusal is a duty rather than a pleasure." —Dr. Samuel Johnson

11. *Something I've Been Meaning to Tell You* by Alice Munro (1974)

"The book is filled with lots of information on who did what to whom and when, and where, but there is little emotional tension arising from the events. Everything is thought out, decided upon. Most of the dialogue, even, seems there for the sake of information, not for its own sake. And much of the writing seems to be designed to win our love rather than stun us with character or prose." —Frederick Busch, *New York Times Book Review*, October 27, 1974

12. *Two Solitudes* by Hugh MacLennan (1945)

"*Two Solitudes* is a novel of many fine peripheral qualities but it seems empty at the centre." —J.R. MacGillivray, *The U. of T. Quarterly*, April 1946

ELMORE LEONARD'S 11 FAVOURITE NOVELS

Born on October 11, 1925, in New Orleans, Louisiana, Elmore "Dutch" Leonard began writing novels while working as an advertising executive. His first successes were Westerns, including The Bounty Hunters *(1953) and* Hombre *(1961), before he turned to crime fiction with such bestsellers as* Stick *(1983),* Glitz *(1985) and* Killshot *(1989). Leonard's novels have been the basis for many hit movies, including Barry Sonnenfeld's* Get Shorty *(1995), Quentin Tarantino's* Jackie Brown *(1997) and Steven Soderbergh's* Out of Sight *(1998). Leonard makes his home outside Detroit, Michigan (the locale for many of his novels).*

1. *All Quiet on the Western Front* by Erich Maria Remarque
The first book that made me want to write, when I was still in grade school.

2. *For Whom the Bell Tolls* by Ernest Hemingway
A book I studied almost daily when, in 1952, I began to write with a purpose.

3. *A Stretch on the River* by Richard Bissell
The book that showed me the way I should be writing: not taking it so seriously.

4. *Sweet Thursday* by John Steinbeck
The book that showed the difference between honest prose and show-off writing.

5. *The Friends of Eddie Coyle* by George V. Higgins
Twenty years ago George showed how to get into a scene fast.

6. *Paris Trout* by Pete Dexter
An awfully good writer.

7. *The Heart of the Matter* by Graham Greene
Especially moving at the time it was written. I like everything he did, from *The Power and the Glory* to *Our Man in Havana*.

8. *The Moviegoer* by Walker Percy
Walker, the old pro.

9. *Legends of the Fall* by Jim Harrison
Wonderful prose writer and great poet.

10. *7 1/2 Cents* by Richard Bissell

11. Collected Short Stories of Hemingway, Annie Proulx, Raymond Carver and Bobbie Ann Mason
Have studied and, I hope, learned from all of them.

14 MEMORABLE SEX SCENES IN CANADIAN LITERATURE

At first glance, sex and Canadian literature hardly seem to go hand in
hand, but on closer consideration, there is indeed a wealth of sex scenes
in our books. At times titillating and at others deeply disturbing, the sex
scenes below indicate that Canadian writers deal frankly with a broad
range of subjects (although, interestingly, there seems to be a trend
towards depicting masturbation).

1. *Lives of Girls and Women* by Alice Munro (1971)
In the title story of this collection, Del Jordan develops a flirtation with
a war veteran that ends with him masturbating in front of her in a field.
In one of Canadian literature's most succinct passages, Del describes his
penis: "Not at all like marble David's, it was sticking straight out in front
of him, which I knew from reading is what they did. It had a sort of head
on it, like a mushroom, and its colour was reddish purple."

2. *The Diviners* by Margaret Laurence (1974)
The zealots who wanted this book banned from high schools and community libraries often point to Morag's dalliance with Harold as a sign of
the book's immorality. Morag is a single woman and Harold is recently
separated—how dare they have a casual sexual encounter? In a letter to
Laurence that appears in *Intimate Strangers: The Letters of Margaret Laurence and
Gabrielle Roy*, Roy discusses the attempts to ban *The Diviners*, as well as her
own book *The Tin Flute*: "Perhaps we offer books of too vast an experience
to young people as yet too young. I know that I always feel a little embarrassed when I hear of adolescents of fifteen or sixteen reading and
studying *The Tin Flute* at school. I don't think we had them in mind—do
you?—when we wrote our books."

3. *Bear* by Marian Engel (1976)

A woman on vacation in the woods gets intimate with a bear. Margaret Laurence describes this powerful, iconoclastic novel as follows: "Fascinating and profound, this novel speaks of a woman's strange (some would say bizarre) and moving journey toward inner freedom and strength, and ultimately toward a sense of communion with all living creatures."

4. *The Wars* by Timothy Findley (1977)

Findley's brilliant excavation of war, and the horror and treachery it makes possible, has one of the most graphically disturbing sex scenes in any novel: Robert Ross's rape. The brutal denouement is the moment when Ross realizes that "his assailants, who he'd thought were crazies, had been his fellow soldiers. Maybe even his brother officers." It is one of the most devastating portrayals of male aggression in literature.

5. *Obasan* by Joy Kogawa (1981)

One of the most studied novels in Canada, *Obasan* is a powerful and searing indictment of the internment of Japanese Canadians during the Second World War and its effect on one family and the community in which they are forced to live. It contains one of the most horrifying scenes of sexual abuse in literature. Naomi, the narrator, recalls the childhood moment when Old Man Gower, a neighbour, took her into his lap and bullied her to be complicit. With harrowing clarity, she asks, "Is this where the terror begins?"

6. *The Handmaid's Tale* by Margaret Atwood (1985)

One of the most chilling moments in this powerful novel is Offred's narration of being pinned between the Commander and his wife, Serena Joy, in order to impregnate her against her will. Atwood's novel about a future dystopia no longer feels so futuristic given the state of sexual politics, women's reproductive rights and religious zealotry in North America.

7. *In the Skin of a Lion* by Michael Ondaatje (1987)

Though Ondaatje's *The English Patient* is a masterpiece infused with erotic desire, the most memorable sex scene in his novels is in this one, about Toronto in the 1920s and '30s. A particularly charged passage details the aftermath of a sexual encounter between Clara and Patrick in which his ejaculate becomes a symbol for their interconnectedness: ". . . they passed it back and forth between them till it no longer existed, till they didn't know who had him like a lost planet somewhere in the body."

8. *We So Seldom Look on Love* by Barbara Gowdy (1992)

A young woman who likes sleeping with dead men gets into a relationship with a live one. He becomes obsessed with her obsession and realizes there is only one way to become truly intimate with her. In a review in the *Boston Globe*, Carol Shields describes the book: "Barbara Gowdy invites herself, and us, into taboo territory where love and disgust mingle freely. Nothing seems to hold back the narrative flow, not propriety, not politics, not even that ambiguity we once called good taste."

9. *Fall on Your Knees* by Ann-Marie MacDonald (1996)

"Under a smoky streetlamp I stood face to face with my beloved and pricked my fingers against the diamond studs of her immaculate shirt front." So begins one of the most sensuous lesbian sex scenes in contemporary literature, Canadian or otherwise.

10. *Wish Book: A Catalogue of Stories* by Derek McCormack (1999)

In "Backward," a young man has sex with another man in the back of a hayloft and inadvertently burns down a barn and, with it, the CanLit pastoral tradition. In "The Ghost," the narrator is caught masturbating while watching Bing Crosby in the change room of a Peterborough department store.

11. *The Pornographer's Poem* by Michael Turner (1999)

This isn't the first Canadian novel to feature bestiality, but it is the first one to offer bestiality, S/M play, voyeurism, porn and sex toys in the same scene.

12. *Happiness™* by Will Ferguson (2001)

When Edwin de Valu's wife, Jenni, gets hold of *What I Learned on the Mountain*, the all-encompassing self-help book whose publication he tries to prevent, their conjugal bed heats up. Unrelentingly so. Jenni goes as far as to indicate with Post-it notes the spots she wants her husband to explore. This is arguably one of the funniest sex scenes in a Canadian novel.

13. *Galveston* by Paul Quarrington (2004)

For 16 pages (possibly the longest sex scene in a Canadian novel), Caldwell and Beverly have sex while a force 5 hurricane rips the roof, walls and doors off their vacation house. Sex (and weather) becomes a metaphor for release and redemption.

14. *A Complicated Kindness* by Miriam Toews (2004)

Near the end of this novel, Nomi Nickel loses her virginity to her boyfriend, Travis, after she's discovered that he has started dating another girl who works with him at the replica pioneer Mennonite village. Nomi's description captures it all: "In a way I think it might have gone better if I hadn't been bald, drunk, depressed and jealous . . . and I hadn't started crying in the truck on the way home and slammed it into reverse for no good reason going fifty miles per hour."

—P.D. & M.S.

10 LAST LINES OF CANADIAN NOVELS

1. "He felt the boy's concerned hand on his. This sweet touch from the world." —*Anil's Ghost*, Michael Ondaatje

2. "'God's in his heaven, all's right with the world,' whispered Anne softly." —*Anne of Green Gables*, Lucy Maud Montgomery

3. "Oh my God, I thought, breaking into a sweat. I'd better call Saul. I owe Kate an apology. But, oh God, it's too late for Barney. He's beyond understanding now. Damn, damn, damn." —*Barney's Version*, Mordecai Richler

4. "Truthfully, this story ends with me still sitting on the floor of my room wondering who I'll become if I leave this town and remembering when I was a little kid and how I loved to fall asleep in my bed breathing in the smell of freshly cut grass and listening to the voices of my sister and my mother talking and laughing in the kitchen and the sounds of my dad poking around in the yard, making things beautiful right outside my bedroom window." —*A Complicated Kindness*, Miriam Toews

5. "Morag returned to the house, to write the remaining private and fictional words, and to set down her title." —*The Diviners*, Margaret Laurence

6. "'Here, dear,' says Lily, 'sit down and have a cuppa tea till I tell you about your mother.'" —*Fall on Your Knees*, Ann-Marie MacDonald

7. "I see that I must give what I most need." —*Fugitive Pieces*, Anne Michaels

8. "His back pained only slightly but he did not feel it so much—not knowing the processes of how this had all happened, only understanding that it was irrevocable because it had." —*Nights Below Station Street*, David Adams Richards

9. "She prayed. But not to the absent God. Never, never again to the absent God, but to the absent clouds, she prayed. And to the empty sky. She prayed for rain." —*Not Wanted on the Voyage*, Timothy Findley

10. "The son has drowned himself in the Seine, the mother is screaming so loudly you can hear her in the street; as for the father, rumour has it that he prowls the city in the hope of getting his wife back and erasing all dishonour from his house." —*A Suit of Light*, Anne Hébert

CHAPTER 12   WORDS

ABOVE: *Inuit hunter Henry Aod-la-taok sports a*
pair of wooden ilgaak in the western Arctic

377

33 NAMES OF THINGS YOU NEVER KNEW HAD NAMES

1. Aglet
The plain or ornamental covering on the end of a shoelace.

2. Armsaye
The armhole in clothing.

3. Chanking
Spat-out food, such as rinds or pits.

4. Columella Nasi
The bottom part of the nose, between the nostrils.

5. Dragées
Small beadlike pieces of candy, usually silver-coloured, used for decorating cookies, cakes and sundaes.

6. Feat
A dangling curl of hair.

7. Ferrule
The metal band on a pencil that holds the eraser in place.

8. Harp
The small metal hoop that supports a lampshade.

9. Hemidemisemiquaver
A 64th note. (A 32nd is a demisemiquaver and a 16th note is a semiquaver.)

10–13. Jarns, Nittles, Grawlix and Quimp
Various squiggles used to denote cussing in comic books.

14. Keeper
The loop on a belt that keeps the end in place after it has passed through the buckle.

15. Kick or Punt

The indentation at the bottom of some wine bottles. It gives added strength to the bottle but lessens its holding capacity.

16. Liripipe

The long tail on a graduate's academic hood.

17. Minimus

The little finger or toe.

18. Nef

An ornamental stand in the shape of a ship.

19. Obdormition

The numbness caused by pressure on a nerve; when a limb is "asleep."

20. Octothorpe

The symbol "#" on a telephone handset. Bell Labs' engineer Don Macpherson created the word in the 1960s by combining *octo-*, as in "eight," with the name of one of his favourite athletes, 1912 Olympic decathlon champion Jim Thorpe.

21. Ophryon

The space between the eyebrows on a line with the top of the eye sockets.

22. Peen

The end of a hammer head opposite the striking face.

23. Phosphenes

The lights you see when you close your eyes hard. Technically, the luminous impressions are due to the excitation of the retina caused by pressure on the eyeball.

24. Purlicue

The space between the thumb and extended forefinger.

25. Rasceta
Creases on the inside of the wrist.

26. Rowel
The revolving star on the back of a cowboy's spurs.

27. Saddle
The rounded part on the top of a matchbook.

28. Scroop
The rustle of silk.

29. Snorkel Box
A mailbox with a protruding receiver to allow people to deposit mail without leaving their cars.

30. Spraints
Otter dung.

31. Tang
The projecting prong on a tool or instrument.

32. Wamble
Stomach rumbling.

33. Zarf
A holder for a handleless coffee cup.

—S.B. & D.W.

35 INUKTITUT WORDS FOR SNOW
The Inuktitut vocabulary for snow has been the source of linguistic controversy for decades—some claim there are only a dozen or so words; others have ventured estimates in the hundreds. It all stems from the fact that Inuktitut speakers are able to make infinite distinctions in ice and snow conditions, distinctions that could, in extreme cases, mean

the difference between life and death. For instance, hunters out on the ice pack need to know whether the slush they're about to step on is *mituk* or *masak*, that is, snow floating in an ice-fishing hole or snow that is merely wet or saturated. Based on studies of the Inuktitut vocabularies, anthropologists concluded that language shapes thought, and this, in turn, was used to explain why people appear to "think differently" across cultures.

Unfortunately, the explanations for the extent of the snow vocabulary missed the most important point: Inuktitut, and its various dialects, features many long, compound words; therefore, it is difficult to say what counts as a separate word. In English, we might consider "book" and "books" the same word, but not "handbook" or "notebook." This classification gets even harder in Inuktitut, in which words often combine several ideas and elements. For example, the single word *"tikitqaarminaitnigaa"* conveys the complex idea "He said that he would not be able to arrive first."

There's no easy answer to the question of how many words the Inuit have for snow, because a native speaker could go on making them up forever with different root words, suffixes and modifiers. With that in mind, here is a list of 35 common Inuktitut words for snow, provided by educator and former languages commissioner of Nunavut Eva Aariak and used by Inuit who live in Canada's Arctic:

1. *Aluiqqaniq*: a snowdrift formed on the side of a steep hill, overhanging at top, concave at bottom
2. *Aniu*: snow often used for drinking water
3. *Aniuvak*: snow remaining in depressions on hillsides long after surrounding snow has melted
4. *Aput*: snow on the ground
5. *Aqilluqqaaq*: new soft snow
6. *Auviq*: a snow block for igloo construction
7. *Isiriaktaq*: yellow or reddish snow
8. *Kanangniut*: a snowdrift formed by a northeast wind
9. *Kaniqtaq*: compact, damp snow
10. *Makpataq*: a snow block cut sideways instead of downward
11. *Masak*: wet, saturated snow

12. *Matsaaq*: snow soaked in water and half melted (either on the ground or in a kettle)
13. *Mauja*: deep, soft snow that makes walking or sledding difficult
14. *Mingullaut*: fine, powdery snow that settles on objects
15. *Mituk*: small particles of snow or ice on a confined area of water, such as a fishing hole
16. *Munnguqtuq*: hard-packed snow that begins to soften slightly in the early spring
17. *Naannguaq*: a smooth, rounded snowdrift
18. *Nataqqurnait*: hailstones
19. *Natiruviaqtuq*: snow drift along the ground, surface drift
20. *Niuma*: hard, corrugated snow on sea ice, remaining after wind has blown away soft, loose snow
21. *Pingangniut*: a snowdrift formed by a southwest wind
22. *Piqsiq*: blowing snow, a blizzard
23. *Pukajaaq*: granular snow crystals
24. *Qaniut*: first snow, before it is swept by the wind
25. *Qanniq*: falling snow
26. *Qannitaq*: covered with fresh snow
27. *Qikirralijarnaqtuq*: snow that is squeaky or crunchy underfoot
28. *Qiksukkaqsimajuq*: soft snow that has been compacted by foot to make snow blocks for an igloo
29. *Qimugjuk*: a tapered snowdrift formed in the lee of a projection (house, igloo, boulder)
30. *Qiqsuqqaq*: snow surface that has thawed and refrozen
31. *Tisilluqqaaq*: very hard snow
32. *Tullaaq*: same as *qiksukkaqsimajuq*, different dialect
33. *Uangniut*: a snowdrift formed by a northwest wind
34. *Uluarnaq*: same as *naannguaq*, different dialect
35. *Uqaluraq*: a tongue-shaped snowdrift

17 WELL-KNOWN SAYINGS ATTRIBUTED TO THE WRONG PEOPLE

1. Anybody who hates children and dogs can't be all bad.
   Attributed to: W.C. Fields
   Actually said by: Leo Rosten (at a dinner, introducing Fields: "Any man who hates dogs and babies can't be all bad.")

2.   Go west, young man!
     Attributed to: Horace Greeley
     Actually said by: John Soule (article, Terre Haute *Express*, 1851)

3.   Everybody talks about the weather, but nobody does anything about it!
     Attributed to: Mark Twain
     Actually said by: Charles Dudley Warner (editorial, Hartford *Courant*,
     August 24, 1897)

4.   Survival of the fittest.
     Attributed to: Charles Darwin
     Actually said by: Herbert Spencer (*Principles of Biology* and earlier works)

5.   That government is best which governs least.
     Attributed to: Thomas Jefferson
     Actually said by: Henry David Thoreau (who put it in quotation marks in
     "Civil Disobedience" and called it a motto)

6.   Cleanliness is next to godliness.
     Attributed to: The Bible
     Actually said by: John Wesley (Sermons, no. 93, "On Dress")

7.   A journey of a thousand miles must begin with a single step.
     Attributed to: Confucius
     Actually said by: Lao-Tzu (*Tao Tê Ching*)

8.   God helps those who help themselves.
     Attributed to: The Bible
     Actually said by: Aesop ("The gods help them that help themselves.")

9.   God is in the details.
     Attributed to: Ludwig Mies van der Rohe
     Actually said by: François Rabelais ("The good God is in the details.")

10. If you can't stand the heat, get out of the kitchen.
    Attributed to: Harry S. Truman
    Actually said by: Harry Vaughn (Truman's friend, whom Truman was quoting)

11. Promises are like pie crust, made to be broken.
    Attributed to: V.I. Lenin
    Actually said by: Jonathan Swift (*Polite Conversation:* "Promises are like pie crust, leaven to be broken.")

12. Wagner's music is better than it sounds.
    Attributed to: Mark Twain
    Actually said by: Bill Nye

13. When I hear the word "culture," I reach for my gun.
    Attributed to: Hermann Göring
    Actually said by: Hanns Johst (1933 play *Schlageter:* "Whenever I hear the word 'culture,' I reach for my Browning.")

14. Winning isn't everything, it's the only thing.
    Attributed to: Vince Lombardi
    Actually said by: Red Sanders (UCLA football coach; quoted in *Sports Illustrated,* 1955)

15. Spare the rod and spoil the child.
    Attributed to: The Bible
    Actually said by: Samuel Butler (*Hudibras,* 1664)

16. Float like a butterfly,
    Sting like a bee,
    Your hands can't hit
    What your eyes can't see.
    Attributed to: Muhammad Ali
    Actually said by: Drew "Bundini" Brown (Ali's good friend)

17. There's a sucker born every minute.
     Attributed to: P.T. Barnum
     Actually said by: David Hannum (referring to people who had been duped by Barnum)

—C.F. & K.A.

13 SAYINGS OF WOODY ALLEN

Born Allan Konigsberg in Brooklyn on December 1, 1935, Allen began writing quips for gossip columnists at the age of 15. After graduating from high school, he landed a job writing for Sid Caesar's classic television comedy series Your Show of Shows. *In 1961 he branched out from writing to stand-up comedy. He also wrote plays and screenplays before directing his first film,* What's Up, Tiger Lily?, *in 1966. Among his many hits are* Annie Hall *(1977),* Manhattan *(1979) and* Hannah and Her Sisters *(1986).*

1. It seemed the world was divided into good and bad people. The good ones slept better . . . while the bad ones seemed to enjoy the waking hours much more. —*Side Effects* (1981)

2. Don't listen to what your schoolteachers tell you. Don't pay attention to that. Just see what they look like and that's how you know what life is really going to be like. —*Crimes and Misdemeanors* (1990)

3. [Intellectuals] are like the Mafia. They only kill their own. —*Stardust Memories* (1980)

4. Sun is bad for you. Everything our parents told us was good is bad. Sun, milk, red meat, college. —*Annie Hall* (1977)

5. The prettiest [girls] are almost always the most boring, and that is why some people feel there is no God. —*The Early Essays* (1973)

6. Sex alleviates tension and love causes it. —*A Midsummer Night's Sex Comedy* (1982)

7. Nothing sexier than a lapsed Catholic. —*Alice* (1990)

8. Love is deep; sex is only a few inches. —*Bullets over Broadway* (1994)

9. I thought of that old joke, you know, this guy goes to a psychiatrist and says, "Doc, my brother's crazy. He thinks he's a chicken." And the doctor says, "Why don't you turn him in?" And the guy says, "I would but I need the eggs." Well, I guess that's pretty much how I feel about relationships. You know, they're totally irrational and crazy and absurd . . . but I guess we keep going through it because most of us need the eggs. —*Annie Hall* (1977)

10. To you, I'm an atheist . . . to God I'm the loyal opposition. —*Stardust Memories* (1980)

11. I don't want to achieve immortality through my work, I want to achieve it through not dying.

12. Someone once asked me if my dream was to live on in the hearts of my people, and I said I would like to live on in my apartment. And that's really what I would prefer. (1987)

13. There's this old joke. Two elderly women are in a Catskills Mountain resort and one of 'em says, "Boy, the food at this place is really terrible." The other one says, "Yeah, I know, and such small portions." Well, that's essentially how I feel about life. Full of loneliness and misery and suffering and unhappiness, and it's all over much too quickly. —*Annie Hall* (1977)

17 PAIRS OF CONTRADICTORY PROVERBS

1. Look before you leap.
   He who hesitates is lost.

2. If at first you don't succeed, try, try again.
   Don't beat your head against a brick wall.

3. Absence makes the heart grow fonder.
   Out of sight, out of mind.

4. Never put off until tomorrow what you can do today.
    Don't cross the bridge until you come to it.

5. Two heads are better than one.
    Paddle your own canoe.

6. More haste, less speed.
    Time waits for no man.

7. You're never too old to learn.
    You can't teach an old dog new tricks.

8. A word to the wise is sufficient.
    Talk is cheap.

9. It's better to be safe than sorry.
    Nothing ventured, nothing gained.

10. Don't look a gift horse in the mouth.
    Beware of Greeks bearing gifts.

11. Do unto others as you would have others do unto you.
    Nice guys finish last.

12. Hitch your wagon to a star.
    Don't bite off more than you can chew.

13. Many hands make light work.
    Too many cooks spoil the broth.

14. Don't judge a book by its cover.
    Clothes make the man.

15. The squeaking wheel gets the grease.
    Silence is golden.

16. Birds of a feather flock together.
    Opposites attract.

17. The pen is mightier than the sword.
    Actions speak louder than words.

—J.Ba.

KATHERINE BARBER'S 11 FAVOURITE REGIONALISMS WITHIN CANADA

As editor-in-chief of the Canadian Oxford Dictionary, *Katherine Barber is one of the country's pre-eminent experts on the development of Canadian English. Along the way, she's come across many regionalisms. Here is a list of her favourites.*

1. Bangbelly
An evocative Newfoundland word for a rib-sticking dessert made from molasses, flour, raisins and salt pork.

2. Bunny Hug
The Saskatchewan term for a kangaroo jacket, which is in turn a Canadianism for what is also known as a hoodie.

3. Dainties
When I first moved to Ottawa from Winnipeg, I caused some consternation by telling an Ontarian that I was going to take my dainties to a shower I had been invited to. Any prairie dweller would know I meant an assortment of cookies and squares, but he thought I was talking about my underwear.

4. Gotch/Gonch
The great linguistic dividing line in Canada is not between French and English, but between these two variants of a word, derived from Ukrainian, for underwear. It seems to fall somewhere in the middle of Lloydminster, with Albertans inserting the *n*, for reasons that are unclear.

5. Jambuster

This is the name we Manitobans use for what Albertans call a bismarck and other Canadians (prosaically, so it seems to us) call a jelly doughnut (though some Haligonians may call it a Burlington bun).

6. Kubie

An affectionate Edmontonian shortening of *kubasa*, a Ukrainian name for garlic sausage.

7. Nicky Nicky Nine Doors/Knock On Ginger

The *Canadian Oxford Dictionary* team took it into their heads to ask Canadians the crucial question of what they called the activity of knocking on someone's door and running away before the door is opened. It seems that mischievous young Ontarians call this "nicky nicky nine doors" whereas western pranksters call it "knock on (or down, or a-door) ginger." Each group thinks the other's name is ridiculous.

8. Shag

This is the delightful term used in Thunder Bay to designate a combined shower and stag, which no doubt would cause considerable confusion to a visitor from Britain, for whom "shag" has a quite different meaning.

9. Smithereen

What else could a resident of Smithers, British Columbia, be called?

10. Storm-Stayed

A term used in Scotland and in areas of Scottish settlement in Canada, such as the Maritimes, southwestern Ontario and parts of the Prairies, to mean "snowed in."

11. Wreckhouse Winds

Another evocative term used in southwestern Newfoundland to designate extremely strong winds that, legend has it, can knock a train off the rails.

SO TO SPEAK—THE TRUTH ABOUT 16 COMMON SAYINGS

1. All the tea in China

The United Nations Food and Agriculture Organization estimates that, in 2003, all the tea in China amounted to 800,345 metric tons.

2. At a snail's pace

The fastest land snail on record is a garden snail named Archie, who won the 1995 World Snail Racing Championship in Longhan, England, by covering 13 inches (33 cm) in 2 minutes. Archie's pace was 0.0062 mph (0.001 kph).

3. Blood is thicker than water

In chemistry, water is given a specific gravity, or relative density, of 1.00 because it is used as the standard against which all other densities are measured. By comparison, blood has a specific gravity of 1.06—only slightly thicker than water.

4. By a hair's breadth

Although the breadth of a hair varies from head to head, the dictionary definition of hair's breadth is 1/48 inch (1/19 cm).

5. Eats like a horse

A 1,200-pound (544 kg) horse eats about 15 pounds (7 kg) of hay and 9 pounds (4 kg) of grain each day. This amounts to 1/50 of its weight each day, or 7 times its weight each year. The real gluttons in the animal kingdom are birds, who consume more than 90 times their own weight in food each year.

6. Faster than a speeding bullet

The fastest bullet is a calibre .50 Saboted Light Armor Penetrator-Tracer M962. Used in M2 machine guns, it travels 4,000 feet (1,219 m) per second. The fastest non-military bullet is the .257 Weatherby Spire Point, which travels 3,825 feet (1,166 m) per second.

7. High as a kite

The record for the greatest height attained by a single kite on a single line is 14,509 feet (4,422 m). The kite was flown by a group headed by Richard Synergy at Kincardine, Ontario, on August 12, 2000.

8. Just a moment

According to an old English time unit, a moment takes 1½ minutes. In medieval times, a moment was either 1/40 or 1/50 of an hour, but by rabbinical reckoning a moment is precisely 1/1,080 of an hour.

9. A king's ransom

The largest king's ransom in history was raised by Richard the Lionheart to obtain his release from the Holy Roman Emperor Henry VI in 1194. The English people were forced to contribute almost 150,000 marks to free their sovereign. Nearly as large a ransom was raised by Atahualpa, king of the Incas, when he offered Pizarro a roomful of gold and two roomfuls of silver for his release in 1532. At today's prices, the ransom would be worth more than $7 million (U.S.). Unfortunately, it was not sufficient to buy Atahualpa his freedom; he was given a mock trial and executed.

10. Knee-high to a grasshopper

According to Charles L. Hogue of the Los Angeles County Museum of Natural History, this figure necessarily depends upon the size of the grasshopper. For the average grasshopper, the knee-high measurement would be about ½ inch (1 cm).

11. Only skin deep

The depth of human skin ranges from 1/100 inch on the eyelid to 1/5 inch on the back.

12. A picture is worth a thousand words

The amount paid by magazines for photographs and for written articles varies widely. Both *Travel & Leisure* magazine and *Harper's* magazine pay an average of $350 (U.S.) for a photograph and $1 a word for articles. Based on this scale, a picture is worth 350 words. When *The Book of Lists* first studied this matter in 1978, a picture was worth 2,000 words.

13. Quick as a wink

The average wink, or corneal reflex blink, lasts 1/10 second.

14. Quicker than you can say "Jack Robinson"

When members of the *Book of Lists* staff were asked to say "Jack Robinson," their speed varied from ½ to 1 second. It is acknowledged that this may not be a representative sample of the world population.

15. Selling like hotcakes

Sales figures for the International House of Pancakes show that their 1,164 U.S. restaurants sold a total of 700 million pancakes in 2003.

16. Since time immemorial

Time immemorial is commonly defined as beyond the memory of any living person, or a time extending so far back as to be indefinite. However, for the purposes of English law, a statute passed in 1275 decreed that time immemorial was any point in time prior to 1189—the year when Richard I began his reign.

28 WORDS RARELY USED IN THEIR POSITIVE FORM

	Negative Form	Positive Form
1.	*Inadvertent*	*Advertent* (giving attention; heedful)
2.	*Analgesia*	*Algesia* (sensitivity to pain)
3.	*Antibiotic*	*Biotic* (of or relating to life)
4.	*Unconscionable*	*Conscionable* (conscientious)
5.	*Disconsolate*	*Consolate* (consoled, comforted)
6.	*Incorrigible*	*Corrigible* (correctable)
7.	*Uncouth*	*Couth* (marked by finesse, polish, etc.; smooth)
8.	*Indelible*	*Delible* (capable of being deleted)
9.	*Nondescript*	*Descript* (described; inscribed)
10.	*Indomitable*	*Domitable* (tameable)
11.	*Ineffable*	*Effable* (capable of being uttered or expressed)
12.	*Inevitable*	*Evitable* (avoidable)
13.	*Feckless*	*Feckful* (effective; sturdy; powerful)
14.	*Unfurl*	*Furl* (to draw in and secure to a staff)
15.	*Disgruntle*	*Gruntle* (to put in good humour)
16.	*Disgust*	*Gust* (inclination; liking)
17.	*Disinfectant*	*Infectant* (an agent of infection)
18.	*Illicit*	*Licit* (not forbidden by law; allowable)

19.	*Immaculate*	*Maculate* (marked with spots; besmirched)
20.	*Innocuous*	*Nocuous* (likely to cause injury; harmful)
21.	*Deodorant*	*Odorant* (an odorous substance)
22.	*Impeccable*	*Peccable* (liable or prone to sin)
23.	*Impervious*	*Pervious* (being of a substance that can be penetrated or permeated)
24.	*Implacable*	*Placable* (of a tolerant nature; tractable)
25.	*Ruthless*	*Ruthful* (full of compassion or pity)
26.	*Insipid*	*Sipid* (affecting the organs of taste; savoury)
27.	*Unspeakable*	*Speakable* (able to be spoken of)
28.	*Unwieldy*	*Wieldy* (strong; manageable)

—R.A.

RUSS GERMAIN'S 10 CONTROVERSIES IN SPOKEN CANADIAN ENGLISH

Russ Germain anchored CBC radio's flagship newscast The World at Six *and* World Report *for more than 20 years. Keenly interested in language usage and pronunciation, Mr. Germain became the CBC's in-house Broadcast Language Advisor for national radio news in 1990. He was responsible for maintaining broadcast language standards for all network newscasters and reporters.*

1. Americanisms
Like the British, many Canadians bridle at the overpowering influence of American culture on our traditional speech and pronunciation patterns. The BBC devotes an entire section in its style guide to avoiding Americanisms.

a. Z (zed). Considered perhaps the foremost linguistic difference between Canadian and American speech, eh? Ironically, Canadian English probably got this pronunciation from the French language.
b. Route. In 1945, Nat King Cole sang "(Get Your Kicks on) Route 66," and he pronounced it ROOT, as in highway or path, not ROWT, as in the disordered flight of a defeated army. But ROWT, meaning road, was until relatively recently almost exclusively an American pronunciation.
c. Railway. Here in Canada we don't have railroads; we have railways.

d. Witness box. Many Canadians don't know that witness stands are found in American courtrooms but not in Canadian ones. The misconception probably started with Perry Mason beaming in on TV from the States.

2. Begs The Question

The true meaning of this phrase seems all but lost. Those who still know the difference shudder every time someone uses it to mean "demands the question be asked." Mavens will tell you the phrase refers to circular reasoning, or, if you want to get fancy, *petitio principii* in Latin. When you use this phrase, you most likely mean to say "raises the question."

3. Et Cetera

If Latin is a dead language, why are so many people still speaking it, and poorly at that? *Et cetera*, meaning "and so on," is increasingly being pronounced "ek cetera." Then there are singular Latin words such as "medium," "criterion," "bacterium," "datum." When they are pluralized, they become "media," "criteria," "bacteria," "data." And they like to have plural verbs to make a matching set: "the criteria are"; "the media are"; "the bacteria are"; "data are."

4. Fewer, Less

Even writers in advertising agencies don't seem to know when to use these words anymore. Specific quantities—grams, elephants, skis, cookies—take *fewer*; unknown quantities—water, land, rubber, salt—take *less*.

5. Fisher

In an attempt to move towards more gender-neutral language, the CBC required its on-air news staff to replace traditional terms such as "fireman," "policeman," "mailman" and "stewardess" with "firefighter," "police officer," "letter carrier" and "flight attendant." There was nary a peep from those engaged in these occupations. But when it came to changing the term "fisherman" to "fisher"—we have bankers, doctors, lawyers, pipefitters, farmers, engineers, etc.—all hell broke loose, especially on Canada's coasts. The last known position of the CBC was that both terms, *fisher* and *fisherman*, were allowable. How Canadian can you get?

6. Kilometre

KILL-oh-mee-ter, that is. It's a unit of measurement pronounced just like *centimetre* (SENT-ih-mee-ter) or *millimetre* (MILL-ih-mee-ter). They all belong to the same Measurement family. Down the street, however, you'll find the Instrument family: *barometer* (bah-RAW-meh-ter), *odometer* (oh-DAW-meh-ter), *thermometer* (ther-MAW-meh-ter). Many Canadians hate this; it's too damned logical. Besides, the Brits all say kill-AWWWW-meh-taw.

7. Lay, Lie

"I cannot tell a lie," said George Washington as he laid his axe down. People lie, in word and in bed. People and things lay objects: hens lay eggs; people lay books on tables. Differentiating between "lay" and "lie" ranks among the top difficulties for many people. Let's not even get into the past tenses.

8. Me, I

It seems no one under 20 these days is capable of saying something other than, "Me and Ashley are going to the movies." Perhaps it's immense linguistic peer pressure that is forcing objective pronouns into subjective roles. And whatever happened to linguistic courtesy? Didn't your mother teach you to put your friend first?: "Ashley and I are going to the movies."

9. Pedophile

The medical community came up with this one by combining two Greek words: *pæd(o)*, meaning boy or child, and *phile*, lover. Classical scholars generally agree the construction "æ," called a digraph, is pronounced EE, so *pædophile* is pronounced PEE-doh-fyl. But those same classical scholars decided some time ago that this digraph was obsolete and dropped its use except for ancient or technical terms, which leaves us with *pedophile*. If you don't know your classics, you'd guess it's pronounced PED-oh-fyl. But that's the same pronunciation as *pedem*, Latin for foot, you know, *pedestrian*, *pedestal*, *pedicure*, etc. So, when you say PED-oh-fyl, you are describing someone who has an unnatural love of feet.

10. Qatar

When the first Gulf War began, this former British protectorate leapt into the news. And newscasters everywhere referred to it as an inflamed condition of a mucous membrane, "catarrh"; hardly flattering for Qataris. Of course, the more accurate pronunciation left many of those same newscasters sounding as if they suffered from catarrh. It was a controversial shift, but eventually accuracy and consistency prevailed. KAW-ter (guttural K) is a lovely country to visit.

13 UNTRANSLATABLE WORDS

Here are 13 words and phrases that have no equivalent in English, edited by the *Book of Lists* authors from Howard Rheingold's *They Have a Word for It*, published by Tarcher, St. Martin's Press, 1988.

1. Bilita Mpash (Bantu)

This denotes blissful dreams. In English, we have nightmares, but no word for waking feeling happy. In Bantu, the word is further defined as a "legendary, blissful state where all is forgiven and forgotten." The Afro-American equivalent for *bilita mpash* is a *beluthathatchee*, believed to be traced to Afro-American slang from its Bantu roots.

2. Cavoli Riscaldati (Italian)

The attempt to revive a dead love affair. Literally, "reheated cabbage." The result of such a culinary effort is usually unworkable, messy and distasteful.

3. Dohada (Sanskrit)

Unusual appetites and cravings of pregnant women. *Dohada* is a word older than the English language. There is a scientific basis for *dohada*: women who want to eat dirt (a condition called pica) or chalk are attempting to ingest essential minerals.

4. Drachenfutter (German)

A gift brought home from a husband to his wife after he has stayed out late. Literally, "dragon fodder." In decades past, men went to bars on Saturday night with the wrapped gifts prepared in advance. This word can also be used for all gifts or acts performed out of guilt for having too much fun, such as gifts from employees to bosses, children to parents, students to teachers, etc.

5. Esprit de l'Escalier (French)
The brilliantly witty response to a public insult that comes into your mind only after you have left the party. Literally, "the spirit of the staircase." Observes author Rheingold, "Sometimes, this feeling about what you ought to have said at a crucial moment can haunt you for the rest of your life."

6. Katzenjammer (German)
A monumentally severe hangover. The inspiration for the early American comic strip "The Katzenjammer Kids." On New Year's Eve, it is common for one German to remark to another, "You're setting yourself up for a real *Katzenjammer*." (The wife of the party in question may require some *Drachenfutter*.)

7. Kyoikumama (Japanese)
A mother who pushes her children into academic achievement. A derogatory term that literally means "education mama." The pressure on Japanese students is severe and intense—but they are hardly the only victims of parental pushing. The American fad for using flash cards, etc., to create infant prodigies is practised by fathers and mothers.

8. Nakhes (Yiddish)
A mixture of pleasure and pride, particularly the kind that a parent gets from a child. It is something one relishes, as in "May you only get *nakhes* from your son!"

9. Ondinnonk (Iroquoian)
This noun describes the soul's innermost desires, the angelic parts of human nature. Listening to one's inner instinct to perform a kindly act is to let our *ondinnonk* be our guide.

10. Razbliuto (Russian)
The feeling a person has for someone he once loved but now does not. In the original Russian it applies only to a man, but it has become applicable for both sexes.

11. Schadenfreude (German)

The literal translation is "joy in damage." It is the pleasure one feels as a result of someone else's misfortune, as when you see a rival slip on a banana peel. *Schadenfreude* is not as strong as taking revenge, because it's a thought or a feeling, not an action. But when your noisy neighbour's car breaks down, and you're secretly pleased—that's *schadenfreude*.

12. Tartle (Scottish)

To hesitate in recognizing a person or thing, as happens when you are introduced to someone whose name you cannot recall. A way out of this social gaffe is to say, "Pardon my sudden tartle!"

13. Zalatwic (Polish)

Using acquaintances to accomplish things unofficially. It means going around the system to trade, to evade exchanges in cash. Since shortages seem to be a fact of social life, these exchanges can range from the profound (a new apartment) to the menial (a new pair of trainers).

—By permission of the author, Howard Rheingold

JANE FARROW'S 14 FAVOURITE WANTED WORDS

Wanted Words was a popular game played on CBC Radio One's *This Morning*. Each week I spotted a gap in the English language and invited listeners to fill it with their clever and often hilarious suggestions. The result—some brilliant new coinages that might just make it into the *Oxford Dictionary* someday. Use them or lose them!

1. Armajello

The saggy underside of the upper arm, commonly found on older women.

2. Bagmata

The red lines that appear on the palm of the hand as a result of carrying heavy plastic shopping bags.

3. Baton Rude

The plastic bar used to divide shoppers' groceries at the checkout counter.

4. Beditate

The act of lying down in bed and letting your mind drift, usually done in the morning.

5. Bragrag

The form letters families send around to each other at Christmas to boast about their travels, social triumphs and career accomplishments.

6. Dinnerloper

The uninvited diner who routinely shows up at mealtimes, looking for some home cooking.

7. Gournot

A person who really wants to be able to cook but just can't seem to get anything right; the opposite of a gourmet.

8. Hameo

The bit part played by people who try to get on television by standing, waving or jumping up and down behind television news reporters or sportscasters.

9. Indian Bummer

The blast of winter that comes after the first few days of spring warmth; the opposite of Indian summer.

10. Namenesia

The inability to recall someone's name, even though you know his or her face.

11. Ponis

The thinning ponytail that balding boomers wear in a desperate effort to stem the ravages of middle-age hair loss.

12. Sheetfaced

Having lines on one's face made by pillow and sheets.

13. Slined

To be stuck in the slowest lineup in a store or bank.

14. Yawncore

The contagious yawn that is caused by witnessing someone else yawn.

7 ADJECTIVES IN WHICH ALL THE VOWELS APPEAR IN ALPHABETICAL ORDER

1. *Abstemious:* practising temperance in living
2. *Abstentious:* characterized by abstinence
3. *Annelidous:* of the nature of an annelid
4. *Arsenious:* of, relating to, or containing arsenic
5. *Casesious:* having a blue colour
6. *Facetious:* straining to be funny or flippant, especially at the wrong time
7. *Fracedinous:* productive of heat through putrefaction

5 REMARKABLE MESSAGES IN BOTTLES

1. Better Late than Never

In 1714, Japanese seaman Chunosuke Matsuyama embarked on a treasure hunt in the Pacific. His ship was caught in a gale and sank, but he and 44 shipmates managed to swim to a deserted coral reef. Matsuyama and his companions eventually died of starvation and exposure, but before they did, Matsuyama attempted to send word home. He wrote the story on chips of wood, sealed them in a bottle and tossed it into the sea. The bottle washed ashore 150 years later on the beach where Matsuyama grew up.

2. Deliver Us This Day

In 1825 one Major MacGregor bottled a message and dropped it into the Bay of Biscay: "Ship on fire. Elizabeth, Joanna, and myself commit our spirits into the hands of our Redeemer Whose grace enables us to be quite composed in the awful prospect of entering eternity." The note was found a year and a half later, but the major and his party had already been rescued.

3. Double Jeopardy

In the 19th century a British sailor, perhaps in an attempt to found a lonely hearts club, threw a bottled marriage proposal into Southampton waters as his ship left port for India. At Port Said, on his return journey, he was walking along the quay and saw a bottle bobbing in the water. He retrieved it, opened it and read his own proposal for marriage.

4. The Last Message from the *Lusitania*

In 1916 a British seaman saw a bottle bobbing in the North Atlantic. He fished it from the water, opened it . . . and read the final message sent from the *Lusitania* before it sank, taking with it some 1,198 passengers: "Still on deck with a few people. The last boats have left. We are sinking fast. The orchestra is still playing bravely. Some men near me are praying with a priest. The end is near. Maybe this note will . . ." And there it ended.

5. A Message from the North Pole

In 1948 a Russian fisherman found a bottle in the sand bordering Vilkilski Strait in the Arctic. A message was inside, written in both Norwegian and English. It was incomprehensible even when translated: "Five ponies and 150 dogs remaining. Desire hay, fish and 30 sledges. Must return early in August. Baldwin." The bizarre message became clear when it was learned that polar explorer Evelyn Baldwin had sealed the note and sent it in 1902. He managed to survive the Arctic without ever receiving the hay, fish or sledges. Whether or not he made it back in August is unknown.

—J.B.M.

21 ABORIGINAL LANGUAGES SPOKEN BY 50 OR FEWER PEOPLE

Although Canada has only two official languages, at least 57 Aboriginal languages have been spoken by First Nations people at some point in our history. Many of these languages are now on the verge of extinction because they lack the critical mass of speakers that will allow the language to be passed on to future generations.

Family	Language	Approximate Number of Speakers
1. Algonquian	Potawatomi/Neshnabémwen	50
2. Athabaskan	Sekani	50
3. Iroquoian	Onondaga	50
4. Athabaskan	Tsúut'ína/Sarcee	40
5. Athabaskan	Tahltan	40
6. Siouan	Teton/Lak(h)ota	25
7. Iroquoian	Seneca	25
8. Salish	Nuxalk/Bella Coola	20
9. Salish	Straits	20
10. Salish	Squamish	12
11. Algonquian	Munsee Delaware	10
12. Athabaskan	Upper Tanana	10
13. Salish	Sechelt	10
14. Wakashan	Ditidaht/Nitinat	10
15. Iroquoian	Tuscarora	7
16. Wakashan	Oowekyala	5
17. Algonquian	Western Abenaki	5
18. Athabaskan	Hän	5
19. Athabaskan	Tagish	2
20. Tsimshianic	Southern Tsimshian	1
21. Isolates	Beothuk	0

Source: Canadian Linguistics Association Committee on Aboriginal Languages (2003).

WORDS

CHAPTER 13   SPORTS

ABOVE: *Quebec strongman Louis Cyr out-muscles two horses (1892)*

11 OLYMPIC CONTROVERSIES

1. Cruising to the finish line (1904, marathon)

The first runner to enter the Olympic stadium at the end of the 1904 marathon was Fred Lorz of New York. He was hailed as the winner, photographed with the daughter of the president of the United States and was about to be awarded the gold medal when it was discovered that he had stopped running after 9 miles (14.5 km) and hitched a ride in a car for 11 miles (18 km) before returning to the course. Lorz was disqualified, and the victory was given to Thomas Hicks. Although this was only the third modern Olympic marathon, Lorz was not the first person to cheat in this way. In the inaugural marathon in 1896, Spiridon Belokas of Greece crossed the finish line in third place, but was disqualified when it was discovered that he had ridden part of the way in a carriage.

2. With too much help from his friends (1908, marathon)

Italian Dorando Pietri was the first marathon runner to enter the stadium in London, England, in 1908. However, Pietri was dazed and headed in the wrong direction. Track officials pointed him the right way. But then he collapsed on the track. He rose, but collapsed again . . . and again, and again. Finally, the officials, fearful that "he might die in the very presence of the Queen," carried him across the finish line. This aid led to his disqualification, and the gold medal went to John Hayes of the U.S.

3. Champion with a dark secret (1932 and 1936, women's 100 metres)

Competing for Poland, Stella Walsh won the 100 metres in 1932, equalling the world record three times in the process. Four years later, at the Berlin Olympics, Walsh was beaten into second place by American Helen Stephens. A Polish journalist accused Stephens of being a man in disguise. German officials examined her and issued a statement that Stephens was definitely a woman. Forty-four years later, in 1980, Walsh, by then an American citizen living in Cleveland, was shot to death when she stumbled into the middle of a robbery attempt at a discount store. An autopsy concluded that, although Helen Stephens may not have had male sexual organs, Stella Walsh did. While Walsh was winning medals and setting records in women's events, she was, by today's rules, a man.

4. Clock vs. Eyes (1960, 100-metre freestyle)

Swimmer Lance Larson of the U.S. appeared to edge John Devitt of Australia for first place in the 1960 100-metre freestyle. Devitt congratulated Larson and left the pool in disappointment. Larson's official time was 55.1 seconds and Devitt's was 55.2 seconds. Of the three judges assigned the task of determining who finished first, two voted for Larson. However, the three second-place judges also voted 2–1 for Larson. In other words, of the six judges, three thought Larson had won and three thought Devitt had won. The chief judge gave the victory to Devitt, and four years of protests failed to change the results.

5. The fog of war (1968, slalom)

French skier Jean-Claude Killy, competing at home in Grenoble, had already won two gold medals and only needed to win the slalom to complete a sweep of the men's alpine events. Killy's main challenge was expected to come from Karl Schranz of Austria. But something curious happened as Schranz sped through the fog. According to Schranz, a mysterious figure in black crossed the course in front of him. Schranz skidded to a halt and demanded a rerun. His request was granted and Schranz beat Killy's time and was declared the winner. But two hours later, it was announced that Schranz had been disqualified because he had missed two gates before his encounter with the mysterious interloper. At a four-hour meeting of the Jury of Appeal, the Austrians said that if Schranz missed a gate or two it was because a French soldier or policeman had purposely interfered with him. The French claimed that Schranz had made up the whole story to cover up the fact that he had missed a gate. The jury voted 3–1 for Killy, with one abstention.

6. Extra shot (1972, basketball)

Since basketball was first included in the Olympic program in 1936, teams from the U.S. had gone undefeated, winning 62 straight games over a 36-year period . . . until the 1972 final against the USSR. In an era before professionals were allowed in the Olympics, and with most of the best American college players taking a pass, the U.S. team was hard pressed to prevail against the seasoned veterans of the Soviet squad. The Americans trailed throughout and did not take their first lead, 50–49, until there were three seconds left in the game. Two seconds later, the head referee, noting a disturbance at the scorer's table, called an administrative time out. The officials in charge had failed to notice that the Soviet coach, Vladimir Kondrashkin, had called a time out. With one second on the clock, the USSR was awarded its time out. When play resumed, they inbounded the ball and time ran out. The U.S. players began a joyous celebration, but then R. William Jones, the British secretary-general of the International Amateur Basketball Federation, ordered the clock set back to three seconds, the amount of time remaining when Kondrashkin originally tried to call the time out. Ivan Edeshko threw a long pass to Sasha Belov, who scored the winning basket. The U.S. filed a protest, which was heard by a five-man Jury of Appeal. Three members of the jury were from Communist countries, and all three voted to give the victory to the USSR. With the final vote 3–2, the U.S. lost an Olympic basketball game for the first time.

7. Wired for victory (1976, team modern pentathlon)

The favoured team from the USSR was fencing against the team from Great Britain when the British pentathletes noticed something odd about Soviet army major Borys Onyshchenko. Twice the automatic light registered a hit for Onyshchenko even though he had not touched his opponent. Onyshchenko's sword was taken away to be examined by the Jury of Appeal. An hour later Onyshchenko was disqualified. Evidently, he had wired his sword with a well-hidden push-button circuit breaker that enabled him to register a hit whenever he wanted. He was for ever after known as Borys Dis-Onyshchenko.

8. The unbeatable Park Si-Hun (1988, light middleweight boxing)

The 1988 Summer Olympics were held in Seoul, South Korea, and the Koreans were determined to win gold medals in boxing, one of their strongest sports. Light middleweight Park Si-Hun made it to the final with a string of four controversial victories, including one in which he disabled his opponent with a low blow to the kidney. In the final, Park faced a slick 19-year-old American named Roy Jones Jr. Jones dominated all three rounds, landing 86 punches to Park's 32. Yet three of the five judges awarded the decision to Park, who won the gold medal. Park himself apologized to Jones. Accusations of bribery lingered for years, and it was not until 1997 that an inquiry by the International Olympic Committee concluded that no bribery had occurred.

9. Say it ain't so, Ben (1988, 100 metres)

It was the best of times that quickly became the worst of times. On Saturday, September 24, 1988, Canadian sprinter Ben Johnson won a gold medal in the 100 metres in Seoul, South Korea, in a world record time of 9.79 seconds. Three days later, Johnson was stripped of that medal after testing positive for anabolic steroids. Ben Johnson was the highest-profile athlete ever caught cheating at the Olympic Games, but in the end, something positive did emerge out of the ashes of Canada's worst Olympic nightmare. In February 1989 the Dubin Commission began hearing evidence that stripped bare the widespread use of illegal performance-enhancing drugs among Canadian track stars and weightlifters. The resulting public outcry led to new policies that put Canada at the forefront of drug-free sport. It would take more than a decade before some other countries, most notably the U.S., undertook a similar purge of their doped-up Olympic athletes. As for the man who started it all, Ben Johnson continues to insist that he did not take steroids in the days before his race in Seoul, and professes to still be mystified how his urine sample came back positive.

10. Scoring Scandal Synchs Swimmer (1992, solo synchronized swimming)

The two leading synchronized swimmers in Barcelona were Sylvie Fréchette of Canada and Kristen Babb-Sprague of the U.S. The competition included a round of figures that counted for 50% of the final score. Fréchette, who was strong in figures, hoped to pick up points to offset the gains that Babb-Sprague was expected to make with her free routine. But one of the five judges, Ana Maria da Silveira of Brazil, gave Fréchette's albatross spin up 180° the unusually low score of 8.7. She immediately tried to change the score, claiming she had pushed the wrong button. But before the referee could be notified, the judges' scores were displayed and, according to the rules, that meant they could not be changed. When the free routine was completed the next day, it turned out that da Silveira's low score provided the margin of victory that gave the gold medal to Babb-Sprague. Fourteen months later, the International Swimming Federation awarded Fréchette a belated gold medal, while allowing Babb-Sprague to retain hers.

11. Impaired judgment (2002, pairs figure skating)

The sport of figure skating has a long history of judging controversies;
however, the problem reached a head at the Salt Lake City Olympics.
Russian skaters had won 10 straight Olympic championships in the
pairs event. In 2002 Russians Elena Berezhnaya and Anton
Sikharulidze were in first place after the short program, with Jamie
Salé and David Pelletier of Canada in second. In the free skate, the
Russians made a series of technical errors, while the Canadians skated
a clean program. Nonetheless, the judges voted 5–4 to award the gold
medals to Berezhnaya and Sikharulidze. The ensuing outrage expressed
by the North American media was so great and so prolonged that the
International Olympic Committee pressured the International Skating
Union into giving a second set of gold medals to Salé and Pelletier.
Subsequent investigations revealed behind-the-scenes deals among
judges and even the possible involvement of organized crime figures.
Lost in the uproar was the possibility that the five judges who voted for
the Russian pair simply preferred their traditional balletic style, while
considering the exuberance of Salé and Pelletier's performance too glitzy
and "Hollywood."

4 CANADIAN SPORTS RIOTS

1. The Christie Pits Riots (1933)

Sometimes sports serves as a pretext for anger that is actually directed
elsewhere. For example, some historians believe the Rocket Richard riot
(see below) was not really about Richard's suspension, but about long-
simmering French-Canadian anger over Anglo domination. Similarly,
the riot that erupted after a softball game at Toronto's Christie Pits on
August 16, 1933, wasn't really about anything that happened on the field
that night. All summer, gangs of young Nazi sympathizers had been
harassing Jews in the city's parks and beaches, and Jewish groups were
determined to fight back.

It all came to a head during a game between two neighbourhood
teams, St. Peter's and Harbord Playground. Thousands of people had
gathered in the park that evening. Most were more interested in what was
happening in the stands than in what was happening on the field.
Skirmishes broke out between the Nazi "Pit Gang" and the Jewish

"Spadina Avenue Gang" while the game was still in progress, but the real fighting began after the final out. Nazi sympathizers unfurled a blanket with a swastika painted on it, and the Jewish gangs were determined to tear it down. Hundreds of combatants battled for hours in the midtown neighbourhood. Police were slow to arrive. Only five people were arrested, and it was 2:30 in the morning before the fighting finally ended. Oh yes, St. Peter's won the game 5–4.

2. The Rocket Richard Riot (1955)

One of the most famous riots in Canadian sports history was precipitated by a violent incident in Boston on March 13, 1955. During a game between the Bruins and the Canadiens, Maurice "Rocket" Richard smashed three hockey sticks over the back and head of Bruins defenceman Hal Laycoe in retaliation for an earlier incident in which Laycoe had given Richard a cut to the head that required eight stitches. Then Richard punched linesman Cliff Thompson in the face. League president Clarence Campbell suspended the Rocket for the rest of the season and the playoffs.

Four days later, against the advice of League officials and police, Campbell showed up at the Canadiens' first home game since the suspension. He came in late, with his young girlfriend on his arm. His appearance sent the crowd into a fury. They threw tomatoes, eggs, shoes and bottles. One fan managed to slip by security and punch the League president. At the end of the first period, someone threw a smoke bomb in the Forum, which resulted in fans streaming out onto Ste-Catherine Street, where they joined up with hundreds of protestors who were gathered in front of the building. The crowd smashed windows, threw bricks and set fires. The riot lasted for seven hours. By the time it ended, 12 police officers and 25 civilians were injured, and 70 people had been arrested.

3. The Montreal Stanley Cup Riot (1993)

You would think that, by the time the Montreal Canadiens had won the Stanley Cup a record 24 times, their fans would have learned how to celebrate peacefully. But given their behaviour after the Habs' last two victories, that doesn't appear to be the case. In 1986, 5,000 people rampaged through downtown Montreal following the team's victory over Calgary. So poorly prepared were the Montreal police to stop the violence that Quebec courts ruled the police criminally negligent. So, with the Canadiens poised to win another Cup on June 9, 1993, Montreal authorities deployed close to 1,000 police officers, many of them helmeted riot troopers. It was not enough. Moments after the game ended, thousands of people descended onto Ste-Catherine Street, setting bonfires, overturning cars, breaking windows and looting stores. By the next morning, 15 city buses and 47 police cars had been destroyed, 168 people had been injured, including 49 police officers, and 115 people were in jail. Damage was estimated at more than $10 million. Few people could argue with Montreal mayor Jean Doré's assessment of it as "a regretful and appalling situation."

4. Vancouver Stanley Cup Riot (1994)

One of the ugliest riots in hockey history was triggered not by a victory, but by a defeat. On the night of June 14, 1994, following the Vancouver Canucks' loss to the New York Rangers in the seventh game of the Stanley Cup final, between 50,000 and 75,000 people jammed the streets of downtown Vancouver. The mood of the crowd was initially upbeat, but things turned ugly when drunken brawls broke out at the corner of Robson Street and Thurlow. Total damage was estimated at $1.1 million. More than 50 plate glass windows at the downtown Eaton's store were smashed. It took several hours before 540 Vancouver police and RCMP officers could restore order. Dozens of people were arrested, and more than 200 were injured. The most seriously injured was teenager Ryan Berntt, who was shot in the head by police with a rubber bullet. He spent nearly a month in a coma and suffered permanent brain damage as a result of the shooting. But that wasn't the end of Berntt's problems. He spent nine months in jail for his part in the riot, and his civil suit against the city of Vancouver and its police force was dismissed in December 2001, more than seven years after the riot.

AL STRACHAN'S 8 GOALS THAT CHANGED HOCKEY

Al Strachan has been covering hockey since 1973 for the Montreal Gazette, *the Montreal* Sunday Express, The Globe and Mail *and* The Toronto Sun, *as well as a number of other assorted publications. He was also a regular on* Hockey Night in Canada's Satellite Hot Stove. *He is the author of* To the Net *(Doubleday, 2005).*

Like any sport, hockey is in a constant state of evolution. Success is emulated and, after that, variations are introduced in the hope of advancing the game to the next level. As a result, there are specific goals that mark the advancing steps. Sometimes, they're series winners. Sometimes, they're goals that turned the tide and set in motion a series of inexorable events.

This is a list of 8 goals that changed the course of the game. There are others, of course, such as Mike Eruzione's goal in the "Miracle on Ice" at the 1980 Olympics, or Paul Henderson's goal in the 1972 Summit Series between Canada and the USSR, but the ones below are goals that I was fortunate enough to witness myself.

1. February 11, 1979. Challenge Cup, Game Three.
Boris Mikhailov (Alexander Golikov), 5:47 second period.

It was the rubber game of a best-of-three exhibition series between the USSR and the NHL All-Stars. Except for three Swedes, all the NHL players were Canadians who were badly outclassed by the Soviets when it came to skill and conditioning. Mikhailov's goal broke a scoreless tie and opened the floodgates for a 6–0 victory. So embarrassing was the defeat that it prompted Canada to examine its hockey priorities and move away from the carnage on ice that had been a large part of the game for the preceding decade.

2. May 10, 1979. Game Seven, Stanley Cup semifinal.
Guy Lafleur (Jacques Lemaire), 18:46 third period.

It's the famous "too-many-men" goal scored after the Bruins, coached by Don Cherry, were on the verge of ending the Canadiens' Stanley Cup string at three but got caught with too many men on the ice. This goal wasn't the winner, but it did send the game into overtime, at which point Yvon Lambert gave the Canadiens the win. It was a watershed goal as both teams—and their coaches—started a long and inexorable downward slide shortly afterwards.

3. September 13, 1984. Canada Cup semifinal.
Mike Bossy (Paul Coffey, John Tonelli), 12:29 overtime.

For the first time, Canadians proved that they could match the Soviets in every aspect of the game. They were able to skate, pass and shoot every

411

bit as well as the vaunted Soviet players, and were unfortunate not to have won this game in regulation time. With the victory, Canada moved back to the pinnacle of the hockey world.

4. September 15, 1987. Canada Cup final, Game Three.
Mario Lemieux (Wayne Gretzky), 18:34 third period.

This was another rubber game, but this time it was arguably the most entertaining series in the history of the sport. The teams had split a pair of 6–5 games and this one was tied 5–5 in the dying moments when the two greatest hockey players of the era, Wayne Gretzky and Mario Lemieux, conspired to score the winner.

5. April 21, 1988. Smythe Division final, Game Two.
Wayne Gretzky (Jari Kurri, Steve Smith), 7:54 overtime.

The Oilers had been written off by everyone, and even though a radically different Edmonton team won the Stanley Cup three years later, this was the last great moment of the dynasty that changed the face of hockey. The Oilers were heavy underdogs, but this goal spelled the end for the Flames and sent the Oilers on the road to the Cup. It also helped cement the opinion of Bruce McNall that he should acquire Gretzky for his Los Angeles Kings. When he did so, he started the exponential rise in salaries that eventually led to the 2004 owners' lockout.

6. September 16, 1991. Canada Cup final, Game Two.
Steve Larmer (unassisted), 12:13 third period.

Canada was under intense pressure from the United States, pressure that was increased when Gretzky was hurt in the series opener and ruled out for the duration. The Americans lost the opener, but had come back from a 2–0 deficit in Game Two. Had they won this game, they might well have won the series. But Larmer stole the puck and scored on a breakaway to give Canada a lead that the Americans could not overcome. At the time, Canada was clearly on top of the hockey world, but, as it transpired, would not win another tournament at this level for 11 years.

7. June 19–20, 1999. Stanley Cup final, Game Six.
Brett Hull (Mike Modano, Jere Lehtinen), 14:51 third overtime.

After a season that had been turned into a travesty by video replays, it was only fitting that controversy would surround the Stanley Cup winner. Hull's foot was clearly in the crease when he scored the Cup-winning goal for the Dallas Stars, and to this day Buffalo Sabres fans insist that it was an illegal goal. The official interpretation, however, was that he was ruled to be in possession of the puck. The debate will rage for years, but the infamous foot-in-the-crease rule was dropped within days.

8. February 24, 2002. Olympic gold-medal game.
Jarome Iginla (Steve Yzerman, Joe Sakic), 16:01 third period.

The Canadians had faced nothing but adversity throughout this tournament, right from an embarrassing opening-game loss to Sweden and a 3–2 win over a German team that had only two National Hockey League players. But they got to the final and the Americans were giving them everything they could handle. Iginla's goal clinched the goal medal, and sparked impromptu celebrations all across the country.

10 FEATS OF STRENGTH BY LOUIS CYR

Quebec's world-famous strongman Louis Cyr was born on October 10, 1863, in Napierville. Both of his parents were large, robust people, and their first child, Louis, seemed to combine their strengths. He was encouraged to eat large quantities of food and developed bulging muscles working on the family farm. By the age of 11 he could carry calves around on his shoulders and at 12 he worked as a lumberjack. He first appeared as a "strongman" at age 15, carrying a horse around on his shoulders near Boston. He soon became an international sensation as a sideshow attraction in the Barnum & Bailey and Ringling Bros. circuses. His storied career took place before professional weightlifting and standardized measures existed, so his feats of strength were often showy and unusual.

1.   He lifted a 485-pound (220 kg) boulder.
2.   Using just one finger, he lifted a 617-pound (280 kg) weight attached to a hook.

3. He lifted a barrel of cement weighing 313 pounds (142 kg) over his shoulder with one hand.
4. He lifted a 273-pound (124 kg) barbell over his head with one hand.
5. He backlifted a platform of 18 men weighing 4,348 pounds (1,972 kg).
6. He backlifted a record 3,536 pounds (1,604 kg) of pig iron.
7. He did a one-handed dead lift of a dumbbell that weighed 525 pounds (238 kg).
8. He resisted the pull of four horses, whom he held back with ropes, two in each hand, while trainers whipped the horses to get them to pull harder.
9. He often balanced a stack of four 50-pound (23 kg) weights in one hand while casually walking around.
10. At his Montreal bar on Notre-Dame Street, he tossed huge beer kegs into the air and caught them with one hand.

11 GREAT NAMES IN CANADIAN FOOTBALL
1. Junior Ah You, defensive end, Montreal Alouettes
2. Jack Bighead, tight end, Hamilton Tiger-Cats
3. Trod Buggs, running back, Hamilton Tiger-Cats
4. Lance Funderburk, quarterback, Hamilton Tiger-Cats
5. Admiral Dewey Larry, cornerback, Ottawa Rough Riders
6. Prince McJunkin III, quarterback, Ottawa Rough Riders
7. Wonderful Terrific Monds Jr., cornerback, Ottawa Rough Riders
8. Yo Murphy, receiver, Ottawa Renegades
9. Goodluck Owi, defensive end, Toronto Argonauts
10. Joe Paopao, quarterback, B.C. Lions
11. Annis Stukus, quarterback, Toronto Argonauts

KURT BROWNING'S 9 TURNING POINTS IN FIGURE SKATING HISTORY
Kurt Browning was born in 1966 in Rocky Mountain House, Alberta, and grew up in nearby Caroline. He is a four-time world champion and Canadian champion, a three-time world and Canadian professional champion and the only skater to win the world title with and without compulsory figures. He landed the first quadruple jump in a sanctioned event, putting him in the Guinness Book of Records.

1. Sonja Henie (Olympic gold medal winner, 1928, 1932, 1936)

Simply put, she was such a huge star on and off the ice and screen that her name alone was a turning point in the sport. One of the biggest stars in Hollywood at the time, she put figure skating in the public eye. And, boy, could she run on her toe picks. Wow.

2. Barbara Ann Scott (Olympic gold medal winner, 1948)

Canada's queen and my adopted gramma, she was the one who made other skaters afraid of Canadians. Of course, they feared her on the ice only; off the ice she is the sweetest person ever, but she could kick butt when it came time to lace up.

3. Prague World Championships (1962)

Only a miracle could have made Donald Jackson the world champion that year, and a miracle he created. Needing to gain back impossible ground lost during the compulsory figure portion of the competition, Donald pulled out all the stops in the free skate to become Canada's first men's world champion. But the historic turning point was his first jump of the program. Donald went for and landed a huge triple Lutz, which had never been done before. Even after he had made history, he kept his cool, adding many more jumps and spins to win the event. The triple Lutz was not duplicated by any other skater for more than a decade. What a leap!

4. Strawberry Ice (1982)

Toller Cranston's outlandish skating style turned the whole sport around and just a little bit upside down. His extension, his music choices, his elegance and his chest hair all made him stand out from his peers. Easily the best skater of his time, he was a hard pill for the judges to swallow. His 1982 TV special, *Strawberry Ice*, gives an excellent illustration of his extraordinary ability.

5. Budapest (1988)

A skinny kid from Caroline, Alberta, with nothing to lose and everything to gain, tried and landed the first four-revolution jump within a competition. Suddenly, three turns was not enough, and soon the "quad" was an expected jump if you were to be champion. This jump changed the boundaries of skating and—possibly more importantly—got the jumper a six-month loan of a slick Audi Quatro car. That made Kurt Browning one cool 22-year-old that summer.

6. Calgary Olympic Games (1988)
Stepping out on the ice in lingerie—I mean her short-program dress—Katarina Witt shocked the world and broke a few camera lenses. Some liked it, others did not, but it's safe to say the world of skating was never the same. The outfit, or lack thereof, helped make her a superstar, and she has transcended the sport to become a legend.

7. Halifax World Championships (1990)
This was the last event that featured compulsory figures. Figures used to take up most of a skater's training time. They were slow, difficult and expensive, and nobody who watched skating really cared about them. When fans turned on the television, they could not understand why a German or French skater was ahead of, say, me, for example, without being able to jump or spin. It was because of figures, and it was confusing for the audience. TV won out, and figures were gone for good. After the Halifax World Championships, skaters took to the streets dancing and singing, all the while wearing their now-unneeded compulsory figure skates. Sparks flew in celebration of the death of figures.

8. Midori Ito of Japan (1988)
Midori Ito could fly with the best of them. Her jumps easily stacked up against any of the men of her time. Actually, make that of any time. Midori was doing triple-triple combos better than the men, and in 1988, when she became the first woman in the world to land the triple axel, she cemented her place in history. In case you don't remember her, she is the skater who jumped out of the rink and into a TV camera at the Worlds in 1991. She got up, jumped back onto the ice, bowed a quick apology to the cameraman and continued with her program. An amazingly gifted, and polite, athlete.

9. Salt Lake City (2002)
The French judge did it. Okay . . . everybody did it, but she's the one who got caught. The pairs event at the 2002 Olympics was basically fixed,

and the media jumped on the story hard. The frenzy was the start of a chain of events that will change the sport. A new, just judging system has to be found; we'll have to wait and see what happens next.

8 REALLY BAD CANADIAN SPORTS TEAMS

1. The 1919–20 Quebec Bulldogs
In 24 games in the 1919–20 season, the Quebec Bulldogs of the NHL won just four times, and all of those victories were on home ice. The Bulldogs had serious problems keeping the puck out of their net. In a game on March 3, 1920, the Montreal Canadiens managed to score 16 goals against the Bulldogs' goaltender, an NHL record that still stands. Over the course of the season, opposing teams scored an average of 7.38 goals per game against the Dogs, another record that remains intact more than 80 years later.

2. The 1949 Hamilton Wildcats
Canadian football has had its share of really awful teams, but only a handful can lay claim to the dubious distinction of going an entire season without winning or tying a single game. The last team to do so was the Hamilton Wildcats (who merged with the Hamilton Tigers to become the Tiger-Cats in 1950). They managed to lose all 12 games during the 1949 season. In fact, this group of players lays claim to the record for the longest winless streak ever in Canadian football. Between September 1948 and September 1950, the boys from Steeltown won no games, tied 1 and lost 19.

3. The 1969 Montreal Expos
The Expos were truly awful in their first year. Although they beat the New York Mets 11–10 at Shea Stadium in their first game and then went on to win their first home opener against the St. Louis Cardinals, they won just 50 more games in the entire season, finishing with a record of 52 wins and 110 losses. That left them a full 48 games behind the division-leading Mets in the National League East.

4. The 1979 Toronto Blue Jays

It took the Blue Jays until their third season to hit rock bottom. Although their record was marginally better than that of the '69 Expos, at 53 wins to 109 losses, they finished a staggering 50.5 games behind the Baltimore Orioles in the American League East.

5. The 1992–93 Ottawa Senators

The worst Canadian professional hockey team of the modern era was undoubtedly the 1992–93 Ottawa Senators. There had been no NHL team in Ottawa since 1934, and the rust was clearly showing on this first edition of the revitalized franchise. Although they managed to beat the Montreal Canadiens 5–3 in their first game in Ottawa, the Senators won just 9 of their remaining 81 games, and all but one of those victories was at home. Their 41 road losses tied an NHL record. The Senators were outscored by their opponents 395–202, and finished 85 points behind the Boston Bruins in the Adams Division.

6. The 1996–97 Vancouver Grizzlies

The NBA returned to Canada in 1995 after an absence of 50 years. In the NBA's first season (1945–46), the Toronto franchise, known as the Huskies, won 22 of their 60 games, finished in sixth place and promptly folded. But the Huskies' performance was positively stellar compared with that of the Toronto Raptors and the Vancouver Grizzlies in the 1990s. Both teams were bad, but the Grizzlies were terrible. After winning only 15 games in their first season, the Grizzlies did what no one thought possible: they actually got worse in their second season. They experienced one of the worst seasons in NBA history, winning just 14 games and losing 68. Their opponents outscored the Grizzlies by an average of 10 points a game. In the short, inglorious history of pro basketball in Canada, they were the worst.

7. The 2000–2001 Mississauga Ice Dogs

You can't get much worse than the 2000-2001 Mississauga Ice Dogs of the Ontario Hockey League, a team partly owned by hockey genius Don Cherry. The team, in its third year of existence, won just 3 games out of 68. They managed to accumulate 15 points, leaving them 66 points behind the division-leading Sudbury Wolves. The Ice Dogs scored 157 goals in 2000–2001; their opponents scored 380. The Dogs finished their dismal season, appropriately enough, with a 24-game losing streak. Owners of Canadian hockey teams might want to think twice before including the word "dog" in their team's name.

8. The 2003 University of Toronto Blues

How bad a football team was the 2003 edition of the U of T Blues? Well, they lost all of the 8 games they played; they scored only 42 points in those 8 games, while their opponents scored 438 points; they lost by scores such as 80–0 and 72–0; and they didn't score a point until their fourth game. U of T is Canada's largest university, with 60,000 full-time students. How could there not be at least a couple of dozen guys who know how to play football? After all, schools such as Acadia and Mount Allison, with only a tiny fraction of the students to draw on, are able to field competitive teams every year. What's wrong with those U of T men, anyway?

25 THESES ABOUT WINTER SPORTS

1. Stuart A. Barbour. "Mental Skills of National Hockey League Players." University of Ottawa, 1994.

2. Daryl E. Boldt. "A Descriptive Analysis of the Joint Reaction Forces and the Ground Reaction Forces in the Lower Limb during the Landing of a Triple Toe Loop." University of Manitoba, 1994.

3. John D. Brice. "Frustration in Ice Hockey: Extent, Antecedents, and Consequences." University of Waterloo, 1990.

4. Ryan Chang. "Lower Limb Joint Kinematics of Hockey Skating." McGill University, 2004.

5. David H. Constable. "Sources of Stress in Hockey Referees." University of Toronto, 1997.

6. Kim D. Dorsch. "The Effects of Presentation Context on Perceptions of the Aggressiveness and Legitimacy of Various Ice Hockey Behaviours." University of Waterloo, 1993.

7. Dan Drouin. "The Effects of Fatigue on the Mechanics of Forward Maximum Velocity Power Skating in Skilled and Less-Skilled Skaters." University of Windsor, 2001.

8. Martin R.A. Duguay. "Comparison of On-Ice versus Laboratory Tests of Skating Speed and Power." McGill University, 1993.

9. Thomas Millard Evans. "Correlates of Team Performance in the Sport of Curling." University of Alberta, 1981.

10. Donald J. Farquhar. "The Effect of Seasonal Training on Selected Physical and Physiological Variables of Junior Male Alpine Ski Racers." Lakehead University, 1991.

11. Susan B. Greenberg. "Control of Subtalar Motion with the Use of Ski-Boot Footbeds." University of British Columbia, 1991.

12. Crystal L. Grinevitch. "Examining the Lived Experience of Forwards from a National Hockey League Team in Breakaway Situations: An Exploratory Study." University of Alberta, 2002.

13. Hugh R. Huber. "Physiologic Response of Cross-Country Ski Racers during Progressive and Steady State Skiing on the Skimill." University of Manitoba, 1992.

14. Gary J. Kirchner. "A Kinematic Description of the Ankle during the Acceleration Phase of Forward Skating." McGill University, 1988.

15. Steven M. Lazarovitz. "Team and Individual Flow in Female Ice Hockey Players: The Relationships between Flow, Group Cohesion, and Athletic Performance." University of Calgary, 2003.

16. Kimberly C. Mansfield. "A Comparison of Peak Blood Lactates following Maximal Upper Body and Maximal Combined Upper and Lower Body Simulated Ski Exercises in Elite Cross-Country Skiers." University of Ottawa, 1991.

17. Stephen McIlwaine. "A Comparison of Oxygen Consumption and Selected Kinematics between and within the 1-Skate, 2-Skate and Offset Techniques." Lakehead University, 2002.

18. Marilyn A. McNeil. "Measurement of Curling Ability through a Knowledge and Skills Test." McGill University, 1974.

19. Kavita Prakash. "Examining the Relationship between Life Stress, Skating-Specific Stress and Figure Skating Performance." University of Ottawa, 1999.

20. Randall W. Reid. "The Relationship of Lower Limb Flexibility, Strength and Anthropometric Measures to Skating Speed in Varsity Hockey Players." Lakehead University, 1977.

21. Thomas Silletta. "The Effects of Pole Length Variation on the Skiing Performance of Elite Cross-Country Skiers Using V-Skating Techniques." McGill University, 1988.

22. Mark Thomas. "A Physiological and Biomechanical Profile of the Athletes Competing in a World Cup Cross-Country Ski Relay Event." Lakehead University, 1999.

23. Gilbert D. Wade. "An Inductive Analysis of Intramural Ice Hockey Officiating: A Case Study." University of Ottawa, 1995.

24. Lyndsay Wheelans. "Ringette Alberta within the Culture of Technology: A Tenuous Existence." University of Alberta, 1995.

25. Robert Allan Gerald Wong. "Conflict between Cross-Country Skiers and Snowmobilers in Alberta." University of Alberta, 1980.

SPORTS

STEPHEN BRUNT'S TOP 10 CANADIAN BOXERS OF ALL TIME

Stephen Brunt has been a sports columnist for The Globe and Mail *since 1989, and has a particular passion for boxing. He is the author of seven books, including* Facing Ali: The Opposition Weighs In, *which was named one of the 10 best sports books of 2004 by* Sports Illustrated. *He lives in Hamilton, Ontario.*

On any list of boxing greats, it's easy to overvalue "world" championships, which are not all created equal, and also to overvalue heavyweights, who always capture the public imagination although they compete in the sport's shallowest talent pool. This list tries to balance achievements on the big stage with the depth of field and the times. There are some notable omissions. Two of the most popular boxers in Canadian history, Shawn O'Sullivan and Willie DeWit, were successful amateurs but burned out quickly as pros. Donnie Lalonde won one of the world light-heavyweight titles, but against dubious opposition, and he was never generally regarded as the best at his weight in the world. George Chuvalo is a trickier case, because his era now looks like a golden age for heavyweights. But when he faced world-class opposition, but for a couple of exceptions (Doug Jones, Jerry Quarry), he lost, which among the big men puts him behind Langford, Lewis, Burns and even the obscure Gains. On the other hand, if this was a list of the toughest, or the bravest, Chuvalo would be number one.

1. Jimmy Mclarnin, Vancouver, 1923–36
A classy, popular welterweight champion from the sport's golden era.

2. Sam Langford, Weymouth, Nova Scotia, 1902–23
Campaigning from welterweight to heavyweight, he took on all comers. But the colour line, drawn both by white champions and by Jack Johnson, prevented him from challenging for the world title.

3. George Dixon, Halifax, Nova Scotia, 1886–1906
"Little Chocolate" was the first to hold titles in three different weight classes.

4. Lennox Lewis, Kitchener, Ontario, 1989–2004
Olympic gold medalist and the dominant heavyweight of his generation. And yes, he is Canadian.

5. Tommy Burns, Hanover, Ontario, 1900–20
Best known for losing his title to Jack Johnson, he was a remarkable athlete, routinely facing and beating fighters who were 30 pounds (14 kg) or more heavier.

6. Lou Brouillard, St-Eugène, Quebec, 1928–40
Held both the welterweight and middleweight championships.

7. Johnny Coulon, Toronto, 1905–20
Won the world bantamweight title in 1910 and successfully defended it five times.

8. Larry Gains, Toronto, 1923–42
British Empire heavyweight champion. Beat two future world champions, Max Schmeling and Primo Carnera, but never got a chance to fight for the crown himself.

9. Arthur King, Toronto, 1945–57
Great lightweight of the 1940s and 1950s. Denied a title shot in the mob-controlled sport.

10. Arturo Gatti, Montreal, 1991–
Mr. Excitement. Two-time world champion, known for his all-out ring wars.

7 NON-BOXERS WHO TOOK ON THE CHAMPIONS
1. Lord Byron (1788–1824), English poet
Byron sparred with John "Gentleman" Jackson, the former bare-knuckle champion, in the poet's Bond Street rooms. Both men wore "mufflers" (mitten-like gloves used for sparring in the early days). The poet boxed in a dressing gown, Jackson in knee breeches and a shirt. Byron, with his legendary temper, was reputedly a tough customer in the ring.

2. Hessie Donahue (fl. 1890s), U.S. housewife
John L. Sullivan, world heavyweight champion from 1882 to 1892, invited Hessie and her husband, a boxing instructor, to join his

entourage, which was staging boxing exhibitions in theatres around the country. As part of an act they worked out, Hessie, wearing boxing gloves and dressed in a blouse and bloomers, would climb into the ring after Sullivan had disposed of his male challengers, and the two would go at it. During one of their sparring sessions, Sullivan inadvertently hit Hessie in the face, and she countered with a right to the jaw that sent him to the canvas for a full minute. The audience was so delighted that Hessie and Sullivan decided to make a "knockout" part of their regular routine.

3. Paul Gallico (1897–1976), U.S. author

Gallico, author of *The Poseidon Adventure*, was a cub reporter in 1923, assigned to Jack Dempsey's camp at Saratoga Springs prior to the heavyweight champion's title bout with Luis Firpo. Against his better judgment, Gallico asked Dempsey to spar with him for one round. It was, for Gallico, a vivid and somewhat terrifying experience as he was "stalked and pursued by a relentless, truculent professional destroyer." He never saw the punch that flattened him; he was aware only of an explosion in his head, and the next instant he was sitting on the canvas, grinning stupidly. He struggled to his feet and finished the round propped up in a clinch with Dempsey, absorbing those taps to the neck and ribs that, as an observer, had seemed so innocuous to him.

4. J. Paul Getty (1892–1976), U.S. entrepreneur

The billionaire oil magnate met Jack Dempsey in 1916, when Dempsey was an up-and-coming young fighter, and the two became good friends. Getty, who kept fit in the fully equipped basement gym in his parents' mansion, used to spar with Dempsey. Dempsey once claimed that, in an altercation over a girl, Getty knocked him out with a left uppercut—the only time Dempsey was ever KO'd by anyone.

5. Ernest Hemingway (1899–1961), U.S. author

During visits to Hemingway's Havana home, former heavyweight champion Gene Tunney would occasionally allow himself to be talked into sparring bare-fisted with the writer, especially if the two had just downed a Thermos of frozen daiquiris. Once, Hemingway, in a rambunctious mood, tagged Tunney with a hard punch. Incensed, Tunney feinted his friend's guard down and then faked a menacing punch to the face, as he issued a stern warning: "Don't you ever do that again!"

6. Hugh Lowther (1857–1944), British sportsman
Outraged that John L. Sullivan had never fought Jem Smith, the English heavyweight titleholder, the fifth Earl of Lonsdale challenged Sullivan to a bout. According to the earl, he took considerable punishment from the hard-hitting champion—they fought bare-knuckle in those days—but dropped Sullivan in the sixth round with a solid blow to the solar plexus. Though at least two people verified Lowther's version, Sullivan's memoirs make no mention of the fight.

7. George Plimpton (1927–2003), U.S. journalist and author
One of Plimpton's early experiments in "participatory journalism" was taking on Archie Moore, the former light-heavyweight champ, in January 1959. The fight lasted only three rounds, during which Moore cuffed Plimpton around gently, bloodying his nose. The referee called it a draw. Moore was asked how long it would have taken him to polish off his opponent had time been a factor. Moore told Plimpton, "'Bout the time it would take a tree to fall on you, or for you to feel the nip of the guillotine."

20 OLD-TIME HOCKEY NICKNAMES
1. Murph "Old Hardrock" Chamberlain, Montreal Canadiens, 1939–49
2. Carson "Shovel Shot" Cooper, Boston Bruins, 1924–27
3. Bert "Pig Iron" Corbeau, Montreal Canadiens, 1917–22
4. Hank "Lou Costello" Damore, New York Rangers, 1943–44
5. Eddie "the Great Gabbo" Dorohoy, Montreal Canadiens, 1948–49
6. Frank "the Shawville Express" Finnigan, Ottawa Senators, 1924–34
7. Jimmy "the Blonde Bouncer" Fowler, Toronto Maple Leafs, 1936–39
8. Bill "the Honest Brakeman" Juzda, Toronto Maple Leafs, 1948–52
9. Alex "Sea Biscuit" Kaleta, Chicago Blackhawks, 1945–48
10. Joe "the Duke of Paducah" Klukay, Toronto Maple Leafs, 1946–52
11. Alex "Mine Boy" Levinsky, Toronto Maple Leafs, 1930–34
12. Herbie "the Duke of Duluth" Lewis, Detroit Red Wings, 1932–39
13. Howie "the Stratford Streak" Morenz, Montreal Canadiens, 1923–37

14. Frank "the Pembroke Peach" Nighbor, Ottawa Senators, 1917–30
15. Alf "the Embalmer" Pike, New York Rangers, 1939–43
16. Fred "Chief Running Deer" Saskamoose, Chicago Blackhawks, 1953–54
17. Wally "the Whirling Dervish" Stanowski, Toronto Maple Leafs, 1945–48
18. Nels "Old Poison" Stewart, Montreal Maroons, 1925–32
19. Lorrain "Larry Half-n-Half" Thibeault, Montreal Canadiens, 1945–46
20. Georges "the Chicoutimi Cucumber" Vezina, Montreal Canadiens, 1917–26

Source: *Total Hockey: The Official Encyclopedia of the National Hockey League.*

12 CANADIAN SPORTS HEROES WHO BECAME POLITICIANS

1. Syl Apps

Syl Apps played 10 seasons in the NHL, all with the Toronto Maple Leafs. He was Rookie of the Year in 1937 and was twice a first team All-Star. In 1963 he was elected to the Ontario legislature as the Conservative member from Kingston, and he served there until 1975. Between 1971 and 1974, he was the minister of correctional services.

2. Lionel Conacher

Lionel "Big Train" Conacher was voted Canada's greatest athlete of the first half of the 20th century, and it is safe to say that no athlete will ever again have a career quite like his. Consider this: he played for 12 years in the NHL, won two Stanley Cups, one Grey Cup in football and one Triple-A baseball championship, and was a Canadian light-heavyweight boxing champ, a star lacrosse player and a member of the Canadian Wrestling Hall of Fame. Conacher finally retired from professional sports in 1937 and was elected as the Liberal member of the Ontario legislature in the riding of Bracondale. He served provincially until 1943. In 1949 he won a federal Liberal seat in Toronto, which he held until his death in 1954.

3. Ken Dryden

Goaltender Ken Dryden helped lead the Montreal Canadiens to six Stanley Cups in eight years in the 1970s. He won the Vezina Trophy for best goaltender five times and has the highest winning percentage of any goalie in NHL history. In 2004 he won the Toronto seat of York Centre for the Liberals and was named minister of social development by Prime Minister Paul Martin.

4. Don Getty

Don Getty joined the Edmonton Eskimos in 1955 as their starting quarterback and led them to Grey Cup wins in 1955 and 1956. He retired from football in 1965. Two years later, he became a Conservative member of the Alberta legislative assembly. He left politics in 1979 and returned to the private sector. In 1985 he was elected leader of the Alberta Progressive Conservatives; that same year, he led his party to victory in the provincial election. Getty served as Alberta's 11th premier from 1985 to 1992.

5. Otto Jelinek

Otto Jelinek and his sister, Maria, formed one of Canada's most successful skating duos, winning the world pairs championship in their native Prague in 1962. In 1972 Jelinek was elected as the Conservative member in the Toronto riding of High Park–Humber Valley. He served in several cabinet portfolios under Prime Minister Brian Mulroney, including minister of state for fitness and amateur sport from 1984 to 1988. He retired from politics in 1993.

6. Red Kelly

Red Kelly played 20 seasons in the NHL (1947–67) with Detroit and Toronto. He accumulated a total of 823 points and won eight Stanley Cups and numerous individual awards. Between 1962 and 1965, while still playing for the Maple Leafs, he served as the Liberal MP for York West.

7. Normie Kwong

Normie Kwong was born in Calgary in 1929 to Chinese immigrants. In 1948 he became the first Chinese-Canadian to play in the CFL and was dubbed the "China Clipper" for his ferocity as a running back. In 13 seasons in the CFL, he won four Grey Cups—one with the Calgary Stampeders when he was only 18, and three consecutive championships from 1954 to 1956 with the Edmonton Eskimos. He is a member of the CFL Hall of Fame and the Order of Canada. In the 1960s Kwong tried his hand at politics but was unable to get elected as a Conservative. In January 2005 he was chosen by Prime Minister Paul Martin to be Alberta's lieutenant-governor.

8. Peter Lougheed

Peter Lougheed was not a great professional football player. He was with the Edmonton Eskimos for only two seasons, 1949 and 1950, and the records show that big number 30 rushed for a total of only 8 yards. So it was probably a smart move when he left football to seek an MBA from Harvard. And although it didn't seem like a good idea at the time, it was also wise of him to accept the leadership of the Alberta Conservative Party in 1965. The party had been out of office for decades, but the ruling Social Credit Party was showing signs of age. In 1971 the Conservatives were elected to office. Lougheed moved into the premier's office, where he remained until he retired from politics in 1985.

9. Frank Mahovlich

Frank Mahovlich played 18 seasons in the NHL (1956–74). He scored 626 goals, was selected to nine All-Star teams and won a total of six Stanley Cups, four with Toronto and two with Montreal. In 1998 he was appointed to the Senate by Prime Minister Jean Chrétien.

10. Howie Meeker

Howie Meeker played eight seasons with the Toronto Maple Leafs, winning the Rookie of the Year trophy in 1946–47. Like Red Kelly, Meeker served as an MP while he was still playing for the Leafs. He won a federal by-election for the Conservatives in Waterloo South in 1951, and remained an MP until the election of 1954, when he decided not to run again. He then went on to a successful career as a hockey analyst on television.

11. Cindy Nicholas

Cindy Nicholas is one of Canada's greatest long-distance swimmers. In 1974, at the age of 16, she became the fastest swimmer to cross Lake

Ontario, with a time of 15 hours, 10 minutes. But that was just the beginning. In 1976 she won the women's world marathon swimming championship. The following year she became the first woman, and the youngest person ever, to swim the English Channel both ways. By 1982 she had crossed the Channel 19 times. Ten of those crossings involved two-way swims. In 1987 she was elected as a Liberal member of the Ontario legislature for the Toronto riding of Scarborough Centre. She served until 1990.

12. Steve Paproski

Steve Paproski was another in the remarkable line of former Edmonton Eskimos who went on to political prominence. He played for four seasons, between 1949 and 1953, which meant he was the teammate of a future premier (Lougheed) and a future lieutenant-governor (Kwong). Paproski's political career began in 1968, when he was elected for the Conservatives in Edmonton Centre. He was responsible for fitness, amateur sport and multiculturalism in the short-lived government of Joe Clark (1979–80). Paproski retired from politics in 1993 and died a few months later.

CHAPTER 14

DEATH

ABOVE: *Jesse Sharp goes over Niagara Falls in a plastic kayak (June 5, 1990)*

16 CASES OF PEOPLE KILLED BY GOD

1. Entire World Population except Noah and Seven Relatives (Gen. 6, 7)

Transgression: Violence, corruption and generalized wickedness

Method of execution: Flood

2. Entire Populations of Sodom and Gomorrah except Lot, His Wife and Their Two Daughters (Gen. 19)

Transgression: Widespread wickedness and lack of respect for the deity

Method of execution: Rain of fire and brimstone

3. Lot's Wife (Gen. 19)

Transgression: Looked back

Method of execution: Turned into a pillar of salt

4. Er (Gen. 38)

Transgression: Wickedness

Method of execution: Unknown

5. Onan (Gen. 38)

Transgression: Refused to make love to his brother Er's widow

Method of execution: Unknown

6. All the First-Born of Egypt (Exod. 12)

Transgression: Egypt was cruel to the Jews

Method of execution: Unknown

7. Pharaoh and the Egyptian Army (Exod. 14)

Transgression: Pursued the Jews

Method of execution: Drowned

8. Nadab and Abihu (Lev. 10)

Transgression: Offered strange fire

Method of execution: Fire

9. Korah, Dathan, Abiram and Their Families (Num. 16)

Transgression: Rejected authority of Moses and started own congregation

Method of execution: Swallowed by earth

10. 250 Followers of Korah (Num. 16)

Transgression: Supported Korah

Method of execution: Fire

11. 14,700 Israelites (Num. 16)

Transgression: Murmured against Moses and his brother, Aaron, following execution of Korah and his supporters

Method of execution: Plague

12. Retreating Amorite Soldiers (Josh. 10)

Transgression: Fought the Israelites

Method of execution: Hailstones

13. Uzzah (2 Sam. 6)

Transgression: Touched the ark of God after oxen shook it while pulling it on a cart

Method of execution: Unknown

14. 70,000 People (2 Sam. 24)

Transgression: King David ordered a census of the population

Method of execution: Plague

15. 102 Soldiers of King Ahaziah (2 Kings 1)

Transgression: Tried to capture Elijah the Tishbite

Method of execution: Fire

16. Ananias and Sapphira (Acts 5)

Transgression: Land fraud

Method of execution: Unknown

DEATH

10 STRANGE DEATHS

1. Killed by Jazz

Seventy-nine-year-old cornetist and music professor Nicolas Coviello had had an illustrious career, having performed before Queen Victoria, Edward VII and other dignitaries. Realizing that his life was nearing its end, Coviello decided to travel from London, England, to Saskatchewan to pay a final visit to his son. On the way, he stopped in New York City to bid farewell to his nephews, Peter, Dominic and Daniel Coviello. On June 13, 1926, the young men took their famous uncle to Coney Island to give him a taste of America. The elder Coviello enjoyed himself, but seemed irritated by the blare of jazz bands. Finally, he could take it no longer. "That isn't music," he complained, and he fell to the boardwalk. He was pronounced dead a few minutes later. Cause of death was "a strain on the heart."

2. Death by Phone Call

A storm burst upon Lumsden and Bonavista, Newfoundland, on June 26, 1930. When the telephone rang at the O'Neil residence, Mrs. O'Neil took the receiver but fell to the floor after getting a shock. Her husband and his brother-in-law, James Clarke, revived her. When the phone rang again, Mrs. O'Neil told Clarke it was for him. It was his wife, so he warned her to hang up. Just then, lightning struck and Clarke dropped dead on the floor.

3. Death by Dynamite

On July 11, 1932, a freak lightning bolt struck a gold mine near Rouyn-Noranda, Quebec, detonating dynamite 200 feet (60 m) underground and killing two miners instantly. The lightning either struck near two locked safety switches on the surface, jumped across and detonated the dynamite, or struck just inside the mine shaft below the safety switch. The men on the surface were not injured.

4. One Bad Swing

On June 5, 1963, clothing executive Harold Kalles was hitting out of the rough at a Toronto golf course when disaster struck. The shaft of his five iron hit a tree and snapped in two. The jagged end flew up, hit him in the throat and slashed his jugular vein. Bleeding profusely, Kalles managed to straggle out of the woods. His two playing partners got him to the hospital, where doctors were initially optimistic about his recovery. "He's fine and dandy now," one of them told the Toronto *Daily Star*. But the 41-year-old Kalles died of his injuries five days later.

5. Hard to Swallow
Twenty-two-year-old Franco Brun of Toronto died when he choked on a bible he shoved down his throat while in custody at the Metro East Detention Centre on June 9, 1987. Dr. Peter Charlebois, an anaesthetist and respiratory specialist, testified at the inquest into Brun's death that the average person "does not have the will to persistently shove something of such a size, such a solidity" down his throat.

6. Last One In . . .
A hog farm near Lucky Lake, Saskatchewan, proved unlucky for three young Prince Albert farmers, who died after they dived into a giant tank of hog manure on September 25, 1998. Investigators believe one of the men went into the tank without a breathing apparatus, apparently trying to clear a clogged line, and was overcome by hydrogen sulphide fumes. The second man went in when the first didn't reappear, and the third man went in to see about the first two. A fourth man followed, but managed to escape before the gas could overcome him. The tank held more than 7,100 gallons (27,000 L) of manure. One investigator commented that being overcome by hydrogen sulphide is "like being hit on the head with a two-by-four."

7. Bad Bounce
In March 2000, 21-year-old Chad Hildebrand was attending a senior men's hockey league game in Winnipeg. A puck flew into the crowd and glanced off a friend's head before hitting Hildebrand in the temple. Hildebrand went home, collapsed, fell into a coma and died a week later.

8. Hat Trick
Forty-four-year-old Derek Keenan of Lethbridge, Alberta, was killed on November 19, 2003, when he crawled underneath a semi-trailer loaded with precast concrete drainage pipe in pursuit of a baseball hat that had blown off his head. The truck began to move just as Keenan dived under

it. He tried to grab the hat and make a quick exit, but the truck's rear wheels rolled over his upper body and killed him.

9. Tree Hugger

Daryl Hatten, 49, was one of British Columbia's most renowned mountain climbers. He had blazed trails in the Canadian Rockies, in California's Yosemite National Park and on the challenging Squamish Chief, north of Vancouver. But on August 21, 2004, Hatten died from severe internal injuries sustained when he fell 65 feet (20 m) out of a rain-soaked arbutus tree while trying to rescue a neighbour's cat. The cat remained stranded in the tree.

10. A Death Unnoticed

Though his death was not strange in and of itself, the fact that Jim Sulkers's death went unnoticed for 21 months was very strange indeed. Sulkers died of natural causes in the bedroom of his Winnipeg condo sometime during November 2002, but nobody noticed his absence until August 25, 2004. His condo fees and bills were still being paid, his phone was still listed, and his pension was still being deposited into his account. The payments had all been set up for automatic withdrawals and deposits. Sulkers had multiple sclerosis and had withdrawn from neighbours and family over the previous decade. Still, when some relatives were in town in the summer of 2003, a few came knocking at his door. "He didn't answer," said Kim Dyck, a cousin. "You assume he isn't home. You certainly don't assume he's dead." His neighbours didn't recall smelling anything, and while they did wonder where Sulkers had gone, they didn't know him well. His mummified corpse was finally discovered after his father called police to ask them to check in on his son.

5 DAREDEVILS WHO DIED GOING OVER NIAGARA FALLS, AND 1 STRANGE TWIST OF FATE

People have been stunting in the Niagara gorge since the 1820s. In September 1827 the Eagle Hotel in Niagara Falls, New York, decided to attract tourists to the area by publicizing a bizarre and cruel spectacle: they bought an old schooner, loaded it with two bears, two raccoons, a buffalo, a dog and some birds and sent it over the falls. Apparently, only a goose survived. Since then, the curious call of the falls has been answered by 16 human daredevils, including two pairs, in contraptions that range from oak barrels to water tanks wrapped in truck inner tubes. In 2003 Kirk Jones of Canton, Michigan, went over wearing nothing but the clothes on his back and suffered only bruised ribs. A friend failed to capture his wild ride on videotape because he didn't know how to work the recorder.

Here are the five daredevils who died trying.

1. Charles Stephens

A renowned stunt man from Bristol, England, Stephens was in a rush to make history at the falls and refused all advice to first try sending his barrel over unmanned. He installed heavy straps inside the barrel for his arms and, in order to keep himself floating upright, tied an anvil to his feet as ballast. He wore padded clothing and reluctantly took a small supply of oxygen with him, in the event that his barrel got stuck in a whirlpool. On July 11, 1920, he was launched into the river. When the barrel hit the base of the falls, the anvil crashed through the barrel, taking Stephens down with it. When the barrel was recovered, only his right arm remained, still strapped into the harness, with a tattoo that read "Forget Me Not Annie."

2. George L. Stathakis

An eccentric Greek chef from Buffalo, New York, Stathakis declared himself a religious mystic, and in an effort to raise funds for the publication of his books, he devised a plan to conquer Niagara. He went over the falls in a huge barrel on July 5, 1930, presumably surviving the fall. However, he suffocated after getting trapped behind the falls for more than 14 hours. His pet turtle "Sonny Boy," whom he had brought along for the ride, survived. No one ever claimed his body from the morgue.

3. William "Red" Hill Jr.

Hill Jr. was the son of a famous riverman who had shot the rapids in a barrel three times and had pulled 177 corpses from the rapids below. Hill Jr. had helped him on many of these rescues and had tried several times to revive the family legend and fortune with his own derring-do.

Down on his luck, Hill Jr. built a flimsy contraption called "The Thing" from fishnets, canvas straps and 13 truck inner tubes. On August 5, 1951, thousands of people, including his family, gathered to watch The Thing go over Horseshoe Falls and get ripped to shreds in the pounding water. Hill Jr.'s mangled body was recovered the next day.

4. Jesse W. Sharp

On June 5, 1990, Sharp rode the fine line between stunting and suicide when he plunged over Horseshoe Falls in a 12-foot (3.7 m) plastic kayak. The unemployed 28-year-old bachelor from Ocoee, Tennessee, had planned the stunt for three years. A veteran whitewater kayaker, Sharp was attempting to give his career a boost with his high-profile stunt. Accompanied by three friends who were there to videotape him, Sharp refused to wear a helmet because he wanted his face to be visible on the video. He also shunned a life jacket, maintaining it would hinder his ability to swim underneath the falls and whirlpools. His body was never recovered.

5. Robert Overacker

On October 1, 1995, Overacker became the latest daredevil to die going over the falls. The 39-year-old man from California was hoping to publicize the plight of the homeless by shooting off Horseshoe Falls on a Jet Ski while igniting a rocket-propelled parachute strapped to his back. Witnesses say the rocket lit, but there is some confusion as to whether the parachute deployed or simply fell away from his body because he had forgotten to attach it. In any event, Robert plunged to his death, and the *Maid of the Mist* picked up his body later that day.

+1. A Strange Twist of Fate

On July 3, 1984, riding inside a cylindrical barrel with two eyeholes and a snorkel, Karel Soucek became the first Canadian to survive the falls. Later that year, the Hamilton, Ontario, native was killed recreating his feat at the Houston Astrodome by being dropped from a platform into a water tank. His barrel hit the edge of the tank.

9 PEOPLE WHO DIED LAUGHING

1. Calchas (*c*. 12th century BC), Greek soothsayer

Calchas, the wisest soothsayer of Greece during the Trojan War, advised the construction of the notorious wooden horse. One day he was planting grapevines when a fellow soothsayer wandered by and foretold that Calchas would never drink the wine produced from the grapes. After the grapes ripened, wine was made from them and Calchas invited the soothsayer to share it with him. As Calchas held a cup of the wine in his hand, the soothsayer repeated the prophecy. This incited such a fit of laughter in Calchas that he choked and died. (Another version of his death states that he died of grief after losing a soothsaying match in which he failed to predict correctly the number of piglets a pig was about to give birth to.)

2. Zeuxis (5th century BC), Greek painter

It is said that Zeuxis was laughing at a painting of an old woman he had just completed when his breathing failed and he choked to death.

3. Chrysippus (3rd century BC), Greek philosopher

Chrysippus is said to have died from a fit of laughter on seeing a donkey eat some figs.

4. Philemon (*c*. AD 236–263), Greek poet

This writer of comedies became so engulfed in laughter over a jest he had made that he died laughing.

5. Pietro Aretino (1492–1556), Italian author

Aretino was laughing at a bawdy story being told to him by his sister when he fell backwards in his chair and died of apoplexy.

6. Thomas Urquhart (1611–60), Scottish writer and translator

Best known for his translation into English of Rabelais's *Gargantua*, the eccentric Sir Thomas Urquhart is said to have died laughing upon hearing of the restoration to the throne of Charles II.

7. Mrs. Fitzherbert (d. 1782), English widow

On a Wednesday evening in April 1782, Mrs. Fitzherbert of Northamptonshire, England, went to Drury Lane Theatre with friends to see *The Beggar's Opera*. When the popular actor Mr. Bannister made his first appearance, dressed outlandishly in the role of "Polly," the entire audience was thrown into uproarious laughter. Unfortunately, Mrs. Fitzherbert was unable to suppress the laugh that seized her, and she was forced to leave the theatre before the end of the second act. As the *Gentleman's Magazine* reported the following week: "Not being able to banish the figure from her memory, she was thrown into hysterics, which continued without intermission until she expired on Friday morning."

8. Alex Mitchell (1925–75), English bricklayer

Mr. and Mrs. Mitchell were watching their favourite TV comedy, *The Goodies*. During a scene about a new type of self-defence called "Ecky Thump," Mr. Mitchell was seized by uncontrollable laughter. After half an hour of unrestrained mirth, he suffered a heart attack and died. His wife, Nessie, wrote to the Goodies thanking them for making her husband's last moments so happy.

9. Ole Bentzen (d. 1989), Danish physician

An audiologist who specialized in developing hearing aids for underdeveloped countries, Bentzen went to see the film *A Fish Called Wanda*. During a scene featuring John Cleese, Bentzen began laughing so hard that his heartbeat accelerated to a rate of between 250 and 500 beats a minute. He suffered a heart attack and died.

13 TIMELY DEATHS

We read so often in the newspapers about "untimely deaths" that it makes one wonder if anyone ever died a "timely death." Well, people have. Here are some examples.

1. Domitian (AD 51–96), Roman emperor

Early astrological predictions had warned that he would be murdered on the fifth hour of September 18, AD 96. As the date approached, Domitian had many of his closest attendants executed to be on the safe side. Just before midnight marked the beginning of the critical day, he became so terrified that he jumped out of bed. A few hours later he asked the time and was told by his servants (who were conspiring against him) that it was the sixth hour. Convinced that the danger had passed, Domitian went off to take a bath. On the way, he was informed that his niece's steward, Stephanus, was waiting for him in the bedroom with important news. When the emperor arrived, Stephanus handed him a list of conspirators and then suddenly stabbed him in the groin. Domitian put up a good fight, but he was overcome when four more conspirators appeared. He died as predicted, on the fifth hour of September 18, AD 96.

2. Thomas Jefferson (1743–1826), American president
The 83-year-old former president was suffering from a bad case of diarrhea, but he had hopes of lasting until July 4, 1826, the 50th anniversary of the signing of the Declaration of Independence. From his sickbed, he asked, "This is the fourth?" When he was informed that it was, he died peacefully.

3. John Adams (1735–1826), American president
Adams, like Jefferson, held on until July 4, 1826, before dying at the age of 90. He is reported to have said, "Thomas Jefferson survives. . . . Independence forever," unaware that his old friend had died a few hours earlier.

4. Dr. Joseph Green (1791–1863), English surgeon
While lying on his deathbed, Dr. Green looked up at his own doctor and said, "Congestion." Then he took his own pulse, reported a single word, "Stopped," and died.

5. Henrik Ibsen (1828–1906), Norwegian poet and dramatist
On May 16, 1906, Ibsen was in a coma in his bedroom, surrounded by friends and relatives. A nurse told the others in the room that the famed playwright seemed to be a little better. Without opening his eyes, Ibsen uttered one word: *"Tvertimod"* ("On the contrary"). He died that afternoon without speaking again.

6. Mark Twain (1835–1910), American humorist

Born in 1835, the year of Halley's Comet, Twain often stated that he had come into the world with the comet and would go out of the world with it as well. Halley's Comet next returned in 1910, and on April 21 of that year Twain died.

7. Arnold Schönberg (1874–1951), Austrian composer

Schönberg's lifelong fascination with numerology led to his morbid obsession with the number 13. Born in 1874 on September 13, he believed that 13 would also play a role in his death. Because the numerals seven and six add up to 13, Schönberg was convinced that his 76th year would be the decisive one. Checking the calendar for 1951, he saw to his horror that July 13 fell on a Friday. When that day came, he kept to his bed in an effort to reduce the chance of an accident. Shortly before midnight, his wife entered the bedroom to say good night and to reassure him that his fears had been foolish, whereupon Schönberg muttered the word "harmony" and died. The time of his death was 11:47 p.m., 13 minutes before midnight on Friday, July 13, in his 76th year.

8. Leonard Warren (1911–60), American opera singer

Warren was performing in Verdi's *La Forza del Destino* on the stage of the Metropolitan Opera in 1960. He had just begun the aria "O Fatal Urn of My Destiny." When he reached the word "fatal," he suddenly pitched forward, dead of a heart attack.

9. Elizabeth Ryan (1892–1979), American tennis player

Ryan won 19 Wimbledon tennis championships between 1914 and 1934—a record that stood for 45 years. On July 6, 1979, the day before Billie Jean King broke her record by winning a 20th Wimbledon title, the 87-year-old Ryan became ill while in the stands at Wimbledon. She collapsed in the clubhouse and died that night.

10. Charles Davies (1927–95), British singer

Davies, age 67, was giving a solo rendition of the old soldiers' song "Goodbye" at the annual dinner of the Cotswold Male Voice Choir in Echington, England, on January 3, 1995. He finished with the words,

"I wish you all a last goodbye." As the crowd applauded, Davies collapsed and died.

11. Charles Schulz (1922–2000), American cartoonist

In 1999 Schulz, the creator of the popular comic strip *Peanuts*, announced his decision to retire because of poor health. He died on February 12, 2000, the night before the last original *Peanuts* ran in the Sunday newspapers. The timing was "prophetic and magical," said close friend and fellow cartoonist Lynn (*For Better or for Worse*) Johnston. "He made one last deadline. There's romance in that."

12. George Story (1936–2000), American journalist

In 1936 the premier issue of *Life* featured a picture of newborn baby George Story under the headline "Life Begins." Over the years, the magazine periodically updated readers about the "*Life* baby," as Story married twice, had children and retired. On April 4, 2000, just days after *Life* had announced that it would cease publication, Story died of heart failure. The final issue of *Life* featured one last article about Story. The headline: "A Life Ends."

13. Pierre Berton (1920–2004), Canadian writer, columnist, nationalist

Berton's politics shaded towards the left. His views on organized religion bordered on the hostile. So it is not surprising that his opinion of the right-wing fundamentalist Christian president of the United States, George W. Bush, was far from positive. On November 30, 2004, President Bush was in the middle of his first state visit to Canada when Berton died at the age of 84. Faced with the choice of covering the visit of a much-disliked American president or the death of a much-loved author, most Canadian media chose to emphasize the latter. The Berton story led the CBC national news that evening. In fact, the network's Berton coverage ran for more than 10 minutes. The next day, Berton all but shoved Bush off the front page of the nation's newspapers. Somewhere, Pierre Berton was smiling.

—D.W. & C.F.

PRESERVING OUR HERITAGE—10 STUFFED OR EMBALMED PEOPLE

1. Tutankhamen

In 1922, while excavating in the Valley of the Kings, English archaeologist Howard Carter discovered the tomb of Tutankhamen, a king of the 18th Dynasty of Egypt, who flourished about 1348 BC. The mummy of the pharaoh was encased in a 6-foot (1.8 m) coffin containing 2,448 pounds (1,110 kg) of gold. Over the bandages on the king's face was a lifelike gold mask inlaid with precious jewels. A dazzling assortment of rings, necklaces, amulets and other exquisite ornaments was found among the body wrappings. The internal organs of the king had been removed, embalmed and placed in a separate alabaster chest. The mummy, coffin and other valuables from the tomb have toured the world and are currently displayed at the Egyptian Museum in Cairo.

2. Charlemagne

This ruler of the Holy Roman Empire died in 814. Embalmed, he was dressed in his royal robes, a crown was placed on his head, a sceptre was placed in his hand, and thus he was propped up in a sitting position on his marble throne. His preserved body remained on that throne for 400 years. At last, in 1215, Holy Roman Emperor Frederick II removed the corpse, which was found to be in excellent condition. It was buried in a gold and silver casket in the cathedral at Aix-la-Chapelle.

3. Richard II

This English king was deposed in 1399 and probably murdered in 1400. In 1413 Henry V had Richard's body embalmed and put on public display in full royal regalia. Three days later Henry was the chief mourner at Richard's second funeral, during which Richard was interred in Westminster Abbey. At one time there was a hole in the side of the tomb through which visitors could put their hands to touch the king's head. In 1776 an enthusiastic schoolboy thrust his hand in and stole Richard's jawbone. The boy's descendants kept the relic until 1906, when it was finally restored to its rightful resting place.

4. St. Bernadette

In 1858, at the age of 14, Bernadette Soubirous saw several visions of the Virgin Mary at a spring in Lourdes, France. Bernadette later joined the

Sisters of Notre Dame of Nevers, and today the site of the apparitions is one of the most famous Catholic shrines. After her death at the age of 35, Bernadette's body was buried and exhumed three separate times in the next 45 years in attempts to verify the incorruptibility of her corpse (according to Catholic tradition, a sign of sainthood). Although there has been some decomposition, owing in part to numerous examinations, Bernadette's remains are remarkably intact. Her body has been on display in the chapel of the Convent of St. Gildard at Nevers since August 3, 1925.

5. Enrico Caruso

During the six years that followed his death in 1921, the great Italian tenor surely qualified for the "best-dressed corpse" list. Each year solicitous friends ordered a new outfit for Caruso's body, which lay on public display in a crystal casket. In 1927 his widow decided enough was enough and had a white granite slab placed over the casket. It now remains sealed and undisturbed, with Caruso in old clothes, at Del Planto Cemetery, near Naples, Italy.

6. Vladimir Ilyich Lenin

On January 21, 1924, Lenin died, reportedly of a stroke, but possibly of poisoning. The deification process began at once. Lenin's brain was removed and cut into 31,000 sections for study by the Moscow Brain Institute, and then his body was embalmed. It was a poor job, and the face became wrinkled and shrunken. A Russian doctor, using new embalming fluid, which he claimed was based on that used by the ancient Egyptians, re-embalmed the body. A younger, more ascetic look was restored to the face. In 1930 a mausoleum composed of red Ukrainian granite and Karelian porphyry was built in Red Square to contain Lenin's body enclosed in a glass sarcophagus. In a poll taken in April 2004, 56% of Russians wanted Lenin buried, while 35% preferred that he remain above ground.

7. Eva Perón

When the wife of Argentine president Juan Perón died in 1952, her husband had her body embalmed. Perón planned to build a mausoleum for his wife, but his government was overthrown in 1955 and he was forced into exile in Spain. Eva Perón's body disappeared, and it was assumed that she was buried in an Italian cemetery under a different name. However, by 1971 Perón had retrieved the body and, according to a friend who dined with Perón, the body was present every evening at the dinner table, along with Perón and his new wife, Isabel. In late 1974, at Isabel's request, Eva Perón was returned to Argentina, where she was placed in an open casket beside the closed casket of her husband. After being briefly displayed, her body was buried in the Duarte family tomb in La Recoleta Cemetery in Buenos Aires.

8. Mao Zedong

After Mao, chairman of the Chinese Communist Party, died at 82 on September 9, 1976, he was embalmed. His corpse was placed in a crystal sarcophagus to be displayed permanently to the public in a mausoleum in Tiananmen Square in Beijing. At night, after visitors have gone home, Mao is lowered into an earthquake-proof chamber below the square.

9. Joseph Paul Jernigan

In 1993 convicted murderer Joseph Paul Jernigan was executed in Texas. Because Jernigan donated his body to science, his body was frozen and shipped to the University of Colorado, where it was "sliced" into 1,800 cross-sections. Two years later, a 59-year-old Maryland woman was similarly sliced, but into 5,000 segments. These two became the subjects of the Visible Human Project, the first computerized library of human anatomy to be made available to medical researchers around the world.

10. Ted Williams

After the Hall of Fame baseball player died at the age of 83 in 2002, he was taken to the Alcor Life Extension Foundation's cryogenics facility in Scottsdale, Arizona. The decision was challenged by his eldest daughter, Bobby Jo, since his will stated that he wanted to be cremated and have his ashes scattered off the coast of Florida. His son, John Henry, produced a note in which he, Ted and Ted's daughter Claudia entered into a pact to freeze themselves after death. The handwritten pact, signed by all three, read, "JHW, Claudia and Dad all agree to be put in Bio-stasis after we die. This is what we want, to be able to be together in the future, even if it is only a chance." The suit was settled in December 2002, and Ted Williams will remain indefinitely in one of Alcor's liquid nitrogen—filled cryogenic tanks.

—I.W., J.Be., C.F. & the Eds.

REMAINS TO BE SEEN—12 PRESERVED BODY PARTS

1. Joseph Haydn's Head

The Austrian composer died in 1809. Soon after his burial, a prison warden who was an amateur phrenologist—a person who tries to correlate head bumps with character traits—hired grave robbers to steal the head. The warden examined the skull, then gave it to an acquaintance, and a remarkable 145-year odyssey began. The theft of the skull was discovered in 1820, when the family of Haydn's patron had the body disinterred. Eventually they got a skull back, but it wasn't Haydn's. The real item was passed from one owner to another, some of them individuals, others organizations. Finally, it found a home in a glass case at Vienna's Society of Friends of Music. In 1932 the descendants of Haydn's patrons once again tried to get it back. But the Second World War and then the Cold War intervened—the body was in Austria's Soviet quarter, but the skull was in the international zone. It wasn't until 1954 that body and skull were finally reunited.

2. George Washington's Hair and Tooth

In June 1793 George Washington gave a locket containing a clipping of his hair to his aide-de-camp, Colonel John Trumbull. When Trumbull died, he willed the lock of hair to a first cousin of the president's, Dr. James A. Washington, who passed it along to his family as a sort of "hairloom." George Washington's dentist, John Greenwood, managed to acquire another collectible that the president shed from his person— the last of his natural teeth. Washington sent the tooth to Greenwood to use as a model in making a new set of dentures. The dentist kept the tooth as a souvenir, and it remained in the Greenwood family for generations.

3. Del Close's Skull

Close was an improvisational comedian who trained John Belushi, Bill Murray and Mike Myers. Upon his death in 1999, he willed his skull to Chicago's Goodman Theater to be used as Yorick's skull in productions of *Hamlet*. Close's former improv partner, Charen Halpern, noted, "It's not the starring role. But Del was always willing to take smaller parts."

4. George Frederick Cooke's Skull

Even though Irish-born actor George Frederick Cooke died in 1812, he continued to get work in bit parts. Cooke's skull was used in productions of *Hamlet* before being retired to the Thomas Jefferson University Medical School library in Philadelphia.

5. Paul Broca's Brain

In one of the less-frequented corners of the Musée de l'Homme (Museum of Man) in Paris are numerous bottles containing human brains. Some belonged to intellectuals, others to criminals. But perhaps the most distinguished of the specimens is that of Paul Broca, a 19th-century physician and anthropologist who was the father of modern brain surgery.

6. Albert Einstein's Brain

What might have been the greatest brain of the 20th century was not buried with the body that housed it. Albert Einstein asked that after his death his brain be removed for study. And when the great physicist died in 1955, this was done. The brain—which was neither larger nor heavier than the norm—was photographed, sectioned into 240 blocks and sent around the country to be studied by specialists. His parietal lobes were discovered to be unusually large.

7. Saartje Baartman's Brain and Sexual Organs

Baartman was born in the Cape Colony (part of modern-day South Africa) in 1789. Around 1810 she was taken to London, England, by a British navy doctor, who exhibited her in Britain and France as the "Hottentot Venus." People paid to gawk at her unusually large buttocks and elongated labia. Baartman was also studied by racial theorists seeking to support notions of the inherent superiority of European races. After she died in poverty at the age of 27, her brain and sexual organs were preserved and put on display at the Musée de l'Homme (Museum of Man) in Paris. After apartheid ended, the government of South Africa began requesting the return of Baartman's remains. In April 2002 the preserved organs, Baartman's skeleton and a plaster cast of Baartman's body that had been on display were handed over at the South African embassy. "She has recovered her dignity, albeit after many years, with a ceremony that has celebrated her as a true person, and I am very happy about it," announced Bernard Chevassus-au-Louis, director of the French Museum of Natural History.

8. José Rizal's Vertebra

José Rizal, the national hero of the Philippines, was accused of sedition, executed by the Spanish in 1896 and buried without a coffin. He was exhumed in August 1898, after the Americans took Manila. Most of Rizal's remains are interred beneath the Rizal Monument in Luneta—all except one of his cervical vertebrae; the vertebra is enshrined like a holy relic in Fort Santiago.

9. Brother André's Heart

Alfred Bessette was born in a small town east of Montreal in 1845. At the age of 25, he was admitted to the brothers of the Holy Cross and became Brother André. He quickly gained a reputation as a "miracle worker." He was said to possess great powers to cure the sick and the afflicted. In 1904 he began construction of a small chapel on Mount Royal devoted to St. Joseph. Today St. Joseph's Oratory is one of the largest basilicas in the world, and a fixture of the Montreal skyline. When Brother André died in 1937, a million people came to pay tribute to him. His heart was removed, placed in a glass jar and kept on display in a small room of the original chapel. In March 1973 thieves stole Brother André's heart and demanded $50,000 for its return. It was found in December 1974 in the basement locker of a Montreal apartment building. No ransom was paid.

10. Lazzaro Spallanzani's Bladder

When Italian biologist Spallanzani died in 1799, his diseased bladder was excised for study by his colleagues. It is currently on display in the Scarpa Room in the University of Pavia in Italy, where it remains a monument to the inquisitive mind.

11. Galileo's Finger

The great astronomer died in 1642, but his body was not interred in its final resting place until 1737. During that final transfer to a mausoleum at the Church of Santa Croce in Florence on March 12, an intellectual admirer, Anton Francesco Gori, cut off Galileo's middle finger as a keepsake. After passing through various hands, it was acquired by Florence's Museum of the History of Science, where it is now encased in glass and pointing skyward.

12. Dan Sickles's Leg

Sickles was a colourful New York congressman who organized and led a brigade of volunteers at the outbreak of the Civil War. He was involved in some of the bloodiest fighting at Gettysburg, losing his own right leg in the battle. That trauma, however, didn't diminish Sickles's personal flair. He had the leg preserved and sent to Washington, where it was exhibited in a little wooden coffin at the medical museum of the Library of Congress. Sickles frequently visited it himself.

—E.F., M.J.T. & Cdn. Eds.

13 BAD ENDINGS IN CANADIAN BUSINESS, POLITICS AND SPORTS

IN CANADIAN BUSINESS

1. Micheline Charest

After years of legal and financial problems, the controversial co-founder of Cinar, the well-known Montreal animation house, finally looked as if she was ready to move on with her life. She had sold her shares in her company and had paid a $1-million fine to the Quebec Securities Commission. On April 14, 2004, she checked herself into a private clinic to undergo a facelift and a nip and tuck to her breasts. But the operation took longer than expected, and Charest was under general anaesthesia for about seven hours. After surgery, she was moved to the recovery room, and the breathing tube in her windpipe was removed. But the muscles in her larynx went into spasm when the tube was removed, blocking her ability to breathe. She went into cardiac arrest and died a few moments later. She was 51 years old.

2. Michael de Guzman

On March 19, 1997, de Guzman jumped out of the back of an Alouette III helicopter over the jungles of Indonesia and plunged 790 feet (240 m) to his death. De Guzman was the chief geologist in Indonesia for Bre-X Minerals Ltd. It was his surveys that had convinced investors that Bre-X had discovered one of the world's largest gold reserves. But, by March 1997, there was growing evidence that there was no gold there and that de Guzman had fabricated his surveys. Rather than live with the consequences of his actions, de Guzman decided to end his life. Rescuers searched for four days through the dense forest before finally locating the body. The injuries caused by the fall, combined with the ravages of the insects and animals in the jungle, left de Guzman's body so grotesque that authorities decided not to allow his family to see it.

3. Guy Lamarche

Guy Lamarche was born in Timmins, Ontario, and made his living promoting dubious stocks and other shady investment deals. The man who shot him to death in the lobby of Toronto's Royal York Hotel on March 9, 1987, was Lamarche's boyhood friend, Timmins Bissonnette, who had made millions running carnival shows and gambling for big stakes in Las Vegas. But business is business, and when Lamarche refused to repay $80,000 that Bissonnette had loaned him two years earlier, something had to be done. Bissonnette confronted Lamarche in the hotel lobby, demanding his money. Lamarche refused to pay. "He called me a bum and a lot worse," Bissonnette later recalled. "That was the end of it. The light went out. I went and got my gun." Bissonnette shot his old friend twice in the heart, then spat on his body. He fled the scene, but was captured by police a few moments later. He was convicted in February 1988, and sentenced to life imprisonment.

4. Ambrose Small

Ambrose Small's disappearance remains one of the most intriguing unsolved whodunits in Canadian history. Small was a wealthy Toronto businessman and socialite. He lived in a Rosedale mansion and owned several theatres that specialized in racy shows about the misadventures of young, single working-class women alone in the big city. He was also a renowned gambler and womanizer. On December 2, 1919, at the age of 53, Small completed the sale of some of his theatres and deposited a cheque for $1 million in his bank account. Later that day, he walked out of his office and was never seen or heard from again. Much speculation focused on his long-suffering wife as a possible suspect in her philandering husband's disappearance, but no proof of her involvement was ever established.

IN CANADIAN POLITICS

5. George Brown

George Brown played a prominent role in the Quebec and Charlottetown conferences that led to Confederation, but he was probably best known as the crusading editor of the Toronto *Globe*. On March 25, 1880, a disgruntled former *Globe* employee came to Brown's office and, after a brief scuffle, shot the editor in the leg. The wound was considered to be minor, and Brown returned home to recuperate. But over the next few weeks, as Brown continued to work from home, the wound became infected. He became feverish, then delirious, and eventually slipped into a coma. He died on May 9 at the age of 61.

6. John Buchan, 1st Baron of Tweedsmuir

On February 6, 1940, Governor General Lord Tweedsmuir suffered a stroke while shaving at Rideau Hall. He fell and severely injured his head. Dr. Wilder Penfield, the renowned Montreal neurosurgeon, was called in and, over the next several days, performed two operations. But it was to no avail. Lord Tweedsmuir died on February 11, becoming the first governor general to die while in office.

7. Elizabeth Shaughnessy Cohen

Shaughnessy Cohen was first elected to the House of Commons from Windsor in 1993, and quickly established herself as one of the hardest-working and most popular MPs in the House. On the afternoon of December 9, 1998, Cohen was seated at her desk in the Commons, chatting with one of her fellow Liberal MPs, when she started bleeding from the mouth and collapsed on the floor beside her desk. She had suffered a massive brain hemorrhage. Efforts to revive her failed, and she died in hospital later that evening. She was 50 years old.

8. Donald Summerville

Donald Summerville was just two years into his term as mayor of Toronto on the night of November 19, 1963, when he donned his goalie pads to take part in a charity hockey game in aid of Italian flood victims. The game was only five minutes old, and the 48-year-old mayor, a former practice goalie for the Maple Leafs, had already made several solid saves, when he skated shakily off the ice. He made it to the dressing room but then collapsed on the floor. He had suffered a massive heart attack. He was pronounced dead on arrival in hospital, the only Toronto mayor to die while in office.

9. Sir John Thompson

On December 12, 1894, Prime Minister Thompson was summoned to Windsor Castle to be sworn in as the Right Honourable Sir John Thompson. After the ceremony, he was invited to stay for lunch with the Queen. Shortly after taking his seat in the dining room, he fainted. He was taken to a nearby room and, after a few moments, felt well enough to return to the table. But before he could eat his first bite of food, he suddenly collapsed, falling into the arms of Sir John Watt Reid, the Queen's doctor, who had been seated beside him. The prime minister had suffered a massive heart attack, and he died moments later.

10. Sir Samuel Leonard Tilley

Sir Samuel Leonard Tilley was premier (twice) and lieutenant-governor of New Brunswick, a minister in Sir John A. Macdonald's first cabinet and a Father of Confederation. Early in June 1896 he cut his foot while vacationing at his summer home in Rothesay, New Brunswick. Within a few days, blood poisoning had spread through his entire system. He died on June 25 at the age of 78.

DEATH

11. Lionel Conacher

Lionel "Big Train" Conacher was the best all-around athlete Canada has ever produced, a star of hockey, football, baseball, boxing and several other sports. On May 26, 1954, as a Liberal MP, Conacher was playing in a softball game between MPs and members of the parliamentary press gallery. In the sixth inning, Conacher hit a long fly ball into left field and started running the bases. Just as he was pulling into third base, he collapsed of a heart attack. Within 20 minutes, the man voted Canada's greatest athlete of the first half of the 20th century was dead at 53 years of age.

12. Owen Hart

On May 23, 1999, Owen Hart, a member of Calgary's famed Hart family of professional wrestlers, was killed when a stunt he was performing at a World Wrestling Federation event in Kansas City misfired. Hart was planning to descend 100 feet (30 m) into the ring from the top of the arena. He was supposed to be guided down by wires attached to his costume, but the release cord mechanism malfunctioned, and Hart plunged into the ring, smashing into the padded turnbuckle. Many of the 16,200 fans in the arena thought the wrestler's crash landing was part of his act. Paramedics quickly rushed in to try to resuscitate Hart, but they were unsuccessful. He was pronounced dead at the hospital.

13. Owen "Bud" McCourt

On March 8, 1907, Owen "Bud" McCourt became the only player in Canadian hockey history to die as a direct result of an on-ice attack. McCourt, who played for the Cornwall Wanderers of the Federal Amateur Hockey League, was clubbed over the head with the hockey stick of a player for the Ottawa Victorias during a fight-filled game in Cornwall. McCourt died several hours later in hospital. Charles Masson of the Victorias was arrested the day after the game and charged with murder. The charge was later reduced to manslaughter, but when the case went to trial, Masson was acquitted because, in those days before video replays, the Crown was unable to prove conclusively which Ottawa player had struck the fatal blow.

10 CELEBRATED PEOPLE WHO READ THEIR OWN OBITUARIES

1. Hannah Snell

When Hannah Snell's husband walked out on her and joined the British army, she borrowed an outfit from her brother-in-law and enlisted as well, hoping to track down her wayward husband. She first served in the army, and later joined the Royal Marines, sailing to India to fight in the battle of Pondicherry. During the battle, she sustained a groin injury, but she managed to keep her sex a secret by treating the injury herself. Upon her return to England, she revealed her sex to her shipmates and sold her story to a London publisher. She became a celebrity, and once out of the army she performed in public houses as the Female Warrior. On December 10, 1779, when she was 56, she opened a copy of the *Gentlemen's Magazine* and read her own obituary, which informed her that she had died on a Warwickshire heath. Perhaps she was superstitious, because reading her death notice snapped something in her mind. Her mental health slowly deteriorated, and in 1789 she was placed in London's Bethlehem Hospital, where she remained insane until her death in 1792.

2. Daniel Boone

The great American frontiersman had retired and settled down in Missouri. In 1818 a newspaper in the eastern U.S. trumpeted the news that the renowned hunter had been found dead near a deer lick, kneeling behind a tree stump, his rifle resting on the stump, a fallen deer 100 yards (90 m) away. The obituary was picked up across the nation. Daniel read it and laughed. Although he could still trap, he was too old and weak to hunt and could no longer hit a deer, even close up. Two years later, at the age of 86, Boone finally did die. His best-known obituary was seven stanzas devoted to him in Lord Byron's *Don Juan*.

3. Lady Jane Ellenborough

She was one of the most beautiful and sexual women in all history. Her name was Jane Digby. At 17 she married Lord Ellenborough, Great Britain's lord of the privy seal, then left him to run off with an Austrian prince. During her colourful career she was the mistress of novelist Honoré de Balzac, King Ludwig of Bavaria and Ludwig's son, King Otto of Greece. Her last marriage, of 26 years, was to Sheik Medjuel, an erudite

Bedouin, head of the Mezrab tribe in the Syrian desert. Returning from a desert trip with Medjuel, the 66-year-old Lady Ellenborough learned that she was dead. Her obituary appeared prominently in *La Revue Britannique*, published in Paris in March 1873. It began: "A noble lady who had made a great use—or abuse—of marriage has died recently. Lady Ellenborough, some 30 years ago, left her first husband to run off with Count von Schwarzenberg. She retired to Italy, where she married six consecutive times." The obituary, reprinted throughout Europe, called her last husband "a camel driver." The next issue of the publication carried a eulogy of Lady Ellenborough written by her friend Isabel Burton, the pompous and snobbish wife of Burton of Arabia. Mrs. Burton claimed she had been authorized to publish the story of Lady Ellenborough's life, based on dictated notes. Appalled, Lady Ellenborough vehemently wrote to the press, denying her death—and having dictated an "authorized" book to Mrs. Burton. Lady Ellenborough outlived her obituary by eight full years, dying of dysentery in August 1881.

4. James Butler Hickok

In March 1873 "Wild Bill" Hickok, legendary sheriff and city marshal in the Midwest and a constant reader of Missouri's leading newspaper, the *Democrat*, picked up a copy and learned that he was a corpse. Hickok read: "The Texan who corralled the untamed William did so because he lost his brother by Bill's quickness on the trigger." Unsettled by his supposed demise, Wild Bill took pen in hand and wrote a letter to the editor: "Wishing to correct an error in your paper of the 12th, I will state that no Texan has, nor ever will, 'corral William.' I wish to correct your statement on account of my people. Yours as ever, J.B. Hickok." Delighted, the editor of the *Democrat* printed Hickok's letter and added an editorial: "We take much pleasure in laying Mr. Hickok's statement before the readers of the *Democrat*, most of whom will be glad to read from his pen that he is 'still on the deck.' But in case you should go off suddenly, William, by writing us the particulars we will give you just as fine an obituary notice as we can get up, though we trust that sad pleasure may be deferred for years." Three years later Hickok was murdered while playing poker.

5. Alfred Nobel

As the inventor of dynamite, Alfred Nobel, a moody yet idealistic Swede, had become a millionaire. When Nobel's older brother, Ludwig, died of heart trouble on April 12, 1888, a leading French newspaper misread the report and ran an obituary of Alfred Nobel, calling him "a merchant of death." Upon seeing the obituary, Nobel was stunned, not by the premature announcement of his passing but by the realization that in the end he would be considered nothing more than a merchant of death. The printed summary of his life reflected none of his hopes for humanity, his love of his fellow beings, his generosity. The need to repair this false picture was one of several factors that led him to establish, in his will, the Nobel Prizes, to be given to those who did the most to advance the causes of peace, literature and the sciences.

6. P.T. Barnum

At 80, the great American was ailing and knew that death was near. From his sickbed, he told a friend that he would be happier if he had "the chance to see what sort of lines" would be written about him after he was dead. The friend relayed this wish to the editor of the *Evening Sun* of New York City. On March 24, 1891, Barnum opened his copy of the *Evening Sun* and read: "Great and Only Barnum. He Wanted to Read His Obituary; Here It Is." According to the preface, "Mr. Barnum has had almost everything in this life, including the woolly horse and Jenny Lind, and there is no reason why he should not have the last pleasure which he asks for. So here is the great showman's life, briefly and simply told, as it would have appeared in the *Evening Sun* had fate taken our Great and Only from us." There followed four columns of Barnum's obituary, illustrated by woodcuts of him at his present age, of him at 41, of his mother, of his deceased first wife, Charity, and of the Swedish singer Jenny Lind. Two weeks later, Barnum was dead.

7. Leopold von Sacher-Masoch

This police commissioner's son, born in Galicia and raised in Austria, was fascinated by cruelty and loved pain and degradation. His first mistress, Anna von Kottowitz, birched him regularly and enjoyed lovers whom Sacher-Masoch found for her. His second mistress, Fanny Pistor, signed a contract with him, agreeing to wear furs when she beat him daily. She fulfilled the contract and treated him as a servant. He had become a famous writer when he met and married a woman named Wanda. She thrashed him with a nail-studded whip every day of their 15-year marriage and made him perform as her slave. After she ran off, Sacher-Masoch married a simple German woman named Hulda Meister. By this time, he was slipping into insanity, and he tried to strangle her. In 1895 she had him secretly committed to an asylum in Mannheim and announced to the world that he had died. The press published obituaries praising his talent. Undoubtedly, in lucid moments, he read some of his death notices. He finally did die 10 years later. Because of Sacher-Masoch's life, psychiatrist Richard von Krafft-Ebing coined the word "masochism."

8. Mark Twain

In 1897 the noted American author and humorist was in seclusion, grieving over a death in his family, when he learned that he too had been declared dead. A sensational American newspaper had headlined his end, stating that he had died impoverished in London, England. A national syndicate sent a reporter to Mark Twain's home to confirm the news. Twain himself appeared before the bug-eyed reporter and issued an official statement: "James Ross Clemens, a cousin of mine, was seriously ill two or three weeks ago in London, but is well now. The reports of my illness grew out of his illness. The reports of my death are greatly exaggerated." Twain finally lived up to his premature obituaries in 1910.

9. Bertrand Russell

Once, in the 1930s, while the English philosopher was visiting Beijing, he became very ill. Japanese reporters in the city constantly tried to see Russell, but were always denied access to him. The journalists decided he must be dead and notified their newspapers of his demise. Word of his death went around the world. Wrote Russell, "It provided me with the pleasure of reading my obituary notices, which I had always desired without expecting my wishes to be fulfilled." One missionary paper had an obituary notice of one sentence: "Missionaries may be pardoned for heaving a sigh of relief at the news of Mr. Bertrand Russell's death." All this inspired Russell to compose his own obituary in 1937 for *The Times* of

London. He wrote of himself: "His life, for all its waywardness, had a certain anachronistic consistency, reminiscent of the aristocratic rebels of the early nineteenth century . . . He was the last survivor of a dead epoch." He told *The Times* to run it in 1962, the year in which he expected to die. *The Times* did not need it until 1970.

10. Edward V. Rickenbacker

The former auto racer turned fighter pilot emerged from the First World War as America's leading ace, with 26 confirmed kills. In peacetime he was an executive in the automobile and aviation industries. With the onset of the Second World War, Rickenbacker volunteered to carry out missions for the U.S. War Department. In October 1942, on an inspection tour, Rickenbacker's B-17 went down somewhere in the Pacific Ocean. An intensive air search of the area was made. There was no sign of survivors. Newspapers across the U.S. declared Rickenbacker dead. The following month, on Friday, November 13, there were new headlines: Rickenbacker and seven others had been spotted alive in the Pacific, having survived on a raft for 23 days. Waiting for Rickenbacker when he returned home was a pile of his obituaries. One, in the *New York Daily News*, was a cartoon showing a black wreath floating on water, with the caption "So Long, Eddie." Another, in the *New York Journal*, bore the headline "End of the Roaring Road?" Grinning, Rickenbacker scrawled across it, "Hell, no!"

Note: Those 10 are the editor's favourite cases, but there have been numerous other celebrated persons who read of their deaths while they were alive, among them U.S. president Thomas Jefferson, magician Harry Houdini, dancer Josephine Baker, singer Jeanette MacDonald, novelist Ernest Hemingway and foreign correspondent Edgar Snow. There have also been many famous people who, if they did not read about their deaths, heard rumours or announcements that they had gone to the Great Beyond. The modern living dead have included singer Paul McCartney, vague hints of whose demise were supposedly traced to several Beatles records; actress Bette Davis, whose attorney told her that word of her death was spreading throughout New York, to which Miss Davis replied, "With the newspaper strike on, I wouldn't consider it"; and India's elderly political dissenter J.P. Narayan, who heard Prime

Minister Morarji Desai mistakenly deliver a eulogy over his still-warm body in April 1979.

—I.W.

LAST WORDS OF 12 FAMOUS CANADIANS

1. "Now, God be praised, I will die in peace." —General James Wolfe, September 13, 1759. He was mortally wounded in the Battle of the Plains of Abraham, but lived long enough to learn that Quebec had been taken.

2. "Push on, brave York volunteers." —Sir Isaac Brock, October 13, 1812, spoken just before he was shot and killed by American soldiers

3. "Good morning. It is morning now." —Thomas D'Arcy McGee, April 7, 1868. A friend had just wished McGee "good night," but since it was already 2:00 a.m., McGee corrected him. Moments later, he was gunned down in front of his Ottawa rooming house.

4. "I am dying." —George-Étienne Cartier, May 20, 1873, spoken to his wife and doctors

5. "In our opinion, his powers of life are steadily waning." —last bulletin issued to the public by Sir John A. Macdonald's doctors, hours before the prime minister died, June 6, 1891

6. "Oh, take me home." —former prime minister Alexander Mackenzie, April 17, 1892, spoken to his wife and daughter

7. "I am feeling very sick." —former premier of Ontario and federal Liberal leader Edward Blake, March 1, 1912, spoken to his family

8. "C'est fini." —Sir Wilfrid Laurier, February 17, 1919, spoken to his wife, Zoë

9. "Hold up my head." —Dr. William Osler, December 29, 1919, spoken to a friend at his bedside

10. "Did I behave pretty well? Was I a good boy?" —Stephen Leacock, March 28, 1944, spoken to the radiologist treating him for throat cancer

11. "I'm afraid to die, but it pains too much to live." —Samuel Bronfman, July 10, 1971, spoken to his doctor

12. "Please, my near and dear ones, forgive me and understand. I hope this potion works. My spirit is already in another country, and my body has become a damn nuisance. I have been so fortunate." —last words of the suicide note written by Margaret Laurence, January 5, 1987

CHAPTER 15

MISCELLANEOUS

ABOVE: *Doukhobor woman bares all and burns her barn in protest (circa 1940)*

14 PRODIGIOUS SAVANTS

Savant syndrome is a rare condition in which people suffering from mental retardation, autism or schizophrenia nonetheless possess an unusual ability in a single field, most often relating to music, art or numbers.

1. Clarence Asham (dates unknown)

Asham is blind and unable to speak, and has an IQ of 32. For 28 years, he lived in an institution in Portage la Prairie, Manitoba. One day, his nurse gave him an accordion, and Clarence immediately proceeded to play hundreds of songs that he had heard on the radio over the years. It turns out that Asham has an extraordinarily highly developed musical memory. He can play any piece of music on the piano, even a complex classical score, after hearing it only once.

2. Thomas "Blind Tom" Bethune (1849–1908)

Although his vocabulary was limited to fewer than 100 words, Blind Tom could play more than 5,000 pieces on the piano, an instrument he had mastered as a four-year-old slave on a Georgia plantation. At the age of 11, he performed at the White House for President James Buchanan. He learned each piece after hearing it only once; his repertoire included Mozart, Beethoven, Bach and Verdi.

3. Alonzo Clemons (1959–)

Clemons, who has an IQ of 40, lives in a home for the developmentally disabled in Boulder, Colorado. An exceptionally talented sculptor, he has sold hundreds of pieces, including one for $45,000 (U.S.). Many buyers have purchased his work unaware that it was created by a mentally handicapped artist.

4–5. George and Charles Finn (1939–)

Known as the Bronx Calendar Twins, the Finns first attracted national attention when they were featured in a 1966 *Life* magazine article. The brothers can give the day of the week for any date over a period of 80,000 years. They can also recall, in detail, the weather for any day of their lives.

6. Thomas Fuller (1710–90)

Born in Africa, Fuller was taken to Virginia as a slave in 1724. He was a calculating wonder who could easily multiply nine-digit numbers. At the age of 78, Fuller, who was never able to learn to read or write, was asked, "How many seconds has a man lived who is 70 years, 17 days and 12 hours old?" Ninety seconds later he gave the answer—2,210,500,800. Informed that he was wrong, Fuller corrected his interrogator by pointing out that the man had forgotten to include leap years.

7. Leslie Lemke (1952–)

Like many prodigious savants, Leslie is blind, was born prematurely and possesses an extraordinary memory. He sings and plays the piano and has appeared on numerous television shows, including *60 Minutes* and *Donahue*. He has also been the subject of two films, *An Island of Genius* and the Emmy-winning *The Woman Who Willed a Miracle*.

8. Jonathan Lerman (1987–)

Lerman, who was diagnosed as autistic at the age of 3, has a tested IQ of 53. He began drawing at 10, shortly after the death of his maternal grandfather, Burt Markowitz, who had always insisted that Jonathan had promise. His charcoal drawings, which critics have compared to the works of George Grosz and Francis Bacon, sell for $500 to $1,200 (U.S.). A book of his artwork, *Jonathan Lerman: The Drawings of a Boy with Autism*, was published in 2002.

9. Kim Peek (1951–)

A mathematical savant, Peek, who lives in Salt Lake City, Utah, was the inspiration for the character played by Dustin Hoffman in the 1988 Academy Award–winning film *Rain Man*. His true story is told in the book *The Real Rain Man* (1997).

10. Christopher Pillault (1982–)

Born in Iran, Pillault is unable to talk, walk or feed himself. He discovered painting in 1993, using his hands, since he can't use his fingers functionally. His paintings, featuring striking, ethereal figures, have been exhibited in France, Italy, Japan and the U.S. He is also a member of several artists' societies.

11. Grant Reimer (dates unknown)

Grant Reimer of Steinbach, Manitoba, is autistic and unable to live on his own, but he possesses one narrow streak of brilliance. Give Grant a date from any year as far back as the 19th century, and he will instantly be able to tell you what day of the week that date fell on. He is also able to tell you, with extraordinary accuracy and precision, what the weather was on any day of his life. When asked to explain his amazing talent, Riemer replied, "I have a computer in my mind."

12. Matthew Savage (1993–)

At the age of three, Savage was diagnosed with Asperger's disorder, a condition similar to autism. He is a professional jazz musician who leads his own trio, has performed at jazz festivals throughout the U.S. and Canada, and has recorded three CDs. He was described as "amazing" by jazz legend Dave Brubeck. Savage is also prodigious in mathematics (he was learning advanced algebra at the age of 11) and geography (he represented New Hampshire in the U.S. National Geography Bee in 2004).

13. Richard Wawro (1952–)

Wawro, who is autistic and moderately mentally handicapped, started drawing at the age of three. He held his first exhibition in Edinburgh, Scotland, when he was 17. Most of his works are landscapes and seascapes based on images he has seen just once in books or on television. Wawro can remember where and when he drew each picture. He was the subject of the documentary *With Eyes Wide Open* (1983).

14. Stephen Wiltshire (1974–)

Although Wiltshire, who lives in London, England, is autistic, he is able to glance briefly at a building and then draw it in exquisite detail. Wiltshire has produced three books of drawings, one of which, *Floating Cities*, was a number one bestseller in Great Britain. In 1993 he was discovered to also be a musical savant, with perfect pitch.

—The Eds.

12 OF THE STRANGEST THINGS FOUND IN THE TORONTO TRANSIT COMMISSION'S LOST AND FOUND OFFICE

1. False teeth, dentures, retainers
2. Oxygen tanks
3. Artificial or glass eyes
4. Wheelchairs, crutches
5. Car baby seats (no babies)
6. French provincial armchair
7. Karaoke machine
8. Computer monitors
9. TVs/VCRs
10. Pets (cats and dogs)
11. Snow shovel
12. Chainsaw

9 DISTURBING TRENDS IN THE CANADIAN ENVIRONMENT

1. Bottled water

Tap water is the cleanest and cheapest source of drinking water for most Canadians, but the growing preference for bottled water or "spring" water has put unprecedented pressure on our aquifers. These naturally filtered underground sources of water are effectively being mined by water bottlers at a rate faster than the aquifers can naturally recharge. When an aquifer is drained, it can cause cave-ins that alter or destroy the gravel layer and water supply. Speculation in and the privatization of Canada's water supply as a "good" to sell on the open market is on the rise. And the ubiquitous empty plastic bottles are yet another strain on the waste stream.

2. Fish farming

Essentially floating feedlots, salmon open-net cages range from 30 to 100 feet (9 to 30 m) in diameter and hold up to 50,000 fish each. Although farmers lace the feed with antibiotics, disease and sea lice infestations break out in the crowded conditions, threatening the wild salmon nearby. Excess food pellets and waste float to the bottom and further disrupt the marine environment. Moreover, salmon farmers have reported that, between 1987 and 1996, over 1 million farmed Atlantic salmon escaped from open-net cages into British Columbia waters. Some of these non-native salmon have done what scientists thought was impossible: they have spawned in the wild. On the Pacific coast, several runs of salmon have collapsed or are endangered because Atlantic salmon have overtaken their spawning grounds, food supply and even mates.

And now there's a new threat to the native salmon. Genetically engineered salmon that mature rapidly are being created for possible use in fish farms. One study undertaken by Fisheries and Oceans Canada demonstrated that coho salmon engineered with a growth hormone ate three times more than normal coho, raising fears that if these fish ever escape into the wild they will decimate the food supply available to native species.

3. Melting icefields and glaciers

Icefields and glaciers in Canada have been gradually but steadily melting away over the past three decades. In Canada's Arctic, the ice pack is 40% thinner than it was in the 1950s, a process that is now accelerating at the rate of 9% a decade. The 1,300 or so glaciers on the eastern slopes of the Rocky Mountains have lost 25% to 75% of their mass since 1850. The permafrost is melting and retreating in some areas, causing instability in buildings, bridges and infrastructure. Inuit are finding it more difficult to get out on the ice to hunt and fish, and are losing traditional culture and know-how. Polar bears are losing critical body mass because they cannot stay out on the ice long enough to gorge on seal pups—and when they do, some get stranded on ice floes because breakup is happening earlier. The Northwest Passage is staying ice-free for longer periods of time in the summer, and Canada's sovereignty is at stake: although Canada has declared it an internal waterway, the Americans do not recognize the claim.

4. Urban sprawl

At more than 435 square miles (700 sq. km), Calgary is about the same size as New York City's five boroughs, but with one-tenth the population. Winnipeg has quadrupled its size in the last 20 years. Sprawling Canadian cities seem like a good deal on the surface—houses are new and comparatively cheap, and there's lots of space for parks and roads. But because it is extremely costly to build the infrastructure—new electrical lines, sewers, shopping centres, roads, schools and office buildings—needed to service these communities, sprawl is an inefficient way to house urban and suburban families. In addition, as cities expand, farmland, forests and wetlands get swallowed up, and air pollution increases with the greater reliance on cars. Some municipalities have attempted to control the degradation of the environment caused by urban sprawl by increasing urban density, establishing urban boundaries and putting moratoriums on new road construction.

5. Disappearing spotted owls

It is estimated that there were once 500 pairs of spotted owls (they mate for life) in Canada, but their numbers declined by at least two-thirds between 1992 and 2002. And only 16 adult spotted owls were recorded in British Columbia in 2004. The medium-sized brown-grey owl lives in the old-growth forests of the Pacific Northwest, where industrial logging has decimated its habitat. The spotted owl was designated "endangered" in 1986 by the Committee on the Status of Endangered Wildlife in Canada (COSEWIC), but the British Columbia government continues to approve logging operations in at least three, and possibly six, of the ten areas where the owl nests and forages.

6. Invasive species and hardwood trees

In the last few years, the Asian long-horned beetle, the emerald ash borer and the brown spruce long-horned beetle have been destroying various species of softwood and hardwood trees across Canada. The ash borer, for instance, has claimed approximately 12 million trees in the U.S. and Canada, essentially eliminating ash trees from southwestern Ontario. The insects likely arrived here in the packing materials of goods imported from China and made the leap to local forests and parks.

7. Disappearing wilderness

Canada's boreal forest runs through the northern reaches of every province from Labrador to the Yukon and provides a great deal of the world's oxygen supply. Home to 600 First Nations communities, the boreal forest is a vast ecosystem that provides essential habitat for thousands of plant and animal species, especially waterfowl. The vast freshwater reserves and lush forests are irreplaceable sources of the necessities of life, and yet only 10% of the boreal forest is protected from development. Mining, farming, logging, pulp and paper plants, pipelines and hydro-electricity dams have all encroached on the boreal, and continue to do so without a politically sanctioned plan for conservation or sustainability.

8. Toxins in breast milk

A chemical compound used as a flame retardant in computers, carpets and furniture has shown up in Canadian women's breast milk. In 2004 Health Canada found that Canadian women's breast milk had the second-highest levels in the world of polybrominated diphenyl ethers (PBDEs); the U.S. is first. The contaminant has been linked to learning disabilities, memory loss and thyroid hormone irregularities. The federal government has concluded that PBDE levels in Canada have not yet reached harmful levels.

9. Extreme weather and climate change

Canada has experienced more weather-related disasters in the past decade than at any other time in recorded history. The occurrence of devastating droughts in the Prairies, tornadoes, hurricanes and floods has increased dramatically. Climate shifts such as these are caused largely by the effects of human intervention on the environment—urbanization, greenhouse gas emissions, clear-cutting, soil erosion, drained wetlands and smog.

9 AMAZING ATTIC EVENTS

1. Thomas Chatterton commits suicide (1770)

As a boy, Thomas Chatterton was a prodigious poet and scholar. An early Romantic, at the age of 10 he wrote on a par with his adult contemporaries. His family was poor, his mother a widowed seamstress, and privacy was difficult to come by in their small Bristol, England, home. So young Thomas set up a writing room in the attic, which he jealously guarded as his secret domain. In the attic room, among his books and papers, stood Ellinor, a life-sized doll made of woven rushes, which his mother used for dress fittings. Thomas loved Ellinor and always took care to powder her face and do her hair. However, when he moved to London to pursue his literary career, he left his beloved Ellinor behind. He rented a garret reminiscent of his attic study at home. Thereafter suffering repeated personal and professional disappointments, including failure to sell a series of forgeries he claimed had been written by a 15th-century monk, Chatterton took arsenic and died at the age of 17.

2. Marconi invents the wireless telegraph (1894–96)

Guglielmo Marconi was 20 years old when he began experimenting in earnest with radio waves. Because his father took a dim view of such "childish" pursuits as physics, and even went so far as to destroy his son's electronic equipment, young Marconi had to set up a secret laboratory in the attic of their villa in Bologna. There, among his mother's trays of silkworms, Marconi determined that radio waves could carry a message in Morse code across the room. In time, he proved that the effectiveness of his invention was not bound by the four attic walls; radio waves could transmit messages over great distances.

3. Baird constructs and demonstrates the first television (1922–26)

In 1922 British scientist John Logie Baird rented an attic room above an artificial-flower shop at 8 Queen's Arcade in Hastings, England, to continue research on his primitive television sets. He used a tea chest as the base for his motor and a biscuit tin to house the projection lamp. He held the whole contraption together with darning needles, scraps of wood, string and sealing wax. In 1924 he took his "working" apparatus to London. There he rented two attic rooms at 22 Frith Street in Soho. He struggled for another two years before he gave the first demonstration of true television on January 26, 1926, for an audience of 50 scientists. The British Broadcasting Corporation inaugurated Baird's system in 1929 and used it until 1935, when a more sophisticated system was adopted.

4. Hitler attempts suicide (1923)

After the failure of his Beer Hall Putsch in Munich, Germany, Hitler hid in an attic bedroom at Uffing, the country estate of his follower Ernst "Putzi" Hanfstängl. Hitler tried to commit suicide by shooting himself when the police came to arrest him. A police agent managed to disarm him before he could pull the trigger.

5. The Kühns commit espionage at Pearl Harbor (1939–41)

Ruth Kühn was only 17 years old when she became the mistress of Nazi leader Joseph Goebbels. But like all of his mistresses, Ruth was soon discarded. When the affair ended in 1939, Goebbels decided to send Ruth out of Germany. He arranged for her and her parents, Bernard and Friedel, to move to Hawaii and act as espionage agents for the Japanese. Ruth set up a beauty parlour in Honolulu, which became her chief source of information, since it was frequented by the wives of American military men. The next step was to figure out a way to transmit this information to the Japanese. The Kühns devised a simple code system and sent signals from the attic window of their small house overlooking Pearl Harbor. On December 7, 1941, towards the end of the Japanese surprise attack, their signals were noticed by two American naval officers. The U.S. Navy Shore Patrol arrested the family, and all were imprisoned for espionage.

6. Anne Frank writes her diary (1942–44)

Forced into hiding when the Nazis overran the Netherlands, Anne Frank, her parents and sister, and four other Jews shared a musty Amsterdam attic above a warehouse and office building. They hid there for two years, obtaining food and other necessities from Gentiles on the floor below. Anne, a precocious girl in her early teens, kept a diary in which she chronicled not only the details of their imprisonment, but also her personal feelings about life, love, the future and her budding sexual awareness. Finally, in August 1944, the Gestapo, acting on a tip from Dutch informers, raided the hiding place. All of the Franks died in concentration camps (Anne of typhus) except Otto Frank, Anne's father. He returned to the attic after the war and found his daughter's diary, which was first published under the title *The Diary of a Young Girl*.

7. Franz Schubert's lost piano score is discovered (1969)

The score for a fantasy for piano by Franz Schubert was discovered in an attic in Knittlefield, Austria, in 1969. The piece is believed to have been written by the Viennese composer in 1817.

8. Frédéric Chopin's lost waltzes are discovered (1978)

Several waltzes dedicated to Clementine de la Panouse were discovered by Vicomte Paul de la Panouse in the attic of the family château near Paris in 1978. The waltzes were stored in a heavy trunk belonging to the French aristocratic family. They had been hidden—along with many other documents—in various locations prior to the German invasion of France during the Second World War.

9. Schindler's list is discovered (1998)

When a German couple found an old grey suitcase in a loft belonging to the husband's late parents in Hildesheim, they didn't think much about it, until they saw the name on the handle: O. Schindler. Inside were hundreds of documents, including a list of the names of Jewish labourers that factory owner Oskar Schindler gave the Nazis during the Second World War. By giving Jewish workers fake jobs and otherwise manipulating the system, Schindler saved 1,200 Jews from extermination. His story inspired Thomas Keneally's novel *Schindler's Ark* (1982) and the movie *Schindler's List* (1993). The documents had apparently been stored in the loft by friends of Schindler and then forgotten. In 1999 the suitcase and its contents were donated to the Yad Vashem Holocaust Museum in Jerusalem.

—L.O. & M.J.T.

15 "REMARKABLE OCCURRENCES" OF 1885

Every year between 1878 and 1887, the federal government of Canada published *The Dominion Annual Register and Review*, an eclectic compendium of stories and information that managed to capture a broad slice of Canadian life. One of the most informative chapters was called "A Journal of Remarkable Occurrences." Here is a sample of some of those "remarkable occurrences" from October to December 1885, as described in the 1885 edition.

1. October 2

The Hudson's Bay Company ship *Princess Royal* is driven ashore at Sandhead beach, near the mouth of Moose River, during a heavy gale. She is laden with furs.

2. October 4

A dispatch to Victoria B.C. announces an accident on the C.P.R. near Kamloops, by which 1 white man and 5 Chinese are killed.

3. October 7

At Halifax, it transpires that H.Y. Clarke, cashier of the Union Bank of Halifax, is a defaulter to the extent of $33,000, and has been dismissed from his position.

4. October 12

In Toronto, Jas. Wilson, 26, is run over by a wagon, and dies in a few minutes.

5. October 20

Kyle & Mustard's roller, flouring and sawmills at Egmondville, Ont., are destroyed by fire. Loss $35,000; insurance $5000.

6. October 28

A meeting in Quebec to express disapproval of the execution of Riel, breaks up in a general row.

At Peterboro Ont., Mr. Wm. Hopkins is killed by being thrown out of his buggy while driving.

7. October 29

At Halifax, a somewhat novel case is tried before the Supreme Court. Dr. Rigby sues Dr. Slayter for $1000 for assault. Slayter, it appears refused to go to the North-West with his batallion when called on for active service. Rigby taunted him upon the fact, and called him a coward, for which Slayter knocked him down. Rigby obtains a verdict for $20.

8. October 30

Mr. C.S. Chapman, a clerk in the Department of the Interior, Ottawa, formerly an officer in H.M.'s 54th Reg., is found in bed suffocated to death, with his wife lying insensible beside him. It is supposed they were overcome by the fumes of gas, generated by a coal stove.

The Montreal Harbour Commissioners tug *St. John*, while proceeding to Pointe-aux-Trembles, takes fire and is run on a sand-bank where she is completely consumed. Some sporting gentlemen on board have a narrow escape from being burned to death.

9. November 12
Three men are dashed to death by falling from the roof of the Montreal drill hall which they were engaged in painting.

Adolphe Sharpe, sailor on board the steamboat *Speedwell* falls from the mast whilst the vessel is at the Niagara dock and is instantly killed.

10. November 18
The existence of 18 cases of smallpox causes much alarm at Charlottetown P.E.I. No services are held at the churches, and all public meetings are forbidden.

11. November 28
The first car of oatmeal exported from Manitoba is shipped to Montreal.

12. December 9
Samuel Perry is killed in the Union Phosphate Mine, Portland West, P.Q., by the falling of a piece of ice, about a ton in weight, into the pit where he is working.

13. December 16
Chief of Police McMillan of Brandon, Man., accidentally shoots himself with a rifle, and dies from the effects of the wound.

14. December 24
The annual Christmas distribution of the Toronto St. George's Society includes 7,000 lbs. of beef and 2,500 4-lb. loaves, besides tea and sugar. 750 families and 200 casuals are relieved.

15. December 31
John Napier, a farmer at Coveyhill P.Q., while lying intoxicated in his farm yard, has his nose and fingers eaten off by hogs.

15 THINGS THAT FELL FROM THE SKY

1. Black eggs

On May 5, 1786, after six months of drought, a strong east wind dropped a great quantity of black eggs on the city of Port-au-Prince, Haiti. Some of the eggs were preserved in water and hatched the next day. The beings inside shed several layers of skin and resembled tadpoles.

2. Toads

One of the most famous toad falls happened in the summer of 1794 in the village of Lalain, France. A very hot afternoon was broken suddenly by such an intense downpour of rain that 150 French soldiers (then fighting the Austrians) were forced to abandon the trench in which they were hiding to avoid being submerged. In the middle of the storm, which lasted for 30 minutes, tiny toads, mostly in the tadpole stage, began to land on the ground and jump about in all directions. When the rain let up, the soldiers discovered toads in the folds of their three-cornered hats.

3. Fire

On the evening of May 30, 1869, the horrified citizens of Greiffenberg, Germany, and neighbouring villages witnessed a fall of fire, which was followed by a tremendous peal of thunder. People who were outside reported that the fire was different in form and colour from common lightning. They said they felt wrapped in fire and deprived of air for some seconds.

4. Judas tree seeds

Just before sunset one day in August 1897, an immense number of small, blood-coloured clouds filled the sky in Macerata, Italy. About an hour later, the clouds burst and small seeds rained from the sky, covering the ground to a depth of ½ inch (1 cm). Many of the seeds had already started to germinate, and all of the seeds were from the Judas tree, which is found predominantly in the Middle East and Asia. There was no accompanying debris—just the Judas tree seeds.

5. The largest meteorite

The largest known iron meteorite, weighing more than 60 tons, crashed to earth in late 1920, landing on a farm in the Hoba district west of

Grootfontein in northern Namibia. It has since been declared a national monument and is visited by more than 20,000 tourists a year. A minor international incident occurred in 1989 when 36 Malaysian soldiers serving in a UN peacekeeping force tried to cut pieces from the boulder for souvenirs.

6. Frogs

It rained frogs in Calgary, Alberta, early on the morning of August 4, 1921. Along 11th Avenue, the frogs were strewn thickly on the pavement. Residents were puzzled as to the source of the amphibians. A few believed they had come out of their hidden retreats to bathe in the shower, but there were no eyewitnesses.

7. Brown rain

On May 18, 1931, in northern Saskatchewan, gale-force winds tossed powdered soil into the air. It started to rain. There was so much dust in the air that "brown rain" beat down from the skies.

8. Wild geese

During an electrical storm on April 22, 1932, 52 wild geese were struck by lightning as they flew over Elgin, Manitoba. The jolt killed the birds, sending them crashing to the ground. Those collected were distributed to townspeople for dinner.

9. Silver coins

Several thousand rubles' worth of silver coins fell in the Gorky region of the USSR on June 17, 1940. The official explanation was that a landslide had uncovered a hidden treasure, which was picked up by a tornado, which dropped it on Gorky. No explanation was given for the fact that the coins were not accompanied by any debris.

10. Mushroom-shaped things

Traffic at Mexico City airport was halted temporarily on the morning of July 30, 1963, when thousands of greyish mushroom-shaped things floated to the ground out of a cloudless sky. Hundreds of witnesses described these objects variously as "giant cobwebs," "balls of cotton" and "foam." They disintegrated rapidly after landing.

11. Soot

A fine blanket of soot landed on a Cranford park on the edge of London's Heathrow Airport in 1969, greatly annoying the local park keepers. The official report of the Greater London Council said the "soot" was composed of spores of a black microfungus, *Pithomyces chartarum*, found only in New Zealand.

12. Beans

Rancher Salvador Targino of João Pessoa, Brazil, reported a rain of small beans on his property in Paraíba State in early 1971. Local agricultural authorities speculated that a storm had swept up a pile of beans in West Africa and dropped them in northeastern Brazil. Targino boiled some of the beans, but said they were too tough to eat.

13. Fish

About 150 perch-like silver fish dropped from the sky during a tropical storm near Killarney Station in Australia's Northern Territory in February 1974. Fish falls are common enough that an "official" explanation has been developed to cover most of them. It is theorized that whirlwinds create a waterspout effect, sucking up water and fish, carrying them for great distances and then dropping them somewhere else.

14. A 3,902-pound (1,770 kg) stone

The largest meteorite fall in recorded history occurred on March 8, 1976, near the Chinese city of Kirin. Many of the 100 stones that were found weighed over 200 pounds (90 kg); the largest, which landed in the Haupi Commune, weighed 3,902 pounds (1,770 kg). It is, by more than 1,000 pounds (450 kg), the largest stony meteorite ever recovered.

15. Human body

Mary C. Fuller was sitting in her parked car with her eight-month-old son on Monday morning, September 25, 1978, in San Diego, California, when a human body crashed through the windshield. The body had been thrown from a Pacific Southwest Airlines jetliner, which had exploded after being hit by a small plane in one of the worst disasters in U.S. history. Mother and son suffered minor lacerations.

9 UNUSUAL DISASTERS

1. The St. Pierre Snake Invasion

Volcanic activity on the "bald mountain" towering over St. Pierre, Martinique, was usually so inconsequential that no one took seriously the fresh, steaming vent holes and earth tremors during April 1902. By early May, however, ash began to rain down continuously, and the nauseating stench of sulphur filled the air. Their homes on the mountainside made uninhabitable, more than 100 fer-de-lance snakes slithered down and invaded the mulatto quarter of St. Pierre. The 6-foot-long (1.8 m) serpents killed 50 people and innumerable animals before they were finally destroyed by the town's giant street cats. But the annihilation had only begun. On May 5 a landslide of boiling mud spilled into the sea, followed by a tsunami that killed hundreds. Three days later, on May 8, Mount Pelée finally exploded, sending a murderous avalanche of white-hot lava straight towards the town. Within three minutes St. Pierre was completely obliterated. Of its 30,000 population, there were only two survivors.

2. The Shiloh Baptist Church Panic

Two thousand people, mostly black, jammed into Shiloh Baptist Church in Birmingham, Alabama, on September 19, 1902, to hear an address by Booker T. Washington. The brick church was new. A steep flight of stairs, enclosed in brick, led from the entrance doors to the church proper. After Washington's speech, there was an altercation over an unoccupied seat, and the word "fight" was misunderstood as "fire." The congregation rose as if on cue and stampeded for the stairs. Those who reached them first were pushed from behind and fell. Others fell on top of them until the entrance was completely blocked by a pile of screaming humanity 10 feet (3 m) high. Efforts by Washington and the churchmen down in front to induce calm were fruitless, and they stood by helplessly while their brothers and sisters, mostly the latter, were trampled or suffocated to death. There was neither fire nor even a real fight, but 115 people died.

3. The Great Boston Molasses Flood

On January 15, 1919, the workers and residents of Boston's North End, mostly Irish and Italian, were out enjoying the noontime sun of an unseasonably warm day. Suddenly, with only a low rumble of warning, the huge cast-iron tank of the Purity Distilling Company burst open,

479

and a great wave of raw black molasses, two storeys high, poured down Commercial Street and oozed into the adjacent waterfront area. Neither pedestrians nor horse-drawn wagons could outrun it. Two million gallons (7.5 million L) of molasses originally destined for rum engulfed scores of people—21 men, women and children drowned or suffocated, while another 150 were injured. Buildings crumbled, and an elevated train track collapsed. Those horses not completely swallowed up were so trapped in the goo that they had to be shot by police. Sightseers who came to see the chaos couldn't help but walk in the molasses. On their way home, they spread the sticky substance throughout the city. Boston smelled of molasses for a week, and the harbour ran brown until summer.

4. The Pittsburgh Gasometer Explosion

A huge cylindrical gasometer—the largest in the world at the time—located in the heart of the industrial centre of Pittsburgh, Pennsylvania, developed a leak. On the morning of November 14, 1927, repairmen with an open-flame blowtorch set out to look for the leak. At about ten o'clock they apparently found it. The tank, containing 5 million cubic feet (1.5 million cu. m) of natural gas, rose in the air like a balloon and exploded. Chunks of metal, some weighing more than 100 pounds (45 kg), were scattered great distances, and the combined effects of air pressure and fire left a square mile (1.6 sq. km) of devastation. Twenty-eight people were killed, and hundreds were injured.

5. The Gillingham Fire "Demonstration"

Every year the firemen of Gillingham, England, would construct a makeshift "house" out of wood and canvas for the popular firefighting demonstration at the annual Gillingham Park fete. A few local boys were selected from many aspirants to take part in the charade. On July 11, 1929, nine boys—aged 10 to 14—and six firemen costumed as if for a wedding party climbed to the third floor of the "house." The plan was to light a smoke fire on the first floor, rescue the "wedding party" with ropes and ladders and then set the empty house ablaze to demonstrate the use of the fire hoses. By some error, the real fire was lit first. The spectators, assuming the bodies they saw burning were dummies, cheered and clapped, while the firemen outside directed streams of water on what they knew to be a real catastrophe. All 15 people inside the house died.

6. The Empire State Building Crash

On Saturday morning, July 28, 1945, a veteran army pilot took off in a B-25 light bomber from Bedford, Massachusetts, headed for Newark, New Jersey. The co-pilot and a young sailor hitching a ride were also aboard. Fog made visibility poor. About an hour later, people on the streets of midtown Manhattan became aware of the rapidly increasing roar of a plane, and watched with horror as a bomber suddenly appeared out of the clouds, dodged between skyscrapers and plunged into the side of the Empire State Building. Pieces of plane and building fell like hail. A gaping hole was gouged in the 78th floor, one of the plane's two engines hurtled through seven walls and came out the opposite side of the building, and the other engine shot through an elevator shaft, severing the cables and sending the car plummeting to the basement. When the plane's fuel tank exploded, six floors were engulfed in flame, and burning gasoline streamed down the sides of the building. Fortunately, few offices were open on a Saturday, and only 11 people—plus the three occupants of the plane—died.

7. The Texas City Chain Reaction Explosions

On April 15, 1947, the French freighter *Grandcamp* docked at Texas City, Texas, and took on some 1,400 tons of ammonium nitrate fertilizer. That night a fire broke out in the hold of the ship. By dawn, thick black smoke had port authorities worried because the Monsanto chemical plant was only 700 feet (213 m) away. As men stood on the dock watching, tugboats prepared to tow the freighter out to sea. Suddenly, a ball of fire enveloped the ship. For many, it was the last thing they ever saw. A great wall of flame radiated outward from the wreckage, and within minutes the Monsanto plant exploded, killing and maiming hundreds of workers and any spectators who had survived the initial blast. Most of the business district was devastated, and fires raged along the waterfront, where huge tanks of butane gas stood imperilled. Shortly after midnight, a second freighter—also carrying nitrates—exploded, and the whole sequence began again. More than 500 people died, and another 1,000 were badly injured.

8. The Basra Mass Poisoning

In September 1971, a shipment of 90,000 metric tons of seed grain arrived in the Iraqi port of Basra. The American barley and Mexican wheat, which had been chemically treated with methylmercury to prevent rot, were sprayed a bright pink to indicate their lethal coating, and clear warnings were printed on the bags—but only in English and Spanish. Before they could be distributed to the farmers, the bags were stolen from the docks, and the grain was sold as food to the starving populace. The Iraqi government, embarrassed at its criminal negligence or for other reasons, hushed up the story, and it was not until two years later that an American newsman came up with evidence that 6,530 hospital cases of mercury poisoning were attributable to the unsavoury affair. Officials would admit to only 459 deaths, but total fatalities were probably more like 6,000, with another 100,000 suffering such permanent effects as blindness, deafness and brain damage.

9. The Chandka Forest Elephant Stampede

In the spring of 1972, the Chandka Forest area in India—already suffering from drought—was hit by a searing heat wave as well. The local elephants, who normally were no problem, became so crazed by the high temperatures and lack of water that the villagers told authorities they were afraid to venture out and to farm their land. By summer the situation had worsened. On July 10, the elephant herds went berserk and stampeded through five villages, leaving general devastation and 24 deaths in their wake.

—N.C.S.

8 REAL BARENAKED LADIES IN CANADIAN HISTORY

1. Bare-Breasted in Battle

Eric the Red's illegitimate daughter Freydis travelled from Iceland to the shores of present-day Newfoundland twice, first as a colonist and then as the leader of an expedition and fighting force. It was during her first sojourn in "Vinland," as they called it, that she engaged in battle with the Natives. For the most part the Vikings had been getting along with the Beothuks, but when relations soured, the newcomers beat a retreat—right past Freydis's house. Vulnerable and outnumbered, the very pregnant Freydis tried to ridicule and shame her Viking countrymen into standing their ground. When that failed, she picked up the sword of a fallen comrade, brandished it at the Natives, then stroked her bare breasts with the blade and charged them. According to legend, the Natives turned and ran.

2. Naked Doukhobor Demonstrations

Seven thousand Doukhobors settled in Saskatchewan in 1898–99 after they were expelled from Russia for resisting military conscription. Their religious beliefs emphasized pacifism, frugality, equality and industriousness. The communal farms they built in western Canada flourished, but within a few years they clashed with the government in their newly adopted country because they refused to assimilate and swear allegiance to the Crown—they felt this contradicted their belief in the omnipotence of God. In May 1903 a small sub-sect of the Doukhobors, the Sons of Freedom, decided to march naked through the towns and villages of Saskatchewan to demonstrate strict adherence to their faith. Several dozen naked men, women and children marched through late spring snowfalls, subsisting on grass, leaves and raw potatoes. They were chased and whipped by neighbours and non-believers until the RCMP stepped in, arresting and imprisoning them for "indecent exposure." Over the next few decades, the Sons of Freedom periodically marched nude to demonstrate their zealous beliefs. They strenuously resisted putting their children in public schools and would come to the schools naked to remove their children. They also began firebombing homes and government buildings. Their actions resulted in mass trials, detainment and prison sentences that were still being handed out into the 1960s. The images of naked Doukhobors splashed across the newspapers of the day forever coloured Canadian perceptions of sect members as religious fanatics.

3. Cinema's first nude scene

Author, actress, director and conservationist Nell Shipman was a woman ahead of her time. Born in Vancouver in 1892, she produced, starred in and directed her own breakthrough film, *God's Country and the Woman*, at the age of 23. As in most of her films, Nell played a strong and brave woman who thrived in the cold northern climate while coexisting harmoniously with wild animals such as bears, wolves and walruses. In 1919 Nell wrote the screenplay for and starred in *Back to God's Country*, a sequel to her first big hit. Nell appeared completely nude in the film as she plunged into the icy waters of Lesser Slave Lake. *Back to God's Country* cemented Nell's free-spirited reputation and became the most successful silent film ever made in Canada. She lost a legal battle to receive royalties for the film, however, and ended up homeless in New York City.

4. The Wreck Beach Nude-In

In the 1960s and into the 1970s Vancouver's "underground" newspaper, the *Georgia Straight*, promoted an annual "nude-in" at Wreck Beach. The sandy shores just under the cliffs of the University of British Columbia campus were a well-known haven for nudists, hippies and counterculture types who routinely suntanned and bathed naked there. The nude-in served to protest the occasional police presence and harassment Wreck Beach regulars had endured over the years. At the nude-in in August 1970, 13 people were arrested, including Sheila Beaupré, who was fined $50 for "committing an indecent act." She fought her case right up to the British Columbia Supreme Court and got it overturned on a technicality (they had charged her under the wrong section of the Criminal Code) in 1971. The Crown then dropped the charges on everyone else who had been arrested that day. The police have never again arrested anyone on Wreck Beach for being naked in a public place. The most recent threat to the nudist preserve is the proposed construction of high-rise student residences that will overlook the beach and its 300,000 annual users.

5. Legally Topless in Ontario

Gwen Jacobs was walking down a street in Guelph, Ontario, on July 19, 1991. It was humid and hot—91°F (33°C)—and Jacobs decided to take off her shirt to cool down, as the men she was with had done. But things heated up considerably when she was ticketed and fined $75 for indecent exposure. An Ontario court judge declared that female breasts were "sexually stimulating to men" and should therefore be covered in public. Jacobs appealed the decision, and on December 10, 1996, the Ontario Court of Appeal made it legal for women to go topless in Ontario. It is still considered "indecent" to bare female breasts in public for sexual or commercial purposes.

6. Legally Topless in Canada

Because the Jacobs decision was provincial in scope, like-minded women across the country have stripped off their shirts in an effort to make the Ontario law apply elsewhere. In August 1997 Regina residents Kathleen Rice, 42, and Evangeline Godron, 64, challenged the law in their province by going topless in a downtown park. They were charged with public indecency, but a year later a Saskatchewan judge affirmed their right to bare their breasts in public, effectively establishing the Ontario ruling as a legal precedent for all of Canada. Victorious defence lawyer James Rybchuk said, "Let's face it, if a woman can walk topless down the streets of Regina, Saskatchewan, she can probably walk topless down any city street in Canada."

7. In Defence of Breastfeeding in Public

Lactation advocates and hungry babies everywhere rejoiced at the 1997 British Columbia Human Rights Tribunal decision that upheld Michelle Poirier's right to breastfeed in a public place. Poirier was asked to leave a staff meeting at her workplace when she began breastfeeding her baby in front of her peers. According to managers, other female staffers were made uncomfortable by the breastfeeding, which Poirier usually did over her lunch break, sitting at her desk. The tribunal decreed that it was against the law to expect Poirier to miss meetings in order to breastfeed her child.

8. Barenaked Ladies Save Gulf Island Paradise

Forty-year-old Briony Penn rode naked through the streets of downtown Vancouver on a horse to bring attention to the campaign to stop logging and development on Salt Spring Island, British Columbia. Wearing only flesh-coloured panties and a blonde wig, Penn took her chilly ride on January 22, 2001. Another 35 Salt Spring Island women posed naked for a calendar that was sold to raise funds to save the Salt Spring old-growth trees and habitat. One week after Penn's ride, the British Columbia government announced its plan to purchase the 1,900 acres (770 hectares) of land in question and turn it into a park. "It did what it was supposed to do," said Penn. "People entered into it with a spirit of fun, and it helped infect the whole island with enthusiasm."

PHILIP PULLMAN'S 10 BEST TOOLS, PLUS 1 MORE

Philip Pullman is one of the world's great storytellers, and his trilogy His Dark Materials, the adventures of Lyra Belacqua and her friend Will Parry in a richly imagined alternative universe, has been widely acclaimed.

Born in Norwich, England, in 1946, Philip Pullman grew up to become a teacher. Unable at first to afford the tools he wanted, he turned to writing as the alternative to a life of crime. His greatest unfulfilled ambition is to present woodworking programs on satellite TV. He is reasonably presentable and articulate, and is open to offers.

1. The Tormek Grinder
It's no good trying to use edge tools that are blunt, so you have to keep them sharp. Of all the ways I've tried, this is the best. An ordinary electric bench grinder spins the stone around at such a speed that the steel you're trying to sharpen gets easily overheated and loses its power to hold an edge. The Tormek grinder overcomes that by having a large wheel that revolves fairly slowly in a trough of water and an ingenious system of jigs that slip onto the tool rest and hold the chisel, or the gouge, or the scissors, or the carving knife, at exactly the right angle to the stone. It produces the sharpest, most reliable edge you can get.

2. The Japanese Pull Saw
It's so obvious: a saw that cuts on the pull stroke instead of the push. The advantage is that you can have a much thinner blade, because it doesn't have to be stiff, and that means you can cut a much narrower kerf much more accurately. It cuts dovetails very well.

3. The Block Plane
This is a little plane that you hold with one hand. I have two of them, but the one I use most often is a metal one: a Record. It's satisfyingly heavy for such a small thing and beautifully designed: there's a hollow in the top of the throat-adjustment knob for your forefinger so that you can press on the front end and guide it more firmly, and hollows on the sides for your thumb and middle finger, and the lever cap curls over precisely to fit the palm of your hand. You can adjust the depth of the blade and the width of the throat, and it's ideal for planing end

grain. I found that what made the most difference (apart from keeping the blade razor-sharp: see the Tormek grinder, above) was grinding the sole until it was as smooth and flat as a mirror. Now it just glides over the wood.

4. The Try Square
My favourite is a little metal engineer's try square with a 4-inch (10 cm) blade. If you need a long one, use a long one, but this is adequate for most jobs; it slips very neatly into the pocket, and it feels good in the hand. I bought it from the Gloucester Green market in Oxford, where there are a couple of stalls that sell second-hand tools.

5. The Gouge
This is a chisel with a blade that's curved in cross-section. The ones I use for carving have a bevel ground on the outside so you can scoop out a hollow. Sharpening on its own isn't enough for these delicate and high-bred creatures: you have to hone the bevel till it shines. Fortunately, the Tormek (see above) has a leather wheel especially designed for that. Once it's so sharp that it hurts the eye to look at it, the gouge will slice through wood with nonchalant accuracy.

6. The Carver's Chops
"Chop" has the same origin as "chap," which means jaw or cheek. It's a heavy wooden vise that holds a big workpiece for carving. I made mine out of beech, following a plan by the excellent and learned Anthony Dew, founder and president of the Guild of Rocking Horse Makers.

7. The X-Acto Knife
In combination with a steel straightedge and a rubber cutting mat, this is unbeatable. Card, paper, leather, even thin plywood all succumb.

8. The Pencil
This is one of those things you don't think of as a tool. But whenever you make something out of wood, you're going to need a pencil at some point, whether to mark a line for cutting or to jot down calculations for the measurements or to sketch a complicated joint and fix the shape in your mind. I have never found those wide so-called carpenter's pencils

with a flat lead any better than an ordinary HB. A few strokes on a piece of fine sandpaper will restore the sharpest of points.

9. The Belt Sander

I had to think hard about which power tool to include. Each one I have is utterly necessary, and so is the next one I'm going to buy, as soon as I decide which it is. How can you cut complex shapes without a band saw? How did we manage to do anything at all before they invented the router? But if you're making a large piece of furniture, the only way to achieve a perfectly smooth surface without loathsome and back-breaking toil is to use a belt sander. It removes all the bumps and hollows and rough patches, and with progressively finer belts you can get a result that would have taken our ancestors hours, if not days. They might have turned their noses up at the biscuit jointer or the radial arm saw, but they would have used one of these like a shot.

10. The Jig

A hammer always looks like a hammer; a screwdriver always looks like a screwdriver. But a jig can look like anything. It's a frame or holding device that's often made specifically for one job and then put away in the corner of the workshop and never used again. But you don't throw it away, just in case. It's used to hold a workpiece in exactly the right place relative to the cutting edge or the drill bit or whatever it might be, to ensure that you cut a perfect semicircle on the band saw, or drill 30 holes at exactly the right angle, or cut several mortises to exactly the right depth, or . . . I love jigs.

+1. The Enigma

This is a beautiful and slender piece of bronze about a foot (30 cm) long. For half its length, it's been beaten out into a flat blade about as wide as a finger, with an edge that's too blunt to cut anything but paper: it's a perfect letter-opener. The other end has been formed into a similar but shorter blade at a right angle to the first, and the shorter blade has been bent halfway along its length into a flat foot, at a right angle to the main shaft, about as long as the middle joint of my thumb. It's been made by hand, and it's worn smooth with use. I guess it was made to tamp down the sand in a mould, but I really have no idea. I use it for scratching my back.

13 BAD PREDICTIONS

1. Canada's Future

"Canadian nationality being a lost cause, the ultimate union of Canada with the United States appears now to be morally certain; so that nothing is left for Canadian patriotism but to provide that it shall be a union indeed, and not an annexation." —Goldwin Smith, in his book *The Political Destiny of Canada*, 1877

Political gadfly Goldwin Smith did not see much hope for the future of the new nation when he published his book. His prediction about the union of Canada and the United States has not come true—yet.

2. Canada in the World

"The nineteenth century was the century of the United States. I think we can claim that it is Canada that shall fill the twentieth century." —Wilfrid Laurier, Canadian prime minister, speech to the Canadian Club, Ottawa, January 1904

Laurier never said "the twentieth century belongs to Canada," although most people think he did. But even his more modest claim that Canada will "fill" the 20th century would probably have to be judged as overly optimistic. It wasn't a bad century, but it would be pretty hard to deny the U.S. the title of Most Important Country for the second century in a row. Any bets on this one?

3. The 1929 Stock Market Crash

"While no doubt a number of people have suffered owing to the sharp decline in stocks, the soundness of Canadian securities generally is not affected. Business was never better, nor faith in Canada's future more justified." —William Lyon Mackenzie King, Canadian prime minister, October 30, 1929

Mackenzie King made this statement the day after the stock market crashed. His optimism about the soundness of the Canadian economy on the eve of the greatest economic downturn in history proved to be completely unjustified.

4. Hitler

"I still stake my belief in Hitler's word that the people themselves do not want war, and that he, himself, has primarily the interests of the people at heart." —William Lyon Mackenzie King, Canadian prime minister, 1937

After their meeting, Mackenzie King confided to his diary that Hitler was "a calm, passive man, deeply and thoughtfully in earnest."

5. The Atomic Bomb

"That is the biggest fool thing we have ever done. . . . The bomb will never go off, and I speak as an expert in explosives." —Admiral William Leahy, U.S. Navy officer, speaking to President Truman, 1945

6. Landing on the Moon

"Landing and moving around the moon offers so many serious problems for human beings that it may take science another 200 years to lick them." —*Science Digest*, August 1948

It took 21 years.

7. Fashion in the 1970s

"So women will wear pants and men will wear skirts interchangeably. And since there won't be any squeamishness about nudity, see-through clothes will only be see-through for reasons of comfort. Weather permitting, both sexes will go about bare-chested, though women will wear simple protective panties." —Rudi Gernreich, American fashion designer, 1970

8. The Montreal Olympics

"The Olympics can no more have a deficit than a man can have a baby." —Jean Drapeau, mayor of Montreal, 1973

The mayor's prediction about the financial legacy of the 1976 Olympic Games proved to be slightly off the mark. The Games ended up more than $1 billion in the red, and Montrealers have spent nearly 30 years paying down the debt. The mayor never did have that baby.

9. The Collapse of the Soviet Union

"We must expect the Soviet system to survive in its present brutish form for a very long time. There will be Soviet labour camps and Soviet torture chambers well into our great-grandchildren's lives." —Newt Gingrich, U.S. Representative (and future Speaker of the House), 1984

10. The Fall of the Berlin Wall

"Liberalization is a ploy . . . the Wall will remain." —George Will, columnist for the *Washington Post*, November 9, 1989—the day the Berlin Wall fell

11. Invasion of Iraq #1

"There is a minimal risk of conflict." —Heino Kopietz, senior Middle East analyst, on the possibility of Iraq invading Kuwait, in *The Times* of London, July 26, 1990

Iraq invaded Kuwait five days later.

12. 9/11

"Who cares about a little terrorist in Afghanistan?" —Paul Wolfowitz, U.S. deputy secretary of defence, dismissing concerns about al Qaeda at an April 2001 meeting on terrorism

13. Invasion of Iraq #2

"I have no doubt we're going to find big stores of weapons of mass destruction." —Kenneth Adelman, U.S. Defense Policy Board member, in the *Washington Post*, March 23, 2003

"[The war] could last six days, six weeks. I doubt six months." —Donald Rumsfeld, U.S. secretary of defence, to U.S. troops in Aviano, Italy, February 7, 2003

"[My] belief is we will, in fact, be greeted as liberators. . . . I think it will go relatively quickly, weeks rather than months." —Dick Cheney, U.S. vice president, March 16, 2003

"We are dealing with a country that can really finance its own reconstruction and relatively soon." —Paul Wolfowitz, U.S. deputy secretary of defence, to the House Budget Committee, February 27, 2003

—K.H.J., C.F. & Cdn. Eds.

12 VENERABLE TREES OF CANADA

1–2. The Carmanah Giant and the Red Creek Tree

The Pacific rainforest is home to Canada's most imposing and majestic trees. Randy Stoltmann was an enterprising environmentalist who found and catalogued many of the biggest and oldest trees in the B.C. Register of Big Trees. His efforts to save them from being logged were successful in areas such as the Carmanah Valley, but when he died in a backcountry skiing accident in 1994, the Register suffered a setback. Only now is it being revived through the efforts of volunteer giant-tree hunters. Two of the trees Stoltmann discovered remain the largest on record. The Carmanah Giant is Canada's tallest known tree. It is a Sitka spruce in the Carmanah Walbran Provincial Park that stands 314.1 feet (95.73 m) tall and has a circumference of 43.57 feet (13.28 m). The largest (height combined with circumference) Douglas fir is the Red Creek Tree, near the San Juan River in B.C. It is 242.1 feet (73.8 m) tall and has a circumference of 75 feet (22.8 m).

3. The Cheewhat Lake Cedar

The Cheewhat Lake Cedar in Pacific Rim National Park is Canada's biggest overall tree. It is a western red cedar 51 feet (15.6 m) in circumference and 182.1 feet (55.5 m) tall. It is considered the biggest because it combines its height and circumference with many branches and a massive crown. A partial core sample of the tree taken by Randy Stoltmann reveals that the tree is at least 1,212 years old and possibly 2,000. The red cedar is revered by the Natives of the northwest coast, who use the wood and bark for clothing, medicine, rituals, totem poles, dugout canoes and housing material. According to the Coast Salish, the Great Spirit created the red cedar to honour a man who was always helping others.

4. Eastern White Cedars

There's an ancient forest of eastern white cedars that grows on the limestone, sandstone and shale cliff faces of the Niagara Escarpment in southwestern Ontario. The trees grow very slowly and as a result are twisted and stunted. A tree survey was done in 2000, and over 73 trees were found to be more than 500 years old; 17 of them were over 700 years old. The oldest cedar, found in Lion's Head, is 1,053 years old, making it the oldest tree in Canada east of the Rocky Mountains.

5. The Golden Spruce

The 300-year-old golden spruce, the only living tree of its kind, stood in the old-growth forest of the Queen Charlotte Islands, British Columbia, until January 1997, when a disturbed "conservationist," Grant Hadwin, took a chainsaw and hacked at it. It fell a couple of days later. This Sitka spruce was unlike all others in that it lacked 80% of the regular amount of chlorophyll, rendering its needles golden yellow instead of green. Considered sacred by the local Haida, the tree, 6.56 feet (2 m) in diameter, stood perfectly straight and conical. Scientists gave the tree its own scientific name, *Picea sitchensis aurea*. In a letter Hadwin sent to environmental groups, the media and lumber companies, he wrote, "I didn't enjoy butchering this magnificent old plant, but you apparently need a message and wake-up call. . . . I mean this action to be an expression of my rage and hatred towards university trained professionals and their extremist supporters, whose ideas, ethics, denials, part truths, attitudes, etc., appear to be responsible for most of the abominations towards amateur life on this planet." Eighty cuttings of the fallen spruce were taken, and many of the grafts have been successful. One tree, now seven years old, sits in its own cage in the centre of Port Clements, beside a church. So far, it has continued to produce golden needles.

6. The McIntosh Apple Tree

The McIntosh apple was developed and nurtured from a wild sapling discovered by John McIntosh in 1801 in Dundela, Ontario. For many years, the original tree produced abundant fruit and healthy grafts for the propagation of the species. In 1893 the original tree was damaged by fire, and it died in 1910. Today, five trees still stand in Dundela that grew from grafts of the original McIntosh apple tree.

7. The Newton Apple Tree

On the front lawn of the National Research Council in Ottawa grows the Newton Apple Tree. A small but sturdy tree, it is believed to be a direct descendant of the apple tree under which Sir Isaac Newton lay on that fateful day when an apple fell on him—the "eureka" moment when he formulated the basis of his theory of gravity.

8. The Hanging Garden

Meares Island, off Tofino, British Columbia, is home to a grove of ancient rainforest hemlock, fir, cedar and spruce trees. Nestled among them is a cedar dubbed the Hanging Garden that is 60 feet (18.3 m) in circumference and approximately 1,500 years old. Supported in its branches that twist and jut off in all directions is an entire ecosystem of mosses, lichens, fungus, shrubs and ferns; it looks like a massive, mossy candelabra. Tourists come from around the world to stare at and photograph it.

9. The Eik Cedar

The Eik Cedar became the old-growth mascot of Tofino, British Columbia, due to a heated campaign to rescue it from the chainsaws in 2001. The 800-year-old western red cedar was the last example of old-growth forest in the town, but was declared a safety hazard by town councillors because of some rot inside its trunk. When Tofino residents heard about the plan to chop it down, they quickly conspired to save the tree with a publicity and fundraising campaign. Two local men, Brad Lindey, 17, and Dominic Beaulieu, 24, scrambled up the trunk and lived in its canopy for 35 days. The standoff allowed everyone time to think up creative options for saving the tree. Ultimately, engineers and arborists encircled the cedar with a $60,000 girdle of steel rods anchored in the bedrock to prevent it from falling, and it should stand for centuries to come.

10. The Swamp Cottonwood

The first known example of a swamp cottonwood growing in Canada was discovered in November 2002 by botanists John Ambrose, Lindsay Rodger and Gerry Waldron. Out for a walk in the woods at Bickford Oak Woods, south of Sarnia, Ontario, Ambrose was amazed when he came across the tree: "Since the late 1700s or early 1800s people have been documenting what is here and we are still finding new trees. And these aren't obscure little orchids or whatever, but big trees."

11. The Burmis Tree

The Burmis Tree, named after a now-deserted village 155 miles (250 km) southwest of Calgary, is said to be Canada's most photographed tree. The twisted and weathered pine, 16 feet (5 m) tall and somewhere between 200 and 600 years old, is a much-loved landmark for people living around Crowsnest Pass. A spectacular example of the limber pine species, its flexible branches and twigs can be tied in knots without breaking. Although the Burmis Tree died 25 years ago, its many fans and defenders have twice rescued it from decay and destruction by rebuilding it. In 1998 the tree fell over in high winds, and it was raised and replanted using steel bands and bolts to anchor it to the bedrock. In 2004 vandals hacked off several branches, which were then reattached to the tree with rods and wooden dowels.

12. The Burford Sweet Chestnut Trees

The Burford sweet chestnut trees represent a botanical find akin to the discovery of a living dinosaur. Arborist and conservationist Bruce Graham stumbled upon four mature sweet chestnut trees growing just outside Burford, a southwestern Ontario farm town. Sweet chestnuts were thought to have been wiped out from the local area due to a deadly disease that has infected an estimated 3.5 million trees in Canada and the U.S. since 1904. Graham collected seeds from the large, robust specimens, and in recent years has planted and raised thousands of them. The public is encouraged to buy seedlings and grow them to help the sweet chestnut re-establish itself in Canada.

10 FUNGUSES THAT CHANGED HISTORY

1. The Yellow Plague *(Aspergillus flavus)*

A. flavus is an innocent-looking but deadly yellowish mould also called aflatoxin. Undoubtedly the cause of countless deaths throughout history, it was not suspected of being poisonous until 1960. That year, a mysterious disease killed 100,000 young turkeys in England, and medical researchers traced the "turkey-X disease" to *A. flavus* growing on the birds' peanut meal feed. Hardy, widespread and lethal, aflatoxin is a powerful liver cancer agent. Even so, people have long cultivated *A. flavus*—in small amounts—as part of the manufacturing process of soy sauce and sake. But *A. flavus* can get out of control easily. It thrives on warm, damp conditions, and as it breeds—sometimes to lethal proportions within 24 hours—the mould produces its own heat, which spurs even faster growth.

Some of *A. flavus*'s favourite dishes are stored peanuts, rice, corn, wheat, potatoes, peas, cocoa, cured hams and sausage.

2. The Mould That Toppled an Industry *(Aspergillus niger)*

This common black mould, most often found on rotting vegetation, played a key role in the collapse of a major industry. Until the early 1920s, Italy produced about 90% of the world's citric acid, using low-grade lemons. Exported mainly to the U.S. as calcium citrate, citric acid was a costly ingredient—about $1 (U.S.) a pound (454 g)—used in food, pharmaceutical and industrial processing. When American chemists discovered that *A. niger*, the most ordinary of moulds, secreted citric acid as it grew in a culture medium, they seized the opportunity to perfect citric-acid production using the easily grown mould. Charles Pfizer & Co., of Brooklyn, New York, became known as the "world's largest lemon grove"—without a lemon in sight. Hard-working acres of *A. niger* were soon squirting out such quantities of citric acid that by 1923 the price was down to 25 cents a pound and the Italians were out of business.

3. St. Anthony's Fire *(Claviceps purpurea)*

A purplish-black spur-shaped mass, *C. purpurea* is a formidable and even frightening fungus that has long plagued mankind. But in addition to its horrible effects, *C. purpurea* also has valuable medical uses if the greatest care is taken to use tiny amounts. The fungus is a powerful muscle contractor and can control bleeding, speed up childbirth and even induce abortion. It is also the source of the hallucinogenic LSD-25. In doses larger than microscopic, *C. purpurea*—commonly called ergot—produces ergotamine poisoning, a grisly condition known in the Middle Ages as St. Anthony's fire. There is still no cure for this hideous, often fatal disease caused by eating fungus-infected rye. The victim suffers convulsions and performs a frenzied "dance." This is often accompanied by a burning sensation in the limbs, which turn black and fall off. Some victims of medieval ergotism went insane and many died. In AD 994 more than 40,000 people in two French provinces died of ergotism, and in 1722 the powerful fungus forced Peter the Great of Russia to abandon his plan to conquer Turkey when, on the eve of the Battle of Astrakhan, his entire cavalry and 20,000 others were stricken with ergotism. The last recorded outbreak of ergot poisoning was in the French village of Pont-Saint-Esprit in 1951.

4. The Nobel Mould *(Neurospora crassa)*

The humble bread mould *N. crassa* provided the means for scientists to explore the most exciting biological discovery of the 20th century: DNA. As anyone with an old loaf of bread in the bread box knows, *N. crassa* needs only a simple growing medium, and it has a short life cycle. With such cooperative qualities, this reddish mould enabled George Beadle and Edward Tatum to win the Nobel Prize in Medicine/Physiology in 1958 for discovering the role that genes play in passing on hereditary traits from one generation to the next. By X-raying *N. crassa*, the researchers produced mutations of the genes, or components of DNA, and then found which genes corresponded with which traits.

5. The Bluish-Green Lifesaver *(Penicillium notatum or Penicillium chrysogenum)*

A few dots of a rather pretty bluish-green mould were Dr. Alexander Fleming's first clue to finding one of the most valuable life-saving drugs ever developed. In 1928 he noticed that his petri dish of staphylococcus bacteria had become contaminated with symmetrically growing, circular colonies of *P. notatum*. Around each speck, all the bacteria were dead. Fleming further found that the mould also killed pneumonia, gonorrhea and diphtheria germs—without harming human cells. The unassuming bluish-green mould was beginning to look more interesting, but Fleming could not isolate the active element. Not until 1939 did Howard Florey and Ernst Chain identify penicillin, a secretion of the growing mould, as the bacteria-killer. The first important antibiotic, penicillin revolutionized treatment of many diseases. Fleming, Florey and Chain won the Nobel Prize in Physiology/Medicine in 1945 for their pioneering work with the common fruit mould that yielded the first "miracle drug."

6. The Gourmet's Delight *(Penicillium roquefortii)*

According to an old legend, a French shepherd forgot his lunch in a cave near the town of Roquefort, and when he found it weeks later, the cheese had become blue-veined and was richly flavoured. No one knew why this had happened until American mycologists discovered the common blue mould *P. roquefortii* in 1918. All blue cheeses—English

Stilton, Italian Gorgonzola, Norwegian Gammelost, Greek Kopanisti and Swiss Paglia—derive their tangy flavour from the energetic blue mould that grows rapidly in the cheese, partially digesting it and eventually turning the entire cheese into mould. Of course, it's more appetizing to say that *P. roquefortii* ripens the cheese instead of rotting it, but it's the same process.

7. The Famine-Maker *(Phytophthona infestans)*
The political history of the world changed as a result of the unsavoury activity of *P. infestans*, a microscopically small fungus that reduced Ireland to desperate famine in 1845. Hot, rainy July weather provided perfect conditions for the white fungus to flourish on the green potato plants—most of Ireland's food crop—and the bushes withered to brown, mouldy, stinking clumps within days. The entire crop was devastated, causing half a million people to starve to death, while nearly 2 million emigrated, mostly to the U.S. *P. infestans* dusted a powdery white death over Ireland for six years. The fungus spread rapidly, and just one bad potato could infect and ruin a barrel of sound ones. British prime minister Robert Peel tried to get Parliament to repeal tariffs on imported grain; while the MPs debated, Ireland starved. Relief came so slowly and inadequately that Peel's government toppled the next year, in 1846.

8. The Temperance Fighter *(Plasmopara viticola)*
A soft, downy mildew infecting American-grown grapes was responsible for nearly ruining the French wine industry. In 1872 the French unwittingly imported *P. viticola* on grafting stock of wine grapes grown in the U.S. Within 10 years, the mild-mannered mildew had quietly decimated many of France's finest old vineyards. But in 1882 botanist Pierre-Marie-Alexis Millardet discovered a miraculous cure for the ravages of *P. viticola*. He noticed that Médoc farmers painted their grape leaves with an ugly paste of copper sulphate, lime and water to prevent theft. Called Bordeaux mixture, this paste was the first modern fungicide. The vineyards of France recovered as the entire world sighed with relief.

9. Merchant of Death *(Saccharomyces cerevisiae)*
Ordinary brewer's yeast, *S. cerevisiae*, used to leaven bread and make ale, was once employed as a wartime agent of death. During the First World

War, the Germans ran short of both nitroglycerin and the fat used in its manufacture. Then they discovered that the usually friendly fungus *S. cerevisiae* could be used to produce glycerine, a necessary ingredient in explosives. Fermenting the fungus together with sucrose, nitrates, phosphates and sodium sulphite, the Germans produced more than 1,000 tons of glycerine per month. According to some military sources, this enabled them to keep their war effort going for an additional year.

10. The TB Killer *(Streptomyces griseus)*

A lowly mould found in dirt and manure piles, *S. griseus* nevertheless had its moment of glory in 1943, when Dr. Selman Waksman discovered that it yields the antibiotic streptomycin, which can cure tuberculosis. Waksman went to the U.S. in 1910 as a Russian refugee, and by 1918 he had earned his doctorate in soil microbiology. He had worked with *S. griseus* before, but not until a crash program to develop antibiotics (a word coined by Dr. Waksman himself) was launched did he perceive the humble mould's possibilities for greatness. Streptomycin was first used successfully on human beings in 1945, and in 1952 Dr. Waksman was awarded the Nobel Prize in Physiology/Medicine.

—K.P.

13 FAMOUS EVENTS THAT HAPPENED IN THE BATHTUB

1. The Poisoning of Pelias

According to Greek mythology, Medea murdered Jason's uncle (Pelias, king of Thessaly) by showing his daughters that they could rejuvenate him if they chopped him up and bathed him in her cauldron of herbs. They believed her, and he died.

2. The Murder of Agamemnon

Shortly after his return from the Trojan War, the Greek hero Agamemnon was murdered by his wife, Clytemnestra, who struck him twice with an axe while he was relaxing in the tub.

3. Archimedes' Discovery

While soaking in the bathtub, the Greek scientist Archimedes formulated the law of physics—known as the Archimedean principle—that a body immersed in fluid loses weight equal to the weight of the fluid it displaces. He became so excited about his discovery that he rushed out stark naked into the streets of Syracuse, Sicily, shouting "Eureka!" ("I have found it!")

4. Franklin's Pastime

Benjamin Franklin is reputed to have imported the first bathtub into America. He improved its design, and contemporary reports indicate that he carried on much of his reading and correspondence while soaking in the tub.

5. Marat's Assassination

Jean-Paul Marat played an active part in the French Revolution. As editor of the journal *L'Ami du Peuple*, he became known as an advocate of extreme violence. The moderate Girondists were driven out of Paris and took refuge in Normandy. There, some of them met and influenced a young woman called Charlotte Corday. Convinced that Marat must die, she went to Paris and bought a butcher's knife. When she arrived at Marat's house on July 13, 1793, he was taking a bath. (He spent many hours in the tub because of a painful skin condition.) Overhearing Corday, he asked to see her. They discussed politics for a few minutes, then Corday drew her knife and stabbed Marat to death in the bathtub.

6. The Bonapartes' Argument

While Napoleon was taking a bath one morning in 1803, his brothers Joseph and Lucien rushed in, seething with rage because they had just heard of his plan to sell Louisiana to the Americans. They were furious because he refused to consult the legislature about it. Lucien had worked hard to make Spain return the colony to France, and now his work would be for naught. Joseph warned Napoleon that he might end up in exile if he carried out his plan. At this, Napoleon fell back angrily in the tub, splashing water all over Joseph. Napoleon's valet, who was standing by with hot towels over his arm, crashed to the floor in a dead faint.

7. Wagner's Inspiration

Composer Richard Wagner soaked in a tub scented with vast quantities of Mild of Iris perfume for several hours every day while working on his final opera, *Parsifal* (1882). He insisted that the water be kept hot and heavily perfumed so that he could smell it as he sat at his desk, clad in outlandish silk and fur dressing gowns and surrounded by vials and sachets of exotic scents.

8. Rostand's Writing

Edmond Rostand, French poet and playwright, hated to be interrupted while he was working, but he did not like to turn his friends away. Therefore, he took refuge in the bathtub and wrote there all day, creating such successes as *Cyrano de Bergerac* (1898).

9. Smith's Murders

George Joseph Smith of England earned his living by his almost hypnotic power over women. In 1910 he met Bessie Mundy, married her (without mentioning that he already had a wife) and disappeared with her cash and clothes. Two years later they met by chance and began living together again. After Smith persuaded Bessie to write a will in his favour, he took her to a doctor on the pretence that she suffered from fits. (Both she and the doctor took his word for it.) A few days later she was found dead in the bathtub, a cake of soap clutched in her hand. Everyone assumed she had drowned during an epileptic seizure. Smith married two more women (Alice Burnham and Margaret Lofty), took out insurance policies on their lives and described mysterious ailments to their doctors. They too were found dead in their bathtubs. When Alice Burnham's father read of Margaret Lofty's death, he was struck by its similarity to his daughter's untimely end. The police were notified, and Smith was tried for murder and sentenced to be executed. His legal wife, Edith, testified at the trial that she could remember only one occasion when Smith himself took a bath.

10. Bennett's Death

R.B. Bennett, who had the misfortune of being prime minister of Canada during the Great Depression, spent most of the 1940s in self-imposed exile at his English estate, Juniper Hill. At 10:30 on the evening of June 26, 1947, Bennett drew a hot bath and climbed in. Shortly thereafter, the former prime minister suffered a massive heart attack and died. He was found the next morning by his butler. The floor of the bathroom was covered with water. His dog, Bill, was asleep on the bed, no doubt awaiting the master who would never return.

11. King Haakon's Fall

On June 29, 1955, the reign of King Haakon VII, who had ruled Norway from the time of its independence in 1905, effectively came to an end when the beloved monarch fell in the royal bathtub at his palace in Oslo. The elderly king lingered on for over two years before succumbing on September 21, 1957, to complications resulting from his fall.

12. A Hiccup in Glenn's Career

The momentum of what contemporary experts considered to be an unstoppable political career was interrupted in 1964 when astronaut hero John Glenn fell in the bathtub and had to withdraw from his race for senator of Ohio. He was finally elected to the Senate in 1974.

13. Morrison's Death

Rock idol Jim Morrison was living in exile in an apartment in Paris. On the morning of July 3, 1971, he was found dead in his bathtub. The cause of death was ruled "heart failure." He was 27 years old.

—P.S.H., L.B., J.Be. & Cdn. Eds.

DAVE EGGERS'S 4 BEST PLACES TO PUT THINGS INTO

Dave Eggers has written four books and three songs and edits McSweeney's.

1. Boxes

Boxes will always be No. 1. I don't care what anyone else says—boxes are the best. I recommend square ones for most occasions except for occasions involving hats. One of the things I like about boxes is that after you put things into a box, you can close the box with tape. They'll stay closed, all right! Boxes = No. 1.

2. Vases
Flowers are best, in terms of things to put into vases, but marbles can create a good look too. The problem with vases is that a lot of things don't fit into them. I guess vases shouldn't be No. 2.

3. Cars
Cars have one advantage over most things you can put things into: once you put something into a car, you can move it to a different place. Cars can go almost anywhere. Cars should be No. 2.

4. The Ground
This takes more effort than the first three, but it's a good choice in some circumstances, e.g., bones. Make sure the ground you put something into is sturdy and dry. If you put something into wet ground, wrap it in plastic first. That'll save you lots of time and headaches later if you need to get the thing you put into the ground out of the ground. The Ground = No. 4.

12 LAST FACTS

1. The Last Beothuk
On June 6, 1829, Nancy Shawnadithit, the last living Beothuk, died of tuberculosis in St. John's, Newfoundland, at the age of 23. She had spent the last five years of her life working as a maid for a white family. She spoke little English, but when encouraged to record details about her ancestors, language and culture, she made many detailed drawings.

2. The Last Duel in Upper Canada
The last fatal duel in Upper Canada was fought in Perth, Ontario, on June 13, 1833. John Wilson squared off with Robert Lyon over the affections of the local schoolteacher, Elizabeth Hughes. Lyon was shot and killed, and Wilson was charged with murder. The place where these events unfolded is now called Last Duel Park.

3. The Last Wish of Robert Baldwin
The last wish of Robert Baldwin, two-time former premier of Upper Canada, was that an incision be made in his corpse below his waistline

that would mirror the surgical scar his long-dead wife had from her Caesarean section. His wish was granted in 1858.

4. The Last Spike of the Canadian Pacific Railway
The last spike connecting eastern and western Canada by rail was pounded into the ground by the Honourable Donald Alexander Smith at Craigellachie, British Columbia, on November 7, 1885.

5. The Last Canadian WWI Casualty
The last Canadian soldier to die in battle during the First World War is believed to be Private George Lawrence Price of Port Williams, Nova Scotia. He was killed on November 11, 1918, at Mons, Belgium, about two minutes before the signing of the Armistice. He was 25 years old.

6. The Last Woman Hanged in Canada
The last woman to be hanged in Canada was Marguerite Pitre, on January 9, 1953, for "abetting" Albert Guay, the man responsible for planting a bomb on a Canadian Pacific airplane that killed 23 people.

7. The Last Men Hanged in Canada
The last men to be hanged in Canada were Ronald Turpin, 29, and Arthur Lucas, 54. Turpin was convicted of murdering a Toronto cop, and Lucas of murdering an FBI informant working in Canada. They were hanged just after midnight on December 11, 1962, at the Don Jail in Toronto, where they had been held.

8. The Last Race of Northern Dancer
The last race run—and won—by the horse Northern Dancer was the 1¼ mile (2 km) Queen's Plate on June 30, 1964. His time was 2:02, capping a career record of winning 14 of 18 starts.

9. The Last Films of Buster Keaton
The last two films of Buster Keaton—*The Railrodder* and *Buster Keaton Rides Again*—were made in Canada in 1965. The first was silent, a comedy about riding a railway scooter across Canada. The second, which had sound, was a documentary directed by John Spotton on how Keaton worked and lived.

10. The Last RCMP Dogsled

The last RCMP dogsled was driven between Old Crow, Yukon, and Fort McPherson, Northwest Territories, between March 11 and April 5, 1969. After that, the RCMP switched to snowmobiles.

11. The Last Direct Link to the Inventor of Insulin

The last and longest-living link to the inventor of insulin was Theodore Ryder. He was close to death from diabetes at age five when he was given an experimental injection of insulin by Dr. Frederick Banting at the Toronto General Hospital in 1922. He instantly revived and recovered. By using insulin regularly to keep his diabetes in check, he lived a long, healthy life. He died at the age of 76 on March 8, 1993, of heart failure.

12. The Last Message from the Authors to the Readers

We hope you have enjoyed the Canadian edition of *The Book of Lists*. If you have any comments or suggestions, please write to:
bookoflists@randomhouse.com

CREDITS

Expert Contributors

"Margaret Atwood's 10 Annoying Things to Say to Writers" Copyright © 2005 Margaret Atwood

"The Clockwatcher's 8 Reasons to Raid the Office Supply Closet" Copyright © 2005 Lisa Ayuso

"Katherine Barber's 11 Favourite Regionalisms within Canada" Copyright © 2005 Katherine Barber

"Kurt Browning's 9 Turning Points in Figure Skating History" Copyright © 2005 Kurt Browning

"Stephen Brunt's Top 10 Canadian Boxers of All Time" Copyright © 2005 Stephen Brunt

"10 Things Douglas Coupland Figured Out about Terry Fox While Doing a Book about Him" Copyright © 2005 Douglas Coupland

"'Is It Something I Said?' John Duffy's 10 Election-Losing Zingers" Copyright © 2005 John Duffy

"Jay Ferguson's 10 Perfect Pop Songs" Copyright © 2005 Jay Ferguson

"Will Ferguson's 15 Favourite Canadian Roadside Attractions" Copyright © 2005 Will Ferguson

"Vicki Gabereau's 10 Favourite People to Interview" Copyright © 2005 Vicki Gabereau

"Russ Germain's 10 Controversies in Spoken Canadian English" Copyright © 2005 Russ Germain

"Charlotte Gray's 10 Women Who Liven Up Canadian History" Copyright © 2005 Charlotte Gray

"Norman Jewison's 10 Most Important Films" Copyright © 2005 Norman Jewison

"Michele Landsberg's 14 Favourite Children's Books" Copyright © 2005 Michele Landsberg

"Ann-Marie MacDonald's 5 Formative Fictional Characters" Copyright © 2005 A. M. MacDonald Holdings Inc.

"Misty MacDuffee's Top 5 Dos and Don'ts When Encountering a Bear in the Wild" Copyright © 2005 Misty MacDuffee

"Margaret MacMillan's 12 Favourite 20th-Century Diplomatic Incidents" Copyright © 2005 Margaret MacMillan

"Ron Mann's 10 Favourite Documentaries" Copyright © 2005 Ron Mann

"Becky Mason's 12 Favourite Rivers to Canoe" Copyright © 2005 Becky Mason

"Aislin's 10 Favourite Faces for Political Cartoons" Copyright © 2005 Terry Mosher

"Mike Myers's 10 Best Things to Do in Toronto" Copyright © 2005 Mike Myers

"Michael Ondaatje's 12 20th-Century Classics in Translation" Copyright © 2005 Michael Ondaatje

506

Contributors

A.E.	Ann Elwood	K.P.	Karen Pedersen
A.K.	Aaron Kass	L.B.	Linda Bosson
A.W.	Amy Wallace	L.C.	Linda Chase
C.D.	Carol Dunlap	L.K.L.	Linda K. Laucella
C.F.	Chris Fishel	L.O.	Laurel Overman
C.O.M.	Carol Orsag-Madigan	M.B.T.	Marguerite B. Thompson
C.Ro.	Christopher Rouse	M.J.T.	Michael J. Toohey
C.S.	Carl Sifakis	M.S.	Michael Schellenberg
D.B.	Danny Biederman	N.C.S.	Nancy C. Sorel
D.L.	Don Lessem	N.P.	Nick Purdon
D.P.M.	David P. Monahan	N.R.	Nicholas Rennison
D.W.	David Wallechinsky	P.D	Peter Darbyshire
D.W.B.	David W. Barber	P.S.H.	Paul S. Hagerman
E.F.	Ed Fishbein	R.A.	Randy Alfred
E.H.C.	Ernest H. Corfine	R.J.F.	Rodger J. Fadness
F.B.	Fern Bryant	R.S.	Ray Spangenburg
I.W.	Irving Wallace	R.W.	Robert Williams
J.Ba.	James Barnett	R.W.S.	Roy W. Sorrels
J.Be.	Jeremy Beadle	S.B.	Sue Berkman
J.B.M.	Joseph B. Morris	S.R.	Steven Raichlen
K.A.	Kayti Adkins	S.S.	Steven Sherman
K.A.M.	Kenneth A. Michaelis	T.C.	Tim Conaway
K.H.J.	Kristine H. Johnson	W.A.D.	William A. DeGregorio

CREDITS

INDEX